In the past twenty years our understanding of the novel's emergence in eighteenth-century Britain has drastically changed. Drawing on new research in social and political history, the twelve contributors to this *Companion* challenge and refine the traditional view of the novel's origins and purposes. In various ways each seeks to show that the novel is not defined primarily by its realism of representation, but by the new ideological and cultural functions it serves in the emerging modern world of print culture. Sentimental and Gothic fiction, and fiction by women are discussed, alongside detailed readings of work by Defoe, Swift, Richardson, Henry Fielding, Sterne, Smollett, and Burney. This multifaceted picture of the novel in its formative decades provides a comprehensive and indispensable guide for students of the eighteenth-century British novel and its place within the culture of its time.

D0764586

THE CAMBRIDGE
COMPANION TO THE
EIGHTEENTH-CENTURY
NOVEL

Cambridge Companions to Literature

The Cambridge Companion to Old English Literature
edited by Malcolm Godden and Michael Lapidge

The Cambridge Companion to Dante
edited by Rachel Jacoff

The Cambridge Chaucer Companion
edited by Piero Boitani and Jill Mann

The Cambridge Companion to Medieval English Theatre
edited by Richard Beadle

The Cambridge Companion to Shakespeare Studies
edited by Stanley Wells

The Cambridge Companion to English Renaissance Drama
edited by A. R. Braunmuller and Michael Hattaway

The Cambridge Companion to English Poetry, Donne to Marvell
edited by Thomas N. Corns

The Cambridge Companion to Milton
edited by Dennis Danielson

The Cambridge Companion to British Romanticism
edited by Stuart Curran

The Cambridge Companion to James Joyce
edited by Derek Attridge

The Cambridge Companion to Ibsen
edited by James McFarlane

The Cambridge Companion to Brecht
edited by Peter Thomson and Glendyr Sacks

The Cambridge Companion to Beckett
edited by John Pilling

The Cambridge Companion to T. S. Eliot
edited by A. David Moody

The Cambridge Companion to Renaissance Humanism
edited by Jill Kraye

The Cambridge Companion to Joseph Conrad
edited by J. H. Stape

The Cambridge Companion to Faulkner
edited by Philip M. Weinstein

The Cambridge Companion to Thoreau
edited by Joel Myerson

The Cambridge Companion to Edith Wharton
edited by Millicent Bell

The Cambridge Companion to Realism and Naturalism
edited by Donald Pizer

The Cambridge Companion to Twain
edited by Forrest G. Robinson

The Cambridge Companion to Whitman
edited by Ezra Greenspan

The Cambridge Companion to Hemingway
edited by Scott Donaldson

The Cambridge Companion to the Eighteenth-Century Novel
edited by John Richetti

THE CAMBRIDGE
COMPANION TO THE
EIGHTEENTH-CENTURY
NOVEL

EDITED BY
JOHN RICHETTI
University of Pennsylvania

CAMBRIDGE
UNIVERSITY PRESS

Published by the Press Syndicate of the University of Cambridge
The Pitt Building, Trumpington Street, Cambridge CB2 1RP
40 West 20th Street, New York, NY 10011-4211, USA
10 Stamford Road, Oakleigh, Melbourne 3166, Australia

First published 1996

Printed in Great Britain at the University Press, Cambridge

A catalogue record for this book is available from the British Library

Library of Congress cataloguing in publication data
The Cambridge companion to the Eighteenth-Century novel / edited by John Richetti.
p.   cm. – (Cambridge companions to literature)
ISBN 0 521 41908 5 (hardback) ISBN 0 521 42945 5 (paperback)
1. English fiction – 18th century – History and criticism.
I. Richetti, John J.   II. Series.
PR851.C36   1996
823′509–dc20   95–43083   CIP

ISBN 0 521 41908 5 hardback
ISBN 0 521 42945 5 paperback

CE

CONTENTS

CONTRIBUTORS

JAMES P. CARSON teaches English at Kenyon College. He has published essays on *Frankenstein*, Samuel Richardson, and Tobias Smollett. He is currently completing a book on the Gothic novel.

MARGARET ANNE DOODY is Andrew W. Mellon Professor of Humanities and Professor English at Vanderbilt University. Her books include *A Natural Passion: a Study of the Novels of Samuel Richardson* (1974), *The Daring Muse: Augustan Poetry Reconsidered* (1985), *Frances Burney: the Life in the Works* (1988), and *The True Story of the Novel* (1996).

JULIA EPSTEIN is Barbara Riley Levin Professor of Comparative Literature at Haverford College. She is the author of *The Iron Pen: Frances Burney and the Politics of Women's Writing* (1989) and *Altered Conditions: Disease, Medicine and Storytelling* (1995). With Kristina Straub, she has edited *Body Guards: the Cultural Politics of Gender Ambiguity* (1991).

J. PAUL HUNTER is Chester D. Tripp Professor in the Humanities at the University of Chicago. Among his books are *The Reluctant Pilgrim: Defoe's Emblematic Method and Quest for Form* (1966), *Occasional Form: Henry Fielding and the Chains of Circumstance* (1975), and most recently *Before Novels: the Cultural Contexts of Eighteenth-Century English Fiction* (1990), winner of the Louis P. Gottschalk Prize for 1991. He is editor of the *Norton Introduction to Literature* and the *Norton Introduction to Poetry*.

JONATHAN LAMB is Professor of English at Princeton University. He is the author of *Sterne's Fiction and the Double Principle* (1989) and *The Rhetoric of Suffering: Reading the Book of Job in the Eighteenth Century* (1995).

JOHN MULLAN is Lecturer in English at University College, London. He is the author of *Sentiment and Sociability: the Language of Feeling in the Eighteenth Century* (1985). He has also edited Defoe's *Memoirs of a*

Cavalier (1991) and *Roxana* (1996) for the Oxford University Press World's Classics Series.

MAX NOVAK is Professor of English at the University of California, Los Angeles. He has written extensively on Defoe, Dryden, and Congreve, as well as more generally on the eighteenth-century novel and Restoration drama. Among his books are *Economics and the Fiction of Daniel Defoe* (1962), *Defoe and the Nature of Man* (1965), and *Realism, Myth, and History in Defoe's Fiction* (1984).

CLAUDE RAWSON is the George Bodman Professor of English at Yale University, and Chairman of the Yale Boswell Editions. He is the author of *Henry Fielding* (1968) and *Henry Fielding and the Augustan Ideal under Stress* (1972), and the editor of *Fielding: a Critical Anthology* (1973). His other books include *Gulliver and the Gentle Reader* (1973), *Order from Confusion Sprung* (1985), and *Satire and Sentiment, 1660–1830* (1994).

JOHN RICHETTI is the Leonard Sugarman Professor of English at the University of Pennsylvania. Among his books are *Popular Fiction Before Richardson: Narrative Patterns, 1700–1739* (1969), *Defoe's Narratives: Situations and Structures* (1975), and *Philosophical Writing: Locke, Berkeley, Hume* (1983). Most recently he has edited *The Columbia History of the British Novel* (1994).

MICHAEL ROSENBLUM is Associate Professor of English at Indiana University in Bloomington, Indiana. He has published scholarly essays on Pope, Sterne, Smollett, and Nabokov.

MICHAEL SEIDEL is Professor of English and Chairman of the Department at Columbia University. He has written extensively on narrative and on satire in such books as *Epic Geography: James Joyce's Ulysses* (1976), *Satiric Inheritance: Rabelais to Sterne* (1979), *Exile and the Narrative Imagination* (1986), and *Robinson Crusoe: Island Myths and the Novel* (1991).

JANE SPENCER is Lecturer in English Literature in the School of English and American Studies at the University of Exeter. Her publications include *The Rise of the Woman Novelist: from Aphra Behn to Jane Austen* (1986) and *Elizabeth Gaskell* (1993). She has edited Aphra Behn's *The Rover and Other Plays* (1995) for the Oxford University Press World's Classics Series.

CHRONOLOGY

1711 Addison and Steele's *Spectator* begins publication
South Sea Company founded

1713 Treaty of Utrecht signed with France, ending War of Spanish Succession
Laurence Sterne born, Clonmel, Ireland

1714 Death of Queen Anne
Accession of George I

1715 Jacobite rebellion
Death of Louis XIV of France

1719 Defoe's *Robinson Crusoe* published

1720 War with Spain declared
South Sea Company fails ("South Sea Bubble")

1721 Smollett born in Dumbarton, Scotland
Robert Walpole appointed First Lord of the Treasury and Chancellor of the Exchequer

1726 Swift's *Gulliver's Travels* published
Death of George I
Accession of George II

1731 Defoe dies

1737 Theatrical Licensing Act passed

1739 "War of Jenkins' Ear" with Spain
David Hume's *A Treatise of Human Nature* published

1740 Richardson's *Pamela* published

1741 Britain involved in War of the Austrian Succession with Empress Maria Theresa of Austria against France, Spain, Bavaria, Prussia, and Saxony

1742 Robert Walpole resigns

1743 George II defeats the French at the Battle of Dettingen in War of the Austrian Succession
Britain at war with France in America and in India

1744 Alexander Pope dies

1745 Charles Edward Stuart ("Bonnie Prince Charlie") "the Young Pretender," lands in Scotland and leads the Jacobite uprising
Jonathan Swift dies
Robert Walpole dies

1746 Battle of Culloden and defeat of the "Pretender" ("Bonnie Prince Charlie") and his allies

1747–8 Richardson's *Clarissa* published

1748 John Cleland's *Memoirs of a Woman of Pleasure* (*Fanny Hill*) published
Smollett's *Roderick Random* published

Treaty of Aix-la-Chapelle ending the War of the Austrian Succession
1749 Fielding's *Tom Jones* published
1751 Death of Frederick Lewis, Prince of Wales
1752 Frances Burney born
1754 Fielding dies in Lisbon
1756 Seven Years' War with France
1759 First two volumes of Sterne's *Tristram Shandy* published
Wolfe defeats the French under Montcalm at Quebec
1760 Death of George II
Accession of George III
Josiah Wedgewood opens pottery works in Staffordshire
1763 Peace of Paris ends the Seven Years' War with France
1764 Horace Wolpole's *The Castle of Otranto* published
James Hargreaves invents the spinning jenny
James Watt perfects the steam engine
1768 Sterne dies
Captain Cook's first voyage to Australia and New Zealand
Royal Academy of Art founded
1771 Smollett dies
Humphry Clinker published
Mackenzie's *The Man of Feeling* published
Walter Scott born
1775 Jane Austen born
1776 American Declaration of Independence
Adam Smith's *Wealth of Nations* published
Edward Gibbon's *Decline and Fall of the Roman Empire* published
1778 Burney's *Evelina* published
France joins the Americans in war against Britain
1781 General Lord Cornwallis surrenders to Washington at Yorktown, Virginia, to close American Revolution
1783 Treaties of Paris and Versailles end the War of American Independence
1785 Edmund Cartwright patents his power loom
1787 US Constitution signed in Philadelphia
1789 French Revolution begins; fall of the Bastille in Paris
1790 Edmund Burke's *Reflections on the Revolution in France* published
1791 Thomas Paine's *The Rights of Man* published
1793 Execution of Louis XVI of France
France declares war against England

I

JOHN RICHETTI

Introduction

The title of this volume is misleading in a usefully revealing sense. As a classification for the many prose narratives produced in Britain over the course of the eighteenth century, "novel" is a convenient label rather than a historically accurate term, which tells us much more about our own late twentieth-century assumptions concerning narrative than about the eighteenth-century sense of what prose fiction was for its contemporary readers and writers. What we now think of as the novel – a long prose narrative about largely fictional if usually realistic characters and plausible events – did not actually solidify in the minds of readers and writers as a literary type or a set of expectations for narrative in the English-speaking world until the beginning of the nineteenth century, when Jane Austen and Walter Scott flourished, and when the novel in our current sense of it was widely accepted in Britain and elsewhere in Europe as a major literary form; as the inevitable and inescapable mode of telling a long fictional story. Eighteenth-century "novels" such as we now read and study represent part of the "prehistory" of novelistic development; they constitute the early and truly formative phase of the novel as a genre of prose fiction that has since then come to dominate readers' sense of what literary narrative should be.

In this early phase, the novel in the current sense of the term does not really exist as a coherent literary institution. Those narratives from the eighteenth century that we call novels include a wide range of distinct books and stories, and they comprise a large variety of rival, competing approaches to the problem of fictional storytelling. "Novel," in fact, is only one of many names floating around in the discourse of writers and readers during those years for prose narratives of various kinds, which were just as often called by other names such as "romance" or "history," or most confusingly "true history" or "secret history." To read fiction from the early and even the middle years of the eighteenth century is to enter a narrative situation in which the boundaries between the ordinary and everyday world of fact and event (such as we now read about in newspapers and watch unfold on television) and the fictional or sensational or even fantastic realm are fluid and uncertain. The divide between fact and fiction that we are pretty confident about is hard to locate in narratives from earlier centuries, and the eighteenth-century novel played with that still blurry division, often presenting fiction as fact and dramatizing fact in ways we would find more appropriate to fiction. Indeed, the novel, the narrative institution, that emerges eventually out of this rich confusion is an outgrowth of the norms of that intellectual development we call the Enlightenment, since with its strict establishment of a categorical and absolute difference between the fictional and the factual, the new novel is a mode of regulation or realignment of those perhaps naturally interpenetrating spheres. Traditional narrative forms such as romance and allegory have a much less strict sense of fact and fiction, and indeed they depend upon a view of the world in which notions of probability and single and stable meaning do not necessarily obtain. For such traditional forms of storytelling, readers agree implicitly that the everyday world of common fact is insufficient, and they take pleasure precisely in the distance between that world and separate narrative realms featuring a fullness of meaning and significance such as quotidian existence radically lacks.

The great issue for most students of the eighteenth-century novel is why expectations for prose fiction seem to have shifted so clearly during the middle of the century, and why by the end of the century something called the novel very clearly exists in the minds of readers and writers. The expectations for narrative that came to dominate the minds of readers in those years, as well as the popularity of such narratives, may be related to larger intellectual and social changes. Most readers and writers from previous centuries would not have shared the essentially secular and materialistic notion of the line that comes in these years to separate the factual from the fictional, the probable or possible from the romantic and unreal. The history of the novel in Britain (like that of the European novel of which it is a part) is precisely the story of the emergence of a new kind of quite distinct fictional narrative, which defines itself, sometimes aggressively and polemically, by a process of rejection, modification, and transformation of previous forms or practices of storytelling, that are seen as insufficiently attentive to a narrow view of what constitutes truth and reality. Eventually, the realistic novel as it develops over the course of the century is a very self-conscious revision and strict reformation of what its authors tend to define as unacceptably loose attitudes toward the referentiality of narrative in relation to the actualities of experience, as the Enlightenment came to define that elusive category. This hunger for actuality and belief that the actual is a separable category are features of Enlightenment thought that are still with us, of course, but which were aggressively articulated in the mid-eighteenth century against what was clearly a lingering older confusion of the realms of the actual and the ideal. In his *Treatise of Human Nature*, published the same year as Richardson's *Pamela* (1739–40), the philosopher David Hume could describe the different expectations readers would bring to the same book according to whether they thought it was a "true history" or a "romance." His evocation of what the reader of a true history does with that feeling of the truth of the tale is a good rendition of what the realistic novel claims to induce in its readers.

> Nothing is more evident, than that those ideas, to which we assent, are more strong, firm and vivid, than the loose reveries of a castle-builder. If one person sits down to read a book as a romance, and another as a true history, they plainly receive the same ideas, and in the same order; nor does the incredulity of the one, and the belief of the other hinder them from putting the very same sense upon their author. His words produce the same ideas in both; tho' his testimony has not the same influence on them. The latter has a more lively conception of all the incidents. He enters deeper into the concerns of the persons: represents to himself their action, and characters, and friendships, and enmities: he even goes so far as to form a notion of their features, and air, and person. While the former, who gives no credit to the testimony of the author, has a more faint and languid conception of all these particulars; and except on account of the style and ingenuity of the composition, can receive little entertainment from it. (I. VII)

To be sure, the eighteenth-century British novel also records in popular subtypes such as the amatory novella, the sentimental, and the Gothic novel a clear and perennial protest against that rationalistic preference for the actual and the historical, with its exclusion from narrative of the improbable, the marvelous or the melodramatic. And in Protestant England, at least, many novels try to cancel or overcome the materialistic and secular implications of the form, dramatizing in the tortured religiosity of heroines like Richardson's saintly Clarissa (for the greatest example) a persistent yearning for transcendence.

One major strain of the novel's revision of past narrative forms follows the example of Cervantes' *Don Quixote* (1605, 1615) by comically substituting local and historical realism for the much less restrictive standards of probability associated with traditional narratives such as the romance and the epic. In Cervantes' case, this means telling the story of a man who is clearly delusional in taking the world represented in medieval romances of chivalry for a description of the actual world of late sixteenth-century Spain in which he lives. Cervantes' famous book looks both ways, of course, since its ridicule of Don Quixote modulates into admiration for his visionary consistency and even nobility in tenaciously preferring the idealized and honorable world of chivalry to the brutal realities of sixteenth-century Spain. In *Don Quixote*, the idea of romance remains alive precisely because of the book's realism, which turns unreal and impossible dreams into psychological rather than literal truth. But at its simplest, the novel as it develops in the eighteenth century substitutes what it sees as the actual for the merely literary, banishing the supernatural and the marvelous in order to tell stories in which only natural or probable causation is admitted; there are, in this new kind of fiction, no miracles or suspension of the physical laws of nature, no angelic visitations, no gods dropping down from heaven, no magicians and no fairy godmothers. In place of the gloriously and deliberately "unreal" world of romance from the Middle Ages and early Renaissance, novelistic narrative in the seventeenth and eighteenth centuries comes to substitute the quotidian world of everyday and common sense experience and to put in place of larger-than-life characters, both good and evil, people who are no different from the implied reader in an ordinary world where everyday common sense prevails. Of course, that ordinary world had always been a part of narrative representations in the prenovelistic world of written storytelling that goes back to classical antiquity, but the ordinary had always been secondary and subordinate in a literary and moral hierarchy to the worlds of epic and romance, a comic supplement to the ideal realm depicted in forms of representation considered higher and nobler.

What is unprecedented about the novel as it emerges in Britain and in the rest of Western Europe in these early modern European centuries is that it very aggressively and insistently seeks to restrict meaningful, significant, and serious narrative to the actual and familiar world of more or less daily experience and to banish or trivialize the older and manifestly unrealistic genres of epic and romance. In this new set of attitudes to narrative, romance and epic are branded as preposterous and irrelevant in their unreality, in their distance from the everyday world and experience of most readers. For the novel, the ordinary and the specifically and concretely experiential (along with the everyday language specific to that realm) come in this new world of narrative to define the absolute boundaries or limits of reality and by extension of moral significance. Such an understanding is, potentially at least, subversive of traditional notions of the individual and his or her decidedly subordinate relation to a communal and often hierarchical reality, and to a supernatural order which upholds that community. But within the materialistic and probabilistic assumptions of the realistic novel, the supernatural can be treated as an object of belief or faith but never presented as a matter of direct and unambiguous experience for the new kind of person who is taken absolutely for granted by modern individualism. The novel tends in these preferences to validate the perspective of the newly conceptualized modern individual, whose particularized and personalized view of the world is explored as if it were somehow prior to a communal or social world. Most readers of novels now, at the end of the twentieth century, take such an individual very much for granted, but the notions of autonomy, agency, and self-consciousness (as well as the skepticism about the ideal or the transcendental) summed up in the persons dramatized in most novels were in fact only emerging as new and controversial ideas for European thought at the turn of the seventeenth century when the modern individual is, in effect, invented and naturalized, that is to say, presented as an inevitable feature of the order of the world rather than as an entity constructed in a cultural moment, conceptualized and in that sense produced by modern historical circumstances.

As the example of Cervantes' *Don Quixote* makes clear, however, imagining this modern individual involves something more complicated than deference to that particularized and phenomenal knowledge that only individuals as we now understand them can possess or experience. Don Quixote is convinced that his chivalric visions are true, and such is the power and consistency of his delusion that for him they are true, so that sheep become armies, peasant girls beautiful princesses, and windmills threatening giants. What is memorably real about Don Quixote is the intense and persuasive individuality that he projects by holding fast to these beliefs, and his story dramatizes what many novels in the years to come will take as their subject or theme: reality is largely the construction of particular minds or wills. The world represented by the new novelistic narrative is not an inert and objective mass somehow out there beyond human experience; the reality the novel tends to deliver is, rather, a record of the productive interaction between a world of facts and heroic individuals who give it shape and meaning. An objective world yields to the insistently differing subjective perspectives of strong and creative individuals. To be sure, there is a difference between the philosophical validity of such constructionism and relativism and the practical and moral consequences of an individual like Cervantes' hero preferring his eccentric vision to that sanctioned by worldly common sense (and of course strongly represented by other characters in *Don Quixote*, notably Sancho Panza, the Don's peasant squire). Novels often enough feature the deflation or cancellation of eccentric individual perspectives by social norms or by the brute factual force of the physical world. At their most complex, novels can dramatize the relationship whereby the lonely or defiant individual is linked by experience in the world to society and discovers his or her implication in history and community, thereby achieving (sometimes) a sort of freedom in that consciousness of necessity.

But the assertion of modern individuality and of the narrative form that expresses it happens very gradually, and for a long time older forms and their fluid assumptions about reality and the nature of the individual coexist with these emerging ideas and tendencies. What we now call the novel, especially in Britain, seems to have been a literary response to profound cultural and social changes, and like those changes narrative evolves over time, over a long century and a half. Slowly but surely the market for print grew in the course of the eighteenth century in Britain, as books in the vernacular dealing with secular topics were now available as a commodity offered to an increasingly larger (although still very small by modern mass market standards) group of literate consumers. Instead of a luxury affordable only by the privileged and educated few, books and especially novels were part of the revolution in the availability of consumer goods that changed the nature of daily life for a large part of the population in Britain as the eighteenth century progressed. Reading matter in English had been since Tudor times mainly religious and didactic – the Bible, collections of saints' and martyrs' lives, sermons and homilies – but with the growth of the London publishing industry in the late seventeenth and early eighteenth century and the emergence of a fairly large urban bourgeoisie and an increasing urban population of servants and other workers in the new metropolitan and imperial center who were at least minimally literate, printed material became increasingly secular in nature and contemporary in its references. Pamphlets, broadsides, cookbooks, medical manuals, almanacs, periodicals, and "novels" come increasingly to share shelf space in the shops with religious and didactic literature. "Novels" in those new bookshops meant a lot of different products: amatory novellas about seduced virgins and rapacious libertines; sensationalized inside accounts of the steamy affairs and scandals of aristocrats, politicians, and courtiers; breathless biographies and last-dying words before execution of criminals, pirates, highwaymen, and whores; yarns by travelers to exotic and faraway places (some like Defoe's *Robinson Crusoe* [1719] pretending to be true stories). To a greater or lesser extent, this exploding mass of popular reading matter caters to a new hunger in an expanding reading public to know about the specific and historical existence of particular individuals and their contemporary doings. Like the newspapers, magazines, and television which feed our appetites for similar revelations, such books provided "news" for the growing public that demanded it.

In a deep cultural transformation that defies efforts to isolate its exact beginnings and causes, the present and the local seem to acquire a primacy in everyday consciousness near the end of the seventeenth century. It may be that philosophers' ideas about the nature of our experience play a role in this transformation, and the influence of a book such as Locke's *Essay Concerning Human Understanding* (1690), which grounds human knowledge in our particular sensory experience, cannot be underestimated. But it is probably the case that Locke's empiricism and his skepticism about innate ideas could only have been conceived within a climate of ideas and feelings in which the particular and the present acquired an urgency and a primacy in people's lives such as they never had before. Baconian empiricism, with its emphasis on experimentation and particular observation of natural phenomena, is in the seventeenth-century intellectual air, and such nascent scientific and secular modes of thought can be regarded as important, even formative influences on the novel and the attitudes that make it possible; but it is hard to measure the results of learned and very specialized speculation in the consciousness of the masses of people.

Perhaps the print revolution taking place in those centuries has a great deal to do with this epistemological shift, since printed matter (as opposed to oral transmission) encourages the isolation and self-enclosure of the silent reader. Or perhaps the growth of urban centers, like London, and the erosion of traditional village society are more important factors, as the novel develops to accompany and to promote a shift in most people's consciousness of life and its possibilities. Many novels not only represent individuals from the middling ranks or classes of society; they depict more often than not attempts to acquire status (or wealth and power) through isolated and individual virtue and action rather than by inheritance or through corporate involvement. And indeed power and social status in the new commercial order of the eighteenth century acquire new meanings, as what historians call the "financial revolution" shifts value away from real property, its concrete embodiments and human relationships toward financial arrangements where wealth exists in the abstract form of stocks, bonds, and other instruments of commercial exchange. In this world, the daring and resourceful investor and entrepreneur is a great hero, and in reality great fortunes were made (and lost), and some men transformed themselves by hard work, luck, or often enough by bribery and corruption into great lords and aristocrats. In this emerging socioeconomic order, in fact but also in imagination, status is for sale, like everything else, and identity is subject to the fluidity and fluctuations of the market. Novels tend to be about leaving home, making a break with the familiar world of childhood, finding your way, and often enough a mate, seeking your fortune, acquiring an identity by making your mark in the world and "doing well"; they dramatize a wider, more open but much more unstable and unpredictable world than that encompassed by the village, the manor house, or the parish. Set in a world where nothing is impossible to virtue and ambition, the novel (taken as a whole) invokes what might be called a middle-class myth of personal possibility, of the individual's potential for growth and achievement (and also of course for failure and obliteration in the unforgiving struggle with other individuals). Indeed, from the beginnings of the century the novel is also frequently a critique of the breakdown of the traditional moral order in the face of this new and ruthlessly dispassionate and impersonal economic world, and the so-called "sentimental novel" that develops in the middle of the century is a celebration of private and domestic virtue and solitary philanthropy in the face of a rapacious and uncompromising possessive individualism.

Modern readers can see such thematic patterns easily in the narratives produced by Defoe, Richardson, and Burney, with their intense focus on the subjectivity of their characters, although we can not help but notice that even those novels are about the limitations (and the moral dangers) of individualism and feature characters who often yearn for a meaning or purpose which is more than merely personal or selfish. Other novels by more traditionalist authors such as Fielding and Smollett, for all their interest in individualized characters and contemporary settings, are deeply critical (and hilariously satirical) of this emerging modern self and the new kind of society that encourages it. A moral comedian like Fielding, in fact, offers his readers an understanding of character and personality that is founded on generalized moral types, and his universalism produces characters quite distinct from the deeply psychologized and intensely individualized characters Richardson imagined. The striking differences between *Tom Jones* (1749) and *Clarissa* (1747–48) encompass not only style and narrative form but nearly opposing notions of character and society. And of course Sterne's *Tristram Shandy* (1760–67) is a profoundly comic analysis of the solipsistic absurdity of individual perception. In other words, even the most well known and successful of the British eighteenth-century novelists display no agreement about what a novel should be; they in fact continue the debate about the nature and function of the novel, even as they narrate differing versions of that new world of secular materialism and individualism, celebrating or deploring its features. One might even say that the central theme and formal obsession of British eighteenth-century fiction is a continuing and unresolved debate about the nature of that evolving narrative convention we now confidently call the novel.

2

J. PAUL HUNTER

The novel and social/cultural history

In their own time they were most often called "histories," these fictional narratives of present time that chronicled the daily experiences, conflicts, and thoughts of ordinary men and women. They went by other names, too – "romances," "adventures," "lives," "tales," "memoirs," "expeditions," "fortunes and misfortunes," and (ultimately) "novels" – because a variety of features and traditions competed for attention in this new hybrid form that in the course of the eighteenth century came to dominate the reading habits of English men and women of all classes. When the term "novel" finally stuck, near the end of the century after several decades in which novels had been the most popular books in England, it represented both the power of a "new" literary form to dominate the reading public and the cultural acceptance of narratives about contemporary life and times.

The term "novel," which originally designated a short tale of romantic love, gradually was broadened to include longer fiction of various kinds and then narrowed again to describe the new "realistic" fictions that featured ordinary people in familiar, everyday, contemporary circumstances. As early as the seventeenth century (see, for example William Congreve's preface to *Incognita* [1692]) the term sometimes was used to describe the then-developing new fictions of ordinary life, but it did not come into general use until late in the eighteenth century following the critical distinctions of Clara Reeve's *The Progress of Romance* (1785). Exactly when and where the novel originated is hard to say. Literary historians variously credit Richardson, Defoe, or Behn as the "founder" of the English novel, thus dating its beginnings from the 1740s, the 1710s, or the 1680s; there are much earlier examples of similar narratives (though with some significant differences) in Spain and France and a few classical precedents in ancient Greece.

But the term that most often labeled these books on their title pages – history – also testifies to an important conception of what the new narratives seemed to contemporaries to be about: the story of a present-day individual in a recognizable social and cultural context. The plot might involve ongoing – or even enduring – human issues, and the hero or heroine might be "typical" or "representative" of its time and place, but the emphasis was on the individual, the local, and the particular. Unlike traditional literary genres, the novel sought to record and privilege the specific details that shaped the daily, contingent lives of ordinary people; unlike essentialist forms that promised universal solutions because human nature was constant across cultures and times, the novel offered varied, circumstantial, and individual outcomes, a freedom from formal determination that left texts open to tell whatever individual stories they chose by referring causes and effects to local choices and cultural particulars. This preoccupation with circumstance over pattern – or rather the interest in how individual circumstances modified, revised, or played variations on the human patterns that literature had traditionally sought to describe – meant from the beginning that here was a genre based on temporal and cultural context, that the social and the adjustable had to be an important part of any narration however concerned it might be with human nature or permanence.

Because they tell stories of familiar human situations and share some structural features across time and culture, novels may sometimes seem "universal," accessible to readers who lack a knowledge of the cultural history they represent. And – because of the ready elements of plot, situation, and character – they are more easily accessible to readers today than most eighteenth-century texts. But they are still deeply involved in a complex and distant social history that can be quite puzzling to modern readers. Novels, in fact, explicitly render manners, habits, customs, and beliefs that differ from culture to culture, and they depend heavily on the particulars of time and place. You can usually follow readily enough the plots of novels and sort out the main features of characters even if you know nothing of the history of their time and place, but often conflicts in the plot – and subtle differences between different characters – derive from interpretations of desires, needs, and values that are culturally based. The subtlety of your reading thus often depends on knowing quite specific things about local particulars in the narrative. Beyond that, many larger questions of literary history – how novels came to be written, who read them and when, the relation of novels to other texts and other cultural phenomena – depend crucially on the specifics of history at the time the novels were written, produced, and circulated.

I

Over the past ten years or so there has been an explosion of academic interest in eighteenth-century studies and especially in the eighteenth-century British novel. The reasons are many and complicated. Some involve the undue neglect earlier this century of eighteenth-century texts generally and especially those written by women or thought to be merely "popular literature" not "literary" enough to merit the serious attention of high-minded scholars. Accounts of literary history, especially those written between World War II and the 1980s, tend to pass patronizingly over everything between Milton and Blake, implying that both texts and contexts are dull and not very important in a larger, and higher, scheme of things. That view, which privileged Romanticism and a particular kind of elitist intellectual and aesthetic history, also prevailed in college and university curricula that similarly relegated the whole eighteenth century to wasteland status.

Other reasons for the earlier neglect – and for the recent resurgence – involve the very historicity of novels themselves, their crucial dependence on cultural particulars. The formalism of the mid-twentieth century and the waves of structuralist and then critical theory that followed in the 1970s and early eighties were generally hostile to historical questions about texts and showed little interest in any text that was not already considered a "great book." One result was that "minor" works (and some once considered "major") slipped out of the curriculum and out of scholars' minds. Frances Burney, for example, who had always been considered a major novelist until well into the twentieth century, disappeared from syllabi and nearly from sight, and scores of other texts formerly read at least occasionally – including the fiction of Aphra Behn, Charles Gildon, Delarivier Manley, Eliza Haywood, Sarah Fielding, Charlotte Lennox, Frances Sheridan, and Richard Graves – sat unregarded on the shelves of rare book rooms. The paperback revolution that transformed English syllabi in most periods and subject areas just after World War II included only a few eighteenth-century novelists (Defoe, Richardson, Henry Fielding, Smollett, Sterne), so that the teaching canon actually narrowed even though more literary criticism was being produced than ever before. By 1970 there was virtually no scholarly work going forward – not editions, biographies, critical studies, or any historical work at all – on "minor" figures who earlier, in a much smaller academic world, had spurred scholars into archival digging and attracted many "common" readers beyond academe.[1]

The relative neglect of eighteenth-century novels for more than half of the twentieth century is due in part, then, to the precarious fortunes of older texts in general, to a lengthy period of antihistoricism in literary studies, to a major-works economy that pushed aside "minor" and "popular" works and that tended especially to marginalize women's texts, and to the vagaries and prejudices of unpredictable academic trends. The renewed interest in novels – and in eighteenth-century studies more generally – marks some major reversals in trends among literary critics and other students of texts who (with newfound support in different kinds of theory from those that flourished in the 1970s) have become deeply interested in the historical dimensions of texts, the social environment and history of those texts, and in historicism itself. Because this sudden, intense, and deep interest in historical questions is relatively new – it began only in the mid-1980s – it is too early to say how sustained its reach will be. But some form of literary historicism seems likely to be around for some time, demanding that texts be interpreted relative to the historical contexts in which they were conceived and first read – as cultural productions that participated as active agents in the ongoing life of their times, not just as verbal constructs with some vague kind of historical "background." That is good news for the detailed study of eighteenth-century novels, but it means hard historical work for those who read them.

The ferment that now characterizes the study of eighteenth-century texts is not, however, altogether (or even primarily) due to changes in the interests, priorities, and premises of literary critics. The present ferment derives from a new – or newly revived – sense of ferment and vitality in the eighteenth century itself, as historians and historiographers have turned to the daily life of the period in order to reconceive the deeper structures of the culture. Once regarded as one of the most stable, placid, and complacent of times – when nothing much happened and when the calm surfaces of the leisure classes stood for the whole social fabric – the eighteenth century now seems a vibrant, unpredictable, troubled, and precarious cultural era that retained its apparent serenity at a deep price and that always teetered on the edge of chaos. The "apparent" serenity was, of course, real in one quite specific sense: after a chaotic seventeenth century, which saw a civil war, a "glorious" revolution in which the king (James II) was sent packing because of his Catholicism, and two separate Protestant solutions to the succession crises that involved imports from Holland and Germany, political stability was in fact achieved in England. The "reign" of Sir Robert Walpole as prime minister (1721–42) epitomizes – in its pragmatism and ruthless suppression of opposition – this "stability," which, ever aware of the volatile recent past, sought to preserve order in the English national consciousness at almost any price. This "new" eighteenth century emerges from the developing picture provided by a variety of historians, especially social and cultural historians, who see a different eighteenth century because they ask different questions and apply them to a broader range of people and institutions. Rather than the history of public life – with its concentration on the powerful and rich – that dominated earlier generations, this new cultural history seeks to provide (like novels) a broad and vivid picture of ordinary daily life as a great variety of people – including women, merchants, members of the working class, servants, and the poor – lived and experienced it.

The title of George Saintsbury's 1916 account of eighteenth-century texts – *The Peace of the Augustans: a Survey of Eighteenth Century Literature as a Place of Rest and Refreshment* – fairly summarizes the older view, and when it held sway it was tempting to many readers to find the age and its literature serene, complacent, and smug – a view that must have been appealing for its escapism in the midst of World War I, but that misreads badly both the rambunctious, difficult, and disturbing texts of the period and the brittle and dangerous times that produced them.

What do you need to know about eighteenth-century Britain in order to read the novels intelligently and with pleasure? And what do you need to know about the way novels fit into eighteenth-century life, how and why they were written and read, and what relation they had to other kinds of competing texts and cultural institutions? How do they reflect, represent, comment on, rhetoricize, and affect eighteenth-century conditions and events, and in what ways does their representation affect subsequent cultural history? These are the central questions I have had in mind in writing this chapter. There are, of course, many other questions (and other *kinds* of questions) that one might appropriately ask in relation to individual works that (typical of novels) raise just about every social or cultural issue one can imagine. But (except incidentally or as examples) I have not tried to address the countless historical questions posed in individual books. In order to gloss particular events and movements (as well as to understand the specific circumstances and issues involved in any particular text), readers will need to use editions of novels that have been fully annotated with historical information.

II

The writing of history, like history itself, always has a past of its own as well as a present. The new cultural history of the eighteenth century is very much a product of what history was *not* a generation ago – or rather of what present historians see as misdirections, simplifications, and oversights in the histories written by earlier generations. The new history reacts mainly against these features of older historiography: its emphasis on political, military, and economic history and its tendency to see history itself as primarily a question of public events and public policy, thus overlooking private activities and unempowered people; the tendency to ignore feelings and opinions not obviously relevant to dominant political and economic directions; and the too-rigid compartmentalization of different kinds or segments of history (political, intellectual, social, etc.). The new, more integrated "cultural" history considers all kinds of documents, texts, and material artifacts in an effort to describe both the dominant values and communal desires that drive individual behavior and those other cultural patterns that, although "minor" or marginalized, have an important bearing on the way things seemed at the time to observers with varying points of view. There is, therefore, more attention to daily life and immediate perspectives and less emphasis on patterns that emerge retro-spectively.

What I am here calling the New Cultural History is actually a loose confederation of many related developments over the past two decades or so in various branches of historiography (social, intellectual, economic, political, and literary history). Major components include:

1   A Marxist revisionism that, led by E. P. Thompson in the 1960s, challenged dominant strains of political, economic, and legal history and offered models and incentives for studying a broadened range of social groups and the behavior of repressed, deprived, or neglected segments of society.

2   The "new" English social history of the 1970s, itself primarily the adaptation to the study of English history of the practices of the *annales* school that had already flourished for several decades in France.

3   A revisionist history of political thought that, led by J. G. A. Pocock, emphasized political philosophy and the sober exchange of ideas (rather than power politics or pure pragmatics) as determining the directions of politics and statecraft.

4   A revised political history, responding to the social theories of Jurgen Habermas, that emphasized the development of a "deliberative citi-zenry" in a "public sphere" where the exchange of ideas across a fairly broad range of the population became both a self-conscious means of transmitting public policy and, often, a determiner of policy.

5   A new intellectual history that, by the late 1970s, had begun to question the traditional "top down" theories of cultural transmission and that broadened the history of ideas to include the directions of

thought in "lower" cultural echelons usually ignored by intellectual historians.

6   The popular culture movement which, while it has so far had little direct impact on the study of crucial eighteenth-century institutions, has furthered the sense that there are a host of unexplored areas, especially involving the history of the everyday. Ironically, most study of popular culture in the eighteenth century takes its impetus from the attacks, launched by defenders of high culture, on the "depraved" taste of the lower classes in such powerful elitist works as Pope's *Dunciad*. In the early twentieth century these historical alternatives to Pope's high culture attracted a lot of scholarship on booksellers, actors, theatrical producers, quacks, and hawkers of various commercial products, and the popular stars of lower-class "entertainments" – but very little work on such figures and materials has been done over the last half-century.[2]

7   The New Historicism of the 1980s, a set of practices adapted from the social sciences (largely anthropology) and employed primarily by literary scholars to locate canonical texts more precisely and resonantly within a broader range of cultural practices and then within specific discourses designed for particular, definable historical ends.

8   An emerging cultural history, growing out of the historical wing of the cultural studies movement, that at its best seeks to be genuinely multidisciplinary in bringing to bear the findings and methodologies of different schools, subject matters, and interests.

9   Theoretical (and some historical) work done in the wake of the career of Michel Foucault – work that takes various forms and that claims contradictory methodologies as distinctively "Foucauldian." What this work has in common is the consistent rejection of any sense of "natural" continuity of ideas or practices and any traditional explanation of cause and effect; it takes as a premise the basic "constructedness" of all identities and ideas.

In practice, these movements overlap considerably, and there is among them (and within each) a lot of infighting and jockeying for emphasis. Foucault's presence may, for example, be felt in varying degrees in almost all of them, even though historians (unlike many of their literary counterparts) tend to dislike Foucault's methods, show disdain for his premises, criticize his use of evidence or find it unpersuasive beyond its local application, and distrust his conclusions. But even with the varied agendas and disagreements about aims, there is reasonable consensus in the direction of the new work, and some common agreement about assumptions. There is, for example, quite a surprising consistency in embracing the following premises:

> that the activities, preoccupations, and needs of all social classes and economic groups (regardless of their power position) must be studied and analyzed and the results absorbed into any attempt at a total picture of the age;
>
> that all available varieties of texts (including nonverbal ones) be considered cultural productions and studied for their implications about the values, distinctions, and structures of the culture;
>
> that recognition be given to varieties of discourses with different assumptions and interests (as for example, the discourse of nationalism, or of moral reform, of mercantilism) and that an attempt always be made to place any text accurately in terms of the particular discourses in which it participates;
>
> that crafts, tools, amusements, media of exchange, bodies, clothing, and all recoverable or describable material artifacts be considered "texts" worthy of study for their power to reveal cultural traits;
>
> that oral habits and traditions be recovered as fully as possible and considered evidence – equal to that of written traditions – of cultural transmissions and codes;
>
> that (at least in theory) all available disciplines and their methodologies be considered possible contributors to the study of any historical culture (although in practice the methods of economics and political science have been little utilized, and there is often open hostility to the physical and biological sciences and to scientism more generally;
>
> that any procedure of investigation begin with a recognition that the past can never be fully enough recovered for a real "history" to be written; that it continue to question evidence and reassess the criteria for evidence in order to retain an awareness of uncertainty and fallibility; and that the "positivism" of the past be rejected in favor of a perpetual openness to new evidence (although in practice dogmatisms old and new often emerge).

Conclusions from this new history are still fluid and have not yet been fully articulated. But ten more or less coherent features have emerged:

1 a concentration on the structures and material conditions of everyday life;

2 a special interest in women, whose roles, interests, feelings, and values had been ignored almost completely in traditional histories that emphasized public life;

3   an interest in home life, household tasks, domiciles, family structures, and the different roles of household members;

4   a concern with groups and classes who tend to be ignored in conventional elitist histories, especially children, servants, outcasts such as criminals or those with incurable diseases, the poor more generally, members of the working class, and those in marginal, scapegoated, or alienated groups (gypsies, beggars, the mad, etc.);

5   an interest in private life, secret lives, lives beyond the law, underground alliances and occult beliefs, and networks of gossip within or about groups with disguised identities;

6   attention to popular literature (including broadsides, pamphlets, cartoons, chapbooks, and journalistic ephemera, as well as conduct books, self-help guides and handbooks for trades, travel books, and narratives of wonder and adventure), public entertainments and recreations, games, festivals and seasonal celebrations, oral culture, and attitudes toward leisure time;

7   attempts to decipher the deep structures of thinking and to sort out how figures of speech, modes of inquiry, and patterns of everyday behavior indicate both conceptual habits and systems of value-making;

8   a concern with print technologies, bookmaking, libraries and the circulation of texts, and the interactions of written and oral traditions in such venues as parliaments, public assemblies, coffeehouses, and private conversations;

9   an interest in the physical layout of houses, streets, gardens, and public buildings and grounds, and the perceptions of physical space in cities and towns, landscapes, estates, and rooms;

10 a willingness to pursue extensive data in all kinds of archives, and a desire to translate as much data as possible into quantifiable conclusions.

The resulting history is more conscious of the domestic, the material, the everyday, and the interconnected, and more ready to study ordinary people who seem powerless and neglected – more anxious that a concept of culture include different varieties of historical methodology and different sites of investigation. This new history does not, of course, deny the importance of public history. It tacitly recognizes the growing importance of Britain as a world power and accepts the march of nationalism and imperialism that constructed a crucial sense of identity and pride. More or less unchanged in the new history is the larger sense of Britain as a nation marching forward internationally – a developing power that increasingly dominated Europe, expanded its commercial and military importance worldwide, and moved into position as a modern industrial state and imperial economy. But it insists that far more is going on in the culture than a blind acceptance of the developing national identity and that the gains in public policy and national image are achieved at a powerful social cost.

What is different here is a sense of what lies behind the large public canvas, of how five to eight million Britons lived their workaday lives while the modern Britain was being forged. The emphasis of the new history is thus on the conditions and perturbations of an individual's daily life rather than on wars, shifting foreign alignments, changes in political policy, or the conduct of public affairs. It stresses what life looked like and felt like to people going about their daily rounds – whether as queen, prime minister, merchant, farm laborer, or maidservant – and details their anxieties and fears. Because of these interests, we begin to know a lot more about such matters as crime (highwaymen haunted the main roads and heaths; the streets of London were unsafe for men or women of any rank or condition; attempts to curb crime meant that by the end of the century more than 500 crimes had become capital offences), disease (epidemics of plague, typhus, smallpox, and cholera carried off thousands of souls year after year; life expectancy, about thirty-seven at the beginning of the century, decreased by nine years by the 1730s), and a variety of other everyday conditions and patterns: poverty, physical hardship, shifts in male and female roles, urban migration, the rigors of various occupations, the implications of moving to a credit economy, changes in the class system that allowed more mobility but which finally rigidified distinctions between classes. Most important, perhaps, is the attempt to understand what it *felt* like to be involved in so much change and uncertainty. This aristocrat or that politician might be shielded, comfortable, or complacent, but life for most people in the eighteenth century was nasty, brutish, and short – just as much so as in the seventeenth century when Hobbes had thus described it. The best thing about the new history for a reader of novels is that it provides a way to grapple with situations and conflicts in novels; the worst thing is that it details change – often rapid change – as the one constant in the age, and that means trying to know not simply what "the eighteenth century" was like but rather what particular decades, or years, or days were like.

III

The enlarged and enriched historiography I have described provides some new information and a wealth of perspective about such matters as demography, literacy, the circulation of printed materials, and the social history of reading. We now have a more focused picture of what early readers of novels were like, what desires their reading satisfied, and what part reading played in their total lives. It is now possible to be fairly specific about the range of readers that novels reached and to suggest the general contours of a relationship between readerly interests and the contents of early novels. Furthermore, the knowledge we now have of competing reading materials provides a rich context for thinking about generic distinctions in literary and paraliterary kinds, the relationship between fiction and fact in the print marketplace, and (ultimately) how and why novels came to occupy such a significant cultural place in eighteenth-century Britain.

Who read novels? Ian Watt's famous "triple rise" thesis about the novel's origins – that the rise of the middle class, the rise of literacy, and the rise of the novel were related and nearly simultaneous – has often been interpreted to imply that the novel's early readers were middle class and that the novel was in fact a middle-class enterprise. Such a formulation represents a caricature of Watt's argument, a misunderstanding of the process of social change and of class history, and a vast simplification of the readership spectrum. It *is* accurate to say that early novels attracted new readers that traditional "literature" – that is, belletristic texts such as poems – did not. But it is inaccurate (and anachronistic) to think of these readers as being exclusively from the merchant class or part of a new bourgeoisie that develops with the Industrial Revolution later in the century.[3] Readership of novels extended down the social scale to include not only clerks, tradespeople, and those who had taught themselves to read for pragmatic purposes, but considerable numbers of domestic servants, both men and women, and people who – with so much new reading material available – had learned to read for pleasure. But the characteristic feature of novel readership was its social range, not its confinement to a particular class or group. "Traditional" readers – even experienced readers and critics like Alexander Pope, Jonathan Swift, Lady Mary Wortley Montagu, and Samuel Johnson, who had a stake in maintaining a literary hierarchy – consumed novels too; what was unusual about the appeal of novels was the way it spanned the social classes and traditional divisions of readers, although different kinds of readers probably read novels with different needs in mind and with different results.

We do not have a "scientific" profile of novel readers; we do not know anything precise about percentages of readers who come from different classes, age groups, or occupational categories, but we can describe quite accurately what the range consisted of and where the largest concentrations of readers were to be found. Here, in summary, is what recent demographic studies of literacy have concluded about readers and reading practices.

Literacy rose sharply during the seventeenth century, with more than twice as many literate Britons in the eighteenth century as at the beginning of the seventeenth.[4]

By 1750 at least 60 percent of the adult men in England (and perhaps more) could read and write.

Female literacy by 1750 had risen even more dramatically (and from a much smaller base); at least 40 percent of adult women (and possibly as many as half) could read. During the eighteenth century literacy increased among women faster than among men.

Literacy was increasingly common, for both men and women, in the middling and lower orders of the population, although substantial numbers of people, especially in rural areas, remained illiterate.

Literacy was higher in some regions of Britain than others: highest in Scotland, the Southeast of England, and (especially) London.

But of those who could read, which ones read novels? That is a harder question to answer statistically. Personal letters and anecdotes, reviews and advertisements, the records of circulation libraries, wills, subscription lists, and booksellers' records provide fragments of information, but nothing that adds up to a reliable profile of "typical" readers. However, what we know about readers in general, combined with what we can tell from title pages and texts about how novels were aimed, provides quite a good sense not only of who read novels but why.

"The young, the ignorant, and the idle": that was how Samuel Johnson described, at mid-century, the readers of novels.[5] But even in so stereotyping them, he showed himself familiar enough with the contents of novels to demonstrate that he himself (though forty-five years old, well-educated, and hard-working) was also among the most extensive of readers (this despite the fact that the essay from which this phrase is taken was largely an attack on the moral disrepute of novels and a warning against their pernicious effects). His opinion of "typical" novel readers, though, was widely shared by older guardians of public taste, and his characterization – if we keep in mind that it is not the *full* story – is accurate as far as it goes.

Certainly many readers of novels were young; most novels were *about* young people on the verge of making important life decisions about love or career or both, and most seem aimed at readers in similar situations; novelists repeatedly set themselves the task of addressing situations in which large numbers of readers had a vital interest. The question of ignorance is relative; what Johnson appears to mean is that such readers were not *traditionally* educated (that is, they did not necessarily know the classics or have a university education),[6] and novels usually do not require – as many eighteenth-century poems do – that their readers have such a store of knowledge. Idleness is relative too. Johnson implies that people who read novels are time wasters, but his standards were high and his point of view that of one who expected the young to be constantly pursuing directly useful tasks. And although novel readers might well steal an hour here and there from their workdays, those workdays were long (twelve hours a day or more for laborers, apprentices and tradespeople, and servants were usually on duty, although they might find breaks, during all waking hours) and without relief (domestic servants typically worked seven days, apprentices six). The time to read had to be stolen from somewhere when life was lived under such difficult and precarious conditions, and young readers must often have read deep into the night, their only private time. Leisure was for the leisure classes, and sleep and work were the only two places from which time for reading, for many readers, could come. Some reading was communal – from the Bible, sermons and devotional books, or occasionally in histories or uplifting poems – and might involve the whole household, with fathers or mothers reading to children and servants. But private reading usually was in solitude, especially when parents or masters disapproved (as most did) of young people frittering away their time on such "useless" reading as that of novels or plays.[7]

But "useless" depends on your point of view too. Moralists who wrote conduct books for the young and provided advice to their parents and employers regularly worry about the effects on the young of the many kinds of popular books readily available at bookshops in London and the leading towns. At best they thought novel reading a waste of time, at worst a serious instrument of evil. Three things especially concerned them: (1) that fictions, with imaginary solutions to problems and with heroes and heroines often rising above the social stations they were born into, could mislead the young in their expectations about life, creating yearnings and dissatisfactions in those who lived ordinary, dull, or predictable lives; (2) that the "sentiments" in novels – their valuing of feelings over rationality and received truths – corrupted the reasoning of readers; and (3) that the depictions of romance and courtship (and the representation of the languages of sexual attraction) might not only warm the imagination but overheat the passions. Didn't novels undermine the traditional authority of parents and elders and subvert conventional social values, including the expectations of hard work, obedience, piety, and contentment? Didn't they encourage passivity and weaken the fibers of independence, initiative, and decision making? Didn't they promote restlessness and dissatisfaction with one's lot and encourage the lowborn to long for richer lives, more satisfying careers, and better lovers? Novelists themselves constantly tried to counter such fears with claims about their own virtuous motives and promises of the power of novels to recommend and enforce good conduct, but questions about the effects of novels on behavior remained open throughout the century, and novels generally – even though individual books were regarded as uplifting and profitable – had an unsavory reputation well into the nineteenth century.[8]

A lot of the worry, among moralists, about the effects of novel-reading centered on young women, especially those of the susceptible lower classes whose heads might be turned and their passions inflamed. Novel reading seems to have been very popular among young women; the most persuasive evidence we have of their desire for novels is not statistical but derives from the ubiquity of warnings in conduct books, sermons, and moral treatises. Besides, the plots of novels suggest that authors envisioned many women readers among their audience, perhaps even *primarily* women readers.[9] Fewer women than men were literate, but a larger proportion of women probably (though we cannot be sure) read novels. No one seemed to have trouble believing that women, in any class, were capable of writing as well as reading. A literate woman, even someone born into the poorest and least promising social and economic circumstances like Moll Flanders, was not difficult to imagine: clearly Defoe's readers did not struggle with the question of credibility over Moll's having written her own life story – or with the supposition that she could engage in wit battles (in verse, yet) with her lover. Even Henry Fielding, who seems (in *Shamela*, 1741) to have deeply resented the idea of a servant girl telling her story of upward mobility, seems not to have doubted that Pamela could write – only that she could spell.

IV

What did readers seek in novels and what did they find? Pleasure, of course, first and foremost: the joy of escape from drudgery or routine; the pleasure of a story well told and a plot carefully built; satisfaction in seeing outcomes (and even solutions) in the recognizable situations of daily life; identification with characters who faced (and often mastered) difficult situations; and, perhaps, the recognition of a part of oneself in a fictional other who might take a different course or come to a different end – as well as the more traditional pleasures (carried over from romances) of compensatory fantasy in contemplating people quite unlike oneself. A lot of the pleasure available, especially to young readers, involved recognizable situations in the contemporary world where decisions about marriage and a course of life were practical ones no longer dependent just on the demands of parents or community; where individual needs and desires counted as much as convention and tradition. The fact that novels usually portrayed ordinary human beings in the midst of ordinary human crises – but crises very much tied to particular circumstances then in the process of social readjustment and historical change – meant that a variety of readers could identify with the problems (and sometimes the heroines or heroes) they met there. And such content also meant that basic cultural facts were available: about courtship, about decision making, about the practical consequences involved in the choices one made about career, marriage partner, and way of life. These stories were "realistic" not just in the way they relied on contemporary norms of ordinariness, probability, and credibility, but also because they represented the implications of choices in local and contemporary terms.

The availability of such "facts" – for, correct or not, they appeared to be "facts" as presently understood by society – provided a ready form of instruction about conventions, social expectations, and community opinion, and they provided especially useful guidance for young readers as yet inexperienced in the world. Because of the persistent and steady migration of the young to London (and away from the smaller supportive communities that provided a familiar – if often coercive – ethos for earlier generations), large numbers of readers turned to novels for information difficult to come by in as attractive a form elsewhere. Other books did offer such information, for example conduct books that spelled out directions fully (though usually in thou-shalt-not form), and many other kinds of narratives: epics and traditional histories, for example, that described the expectations of past ages, and Continental romances that recorded the norms in contemporary France or Italy. But novels became, for tens of thousands of young men and women in eighteenth-century England, guides to many practical decisions about life, the equivalent of family stories and oral tradition in earlier generations and of self-help books and films in later ones.

One reason that the social norms of novels had such cultural power in the eighteenth century was that they usually reflected the values of "modern" London life and represented to those – especially the young – who aspired to migrate to London what sophisticated lives could be like. Not all novels are set in London – though an astonishing number are either centered there or can hardly wait to get there, setting up their plots to fulfill the promise of London excitement and sophistication early on in the text[10] – but they describe modern urban conflicts and enact the cosmopolitan rituals that offer urban fantasy to rural would-be emigrants.

London was the center of the book trade as well as the hub of economic, political, and intellectual life. It was where most authors (novelists and otherwise) did their writing and where a disproportionate number of readers lived. Londoners were not only more literate and more cosmopolitan, but also more apt to talk publicly about their reading and to be influenced in what they read by conversations and their sense of public trends and intellectual directions. The coffeehouse served this function throughout the century for most London men, especially those who fancied themselves in the "public sphere"; by mid-century the phenomenon had spread into the countryside so that any town of any size had at least one coffeehouse. Women were not barred from coffeehouses, and their presence there may have been more significant than we have been led to believe. But women's conversation about their reading (and other matters) usually took place at levees, balls, and at other private gatherings. More important, though, than what Londoners actually did or thought of themselves was what those in other parts of Britain thought of them. Most Britons thought of London as a bellwether of modernity, the place where what was new – in material goods, economic ideas, or intellectual capital – was available first. It was connected closely to Europe and the rest of the world by diplomacy and trade, and it set the tone for the rest of the nation. Older Britons tended to hate its trendiness and distrust its fickleness and shifting standards; younger ones looked to it hopefully for their own futures, and the young migrated there with increasing frenzy through the late seventeenth and early eighteenth century, even though the dangers of the city – crowding, bad sanitation, disease, vice, and violence – were legendary.[11] It represented – to the young – change, excitement, and promise and, for the same reasons, represented to older generations the road to hell. The symbolic importance of London to the rest of Britain was out of all proportion to its size and population, and the systems of intellectual circulation – centered in the print and book trade – found many ways, including the printing of novels and distribution of them to the provinces, to exploit the developing sense of cultural hegemony. One reason, among many others, that critics distrusted novels and other books with similar appeal was that they seemed to threaten – indeed did threaten – the older, rural, land-centered, solid, stable, and predictable Britain of earlier generations. Theorists from the left and right have long debated whether novels were subversive or regressive in their implications, but there has never been much agreement about the political implications of the genre, perhaps because it has performed different functions and served different masters at different times. The novel's radical tendencies seem to have been most heavily influential early on when it was broadly disapproved of and distrusted. Novels represented (among other things) new and upsetting values and unpredictable ways of living, thinking, and believing.

To readers like Pope or Johnson (conservative protectors of the tradition who wanted to preserve literature from the incursions of popular culture), novels were – quite apart from whatever values they represented or espoused – trash reading. Reading a novel was equivalent to spending one's time with ephemeral tracts, sensational journalistic stories, or the many kinds of cheap popular books that appeared every new day in booksellers' stalls: how-to guides on ethics and the practical needs of different trades, biographies of notorious thieves and pirates, political pamphlets, travel books, accounts of crime, popular summaries of history or antiquity, and anthologies of thematic anecdotes, cautionary tales, or heroic lives.[12] Such books were cheap compared to books bought to be kept elegantly in an aristocrat's library (early in the century, short pamphlets of ephemera were priced between one penny and one shilling, whereas a volume of Pope's poems could cost a thousand times as much). But wages were low too. *Robinson Crusoe* in 1719 cost five shillings (the bookstall price for its 364 pages in unbound sheets), and that was the equivalent of almost a week's wages for a young laborer.

How, then, could young, poor people afford novels? Most could not, strictly speaking, and there is little evidence that a typical youth had much of a library of novels or anything else. But novels could be borrowed or shared; by mid-century a series of "subscription libraries" had begun to spring up both in London and most towns. In Bath, for example, for one pound a year a patron got the right to borrow a volume a week. Since novels after 1740 were usually published in multiple volumes (*Clarissa*, for example, was published in seven volumes; *Betsy Thoughtless* in four), that process could mean awkward reading if, say, when you returned the first volume, someone else had checked out volume 2; readers often had to cope by reading volumes out of order. Also, one pound was a considerable sum for a servant whose annual wage amounted (besides room and board) to only seven or eight pounds, so that less formal systems of borrowing developed, especially among the young, in which volumes were traded back and forth within a household or among friends. In a context in which novel reading was generally disapproved of anyway by parents and masters, the surreptitious trading of novels (and the hiding of them in one's private closet where private reading took place) became an economy of its own, a form of print circulation that – however unofficial – was an important part of daily life both before and after the institution of accessible quasipublic libraries.[13] In the early part of the century when there were relatively few novels around and a somewhat more specialized reading economy,[14] such unofficial circulation of novels included other kinds of disapproved contraband as well, including printed plays and Continental romances, and the system was rather primitive. By the 1750s, however, new novels appeared every week and when the accumulated list of titles began to be extensive, the network of readers became larger and provided more choices.

Only gradually over the century did novels lure readers away from the traditional "higher" forms of literature.[15] At first, novels competed with strictly pragmatic reading about manners and conduct, journalistic ventures describing contemporary events, sensational popular accounts of crime and adventure, and exotic escapist tales. Few took the literary pretensions of novels seriously, even when, near mid-century, Henry Fielding pretended to give the new upstart tradition an ancient pedigree by claiming Homer as the original model and setting himself up as arbiter for this "new province" of writing.[16] But literary protectionists had, early on, begun to worry about competition from the popular culture that novels represented. At opposite ends of the century, Pope and Wordsworth argue quite differently about the proper subjects and designs of poetry, but they share a concern that prose fiction is making territorial gains at the expense of poetry. For Pope, literature is threatened by the debased taste and sheer volume of print trying to satisfy popular demand. *The Dunciad* (1728) does not single out novels for special wrath but merges them with other products of the "Smithfield Muses"[17] that threaten to displace better books; his worry is that there will be no space for the more demanding and sophisticated texts that he and his talented friends were writing. He thinks that bad literature drives out good, and he associates the good with traditional genres, educated tastes, and established standards. For Wordsworth, writing in 1800 in the preface to the second edition of *Lyrical Ballads*, the worry is that novels have taken over the subjects, stories, tones, and language that poetry needs to reclaim for itself.

The literary objections to novels never were as shrill in the eighteenth century as religious and moral objections, but judges like Pope early in the century, Johnson in mid-century, and Wordsworth at the end did see plainly the threat to traditional genres posed by writing that was more accessible to larger numbers of readers. What is especially interesting, however, is how clearly and quickly the writers came to see, and grasp, the popular literary opportunity. If it is true – as most recent literary theory and present cultural history tend to argue, and as I have assumed throughout this chapter – that readerly needs and desires have as important a role in the creation of books as the specific aims and intentions of authors, then writerly directions are chiefly interesting for what they tell us about the way the wind was blowing. And the writing careers of the early novelists that are looked at that way, are quite fascinating.

V

A few writers in the eighteenth century kept themselves "pure" from novelistic writing – Pope, for example, although even he can be seen, in theorizing the epic or in narrativizing the powers of Dulness, to have been reacting defensively. But it is surprising how many writers, opposed in spirit to the subjective directions and representational ideologies of the novel, were sucked into its field. *Gulliver's Travels* (1726) is not, by the usual definitions, a novel, but it reacts to the prosperity of novels in withering ways. Swift clearly is writing in the wake of narratives of a particular kind that he despises, and answering those narratives with a satiric alternative that rejects subjectivity and everything that goes with it.[18] Similarly Johnson, distrusting the moral ambiguities inherent in fictions that rendered the complexities of real life, offered in *Rasselas* (1759) a narrative alternative that had very different features from the novels he criticized.[19] The careers of Defoe and Haywood, the two leading producers of popular fiction in the 1720s, are also instructive, in quite different ways. Defoe, although he had several other careers as well, clearly thought of himself as a man of letters (he was especially proud of his poetry) and wrote in practically every literary and paraliterary genre imaginable, producing some of the most popular titles of his time for widely varied audiences. At age fifty-nine, when he had already authored 300 or so published titles, he wrote *Robinson Crusoe* and then followed it with half a dozen other novelistic fictions – perhaps his most dense genre concentration in his long and varied career. Haywood wrote mainly fiction throughout her career, although she did other writing as well, but her later fictions are quite different from the early ones. Between 1719 and the late twenties, she produced at least a dozen works of fiction, most of them bearing a conscious debt to Continental romances and largely (but not wholly) resisting the "realistic" directions of the newer fiction. When she resumed writing fiction later, after a hiatus of almost ten years, her work is much more like that of the mainstream novelists.

But even more instructive are the careers of literally dozens of writers who set themselves up for different kinds of writing careers but who found themselves inevitably tangled in the enlarging web. Some (especially late in the seventeenth century and early in the eighteenth) wrote novels simply as one of several ways to make a living by their pens; Francis Kirkman, Aphra Behn, John Dunton, William Congreve, Charles Gildon, Delarivier Manley, and Catherine Trotter are examples of those who produced novels but whose primary writing was of some other kind. Plainly they sensed the developing audience for "realistic" narrative fiction and took advantage of it, but none of them found novel writing compelling as a career direction. A little later, though, writers who intended to concentrate on other kinds of writing found themselves mainly writing novels: Henry Fielding, for example, was London's best-known playwright in the 1730s before turning primarily to novel writing in the forties, and Tobias Smollett came to London in the 1740s to write plays but then made a long career in novel-writing instead. Novels were so popular in the 1750s and sixties – and so challenging to write in the wake of the competing successes of *Clarissa* and *Tom Jones* at the end of the forties[20] – that writers from all kinds of backgrounds turned to novels and proved to be novelists of interest and talent: Sarah Fielding, Charlotte Lennox, Laurence Sterne, Horace Walpole, Frances Sheridan, Richard Graves, and Oliver Goldsmith are important examples. By 1750 the novel had become culturally significant enough to influence (and in many cases determine) the careers of anyone, male or female, interested in writing.

VI

There is an important danger inherent in speaking of "the eighteenth century" or "the eighteenth-century novel": the tendency to think in synchronic and generic terms as if all novels were more or less alike and no major changes took place within the century. The greater specifics of history – decade by decade, year by year, and even day by day – are often important to both the reading of individual texts and considerations of patterns and directions, but it is very hard, even for experts in the field, to sort out trends thoughtfully and apply sensibly the criteria of difference to accounts of continuity and definition. Cultures change as rivers do: you never step into the same culture twice. Yet we need to generalize about "characteristic" texts, gestures, and events in order to distinguish patterns in the passage of time and keep everything from seeming no more than flux.

By 1800, when the novel had an established (if still suspected and precarious) literary and cultural place in Britain, the world looked very different than it had in 1700. Britain, like the rest of Europe, was abuzz with significant social change that involved not just evolutions and shifts within a society but total inversions of power. Revolutions had taken place in America and France, and reverberations threatened every European nation and people. Although Britain itself was physically untouched by both, the intellectual and psychological climate had undergone enormous change, and important internal "revolutions" had begun to take place: the Industrial Revolution first and foremost, but also vast changes in social habits, agricultural methods, and relationships among classes. For many, material life had improved considerably; life expectancy was on the rise, new methods of policing and punishing seemed to have crime more nearly under control,[21] and strong new ideological movements were under way – feminism, pacifism, antislavery. Still, however, education at the highest (university) level remained scandalously poor in quality and, of course, severely limited to the privileged few, and literacy had actually begun to slip in the new industrial parts of the nation.

Novels in 1800 reflected a more sophisticated and demanding reading public and a broader awareness of larger social and political issues. Late eighteenth-century novels weren't necessarily better than early ones, but they had almost a century of solid experimental history behind them, and reader expectations were more firmly set. They had become more "literary" too, and typically they were more demanding of readers, counting on more knowledge and a wider range of "life" experience. It was not that they had forsaken their heritage in popular culture – they retained a broad spectrum of strategies and readers – but their greater respectability meant more readers in the top range who read them as "literature." Serious readers now often did record in their diaries the details of their reading, and well-educated folk corresponded about novels as well as poems and other serious texts – so much so that an intellectual rebellion was brewing against the novel among the rising Romantic poets.

Changes in eighteenth-century novels roughly trace the changes in eighteenth-century social and cultural history, but *only* roughly. In the shifting concerns of novels at the end of the century – toward politics, transnational awareness, and concern with radicalism and revolution and (at the same time) toward concentration on the domestic household and a narrowed female sphere – one can get a powerful sense of cultural preoccupation and direction, but there is a danger in trying to move from the concerns of any one novel, or any group of novels, to large conclusions about cultural characteristics or movement. Even the most "faithful" or "realistic" of novels about contemporary life take a particular slant on events and values and offer perspective and conclusions. And all novels select ruthlessly, they do not try to characterize a century or a culture. Thus, the powerful sense of distrust, uncertain identity, deception, and intrigue that characterizes Godwin's *Caleb Williams* may be important to the culture of the 1790s, but it need not *define* the culture or be the most significant feature of the culture just because Godwin used it so successfully to make the plot of his novel work for its first readers. The theoretical risk of deriving conclusions about any culture from its novels may be no greater than the difficulties arising from the interpretation of any set of texts or from any other particular kind of reconstructed evidence or factual data. Social historians have always used novels extensively to help get a handle on both the details of everyday life and their sponsoring patterns and directions, and the evidence they offer is important. But novels also have a special kind of danger because of the particular coherence, clarity, and appeal of their presentation; the illusion they offer of a complete world can easily be mistaken, even by experts, in sorting evidence, as more complete and more accurate than it really is. Novels – like any other kind of textual or documentary evidence – have to be used carefully and sensibly not only because they are selective but because they are themselves – in their rhetorical aspect – part of the mechanism of development and change. Although they are, in themselves, a kind of social history[22] – an attempt to record contemporary life and write its story according to some coherent pattern – novels are also players within the culture, agents as well as portrayers. Novels sometimes reach for radical or reformist ideals through their didactic tendency. They try to make things happen as well as reflect what has already happened; they embody rhetoric as well as representation.

The word "representation" has in recent years become a very popular term for describing what texts do for their culture. It conceptualizes rather differently the way texts try to render or recapitulate the world they grow out of and try to describe. Critical terms formerly used to define this process – verbs such as "reflect," "mirror," "portray," and "picture," and their noun equivalents – had tended to suggest accuracy and exactitude, even a slavish adherence to trying to describe things as they are. In such a conception, writers become a recorder or photographic mechanism for preservation rather than an active agent *within* history as well as a scribe of it. To "represent" thus means to approximate in another medium what a novelist sees and wishes to preserve, but it also means to be a substitute, an advocate, someone who acts on behalf of, as do representatives in a legislature. The role of the writer as an agent – though not always an altogether conscious one – of the culture is thus underscored; the term admits the cultural condition of the writer as part of an ongoing process.

But, more, when novelists become a culture's representative, they also become part of the process of change itself; just as culture is never static but always in motion toward a later point in time when it will be something definably different, any text that has readers participates in the process of change. Readers read, respond, react; the culture itself is altered, made different as a result of the text. And writers to some extent anticipate – and to some extent control – the process. They have positions to uphold, causes to support, axes to grind, things they want to happen. They rhetoricize as well as report and record. Novels, then, may be said to "represent" the culture both in rendering a version of it and in being a vehicle of ongoing self-adjustment and change.

The "accuracy" of novels as a record of social history is thus doubly, even quadruply, complicated. Novels rely on a context of which they are a part, and they address it with a design to modify it, make it move on. And then there is the issue of intention that overlays the other two: novels like any other texts may produce effects either consciously wrought or not. That is, they may have effects either that their author "intended" or those beyond what the author could control. Accuracy is thus always an issue but never *the* issue because what is being represented is also being altered.

VII

Let me try to illustrate the issues of representation and accuracy by suggesting, briefly, the social and textual implications of two novels written half a century apart, *The Fortunes and Misfortunes of Moll Flanders* (1722) and *Evelina, or the History of a Young Lady's Entrance into the World* (1778). *Moll Flanders* tells us a lot about what it would have been like then to be a woman in the London underworld; Moll has to make her way – without many resources of family, upbringing, education, social position, or material well-being – in a hostile urban world. But she is clever, persevering, and alert to opportunity, and she manages to make do, at last becoming both penitent and rich. The novel gives us a clear sense of daily life and the anxieties that go with economic and social uncertainty, and it is quite detailed about the specifics of being female in the criminal world. The author, Daniel Defoe, was not female, an orphan, or a prostitute and pickpocket; he was, however, a lifelong Londoner, someone who lived by his wits, and for much of his life a social "outsider." He spent years living from hand to mouth, and he knew what prisons were like. He was also a solitary and furtive figure, used to being pursued by creditors or enemies, and he knew what it was to have to wrestle one's conscience when faced by dilemmas of survival and honesty.

The social detail in *Moll Flanders* seems largely accurate when measured against what we know from other texts, and is often circumstantial and specific. Even the scenes in Virginia, the "new" (but not totally untroubled) world where Moll grows rich and penitent after being "transported" there as a convicted felon, are full of geographical and sociological detail, though Defoe never traveled to America and knew what he knew second hand. In short, the more we know about the London of Defoe's time, the more likely we are to be impressed with his ability to render it accurately and sympathetically – to give us "social history" even though writing fiction.

But Defoe was not just giving us social history, nor was he just telling a good story. His novel has political and economic implications as well as aesthetic and emotional ones.

Moll's fortunes improve permanently only in Virginia. Before that, she has ups as well as downs, but her criminal past finally catches up with her so fully that execution seems the only possibility. Once her sentence is commuted to "transportation," however, she has a new chance in the New World, and even though the Old World (and her past) still haunts her (the incest episodes), she is finally able to show her worth: "at last [she] grew *Rich*, liv'd *Honest*, and died a *Penitent*." The new and prosperous life in the New World resolves thematically the pattern of transgression, repentance, and redemption that in part structures the narrative (especially for someone born in the prison called "Newgate"), but it also comments on the social constructions of crime and punishment and suggests the social possibilities of regeneration and reform, especially as they bear on the demography of the American colonies. Just four years before Defoe wrote *Moll Flanders*, Britain enacted a new law – the so-called "Transportation Act" of 1718 – the explicit design of which was to rid London of convicted criminals and (at the same time) send to America (mostly to Virginia and Maryland) new white colonists.[23] Virginia especially resented the move and quickly passed a law refusing such immigrants, though that law was first ignored and then dissolved by parliament; after 1718 the British regularly sent several shiploads a year of prisoners to the New World, a practice that continued until American Independence.

Seen in this context, the "happy" ending of Moll Flanders is not just a gratuitous nod to prevailing notions of poetic justice and a sop to sentimental belief in religious conversion, but a working out of larger social problems in urban England and the population-poor colonies: you expunge criminals from their corrupt environment, free them from their pasts, assign them regenerative work, and *voila!* they renew themselves as productive citizens. Whether reading such books made Virginians feel better about their new neighbors may be doubtful, but we do know that (although they found Britain's new policy at first unbearable) they ultimately had to accept many thousands of convicted felons, some of whom did reform and construct productive new lives in a new place and many of whom became sons and daughters of the American Revolution.[24] The effects of books cannot easily be calculated, and no one can say exactly what impact Defoe's popular novel had on London or Virginia readers; what we do know is that "transportation" became an accepted policy for dealing with crime and colonization and that *Moll Flanders* was one of the cultural components bearing on the public response to legal and social policy. Among other things, *Moll Flanders* is an intervention in the public discussion of public policy, a rhetorical statement, a social agent as well as a response and representation.

The social history in *Evelina* seems more straightforward and conventional, but this novel too involves not only representation of contemporary life but also notable intervention in it. When *Evelina* first appeared it was regarded as having represented the "history of a young lady's entrance into the world" in an especially telling way, explicitly rendering both the hidden rituals and the feelings, manners, and private behaviors of young women in the process of coming of age socially and sexually. Recording particulars in a vivid, familiar, and persuasive way was, of course, what by 1778 the novel was generally regarded as doing in almost every instance. What made *Evelina* such a revelation to its early readers is the way it opened a view to things that women did not talk about to men, matters that had, up until then, escaped full disclosure even in the most intimate stories of private personal life. It was not that Burney was physiologically or sexually explicit, but she managed to reveal in astonishing detail what it felt like to be female, insecure, vulnerable, innocent, and in love, and what it meant for an ingenue to learn acceptable habits. The first readers of *Evelina* felt as if they were being let in on secrets – especially secrets of courtship ritual and the female heart – that had never before been so fully revealed. Readers at the time repeatedly commented on the way Burney represented these details because no previous account had offered quite so intimate and detailed a picture of how young women acted in private in circumstances like hers. Because the novel was published anonymously and even Burney's most intimate friends did not know she had written it, the author herself often overheard her book praised for describing details of dressing and preparing for visits and balls, and she described these conversations in her diary. Men (and some women) who had not themselves witnessed this behavior reported themselves astonished and reacted as if the scales had just fallen from their eyes; those who already "knew" found it a kind of public exposure.

Such a representation in a novel changed perceptions and to an extent practice; a reader who had read Burney could never again be "surprised" in the same way by subsequent reading, and (besides) knowledge of the behavior modified actual social practice. Some of the "secrets" of women's life beyond men's gazes were now "out"; in the representation, Burney both shrank what could be done in subsequent novels and affected how women behaved after reading her book. Those young women readers in the country who read novels to find out how to act (or even how to feel) in particular life circumstances, here acquired behavior-affecting knowledge.[25] Burney may or may not have *intended* such effects; her novel may or may not

33

involve a conscious social and ethical rhetoric for its time, but its social impact transcended the solitary, contemplative, and usually passive act of reading. We still know too little about the "affect" of reading – how books can make things happen – and we have no reliable way of measuring the social impact of literature.[26] But in some instances – *Evelina* is a concrete example – we can sometimes trace at least generally the outcome as well as the input of social and cultural history.

Social history is often complicated and is always – at least to some extent – unknown. Novels help reveal it to historians (or to any readers, for that matter), and they participate in it, whether they mean to or not. "Knowing" history is never the sure activity scholars would like, but even a partial sense of it can be an enormous help in understanding how people in other cultures behave. The past is another culture – or rather a whole series of cultures – just as surely as Jamaica, Nigeria, or Beijing, and it takes precise knowledge as well as a sympathetic imagination for readers to confront that culture intelligently in their reading. One can generalize and theorize to some extent about the readerly process, but ultimately the process, like social history and like novels themselves, is best left to particulars.

NOTES

1 Early in the twentieth century, for example, scholarship on Burney far exceeded in quantity that on Tobias Smollett, but by the 1950s Smollett had for some reason become a "major" figure and Burney a "minor" one. It is instructive to look at the early twentieth-century volumes of the *PMLA Bibliography* to see how much more varied scholarship on literary figures was then; the narrowing of interest to major figures took place at mid-century and was more pronounced in American than British scholarship.

2 Interesting exceptions are Richard Altick, *The Shows of London* (Cambridge, Mass.: Belknap Press of Harvard University, 1978), Ronald Paulson, *Popular and Polite Art in the Age of Hogarth and Fielding* (Notre Dame, Ind.: University of Notre Dame Press, 1979), and Pat Rogers, *Literature and Popular Culture in Eighteenth-Century England* (Brighton: Harvester, 1985). Recently there are again signs that such interest has been renewed; see especially Dennis Todd, *Imagining Monsters* (Chicago: University of Chicago Press, 1995).

3 Peter Earle has recently argued that a kind of "middle class" – that is, an identifiable group of a "middling sort" – did begin to develop in England before the Industrial Revolution (*The Making of the English Middle Class: Business, Society and Family Life in London, 1660–1730* (London: Methuen, 1989)). But see, too, L. Davidoff and C. Hall, *Family Fortunes: Men and Women of the English Middle Class, 1780–1850* (London: Hutchinson, 1987). The powerful connotations of the term "middle class" inaccurately type the readership of early novels.

4 Figures offered by literacy experts vary considerably, in part because of definitions of literacy (is it the ability to sign one's name, or to read at a certain level?) and in part because hard data are difficult to come by before 1753, when Lord Hardwicke's Marriage Act required that both men and women sign marriage registers (thus giving modern researchers a consistent set of records to work with). The figures in Lawrence Stone's influential account ("Literacy and Education in England, 1640–1900," *Past and Present*, 42 (1969): 69–139) now seem to most observers too optimistic, but equally suspect are the probably too conservative figures of David Cressy ("Literacy in Context: Meaning and Measurement in Early Modern England," in *Consumption and the World of Goods*, ed. John Brewer and Roy Porter (London: Routledge, 1993) and *Literacy and the Social Order; Reading and Writing in Tudor and Stuart England* (Cambridge: Cambridge University Press, 1980). Sir Keith Thomas has suggested that "There is some reason . . . to think that Dr. Cressy's figures for illiteracy . . . are not just an underestimate of those who could read, but a spectacular underestimate" ("The Meaning of Literacy in Early Modern England," in *The Written Word: Literacy in Transition*, ed. Gerd Baumann (Oxford: Clarendon, 1986), 103). For a lucid account of the working procedures in historical studies of literacy, see R. S. Schofield, "The Measurement of Literacy in Pre-Industrial England," in Jack Goody, ed., *Literacy in Traditional Societies* (Cambridge: Cambridge University Press, 1968), 311–25. Most literacy experts now concede, however, that the standard procedure of analyzing signatures in public documents is especially unreliable for women early on in the century, for there is independent evidence that women unable to write were sometimes avid readers.

5 *Rambler*, 4 (1754).
6 A university education was not, however, necessarily very good. Oxford and Cambridge were at their nadir, with a very low quality of instruction and diminishing enrollments. Many observers believed that Academies founded by the Dissenters (who were barred by law from attending the universities) were far superior in quality, and the aristocracy often sent their sons to universities (such as Leyden) abroad. Daughters were educated privately.
7 Household design was such that people of all classes had small private spaces ("closets") of their own; most solitary reading and writing took place in these closets, and books and diaries were usually stashed there.
8 See Kathleen Tillotson, *Novels of the Eighteen Forties* (Oxford: Clarendon, 1954), 15–16.
9 Critics sometimes assume that women writers wrote for women readers and men for men, but the texts themselves suggest that such a simple division was unlikely. Some individual novels were probably aimed at limited groups (by gender, class, religion, etc.), but most novels seem to have tried for a wide audience, at least by the 1750s when novels had a broadly varied readership. Sarah Scott's *Millenium Hall* (1762), for example, although mostly about women's issues, goes out of its way to include male observers as part of its way of evaluating a special, segregated house for women – apparently to make male readers feel included and comfortable.
10 Eliza Haywood's *History of Miss Betsy Thoughtless* (London: T. Gardner, 4 vols., 1751), for example, takes only sixteen pages (of its total of almost 1,200) to transport readers to London, and London is clearly the "hook" for readers: "Miss Betsy had never seen this great metropolis; but had heard so much of the gay manner in which the genteel part of the world passed their time in it, that she was quite transported at being told she was to be removed thither" (II: 16).
11 A social historian of three generations ago, M. Dorothy George, still has the most graphic account of grisly life and death in early eighteenth-century London; see *London Life in the Eighteenth Century* (London: Kegan Paul, 1925). Contemporary travelers describe the exact place, miles away, where those on their way to London could pick up the stench of the city – largely the product of the sloppy, and dangerous, open sewers.
12 According to Joseph Spence, Pope once said that "Defoe wrote a vast many things; and none bad, though none excellent except [*Robinson Crusoe*]." (*Anecdotes, Observations and Characters of Books and Men* [1819; Carbondale: Southern Illinois University Press, 1964.]) Charles Gildon, a jealous rival of Defoe, claimed that any poor old women who could manage the price bought *Robinson Crusoe* and placed it on a bookshelf next to other works of popular piety such as *Pilgrim's Progress* (*The Life and Strange Surprizing Adventures of Mr. D — DeF —, of London, Hosier* (London: J. Roberts, 1719)). He did not mean it as a compliment.
13 I have discussed this in more detail in "The Loneliness of the Long-Distance Reader," *Genre*, 10 (1977): 455–84.
14 Gendered reading habits seem, then, to have been more distinct, perhaps because most books were plainly designed for male readers, and those that had women in mind were specifically directed to them through clear title-page indicators. Early in the history of the novel, Defoe's adventure novels and Haywood's early love

stories seem to have had fairly distinct audiences defined by gender, though Defoe obviously tried, especially in *Roxana: the Fortunate Mistress* (1724), to gain a female audience as well. And there are strong indications that even so male-centered a novel as *Robinson Crusoe* found many female readers. But the cross-reading seems to have gotten stronger as the century progressed, something that is obscured when "woman's" novels are discussed separately as in the otherwise excellent studies by Jane Spencer (*The Rise of the Woman Novelist, from Aphra Behn to Jane Austen* [Oxford: Blackwell, 1986]) and Ros Ballaster (*Seductive Forms: Women's Amatory Fiction from 1684–1740* [Oxford: Clarendon, 1992]).

15 Where the "origin" of the novel is sited depends on one's definition. It is easy enough to construct a plausible definition of the novel that makes Behn the originator (*Love Letters Between a Nobleman and His Sister* [1684–87] and *Oroonoko* [1688]), or Defoe (*Robinson Crusoe* [1719] and *Roxana: the Fortunate Mistress* [1724]), or Richardson (*Pamela* [1740] and *Clarissa* [1747–48]). But recent theorists of origins are, relatively speaking, less concerned to find a specific first instance than to try to explain the total cultural context that created a desire for novels. Ian Watt (*The Rise of the Novel: Studies in Defoe, Richardson and Fielding* [1957; Berkeley: University of California Press, 1964]) argued that a new "formal realism" develops from the rise of literacy and a new class of readers. Lennard J. Davis (*Factual Fictions: the Origins of the English Novel* [New York: Columbia University Press, 1983]) sees the key in journalism. Michael McKeon (*The Origins of the English Novel, 1600–1740* [Baltimore: Johns Hopkins University Press, 1987]) stresses conceptual changes that over two centuries create a philosophical climate of receptivity for a different kind of hybridized literary form. Nancy Armstrong (*Desire and Domestic Fiction: a Political History of the Novel* [London and New York: Oxford University Press, 1987]) argues that the creation of a separate domestic sphere opens the door for female fictions of home life. My own *Before Novels: the Cultural Contexts of Eighteenth-Century English Fiction* (New York and London: W. W. Norton, 1990) argues that genre construction involves permutations among many different kinds of available forms and materials, and sees the novel developing out of cultural needs that had earlier been divided among a combination of popular reading materials. There has not yet been a good study tracing the relationship of the early English novel to its Continental predecessors, though Ros Ballaster (*Seductive Forms*) has argued sensibly that a common feminized sphere unites early women's novels with a coherent group of French narratives.

16 See especially the preface to *Joseph Andrews* (1742). Henry Fielding, again took up issues of definition and origin in the "interchapters" (that is, the first chapters of each book) of *Tom Jones* (1749).

17 The *Dunciad* purports to trace the movement of taste that brought the "Smithfield" muses – that is, the products of popular culture – to the polite end of town (Westminster) where kings and courtiers adopted the "lower" tastes of their social inferiors.

18 Swift had earlier (in *A Tale of a Tub*, published in 1704 but probably written about 1697) attacked the subjective and modernist drift in popular fiction.

19 On the relation of this kind of narrative (which he calls "apologue") to the

novel, see Sheldon Sacks, *Fiction and the Shape of Belief* (Berkeley and Los Angeles: University of California Press, 1964).

20 The extensive experimentation in the 1750s, perhaps the most broadly creative decade in the first century of the English novel, has oddly enough not yet been much studied. Later directions – involving sentimentalism, Gothicism, and *fin de siècle* politics – have attracted most of the critical attention to novelistic development and change.

21 For an interesting argument about the novel's role in this cultural change, see John Bender, *Imagining the Penitentiary: Fiction and the Architecture of Mind in Eighteenth-Century England* (Chicago: University of Chicago Press, 1987).

22 See Morroe Berger, *Real and Imagined Worlds: the Novel and Social Science* (Cambridge, Mass.: Harvard University Press, 1977).

23 See J. M. Beattie, *Crime and the Courts in England, 1660–1800* (Oxford: Clarendon, 1986).

24 Information about criminal transportation here derives from research I under-took in preparing the Bedford Cultural Edition of *Moll Flanders* (Boston: Bedford Books, 1995).

25 Anthea Zeman (*Presumptuous Girls: Women and Their World in the Serious Woman's Novel* [London: Weidenfeld and Nicolson, 1977]) makes the useful point that novels such as Burney's provided practical and quite specific advice for young women about how to get on in unfamiliar social situations: how to refuse an unwanted dance partner, for example, or how to exercise discretion in public places.

26 For some interesting speculations see Diana Spearman, *The Novel and Society* (London: Routledge and Kegan Paul, 1966).

READING LIST

Buck, Anne, *Dress in Eighteenth-Century England* (London: Batsford, 1979).

Clark, J. C. D., *English Society, 1688–1832: Ideology, Social Structure and Political Practice During the Ancien Regime* (Cambridge: Cambridge University Press, 1985).

Clarkson, L. A., *Death, Disease and Famine in Pre-Industrial England* (Dublin: Gill and Macmillan, 1975).

Cockburn, J. S. (ed.), *Crime in England: 1550–1750* (London: Methuen, 1977).

Colley, Linda, *Britons: Forging the Nation, 1707–1837* (New Haven: Yale University Press, 1993).

Dickinson, H. T., *Liberty and Property: Political Ideology in Eighteenth Century Britain* (London: Weidenfeld and Nicholson, 1977).

Eisenstein, Elizabeth L., *The Printing Press as an Agent of Change* (Cambridge: Cambridge University Press, 2 vols., 1979).

Hay, Douglas *et al*, *Albion's Fatal Tree: Crime and Society in Eighteenth-Century England* (London: Allen Lane, 1976).

Hecht, J. Jean, *The Domestic Servant Class in Eighteenth-Century England* (London: Routledge and Kegan Paul, 1956).

Holmes, Geoffrey, *Augustan England: Professions, State and Society, 1680–1730* (London: Allen and Unwin, 1982).

Mason, Philip, *The English Gentleman: The Rise and Fall of an Ideal* (London: Andre Deutsch, 1982).

McKendrick, Neil, John Brewer and J. H. Plumb (ed.), *The Birth of a Consumer Society: The Commercialization of Eighteenth-Century England* (London: Europa, 1982).

Plant, Marjorie, *The Domestic Life of Scotland in the Eighteenth Century* (Edinburgh: Edinburgh University Press, 1952).
The English Book Trade: an Economic History of the Making and Sale of Books (London: Allen and Unwin, 1939).

Plumb, J. H., *The Commercialization of Leisure in the Eighteenth Century* (Reading: Univ. of Reading, 1973).
The Growth of Political Stability in England, 1675–1725 (London: Macmillan, 1967).
"The New World of Children in the Eighteenth Century," *Past and Present*, No. 67 (1975), 64–95.

Rivers, Isabel (ed.) *Books and Their Readers in Eighteenth-Century England* (Leicester: Leicester University Press, 1982).

Rogers, Pat, *Grub Street: Studies in a Subculture* (London: Methuen, 1972).

Rudé, George, *The Crowd in History: a Study of Popular Disturbances in France and England, 1730–1848* (New York: John Wiley, 1964).

Rule, John, *Albion's People: English Society, 1714–1815* (London: Longman, 1992).

Speck, W. A., *Stability and Strife: England 1714–1760* (London: Edward Arnold, 1977).

Staves, Susan, *Married Women's Separate Property in England, 1660–1833* (Cambridge, Mass.: Harvard University Press, 1990).

3

MAX NOVAK

Defoe as an innovator of fictional form

That the novel began in either 1719 with Daniel Defoe's *Robinson Crusoe* or in 1740 with Samuel Richardson's *Pamela* is a commonplace familiar to all students of English literature. Both assertions are based upon the notion that an entirely new literary form emerged in the first half of Britain's eighteenth century, for no one familiar with early fiction would deny that an extensive body of prose fiction existed before either of these two dates. Without attempting to show that the so-called "Greek romances" of antiquity contained almost all the possibilities that the eighteenth-century novelists were to explore, as a recent critic has maintained,[1] I find it difficult to disqualify Cervantes's *Don Quixote*, some of the many picaresque fictions of the sixteenth and seventeenth centuries, and many of the extremely popular "novels" (a work of prose fiction often as long as a modern novel and frequently about contemporary life)[2] written mainly in France and Spain during the latter century merely because they were not written in English. All might claim precedence. From the middle of the nineteenth century to what is nearly the end of the twentieth, this debate over origins has been confused by privileging the word "novel" as the highest form of prose fiction in an evolutionary sense. For a time, those works, of say Scott and Dickens, considered worthy of being read and taught were those that appeared to be closest to the ideal of the novel as formulated by particular critics. With the recent questioning of the power relationships and the privileging of certain works in canon formation, and the expansion of the canon to include more works by women, such a formula no longer seems tenable. But if prose fiction now appears to us as a highly variable form, it certainly had its periods in which authors discovered new ways of writing and in which such realizations influenced those who followed. In this chapter, I want to emphasize Defoe's discovery of a particular way of writing prose fiction and his exploration of a variety of forms. We may see that he derived certain techniques from some already existing traditions, but like so many writers, Defoe composed under the impression that what he was doing was entirely new. And as far as we can ascertain from the popularity of his works of fiction as well as the outcry against them, his readers felt that they too were experiencing something new.

In his detailed and lively discussion of John Dunton's literary career in *Before Novels*, J. Paul Hunter stresses the urge to novelty in Dunton that produced a body of didactic, proto-fictional works which first aroused the wonder, and after a short time the amusement, of his contemporaries. Hunter stresses the possibilities inherent in some of Dunton's works, but his contemporaries were not half so kind. Rumor had it that the reason Dunton was not punished by the Tory government in 1714 for his attacks upon the ruling party was that he was regarded as an object of pity – a harmless madman. These texts sometimes appear to be distinguished not so much by an endemic chaos as by their marked evidence of hysteria and compulsion. Daniel Defoe, an acquaintance of Dunton, took a more constructive attitude toward novelty. I want to suggest that the great creative period of his life, between 1715 and 1724, a period that produced a literal explosion of fiction, was one of deliberate exploration and experimentation. If Fielding and Richardson laid claims to having created a "new species" of writing; so, in his own way, did Defoe. The narratives he produced during this nine-year period were written at a time when he believed that novelty was essential for gaining a contemporary audience, and if the modern reader senses what might seem to be a completely common ground between the forms of Defoe's fiction, between a *Moll Flanders* and a *Colonel Jack*, the reason has more to do with the erosive effect of time upon the sensibility of the modern reader than to any entire similarity of form. In suggesting such an approach, my arguments run counter to those of critics who see Defoe novels as the product of past nonfictional forms, such as the spiritual autobiography or the many didactic religious treatises employing some fiction, as well as to those arguments of critics who think he put down whatever came into his head and produced whatever artistic effects may be found in his works "unconsciously." The Defoe I intend to present may have had little resemblance to those painstaking creators of fiction who were products of the aesthetic movements of the second half of the nineteenth century, but he sometimes revised his manuscripts extensively and worked hard at producing well-crafted, energetic prose fiction.

Although his career as a writer of book-length fiction takes off around 1715, his fame as a journalist depended upon his ability as a writer of narrative. He could charge a description of a battle such as Blenheim with a sense of action and movement lacking in accounts in other journals, and his *Review* was filled with illustrative stories and short allegories. He was attracted to some of the devices identified by Mikhail Bakhtin as typical of Menippean satire, especially dialogues with characters identified as "Madman" or with "Truth" whose wry views of the world were allowed to contrast with the "accepted" attitudes of his questioner.[3] And in 1705 he published *The Consolidator*, a lengthy voyage to the moon in the manner of Lucian and Cyrano that used the more sensible and ethical lunar world to criticize contemporary England. The obscurity of Defoe's references prevented the work from achieving the impact that he expected, but it did help to give him a dubious reputation as a somewhat harebrained writer of fantasy. He was not to return to anything like this until the "vision" at the end of the third volume of *Robinson Crusoe*.

Since all of the major fictions were written as if they were autobiographical (through the first person) and masquerade (however thinly) as true accounts, the best place to begin is with the two volumes of the *Family Instructor* that he produced in 1715 and 1718. These works were written as dialogues, but the author, writing as an observer and commentator, sets the scene at the beginning and in between the dialogues he discusses the import of what has been said, adds a narrative summary that attempts to make connections between the dialogues, and thrusts the work into the future. In the first editions, such commentary might involve several pages and though written some thirty years earlier, bears some relation to the "editor's" notes to *Clarissa* in which Richardson, using the voice of the editor, attempted to guide the opinions of his readers. Defoe seems to have understood the importance of an appearance of authenticity in a first-person account of events just as he understood the immediacy of the dialogue form. The combination of dialogue and commentary in the two volumes of *The Family Instructor* may have been an experiment at having the advantage of both.[4]

Despite a resemblance to the "guide" tradition, *The Family Instructor* was offered to his audience by Defoe as completely original. He wrote in the introduction to the first volume:

> The way I have taken for this, is *entirely New*, and tho' at first Sight it may appear something *Odd*, and the Method perhaps may be contemned by some; yet let such blame their own more irregular Tempers, that must have every thing turned into new Models; must be touch'd with *Novelty*, and have their Fancies humour'd *with the Dress* of a thing; and if it be what has been said over and over a thousand times, yet if it has but a different colour'd Coat, or a new Feather in its Cap, it pleases and wins upon them, whereas the same Truths written in the divinest Stile in the World, would be flat, stale and unpleasant without it.[5]

Defoe's aggressive stance toward his reader should not be taken too seriously, since he prided himself on his inventiveness and took pleasure in his capacity to meet challenges of this kind as both a thinker and writer. The first volume of this series was supposed to serve as a catechism for the young, a way of instructing children at home to avoid the penalties that might have afflicted the Dissenters with the recent passage of the Schism Act that forbad home instruction, and its theology was shaped in a manner that was deliberately ecumenical in order to reach a wide audience. His separation of form from content was traditional enough at this time, and his use of the term *"Dress"* for formal structure is the same metaphor employed by Pope in the *Essay upon Criticism*. But after seeming to blame the taste of the age that cannot learn directly from old, inspirational texts, he asserts that if his attempt at instruction is successful, "it will be a happy undertaking."

This alternation, between blaming the modern audience for its insistence upon novelty and taking credit for his success, is a method pursued through the entire introduction. He accused his readers of desiring to have "a Toy, a Novelty." In order to do a good deed, he has complied with the "humour of the times," but the "Crime" for doing so was blamed upon the reader rather than the writer. He was merely doing his duty in presenting traditional Christianity in *The Family Instructor*. That the age required entertainment with their religion was not his fault. For all this effort at what one might call a non-apology, and his insistence that the content was no different from equivalent passages in the Bible, some of the introductions to the stories have all of the feel of a novel:

> There was in the same Town a wealthy Shop-keeper, a man in great Business, a Magistrate or Alderman of the Corporation, who has likewise a large Family of Children and Servants: The Man was bred to business, drove a great Trade and grew Rich apace; he was a morally honest sober man, had the Reputation of a very fair Dealer, the Credit of what we call a good Man, that would do no body any wrong; but as to Religion, he made no great Stir about it, he served God *a Sunday* as other People did, and troubled his head very little with any thing else that was Religious all the Week after; indeed he liv'd in a constant hurry of Business, so that he really had no time to think of, or to spare about Religious Affairs. (1: 191)

The irony of the passage depends on the distinction between what passes in the world for ethical and religious behavior and what Defoe establishes as the ideal – the clothier who was "of an exact upright Conversation, of a most devout and religious Behaviour, but more especially in his Family." Defoe's book is devoted to establishing education within the home through a return to what was becoming a somewhat old-fashioned concept of the family – one in which all the members, including the servants, were called together for prayers every morning. Defoe's irony would certainly have been grasped a century later by Jane Austen, whose Anne Eliot in *Persuasion* finds that her cousin's willingness to travel on Sundays is almost sufficient to disqualify him as a potential suitor. Austen's world was very different from Defoe's, but she too liked to make distinctions between what passed in the world for virtue and the genuine article.

When Defoe published the second volume of *The Family Instructor* in 1718, he knew that the Schism Act, which was about to become law on the day that Queen Anne died, would probably never be enforced and that its repeal was imminent. The second volume still preserved its high religious tone, but Defoe's interests had taken a distinct turn toward social problems within the family. He is not above criticizing the treatment of slaves in Barbados and the fear of the owners that if they convert them to Christianity, they will have to give them their freedom.[6] And the longest section is devoted to an attempt of a neighbor to turn his friend from passions that are destroying the peace of his family. The man is dominated by anger toward his son, whom he punishes frequently and with great violence. His neighbor, in an effort at convincing him of the potential evil that might arise from such behavior, tells him stories of various families that have been destroyed by a variety of passions – wrath, suspicion, and jealousy. No wonder, then, that Defoe should have introduced this volume with a promise that the form would be entirely different from the first. Once more he blames the reader for demanding novelty, but he is also intent upon promising that reader just what he desires:

> for if Novelty, the modern Vice of the reading Palate, *is to judge of our Performance, the whole Scene now presented, is so perfectly new, so entirely differing from all that went before, and so eminently directed to another Species of Readers, that it seems to be more new than it would have been, if no other Part had been publish'd before it; nay, to any considering People that reflect upon the different Scenes of Human Life, and the several Stations we are plac'd in, and Parts we act, while we are passing over this Stage; cannot but be known, that there are Follies to be exposed, Dangers to be caution'd against, and Advices to be given, particularly adapted to the several Stages of Life.* (III: iii)

Defoe had apparently grasped that the real attractiveness of the first volume was its modern setting in a real Britain, and he was now ready to direct the second volume to that very person who "served God *a Sunday*" but who enjoyed reading accounts of family life. Defoe argued that there was an inexhaustible supply of such material because his stories were "historical" even if the names were concealed. He instanced Marana's *Letters of a*

Turkish Spy as an example of a work drawing upon the life of the time that "from the known Variety of them, have pleased and diverted the World, even to the Seventh or Eighth Volume." Defoe, who, as formerly mentioned, had achieved fame by his ability to tell stories of modern life in journals such as the *Review*, was now ready to expand in the direction of fiction. He was to discover, despite his puff about the originality of his work, that the second volume did not sell as well as the first. The series of interlocking stories narrated by the neighbor certainly lacked the unity of the first, which was held together by the disastrous relationship between a reforming father and his scapegrace son. At any rate, Defoe was soon searching for new areas to explore.

His *Continuation of Letters of a Turkish Spy*, published in 1718, was an effort at testing the waters for more historical accounts in the manner of Giovanni Marana, the original author of at least the first volume, but whereas the original spy, Mahmut, was intriguing for his skepticism, his francophilia, and his sense of wonder at what he discovered in Europe, Defoe's spy was mainly a vehicle for anti-Jacobite propaganda. The French were revealed as hypocrites ruled by self-interest and the principle of *raison d'état*, and the moral to be drawn from his analysis of French culture during the 1690s was that the Jacobites might as well give up any idea of French assistance in their effort to restore the Stuarts to the throne of Great Britain. What is more interesting than the letters themselves is the preface in which Defoe established the grounds for his attitude toward character and narrative. If his Turk speaks disparagingly of Christianity, the very nature of the character and his situation demand it. Mahmut must be either "Turk or no Turk," either believable and consistent or entirely unreal. If creating a narrative through the angle of vision of such a character meant depicting the ugly as well as the beautiful, so be it. As a critical statement, it had Defoe coming out on the side of the true and the historical rather than idealized representations – on the side of the aesthetics of realist Dutch painting rather than on that of ideal form, which was usually illustrated by the practice of Italian painting. Although Defoe's argument for realist art over ideal and classical form had few defenders in his day, he was not entirely alone in this point of view.[7]

Utilizing fiction for anti-Jacobite propaganda also seems to have been the motivation behind his creation of the character of Major Ramikins in his next work of fiction. Ramikins, who is supposed to be writing his memoirs, joins the ranks of the Jacobites when he is just a teenager and continues working for the cause until he finally realizes that the French will not help the Stuart cause. He is reformed from Jacobitism at the end, and his experience is offered as a model for those who continue to live under the illusion that an invasion aided by France will find a British population eager to receive them and ready to throw off their allegiance to George I. If *Continuation of the Letters of a Turkish Spy* was hoping to attract attention from an audience intrigued by the recent defeat of the Turks by the Austrian general, Prince Eugene, *Memoirs of Major Ramikins* was still capitalizing on the aftermath of the Jacobite rebellion of 1715. The trials of the rebels extended well into 1717, and debates over what to do with their lands and property into the following year. Although Defoe sketched some of the duels and scrapes into which Ramikins manages to become involved, probably the adventure that seemed to grip Defoe's imagination most of all was the Major's encounter with a highwayman and the lecture delivered by the innkeeper on robbery as a form of "Gentleman-like Employment" within the British economic system:

> these Gentlemen approach you decently and submissive, with their Hat in their hand to know your Pleasure, and what you can well afford to support them in that Dignity they live in: 'Tis true, says he, they often for Form sake have a Pistol in their hand, which is part of their riding Furniture; but that is only in the nature of a Petition, to let you know they are Orphans of Providence just fallen under your Protection. In a Word, demanding Money upon the Road, is now so agreeably perform'd, that 'tis much the same with asking an Alms. The poor Begger wou'd rob you if he durst, and the Gentleman Begger will not rob you if you will but give a decent Alms suitable to his Quality.[8]

That kind of thinking signaled the growing turmoil that was taking place in British financial circles. During 1718, under the influence of the Scottish economist John Law, France began to experiment with paper currency and with economic expansion in its North American colonies, and the South Sea Company began the cycle of speculation that would culminate in Britain's first major financial crash, the bursting of the "South Sea Bubble" in 1720. The mania over the buying and selling of stocks seemed to signal to Defoe a revolution in British life – a lurch toward the secular and toward a form of greed that seemed to be sanctioned by the state itself. These events had been proceeded by a series of events in the religious life of the nation that also had lasting effects. Benjamin Hoadly, one of the leading propagandists for the Whig notions of a government based on property rights, liberty of action, and parliament's predominant position in government, had been made a bishop by George I and preached a diminished role for the Anglican church in Britain's political affairs. The conservative wing of the Church counterattacked and began the series of events that saw an end to the power of the High Church and a debate which saw some of the most important members of the Church of England at each other's throats over accusations of lying and professions of "sincerity," a term that took on particular significance at the time. As a Dissenter, Defoe watched the infighting among the members of the established church with a mixture of mischievous glee and considerable satisfaction at the discomfort of the High Church. But the Dissenters were soon to have their own problems. A quarrel known as the "Salter's Hall Controversy" broke out over the question of belief in the Trinity. When a majority of those associated with the Presbyterians refused to sign a statement avowing their continued belief in this doctrine, the split in the group seemed to doom any future unity, and despite Defoe's pamphlets on the side of ameliorating the dispute, it turned preacher against preacher, congregation against congregation. The failure of organized religion and the decline in a standard of honesty in economic life set the stage for Defoe's creation of fictions that showed pirates often more honest than bankers and ordinary men such as Crusoe and Jack, cut off from the influence of particular church doctrines, more capable of finding a truly Christian faith than their churchgoing fellow citizens in Great Britain.

Although explanations such as these provide a kind of background to Defoe's major fictions, they are hardly adequate ways of accounting for the peculiar originality of *The Surprising Adventures of Robinson Crusoe* published on 25 April 1719. Accounts of men cast on unpeopled islands were hardly new. Alexander Selkirk, who lived on the island of Juan Fernandez for five years with only the island's goats for company, had provided a well-publicized model for Defoe, but fictional versions of such an event appear in numerous works of fiction published during the seventeenth century from Grimmelhausen's *Simplicimus* to Gracian's *The Critick (El Criticon)*. In striking a balance between material that easily lent itself to allegory and the marvelous and a world of real experience, Defoe gave the novel a peculiar identity that it has retained ever since.

Crusoe's world is filled with dreams, prophecies and remarkable portents in the form of earthquakes, storms, and the seemingly remarkable single footprint that sends him scurrying to his cave out of "Snare of *the Fear of Man.*"[9] And at the same time that the footprint makes Crusoe believe, at first, that the Devil may have landed on his island, he approaches its appearance as a scientist might, measuring it, comparing it to his own foot, and looking about for evidence of the presence that might have produced it. His responses resemble a cross between a scientist attempting to ascertain the truth through experiment and a detective determined to discover a criminal through a small piece of circumstantial evidence.[10] But between this metaphysical and scientific analysis of evidence of the presence of some alien other, Crusoe behaves as we would expect of a man of his character and situation. He hides himself in his cave quaking in terror. In short, *Robinson Crusoe* is a work of prose fiction that lends itself to the kind of multilayers analysis that Roland Barthes provides in his *S/Z*, a fiction that resonates simultaneously on many levels, providing the reader with divergent codes of significance and leading him forward with a variety of enigmatic questions that demand answers.[11] The variety of structures – spiritual autobiography, traveler's narrative, do-it-yourself utopia, political and economic allegory – fuse into a unity under the realist surface of the narrative but provide a text that opens itself to a myriad of possible readings.

Defoe turned the second part of *Robinson Crusoe* into a mixture of adventure story and ideological commentary on human nature and the third into a combination of essay and baroque spiritual vision. The second volume takes Crusoe on a voyage back to his island and then, by stages, around the world. Defoe took the opportunity to illustrate some of his favorite ideas: on the imperative of self-preservation; on the needless and mindless cruelty of Europeans against indigenous populations; and upon the overvaluation of Chinese culture. Crusoe's encounter with one ship gave Defoe an opportunity to expatiate on the effects of starvation; Crusoe's return to his island an occasion for observations on the natural progress of society. It lacked the power of the original but was still very readable fiction, whereas the final volume abandoned all but the veneer of fiction (Crusoe as narrator) in favor of the essay. The preface to the last volume may appear to be a muddled piece of literary criticism, but it is a valuable document for all that. Defoe never stops being Robinson Crusoe, yet he appears to admit that this character is one aspect of himself. Adapting one of the main accusations in Charles Gildon's *Surprising Adventures of D—l D—e*, Defoe argued that the work was "true," a form of "History," "real" and factually accurate while being an "allegory" and a "satire" in the manner of *Don Quixote*.[12] And he makes a remarkable claim for the validity of representation with the phrase picked up by Camus and used at the beginning of *The Plague*: "it is as reasonable to represent one kind of imprisonment by another, as it is to represent anything that really exists by that which exists not" (xii). In some ways, Defoe was genuinely trying to describe the kind of fiction he had begun to write – a type of fiction that functioned on both a realistic and a symbolic level. But the key words in this preface are "serious" and "sincere" (ix). Although these words are applied to the intention of the author (Crusoe/Defoe), they are also intended to describe a type of fiction that was quite different from the romance. *Don Quixote* is praised as a "satire" on the Spain of Cervantes's time, as a work that was at once amusing, serious, and sincere.

Like most of his contemporaries, Defoe found it easier to discuss the didactic functioning of his text rather than the pleasure that it might give the reader. But this does not mean that he was unaware of the aesthetic pleasure in his fiction – in his vivid representation of the real, his often exciting situations intended to arouse the interest of the reader. "Facts," writes Crusoe/Defoe, "that are formed to touch the mind must be done a great way off, and by somebody never heard of" (xiii). In order to move the reader, a writer of fiction must invent stories that are exotic and exciting as well as new and intriguing characters. Michael McKeon speaks of Defoe's fictions and of the eighteenth-century novel as being on the brink of the aesthetic, whereby the novel and other literary forms are self-validating.[13] But the novel has always been an impure form, enmeshed with life and authorial meaning. If Crusoe/Defoe argues in this preface to the third volume that he is now providing the pure didactic material behind the fiction in the form of individual essays on subjects such as "Necessity" and "Solitude," this does not mean that Defoe actually believed that the fictive material was so much dross, the honey (fictional narrative) to attract the flies (readers). Rather, in the essays of *Serious Reflections*, he has shifted from narrative to a form of discourse in which he allows himself to expatiate over social and ethical questions and draw upon experiences and knowledge about which the Crusoe with whom the reader was familiar would have had little information. Nevertheless, the Crusoe of volumes 1 and 2 was certainly given to meditations upon his experiences. What Defoe does in *Serious Reflections* is similar to what Richardson did when he published a volume of "Sentiments" drawn from his fiction. That Defoe had to write a separate volume of such material suggests that many of his readers did not read him for such bits of wisdom but rather for the pleasure of the narrative.

For the modern reader, *Robinson Crusoe* inevitably raises the problem of colonialism, and two brilliant adaptations of the novel, Michel Tournier's *Friday (Vendredi)* and J. M. Coetzee's *Foe* both focus on Crusoe's inability to address the cannibal Friday in a manner that is cognizant of his otherness. Tournier's Friday eventually overcomes Crusoe's colonial attitudes – his possessiveness, his desire to exploit others, his willingness to enslave another human being, leaving the message that we may yet transform the consciousness of Western man to absorb new ways of seeing and living. Coetzee's *Foe* has a Crusoe and Friday seen from the outside by a Susan Barton, who is herself a version of Roxana, a fictional character drawn from another novel by Defoe. Coetzee's Foe is cold and mechanical. He spends his time building terraces to be used by some future settlers; he does not plant them himself. This sterile image of Crusoe the colonialist is accompanied by a Friday whose tongue has been cut out. Friday's message does not come through the odd English that Defoe gave him, but is rather the message of the body itself and its sufferings – the body of the victim of colonialism.

That Defoe has been able to inspire writers from Rousseau to Coetzee is a testimony to his ability to pose important problems in his fiction, even if he was unable to solve them himself. *Robinson Crusoe* is less a defense of colonialism than it is a direct attack upon the treatment of the natives by the Spanish in their conquest of America. When Crusoe is ready to give in to his hatred and fear of cannibalism, he pauses long enough to weigh the horrors that the Spaniards had committed and to consider how an attack on his part would be a return to the kind of barbaric treatment of savage nations that all of Europe had rejected:

> That this would justify the Conduct of the *Spaniards* in all their Barbarities practis'd in *America*, where they destroy'd Millions of these People, who however they were Idolaters and Barbarians, and had several bloody and barbarous Rites in their Customs, such as sacrificing human Bodies to their idols, were yet, as to the *Spaniards*, very innocent People; and that the rooting them out of the Country, is spoken of with the utmost Abhorrence and Detestation, by even the *Spaniards* themselves, at this Time; and by all other Christian nations of *Europe*, as a meer Butchery, a bloody and unnatural Piece of Cruelty, unjustifiable either to God or Man; and such, as for which the very Name of a *Spaniard* is reckon'd to be frightful and terrible to all People of Humanity, or of Christian Compassion: As if the Kingdom of *Spain* were particularly Eminent for the Product of a Race of men, who were without Principles of Tenderness, or the common Bowels of Pity to the Miserable, which is reckon'd to be a mark of generous Temper in the Mind. (172)

What Defoe wanted was a form of colonialism that would be distinguished by this "generous Temper in the Mind." If the slave trade was part of the economy of England and therefore economically important to British prosperity, then it should be carried out as humanely as possible. After a period, the captive savages should be converted to Christianity and given their freedom.

Such a vision hardly appears attractive to the modern mind, but it was certainly in advance over most contemporary thought. On a purely moral level, Defoe would have acknowledged its weakness. Insofar as Crusoe is representative of the colonizing mind, he is clearly not entirely a sympathetic figure. Like Columbus and the Spaniards who followed him, Crusoe understands the "power of naming" as a form of possession. He names the island ("the Island of Despair") and its various sections ("Castle," "Country House,"), and he names Friday as well.[14] Although the description of

Friday has been considered condescending in its attempt to picture him along classical lines of beauty and different from those with Negroid features, this set piece has to be set alongside the one detailed "Sketch" of Crusoe's appearance on the island, with its massing of negative emotional words such as "shapeless," "barbarous," "clumsy," "monstrous," and "frightful," a description that belongs to the category of the grotesque. Crusoe is a representative Western man in his lust for power and control. Defoe, as a merchant himself, could certainly understand Crusoe's motivation, his consistent self-interestedness. But when, following his successful effort at converting Friday to Christianity, Crusoe remarks that Friday was a better Christian than he, we should not ignore the compliment. Friday is clearly the superior human being, more loving, more giving, more capable of gratitude. These were the qualities Defoe admired above all. There was much about the evils of colonialism that Defoe did not grasp, but, as Coetzee and Tournier recognized, *Robinson Crusoe* provided the materials for mounting an attack against it.

Defoe followed the first two volumes of *Robinson Crusoe* with his brilliant *Memoirs of a Cavalier*, published in May 1720. He had mentioned several times in print that he possessed a manuscript account of the participation of Scottish officers in the army of Gustavus Adolphus, but *Memoirs of a Cavalier* achieves its power from the balance of the narrative account of two wars: the Thirty Years' War and the English Civil War. The Cavalier's initial experience with battle involved him with Gustavus Adolphus's brilliant victories over the Catholic forces led by the armies of the Austrian Empire. The Cavalier cannot speak too highly of the Swedish king. Indeed, as Walzer suggests, the "Swedish Discipline" became the ideal for the English Puritans – a way of conducting war that involved an ordering of mind, body and spirit. It is clear from his enthusiasm, that the Cavalier will be unhappy under Prince Rupert, whose disorganized, romantic cavalry charges gain the field but lose the war for the forces of Charles I. The Cavalier emerges with a contempt for the Anglican Clergy, who lead Charles astray, and an admiration for Lord Fairfax, the leader of the Parliamentary forces. The Cavalier was not enough of a "character" for a nineteenth-century critic such as Macaulay, who complained that there was none of the filling out of plot and character that might be seen in Scott or Ainsworth, but Ainsworth's quaint exploitation of history that Macaulay and his age so admired is likely to make the historical novel of their period tough going for a modern reader, while Defoe's understated account appears to treat history seriously.

The preface to the work makes a special point of praising it for the descriptions of the various battles:

The Accounts of Battles, the Sieges, and the several Actions of which this Work is so full, are all recorded in the Histories of those Times; such as the great Battle of *Leipsick*, the Sacking of *Magdeburgh*, the Siege of *Nurembergh*, the passing the River *Leck*, in *Bavaria*; such also as the Battles of *Keynton*, or *Edge-Hill*; the Battles of *Newberry*, *Marston-Moor*, and *Naseby*, and the like: They are all, we say, recorded in other Histories, and written by those who lived in those Times, and perhaps had good Authority for what they wrote. But do those Relations give any of the beautiful Idea of things formed in this Account? Have they one half of the Circumstances and Incidents of the Actions themselves, that this man's Eyes were Witness to, and which his memory has thus preserv'd? He that has read the best Accounts of those Battles, will be surprized to see the Particulars of the Story so preserved, so nicely, and so agreeably describ'd; and will confess what we alledge, that the Story is inimmitably told.[15]

In the same year as this, Defoe published a translation of Du Fresnoy's poem on painting, and there is reason to believe that his interest in description is closely related to painting itself. The battle-piece had emerged as an important part of history painting, and Defoe attempts to transfer the visual power of the battlefield to his page. This was not easy since painting has the advantage of a total view of everything happening at one time. Defoe concentrated his description and the mind of the reader on one aspect of the battle. The Cavalier experiences only what he can see, and Defoe gives us only partial views of what is happening on the entire field. He recounts the entire struggle only after we experience the particular angle of vision of the Cavalier.

If *Memoirs of a Cavalier* attempted to join together two campaigns by seeing them through one man's eyes, Defoe had a different task to achieve with his narratives of piracy. In the *Review*, he had recounted stories of the riches gathered by the British pirates operating out of Madagascar, and had suggested that the nation might take advantage of the wealth they had obtained by pardoning them for a large sum of money. But Defoe recognized from the very beginning that the accounts of their loot and power were exaggerated. His first full-length fiction about piracy was *The Life, Adventures, and Pyracies of the Famous Captain Singleton*, published on 4 June 1720; but in the year before this he had published an account of a real pirate, Captain Avery. Avery was rumored to have become enormously wealthy, but Defoe's account is skeptical. He noted in the preface, "There is always a great difference between what men say of themselves, and what others say for them, when they come to write historically of the transaction of their lives."[16] Though he claims his version as that which is closest to the truth, he never states unequivocally that his is a genuinely true account; it is merely more probable than any that had been published previously. Avery is shown to be a man with a thirst for adventure and for the loot that might occasionally accompany daring exploits. He completes his second letter from Constantinople, where he has brought all of his wealth with a promise of future adventures. *The King of the Pirates* is a perfect example of "story" in the sense that E. M. Forster defined that term by way of distinguishing it from "plot," or a narrative based on cause and effect.[17] In Defoe's narrative one event follows another with little commentary. It was a wonderful outline for a work of fiction, but Defoe gave nothing in the way of character or motivation. *Captain Singleton* is mainly Avery's story novelized, for while it may be said that "novelization of experience" described by Bakhtin is already present enough in *The King of the Pirates*, Defoe was constrained in composing the latter work by whatever facts about Avery were available.[18] Here was a story about a pirate who had sailed with Sharpe in the Darien expedition and who then joined with Redhand and eventually grew enormously rich. Defoe's imagination required the freedom that would be afforded by a simple change of name from that of well-known historical figure to a creation of his own.

Defoe did not write a preface for *Captain Singleton*, but much of what he had remarked in the preface to *The King of the Pirates* about first-person narrative applied here as well. Captain Singleton now narrates his autobiography with appropriate silences and a particular angle of vision. Like *Memoirs of a Cavalier*, he has two sections to his story, but whereas the Cavalier engages in war out of a desire to discover both himself and his occupation as a soldier, Captain Singleton is close to being a born pirate. He enjoys the freedom and the adventure in such a life; the trek across Africa is an example of Defoe's investigation of the possibilities inherent in the adventure novel, including an exploitation of the sublime in the form of horrific scenery and equally horrific wild beasts. One commonplace about the novel is that the use of scenery does not develop until Ann Radcliffe and the Gothic, but *Captain Singleton* sets the scene for an imaginary Africa with fertile plains filled with animals and vast deserts empty of vegetation. Defoe did not exploit his scenery quite as fully as Ann Radcliffe did much later in the century, but he does render an imaginary African landscape in a convincing manner and peoples a relatively unexplored world filled with a variety of savage human beings and savage beasts.

When Captain Singleton and the other members of the crew encounter the colonial mentality in an Englishman – a figure similar to Joseph Conrad's Kurtz in *Heart of Darkness* (1899), they are puzzled by his single-minded effort at extracting gold. And he is equally dismayed by their seeming lack of interest. But Singleton and his crew are sailors and spend their money with proverbial recklessness. Singleton and his party are certainly willing to take the gold that they find in their trek across Africa, but Singleton regards it with suspicion, as a source of contention ("the *Makebait* of the World").[19] Defoe was once more setting up a dialogue about the uses of wealth. If Crusoe discovers that gold is worthless on his island, Singleton and the twenty-six crewmen set ashore on Madagascar after a mutiny discover much the same thing. They are able to barter their money for food only after one of their group makes their silver coins into jewelry. One small coin beaten thin and shaped into the form of a diamond or a bird and attached to a chain has the equivalent worth of a cow to the natives of Madagascar, but as money it has no value. These themes – piracy, the value of money, exploitation – are all reflections on what was happening in Britain during the furor over the collapse of the South Sea Company's manipulation of stock. Defoe was to make the connection explicit in his *History of the Pirates* a few years later, but the paradox of business as crime and crime as a business was a driving force behind almost all of his fiction.

As for Captain Singleton, only through his encounter with William Walters, the Quaker ship's surgeon, is he gradually forced to rethink his priorities. In some ways William is almost as single-minded as the Englishman encountered in Africa, a figure modeled on a very real representative of Britain's African Company.[20] But William exemplifies Defoe's notion of the "honest" tradesman–merchant in both his diligence while engaged in business and his notion of retiring once he has made enough. His Quaker creed has been reduced to a few speech mannerisms, a conviction that warfare for its own sake was not an efficient way of getting money or of conducting relationships with his fellow human beings, and a drive toward making as much money as possible and with a maximum of efficiency. In furthering this purpose, he is willing to participate in the dirty business of selling slaves and engages in stretching truth as far as possible, indeed to the limits of hypocrisy. Yet in the end he is true to his promise to the pirate, Captain Wilmot, with whom Captain Singleton is serving. "I shall be moderate" (144), he states when they accuse him of being interested in money while being unwilling to fight actively in their battles. But from the very beginning William provides practical advice on capturing ships, and when he suggests that the pirates appear to be avoiding encounters and might consider becoming Quakers, Singleton responds to the effect that such a conversion would clearly result in his becoming "*an excellent Pyrate.*" At the end of his account, when Singleton falls into a state of self-examination and near despair over the ways in which he has accumulated his vast wealth, it is William who convinces him that since pirate and merchant alike are guilty and imperfect, all must rely upon God's mercy.

William quickly becomes the source of rationality among these pirates, applying the equivalent of scientific reasoning to human actions which, so far as ethics were concerned, amounted to the application of contemporary natural law. But he also has the curiosity that was the sign of the "new science." When Singleton and the crew hear of a group of mariners stranded in Japan who have apparently discovered the Northwest Passage between the Atlantic and Pacific Oceans, William tries unsuccessfully to persuade his shipmates to attempt to rescue them. He couches his appeal in a variety of ways, but his real reason – an interest in new knowledge – is apparent enough to his pirate audience to allow them to reject his arguments. He is very much the merchant explorer to whom the Royal Society appealed as the kind of person who would prepare the way for both scientific exploration and colonization.

Captain Singleton has many of the classic contours of an "adventure novel," and if Defoe is not to be credited with inventing this genre, he certainly has to be acknowledged to have developed its possibilities. Admittedly, extrapolating from the often inflated accounts of pirates and piracy to a more exciting, fictionalized form was not all that difficult. If critics have suggested that the form always already existed, in the sense that the already exciting narratives of real pirates who had gained both fortune and fame would have prepared the reader for adventures that might be even more satisfying to a daydreaming reader, this should not deny Defoe the credit for satisfying reader desire for such a narrative.[21] Defoe's next significant work of fiction, *Moll Flanders*, might be seen as fulfilling the expectations already established by picaresque narratives such as *La Picara Justina* or various chapbook heroines such as Moll Cutpurse, but Defoe's treatment of a woman's attempt to survive and thrive under difficult conditions showed his ability to transform previous forms into fictions that were entirely unique. Defoe certainly drew upon previous accounts of female rogues, but just as Captain Singleton emerged as an archetypal pirate modeled upon Captain Avery and embodying the mixture of desperation and adventurousness that drove the poor out of a too rigid society and into a life of freebooting, so Defoe made Moll into the thief she calls "the greatest Artist of my Time."[22] In shaping such materials into a new form of prose fiction, Defoe (in some ways) resembled Robert Burns, who later in the eighteenth century transformed despised popular ballads into poems and songs that were popular with critics and the masses alike, or with Charles Dickens a century after Defoe, whose success in appealing to a mass audience was sometimes held up to scorn by the critics. And not the least of Defoe's accomplishments was to create heroes and heroines whose rise from abject poverty and anonymity to wealth and security provided hope for those among the dispossessed lower and lower middle orders literate enough to read or patient enough to listen.

In *Moll Flanders*, Defoe did not abandon his method of creating archetypal, mythic figures, but he succeeded in deepening the character of his protagonist. The internalization of experience that he had already exploited in *Robinson Crusoe* was not put to use in creating a woman who questions everything about her society, from its institutions to the very language in which the usual exchanges of life are enacted. Moll frequently uses the phrase, "as they call it," after various words to indicate the way language may be used to cloak the realities of experience. Nothing is so bad but that language can function in a manner to make it seem acceptable. The realities behind the linguistic concealments are often harsh enough. And just as she questions the meaning of rank and privilege and the economic workings of her world, so she also interrogates herself about her motives and her understanding of her motives. Defoe seems to have wanted Moll to affect the reader in many ways. She was to be an object lesson, a satirist upon herself and those of her tribe, an experienced thief trying to teach her readers to guard themselves against the tricks of pickpockets and shoplifters, a young, partly innocent girl ever in danger from men, a woman cynical about love and marriage, and a real woman struggling against an indifferent society. Somehow Defoe makes all of these different elements work together. The split between the wise, experienced female narrator and the young Moll seems to make everything possible. Sometimes she achieves an ironic distance about herself, as in her account of herself as a young girl desiring to become a gentlewoman or in the beginning of her relation about how she was seduced by the elder son of the Colchester family where she served as the chambermaid. Yet such distancing is likely to collapse, as in her account of her suffering when she finds her lover is unwilling to marry her, or later in the novel when she tells of her urge to murder a girls he has robbed. At such moments the past comes rushing into the present and narrative distance is almost entirely lost in the violence of the recreated emotions.

The events of Moll's life come across to the reader as vividly lived experience partly for the reasons already stated and partly because her responses to the occurrences of her life seem so natural, so believable. The reader may find the events that take her to North America and lead to her discovery of the mother who gave birth to her while in prison, and her consequent realization her own marriage is incestuous, strangely miraculous for a work rooted in a realistic view of her society. But there is nothing unnatural about the sexual disgust that she feels toward her brother/ husband. She prefers handsome men with a gentlemanly air, but she under-

stands the dangers of poverty and is willing to settle for less. She says that
she made a good wife to the Bank Manager, whom she takes as a distinctly
second best, but she also finds his passivity in the face of bankruptcy
somewhat contemptible. Moll views life in her world as a battle for survival,
a battle in which nothing is certain. Marriage to Jemmy, who proves to be a
highwayman, might prove as safe as marriage to her bourgeois Bank
Manager. Defoe seems to be saying that a woman needed to be as tough as
nails to survive in Moll's world. After the death of the Bank Manager,
when, in her poverty, she turns to stealing, this message becomes particularly cogent. Though Moll tends to stress the warmth of her heart, there are
moments when the heart of a criminal shows through. Readers tend to like
her, but we are never really certain about the honesty of her account. She
can be witty about her past one moment and serious the next. What is clear
is that her narrative is meaningful to her. For all her tricks and schemes, this
is her one creative act, and because it is so important she lies, conceals,
distorts the truth, and forces the reader to interrogate the text, to search
behind the explanations for the real Moll Flanders.

There has been much speculation recently about Defoe's creation of
women characters, or his "narrative transvestitism," as Madeleine Kahn
called it.[23] Some of this grows out of Leslie Stephen's comment to the
effect that Defoe merely created men in women's clothing and asked
himself, "What would I do if I were in such a situation?" For Stephen and
other Victorian critics, Moll was impossibly unfeminine, utterly lacking in
the sensibility to be expected of women.[24] By these standards, Moll should
not have outlived her first seduction. Stephen was trying to establish a
difference between what he considered well-crafted and ideologically sound
nineteenth-century realism and Defoe's fiction. It was another case of the
nineteenth century attempting to convince itself that it owed little debt to
the past. The important question raised by studies such as Kahn's is, what
did Defoe gain in assuming the role of a woman? Certainly a "tough-guy"
pirate such as Captain Singleton deprived Defoe of a proper center of
consciousness and sensibility for dealing with the private sufferings of
those ruined by the "South Sea Scandal." Both Moll Flanders and Roxana
suffer from the bankruptcies of various husbands, and since married
women were deprived of any control over property, they are unable to
respond to such situations directly. They have to pull themselves together
after their husbands have made complete disasters of their lives. Defoe
believed that women were as capable as men in most things; it was society
that had deprived them of an education that might have made them more
capable of dealing with such situations. If those capable women, Moll and
Roxana, succeed in surmounting their difficulties, this does not mean that

Defoe merely made them men in women's clothing or merely versions of himself.[25]

In 1722, the same year as that in which he produced *Moll Flanders*, Defoe also published two volumes of moral dialogues, *Religious Courtship* and *Due Preparations for the Plague*, and two works of fiction, *A Journal of the Plague Year* and *The History and Remarkable Life of the Truly Honourable Col. Jacque*, usually known as *Colonel Jack*. Though the latter bore a 1723 date on its title page, it was published in December 1722 and was part of Defoe's amazing productivity during this single year. I suggested earlier in this chapter how closely Defoe's novels were tied to his moral dialogues, and it might be pointed out that he could never have written, say, the seemingly effortless dialogue between William and the Dutch captive in Ceylon in *Captain Singleton*, a dialogue with no religious import whatsoever, without having mastered that form so thoroughly in his didactic writings. Yet Defoe clearly knew the difference between a jeremiad such as *Due Preparations for the Plague*, with its call to repentance, and *A Journal of the Plague Year*, with its predominantly secular concerns.

A Journal of the Plague Year, published in 17 March while a plague ravaged southern France and threatened to make a seemingly inevitable progress to England, saw Defoe's narrative inventiveness at its height. In *Due Preparations for the Plague*, he had complained that the writings about the plague at such an anxious time had the effect of "amusing the people so that . . . they know not what to conclude" about the various opinions concerning the plague's origins and its cures.[26] There was a debate over the usefulness of attempting to quarantine all of London during this crisis, with the government falling first on the side of a quarantine and finally deciding not to insist upon it. Although Defoe is often seen arguing in favor of the quarantine, and although his narrator H. F., however much he may favor quarantining individual houses, is uncertain about its usefulness, almost everything in the novel as well as Defoe's journalism at the time moves toward viewing the quarantine of the entire city as inhuman and ultimately useless. Defoe saw the plague as a force that broke down any notion of society functioning in a usual manner. Some of the finest scenes in the work involve just these tensions between a city government trying to keep law and order and a populace with little to lose. The scene in which H. F. finds that people have broken into his brother's warehouse – with its image of women trying on hats in the midst of death and despair – is superb, as is the completely human and moving depiction of the Waterman whom H. F. encounters in his wanderings through London. The Waterman seems barely able to get out his words as he speaks of the child he has already lost and those yet alive but sick.

Insofar as the novel is about the plague of 1665, *A Journal of the Plague Year* may be regarded as one of the earliest historical novels; insofar as Defoe depends upon readers recognizing that the narrative is a warning about the threat from plague in 1722, the novel functions much like the modern documentary novels of Truman Capote and Norman Mailer. It is at times grimly realistic in its details and its exact information about the number of deaths, the ordinances passed to keep order and supply the poor with food, and vignettes of the city choking on smoke from the fires set to fend off the plague; at other times the horror of the pits in which the bodies of the dead are hurled evokes the ineffable and the sublime. Language fails to convey the overwhelming horror as H. F. is reduced to saying the sight was "*very, very, very* dreadful."[27] At times, the stories of families who suddenly find themselves faced with inevitable death evoke the literature of sensibility in their images of overwhelming love between family members. Then Defoe will switch to the comic story of the drunken piper who fell in the pits only to survive, or evoke the grotesque in the scene of the man who kisses an unwilling lady on the street only to reveal that he has the plague. In some parts, the work reads like a medical treatise, and of all the narrative forms that provide some resemblance to Defoe's vivid picture of the plague and its effect upon society, probably the medical case studies and dissections of plague come closest to providing that sense of individual character that Defoe gives us.[28]

A Journal of the Plague Year is clearly not easy to classify from a variety of standpoints. For example, Hester Thrale, who might stand for our eighteenth-century common reader, thought that the heroes were the artisans who manage to struggle out of London to Epping Forest where they establish something resembling a self-sufficient community composed of those who have fled the plague, and particularly John, formerly a soldier but now a biscuit maker.[29] Indeed, as the leader of the expedition, he resembles Captain Singleton in his voyage across Africa. One modern critic has argued that it may be seen as an extended meditation by H. F., with all events contained in his mind,[30] and I have argued elsewhere that the real focus of the work is upon the inhabitants of London who heroically struggle against an invisible enemy and gain the triumph at the end.[31] Insofar as my concept of a collective hero encompasses the other two, I still prefer it. Though H. F. is the narrator and John the more traditional hero of saga or adventure story, the numerous anecdotes concerning a wide variety of London's citizens – their individual suffering and courage – suggests a collective hero.

Like *Robinson Crusoe*, *A Journal of the Plague Year* is a story of survival against all odds. Defoe did not believe that the struggle to sustain life was heroic under every circumstance. Indeed, the story he tells of the tradesman in East Smithfield who dies of grief after he fails to find a midwife to help his pregnant, plague-stricken wife, shows admiration for what might be called love unto death:

> The poor Man, with his Heart broke, went back, assisted his Wife what he cou'd, acted the part of the Midwife, brought the Child dead into the World, and his Wife in about an Hour dy'd in his Arms, where he held her dead Body fast till the Morning, when the Watchman came and brought the Nurse as he had promised; and coming up the Stairs (for he had left the Door open, or only latched), they found the Man sitting with his dead Wife in his Arms, and so overwhelmed with Grief that he dy'd in a few Hours after without any Sign of the Infection upon him, but meerly sunk under the Weight of his Grief.[32]

But Defoe did regard self-preservation as something close to a command of nature, and admired those who answered that command with firm courage. This is why H. F. comes to the conclusion that running away from the plague is the wisest act. Short of that, his admiration went out to John, the former old soldier, who affirms his right to leave the city with the affirmation, "*You may as well say I must not go out of my house if it is on fire as that I must not go out of the Town I was born when it is infected with the Plague*" (124). Yet John's victory over the plague is ultimately no greater than the rest of the citizens whose faces revealed their "Smile of Joy" (245).

Colonel Jack rounded out this remarkably productive year for Defoe, and it too broke new ground in a variety of ways. In his preface, Defoe, in the role of "Editor," moderated his claims for authenticity that had produced the ambiguous remarks before *Serious Reflections of Robinson Crusoe*. Whether it was a true history or a work of fiction, a "History *or a* Parable,"[33] was of no significance, he argued. What was important were the lessons to be drawn from the work. It was not what Defoe referred to as "a meer romance," but a narrative with meaning and ideas. Although the preface couches the ethical significance of the work in religious terms, Defoe's main intent was essentially secular – an attempt to illustrate upward mobility in his society by the ideals of ingenuity, hard work, perseverance, and education. *Colonel Jack* fits the formal pattern outlined by Bakhtin as "the novel of emergence," a subgenre within the larger category of the *Bildungsroman*.[34] Although *Colonel Jack* shared with *Moll Flanders* Defoe's involvement with reform of the system of punishment to allow convicted felons an opportunity to go to Britain's colonies where they might begin a new life without concern for their past life of crime, the two novels are very different in tone and purpose. Colonel Jack is certainly involved in criminal activities from his childhood, but he offers what J. L. Austin calls reasonable "excuses" to explain his actions: his ignorance, his being brought up to think that picking pockets was a trade, etc., while Moll's attempts to ingratiate herself to her audience tend toward "justifications," or self-exonerations.[35] He details how he makes amends for stealing money from a poor old nurse, who must still labor like a "Slave" at sixty, by restoring the original sum and even giving her a little extra. On the other hand, he is not ready to restore money to those who were well enough off. He travels to Scotland, where he learns to read and write and has a brief flirtation with a career as an army private until he realizes the folly of risking death for so little reward. Unlike Moll, Colonel Jack is not sentenced to transportation but rather sold as an indentured servant after being kidnapped. He is forced to work in the fields along with indentured servants and slaves, but his condition is more or less an accident. That he turns it into a step in his upward path toward success is the more credit to his ability to accept what life has to offer and improve upon his initial situation, and he moralizes upon the possibilities open to criminals:

> As this is a foundation, which the most unfortunate Wretch alive is entitul'd to; a Transported Felon, is in my Opinion a much happier Man, than the most prosperous untaken Thief in the Nation; nor are those poor young People so much in the wrong, as some imagine them to be, that go voluntarily over to those Countries, and in order to get themselves carried over, and plac'd there, freely bind themselves there; especially if the Persons into whose Hands they fall, do any thing honestly by them; for as it is to be suppos'd that those poor People knew not what Course to take before, or had miscarried in their Conduct before; here they are sure to be immediately provided for, and after the expiration of their time, to be put into a Condition to provide for themselves. (174)

Jack shows his master that slaves will work harder when tied by gratitude to their masters rather than by ill-treatment. By this Whiggish myth of combining goodwill with increased productivity, he becomes an overseer and friend to the plantation owner who starts him on a prosperous career as an independent plantation owner and entrepreneur. And although Jack's method of getting more work out of his slaves through kind treatment will hardly satisfy the modern reader, both Jack and Defoe are aware of the horrible treatment of slaves on other plantations, commenting on the "horrible Out-cryes, Roarings and Yellings of the Servants, either under Torture, or in Fear of it" (159).

Having attained wealth, Jack passes the rest of his life in a quest after education, gentility, and a good wife. He achieves the first with the help of a

"Tutor," a learned prisoner who ultimately becomes the manager of his plantation. The second is somewhat more problematic as he earns the post of colonel in the Jacobite, Irish divisions serving with Louis XIV. And his quest for a good wife, or good wives, ends in a futile search. All of his wives are unfaithful, but the first wife, whom he divorced for her infidelities, in the end proves to be the best. She arrives at Jack's plantation as a transported felon after a career that brought her to complete poverty, prostitution, and thievery. But she has learned to understand morality by this difficult path. Jack remarries her, and she proves to be as faithful a wife as he could wish. For Defoe, Christian charity was more important than the manners of society. That is why we have to look to Dostoevsky's *Crime and Punishment* for a similar gesture in the novel. The English novel of manners was hardly ready to admit back into society a woman who might have made a single sexual transgression. With the exception (at the very end of the eighteenth century) of Mary Wollstonecraft's *The Wrongs of Women*, prostitutes were unlikely to have a fair hearing. As for one marrying the hero, it was beyond consideration.

Had Defoe concentrated more on this material, *Colonel Jack* might have been as good as *Moll Flanders*, but he dissipated the energies of the work by following Jack's military career and then involving him in what Defoe called the "thieving, roguing Trade" to the Spanish colonies. Jack's military career, particularly the account of the war in Italy around 1701 involving one of Defoe's heroes, Prince Eugene, against the forces of Louis XIV, is written with considerable skill but it was hardly an improvement over his accounts of battles in *Memoirs of a Cavalier*. And his dealings with the colonists in Cuba and Mexico have little intrinsic interest for the modern reader. Jack earns a great deal of money from this illicit trade, and his encounters with the colonial officials in evading the prohibitions against such a trade have a certain amusement, but for the most part, this final section suffers from the faults of the worst parts of *Captain Singleton*, a feeling of randomness and drift. Jack embarks on this adventure because he fears being recognized by some of the Jacobite prisoners who have been sent to Virginia after the defeat at Preston, but nothing at all is made of this potentially interesting plot development. Jack's conversion after his sloop has been wrecked off Florida is of importance to him, but many of his readers may have abandoned ship long before.

Defoe's treatment of Colonel Jack's trading activities signaled a shift in his interests toward subjects such as economic geography, and in addition to publishing the first volume of the *Tour thro' the Whole Island of Great Britain* in 1724, before the year was out he was also to create a fictional circumnavigation of the globe in *A New Voyage Round the World*. But

Defoe continued to be interested in the wave of crime that was to infect Great Britain from the end of the War of the Spanish Succession in 1714 until the year of his death in 1731. Eventually the presence of master criminals such as Jonathan Wild, who managed a stable of criminals while pretending to be a middleman between those victims of crime who were eager to recover their stolen goods and the thief, and Jack Shepherd, who succeeded in escaping from Newgate several times, were to occupy him in journalistic accounts of their lives, but the social subjects he had raised in *Moll Flanders* and *Colonel Jack* still interested him enough to involve him in the publication of *The Fortunate Mistress*, commonly known as *Roxana*, after the name of its female narrator. Published on 29 February 1724, *Roxana* already reveals Defoe's desire to comment directly and forcefully upon his own age. Roxana speaks of herself as "apt to be Satyrical," and her attacks upon the laws of marriage that victimize women by giving all of their property to foolish husbands clarify what was already a strongly suggested theme in *Moll Flanders*. But Roxana was a far more transgressive work than the former. Defoe had always been fascinated and repelled by the libertinism of the Restoration. Although he condemned in heavily moralistic terms the wickedness of the period, he also regarded its best poets – Rochester, Dryden, and Sedley – as brilliant satirists, and in the last fifteen years of his life he displays an admiration for the literature produced during his youth, as well as a lingering hostility to the sexual looseness of the upper classes. A curious feature of *Roxana*, for example, is the time scheme that hovers between the masquerades that the impresario Heidegger had started in 1722 and the world of masquerades promoted within the court of Charles II during the 1660s. Events such as the murder of Roxana's lover in France evoke the sensational murders of some English travelers in France in 1723, while her involvement with the court seems to allude to the lives of many of Charles II's mistresses, particularly Louise de Keroualle, Duchess of Portsmouth. The scandalous (and glamorous) past thus evoked by the narrative serves as an escape hatch in case of any accusations of libel.[36]

The main title of Defoe's work was probably an allusion to *The Unfortunate Mistress* by Eliza Haywood, whose novellas about sex and intrigue achieved great popularity at this time, but the tone of Defoe's work bears little resemblance to the writings of Haywood. Roxana never forgets the ethical import of her actions and the text interrogates the reader constantly. The function that Roland Barthes described as a narrative's ability to raise "enigmas" in the reader is constantly present.[37] Deserted by her foolish husband and completely destitute, she debates with her maid Amy the possibility of becoming the mistress of her landlord the Jeweler. Amy insists that giving in to "Necessity," averting starvation by accepting the arrangement proposed by the Jeweler, is what she must accept. She feels that to exchange sexual favors for "Bread" is beneath her. What are we to think? By the ethos of the upper orders during the Restoration, she could justify such an action if she were madly in love. Amy's notion that Roxana could not defy the laws of self-preservation might make sense to most readers. Roxana gives in, but she insists that reality be faced. Amy might want to think better of things by accepting the idea that her mistress is actually married, as the Jeweler insists, but Roxana will have none of it. And to prove that she is nothing but a "Whore," she forces Amy into sexual intercourse with the Jeweler while she remains as a voyeur for the entire scene. Not only does she insist that the situation be confronted without illusions, she adds that if she was to assume the role of a prostitute, in her own eyes, she felt that Amy would have to join in. Moll Flanders tells the story of her life because she knows it is an amusing narrative, but Roxana's story is part of what Michel Foucault describes so well – that historical process by which the confession of sexual transgressions was transferred from the religious to the secular realm.[38] She turns the reader into a voyeur.

This is not the only enigma of this kind. What are we to think of Roxana's arguments concerning the sexual and financial freedom of women? Some critics have accepted Roxana's remark that she did not really believe what she was saying. At the same time, it is clear that the wealth she accumulates under the direction of the vicious and greedy Sir Robert Clayton leads her in the direction of genuine empowerment. Money is power in Defoe's society, and Roxana, once reduced to a state of misery paralleling that of Job, can choose how and where she wishes to live and in what state of opulence. After her marriage to the Dutch Merchant, she even achieves the title of "Countess," satisfying the "Ambition" that is one of the passions driving her. Of course she ends unhappily, and of course what happiness she achieves appears to be in defiance of that spiritual happiness that she ignores. But Defoe is less interested in making *Roxana* into another version of *Pilgrim's Progress* than in showing what her world is like and what it takes to succeed in it. Defoe provided some answers (as well as questions) for his religious readers, but he also wanted us to appreciate how powerless women were in his world and what it took for a woman such as Roxana to achieve a degree of power. Defoe liked to allude to Hercules' advice to the carter whose wagon fell in a ditch and who prayed to the god to rescue him. Hercules advised the carter to put his shoulder to the wheel if he wanted to get out, and Roxana, who has her shoulder to the wheel from the time she takes Amy's advice, could never be wholly villainous in Defoe's mind.

Roxana's relationship with Amy has raised many a critical eyebrow. In the argument about self-preservation, Amy clearly represents the voice of the practical lower orders reminding the bourgeois Roxana of basic human needs, but as Roxana herself remarks, Amy is like a part of herself, a double. When the situation becomes complicated by the extraordinary emergence of Roxana's daughter Susan, as a child in search of the mother who was forced to abandon her, the situation between the three is charged with the kind of raw anguish that the British novel usually avoids. As chance would have it, Susan was a servant in Roxana's household at the time that she succeeded in capturing the attention of the courtiers attending her parties with a dance in Turkish costume. She is in the dangerous position of being capable of revealing Roxana's lurid past at the same time as she arouses in Roxana a passionate sense of motherhood. Seeing only the peril of exposure in Susan's impetuous quest for the identity of her mother, Amy plots to remove Susan from the scene by any means available including murder. But Roxana threatens Amy with an even worse fate if she attempts anything rash. Roxana warns us of her own emotional instability in introducing this part of the story, and the mixture of anxiety, anguish, and despair gives an unusual power to the last section of the novel. If, as Leopold Damrosch has suggested, *Robinson Crusoe* gains some of its power over the reader by its balance between the island as punishment and the island as earthly paradise,[39] *Roxana*, too, keeps the reader in doubt. We are asked to admire her energy, her resolve, and her daring at the same time as we know that she has taken on the corruption of the society that she exploits. I once suggested that Defoe possessed a high degree of what Keats called "negative capability," the dramatist's ability to suspend judgment about his characters and their experiences. However dogmatic Defoe may have been in his moral conduct books about what constituted proper ethical and religious behavior and what did not, his fictional works were almost paradoxical in their tendency to allow such matters to remain unresolved.

Defoe did not abandon narrative after *Roxana*; what disappeared was the interest in creating a complex character and seeing the world through his or her eyes. *A New Voyage Round the World*, which Defoe wrote at the end of 1724, is truly not only a novel without a hero, it is a novel without any real characterization. The captain of the ship never assumes a character beyond that of a person interested in exploration and colonization. Indeed, the anonymous narrator of the *Tour thro' the Whole Island of Great Britain*, whose opinions, tastes, and judgments are quirky enough, gives to that work more character and interest than the narrator of *A New Voyage*, and at least one critic has argued that, in some ways, Defoe's three volumes were closer to a work of fiction than to a travel book.[40] His balanced presentation of the pirates Captain Misson and Captain Tew in *The History of the Pyrates* employs fiction in a way that contrasts Misson the ideologue, whose attempt at a communist colony fails, to Tew, whose practical ideas on colonization succeed. And there are numerous fictional anecdotes in his *System of Magic* and *History of Apparitions*. But in all of these cases fiction is used for a specific purpose – to enliven and clarify a discussion.

The purely fictive impulse in Defoe – the will to create independent characters who tell their stories as emanations of their character and experiences – ended in 1724 with *Roxana*. But Defoe had not run out of things to say. He even created a character, Andrew Moreton, through whom he could express his feelings about a world in which the young mistreated their parents, servants were saucy, masters unable to control their passions, and atheistical philosophers denied the existence of spirit and the soul. But Andrew Moreton was somewhat like Defoe's earlier personae, "The True-Born Englishman" and "Mr. Review," masks through which he could express certain aspects of his personality. He created the curmudgeonly Moreton not only because he wanted to complain about the world of Britain between 1725 and 1730, but also because he had certain improvements to suggest. From the time he composed *An Essay upon Projects*, in 1697, Defoe was a writer who could imagine social constructs such as pension offices and academies for the education of women, replete with ideas and always ready to illustrate his proposals with a variety of narratives. In such works, Defoe revealed something like the same imagination that went into the fiction, but his didactic purpose on every page is hardly to be questioned.

The major fiction was very different. It arose out of a conscious application of Defoe's imagination to the creation of narratives for their own sake – narratives that derived their power directly from the representation of characters experiencing a vividly realized world. Only in these works did he exert a constant effort at rendering that distinctive way in which his characters interacted with their environments, from Moll Flanders amid the ordinary crowds in London, to Roxana emerging in her Turkish costume to dance before the courtiers; from Crusoe's bewilderment at the footprint in the sand, to Colonel Jack's wonder at discovering his former wife among the criminals transported to America from British jails. As a journalist and miscellaneous writer, Defoe specialized in powerful scenes. His depiction of his own experience in witnessing the riots in Scotland during the events of 1705 and 1706, associated as they were with the union of England and Scotland, are a good example of this type of writing. But Defoe was not the center of these events in the same way that Moll Flanders is the center of her world. And his *History of the Union* is not a work of fiction.[41] Unless we grasp the uniqueness of Defoe's brief turn to the novel, we will never grasp his achievement.

NOTES

1 Margaret Doody has been arguing this position in a series of lectures; for example, "Madness and Passion in Novels Ancient and Eighteenth Century," presented at a meeting of the American Society for Eighteenth-Century Studies on 26 March 1992 in Seattle, and "The Classical Novel in the Enlightenment," presented before a meeting of the same organization on 24 April 1993 in Providence.

2 For a definition of this form of "novel," see William Congreve, *Incognita*, reprinted in Philip Henderson, ed., *Shorter Novels: Seventeenth Century* (London: J. M. Dent, 1962), 241–43.

3 See Mikhail Bakhtin, *Dostoevsky's Poetics*, trans. Caryl Emerson (Minneapolis: University of Minnesota Press, 1985), 114–18; and Gary Morson and Cary Emerson, *Mikhail Bakhtin* (Stanford: Stanford University Press, 1990), 490–91.

4 Although Gérard Genette rightly criticizes the division between first person and third person as inept characterizations of what happens in a narrative, I have preferred to use these more familiar terms rather than heterodiegetic, homodiegetic and extradiegetic voices, terms that are not yet stable in the still fluid field of narratology. See *Narrative Discourse*, trans. Jane E. Lewin (Ithaca, N.Y.: Cornell University Press, 1972), especially 185–94, 248–49.

5 *The Family Instructor* (2 vols., London, 1715 and 1718), I: 2. Subsequent references to these volumes will be included within parentheses in the text.

6 A number of judicial rulings during the reign of William III and during the early part of the century suggested that this was correct. See *Modern Reports, or, Select Cases Adjudged in the Courts of King's Bench, Chancery, Common-Pleas and Exchequer*, 5th edn (London, 1794), V, roll 123 for Michaelmas term, 7 William III; and "Chamberlaine against Harvey," *Reports of Cases Adjudged in the Court of the Kings Bench*, ed. William Salkeld, 6th edn (London, 1795), II: 666, Easter term, 8 William III, cases 91 and 92.

7 See for example Bernard Mandeville, *The Fable of the Bees*, ed. F. B. Kaye (Oxford: Clarendon, 1924), II: 32–36. It is not at all clear that Fulvia has the worst of her defense of realist art against Cleomenes' arguments for "*la belle nature.*"

8 *The Memoirs of Majr. Alexander Ramkinds, a Highland-Officer, now in Prison at Avignon* (London, 1719 [for 1718]), 151–52.

9 *Robinson Crusoe*, ed. J. Donald Crowley (London: Oxford University Press, 1972), 163.

10 For a comparison of the conclusions drawn about the footprint and the use of circumstantial evidence as used in a court of law, see Alexander Welsh, *Strong Representations* (Baltimore: Johns Hopkins University Press, 1992), 3–6. Welsh not only analyzes the scene from this viewpoint but shows how the prosecutor in the famous case of Lizzie Borden (accused in late nineteenth-century Massachusetts of murdering her parents with an axe) used it to illustrate how proper conclusions might be drawn from a single piece of evidence. For a connection to establishing "matters of fact" through scientific experimentation, see Steve Shapin and Simon Schaffer, *Leviathan and the Air Pump* (Cambridge: Cambridge University Press, 1985), 17–18, 30–40.

11 Although Barthes denied that he was providing a method for analyzing fiction, his analogy between the experience of reading fiction and listening to a complex musical work is probably the most accurate description of how the novel may operate on many levels. And while Barthes seems to have thought he was revealing some of the failures of "popular" fiction, Genette found many of the same devices in Proust's work. See Genette, *Narrative Discourse*, 57.

12 Daniel Defoe, *Serious Reflections of Robinson Crusoe*, reprinted in *Romances and Narratives*, ed. George Aitken (London: J. M. Dent, 1895), III: xii.

13 Michael McKeon, *The Origins of the English Novel, 1600–1740* (Baltimore: Johns Hopkins University Press, 1987), 63, 120, 361, 408.

14 Although I have borrowed the concept of the "power of naming" from Pierre Bourdieu, *Hastings Law Journal*, 38 (1987): 837–38, I have also drawn upon suggestions from Jean-François Lyotard, *The Differend*, trans. Georges Van Den Abbeele (Minneapolis: University of Minnesota Press, 1988), 32–48.

15 *Memoirs of a Cavalier*, ed. James Boulton (London: Oxford University Press, 1972), 2.

16 *The King of Pirates: . . . Captain Avery*, reprinted in Aitken, ed., *Romances and Narratives*, XVI: 3. This work appeared on 10 December 1719.

17 E. M. Forster, *Aspects of the Novel* (New York: Harcourt Brace, 1958; first published, 1927), 86. For a more detailed consideration of change without the implication of cause and effect or significant embedded materials, see Mieke Bal's discussion of "events" in *Narratology*, trans. Christine van Boheemen (Toronto: University of Toronto Press, 1985), 13–25.

18 For a thorough development of Bakhtin's concept, see John Bender, *Imagining the Penitentiary: Fiction and the Architecture of Mind in Eighteenth-Century England* (Chicago: University of Chicago Press, 1987), 87–89, 103–9. For Bakhtin's original suggestion, see *The Dialogic Imagination*, ed. Michael Holquist, trans. Caryl Emerson and Michael Holquist (Austin: University of Texas Press, 1985), 6–7.

19 *Captain Singleton*, ed. Shiv K. Kumar (London: Oxford University Press, 1969), 94.

20 See Peter Knox-Shaw, *The Explorer in English Fiction* (New York: St. Martin's Press, 1986), 62–64.

21 See Ian Bell's discussion of genre expectation in *Defoe's Fiction* (Beckenham: Croom Helm, 1985), 42–71. Bell dismisses *Captain Singleton* for its relatively simple story form, but if Captain Singleton is a relatively nondescript pirate, William, who functions in the guise of the merchant-as-pirate, is never dull.

22 *Moll Flanders*, ed. G. A. Starr (London: Oxford University Press, 1971), 214.

23 Behind Madeleine Kahn's interesting discussion there appears to lie a certain indignation over Defoe's usurpation of the voice of a woman along with a notion that only a woman could truly write about a woman's problems. As she defines "narrative transvestitism," it is an aspect of male assertiveness and perhaps for that reason even more offensive. See *Narrative Transvestitism* (Ithaca, N.Y.: Cornell University Press, 1991), especially, 28–54, 79–102.

24 I know from having taught *Moll Flanders* for more than three decades that students find Moll's abandonment of her children extraordinarily callous, but we now know from several books on the subject that child abandonment was common enough at the time. When her survival is at stake, when she has no way

of caring for her children, Moll abandons them. When her prospects appear good, she shows a proper concern for their care.

25 The South African novelist J. M. Coetzee in *Foe* has Defoe speak of himself metaphorically as an "old whore," a writer who sells himself to anyone who will pay. If Defoe ever actually felt that way, he might have gained some insight into the lives of Moll and Roxana. Certainly, he knew the meaning of being at the mercy of others and of the inherent danger in such a position. He had experienced that both as a bankrupt merchant and as a mercenary writer for the Tories in 1714. But how his translation of such emotions into an understanding of the psychology of his characters differs in any way from what is usually expected of the imagination of any novelist escapes me. See *Foe* (Harmondsworth: Penguin, 1986), 151.

26 *Due Preparations for the Plague*, reprinted in Aitken, ed., *Romances and Narratives*, 82.

27 *A Journal of the Plague Year*, ed. Louis Landa (London: Oxford University Press, 1969), 60. For a discussion of Defoe's use of the ineffable as a literary device in his novels, see Maximillian Novak, "The Unmentionable and the Ineffable in Defoe's Fiction," *Studies in the Literary Imagination*, 15 (1982): 85–102.

28 See, for example, the grotesque story of the man whose order for ale is forgotten by the servant at an inn. He has died before any one remembers the order and is found "stark dead, and almost cold, stretch'd out cross the Bed; his Cloths were pulled off, his Jaw fallen, his Eyes open in a most frightful Posture, the Rug of the Bed being grasped hard in one of his Hands; so that it was plain he died soon after the Maid left him, and 'tis probable, had she gone up with the Ale, she had found him dead . . ." *Journal of the Plague Year*, 72.

29 Hester Thrale, *Thraliana*, ed. James Clifford (Oxford: Clarendon, 1951), II: 719.

30 Everett Zimmerman, *Defoe and the Novel* (Berkeley and Los Angeles: University of California Press, 1975), 107–25.

31 See Maximillian Novak, "The Disordered City," *PMLA*, 92 (1977): 241–52.

32 *Journal of the Plague Year*, 119–20.

33 *Colonel Jack*, ed. Samuel Monk (London: Oxford University Press, 1965), 2.

34 See Bakhtin, *Dialogic Imagination*, 114–18; and Morson and Emerson, *Mikhail Bakhtin*, 407–13.

35 See J. L. Austin, *Philosophical Papers*, 3rd edn (Oxford: Oxford University Press, 1979), 175–204.

36 For a discussion of the particulars of these relationships, see Maximillian Novak, *Realism, Myth, and History in Defoe's Fiction*, (Lincoln: University of Nebraska Press, 1983), 13–17. The murders of several English gentlemen in France occurred on 21 September 1723. Defoe was to publish *An Account of the Cartoucheans in France*, about the crime wave in France associated with the master criminal Cartouche, in the same year as *Roxana*.

37 See Roland Barthes, *S/Z*, trans. Richard Miller (New York: Hill and Wang, 1974), 18–22.

38 See Michel Foucault, *The History of Sexuality*, trans. Robert Hurley (New York: Vintage, 1978), I: 63–65.

39 Leopold Damrosch, Jr., *God's Plot and Man's Stories* (Chicago: University of Chicago Press, 1985), especially 197–99.

40 See Lynn Batten, *Pleasurable Instruction* (Berkeley and Los Angeles: University of California Press, 1978), 26.
41 For a full discussion of the relation between history and fiction in Defoe's writings, see Novak, *Realism, Myth, and History*, 47–70.

READING LIST

Alkon, Paul. *Defoe and Fictional Time.* Athens: University of Georgia Press, 1979.
Backscheider, Paula. *Daniel Defoe: a Life.* Baltimore: Johns Hopkins University Press, 1990.
Bell, Ian. *Defoe's Fiction.* Beckenham: Croom Helm, 1985.
Blewett, David. *Defoe's Art of Fiction.* Toronto: University of Toronto Press, 1979.
Brown, Homer O. "The Displaced Self in the Novels of Daniel Defoe," *ELH*, 38 (1971): 562–90.
Damrosch, Leo. *God's Plot and Man's Stories: Studies in the Fictional Imagination from Milton to Fielding.* Chicago: University of Chicago Press, 1985.
Earle, Peter. *The World of Defoe.* London: Weidenfeld and Nicolson, 1976.
Hunter, J. Paul. *The Reluctant Pilgrim: Defoe's Emblematic Method and Quest for Form in Robinson Crusoe.* Baltimore: Johns Hopkins University Press, 1966.
Novak, Maximillian E. *Defoe and the Nature of Man.* Oxford: Oxford University Press, 1965.
  Realism, Myth, and History in Defoe's Fiction. Lincoln: University of Nebraska Press, 1983.
Richetti, John. *Defoe's Narratives: Situation and Structures.* Oxford: Oxford University Press, 1975.
  Daniel Defoe. Boston: G. K. Hall, 1987.
Schonhorn, Manuel. *Defoe's Politics: Parliament, Power, Kingship, and Robinson Crusoe.* Cambridge: Cambridge University Press, 1991.
Starr, George. *Defoe and Spiritual Autobiography.* Princeton: Princeton University Press, 1965.
  Defoe and Casuistry. Princeton: Princeton University Press, 1971.
Sutherland, James. *Defoe: a Critical Study.* Cambridge, Mass.: Harvard University Press, 1971.
Zimmerman, Everett. *Defoe and the Novel.* Berkeley and Los Angeles: University of California Press, 1975.

4

MICHAEL SEIDEL

Gulliver's Travels and the contracts of fiction

I FICTIONAL BONA FIDES

Mariners lie like old sea dogs. In James Joyce's *Ulysses* (1922), the adventuring hero, Leopold Bloom, never leaves the confines of his native city, but he does run into an old sailor named Murphy who boasts of his travels to several remote regions of the world. Bloom has his doubts about Murphy, "assuming he was the person he represented himself and not sailing under false colours after having boxed the compass on the q.t. somewhere."[1] Listening to the yarns and finding something out of joint about them makes Bloom "nourish some suspicions of our friend's bona fides" (512).

What does it mean to nourish suspicions about a narrator's bona fides? This is the very question that haunts Jonathan Swift's *Gulliver's Travels* (1726), and for good reason. *Gulliver's Travels* has been a notable gathering place, almost a convocation, for the severer sort of Western Critic who sees its satiric action as a vicious attack on the political and cultural institutions of eighteenth-century British civilization in the guise of a satiric send-up of travel literature.[2]

But what if Swift's satiric travel narrative is directed not simply at the experience of modern political, social, and intellectual life in England and Europe, but at the narrative bona fides of those middling fictional subjects who emerged during the early decades of the eighteenth century in England precisely to endorse the modern, progressivist, commercial vision of the world that Swift's satire bemoans? The novel is the literary form positing the fitness of a low-life, pseudoprofessional, or merchant-class narrator – Moll Flanders, Robinson Crusoe, Colonel Jack, Captain Singleton – to record the contingencies and changing valences of modern life. As such, it was a likely and predictable Swiftian target.[3]

In most of his work, Swift is a master at what might be called satiric deauthentication. His satire cuts to the core of self-representation in the

72

literature of his age, and offers complex challenges to the supposed bona fides of a host of figures whom he sets up as representatives of modern consciousness. No satirist has ever been craftier at allowing his satiric subjects free voice in their own annihilation. His career is based on a kind of satiric ventriloquism where egophiliac narrators talk themselves into states of exhaustion or lunacy. In *A Tale of A Tub* (1704), Swift worms into the voice and rots out the discursive ramblings of a hack for hire; in the *Bickerstaff Papers* (1708-9), he finishes off a scandal-mongering, lying astrologer; in *Argument Against the Abolishment of Christianity* (1708), he turns inside out the equivocations of a trimming, secular, free-thinking religious apologist; in *A Modest Proposal*, he reveals the motives of an ambition-driven, calculating political economist; in *Gulliver's Travels*, he ruins the life of a one-time ship's surgeon turned professional merchant adventurer. Swift's best satire always recreates the manner in which the modern mind conceives, writes up, and enervates its own condition.

For Swift, the early novelistic experiments of the 1720s in England provided a tantalizing space for his satiric powers to run loose over new terrain. He distrusted virtually everything represented in the early novel: its individualistic psychology; its brief for class mobility; its delight in a burgeoning of the British economy; its adjustable ethics and morality; its increasing tolerance of opinion; its role in the proliferation of knowledge; its success as a product of the increasingly commercial literary industry. From Swift's satiric viewpoint, the novel was exactly the narrative form his age deserved, one that removed the time-tested values of cultural inheritance and substituted the subjective experience of a serviceably dim and limited commercial intelligence.

Though first-time readers are more likely to set the satiric perimeters of *Gulliver's Travels* around all of European civilization, there is a way of reading the narrative and drawing the loop around Gulliver as parody of the middling fictional subject as well. In this sense – one perfectly confirmed by other works of Swift – it is less Gulliver's rendition of his civilization that exists at the narrative center of the *Travels* than what the *Travels* tell us about Gulliver as representative of his civilization. Gulliver may be the primary critic of civilization by the end of his account, but he is also, and this is crucial to any productive reading of the work, the primary product on display of that civilization from the beginning of his account. The first items the Lilliputians discover in Gulliver's pockets are a watch and some loose silver coin and gold: time and money, the modern Englishman's credo.

Gulliver is a blustering modern figure at the beginning of his voyages: his middle-class cocksureness, his professional acumen, his receptive linguistic ear, his interests in politics, social values, civic engineering, and military strategy are all inestimable resources for the contemporary subject nego-tiating the early eighteenth-century world. Gulliver in Lilliput is an outsized version of the new man of his age. By the time we begin to understand the satiric focus of the narrative, we also begin to understand the satiric implication of what Swift has done to and with Gulliver in the first adventure. Gulliver's physical size is partly a satiric image of the inflated status of the subject in modern fiction. In Swift's writing, to blow something up is to set it up for satiric action, as deflation necessarily follows inflation. The more complex pattern (exercised on Gulliver's mind) is, of course, previewed in the second book of the adventures in the land of giants. Gulliver the maximalist becomes, for purposes of the satiric narrative, Gulliver the minimalist. This has a structural role in the plot of the fantasy, and also a subtle role in the more ranging satire on the fictional bona fides of the narrator in the early eighteenth-century novel. Where the novel generally works to render its authenticating subject secure, Swift's satire destabilizes the body and then the mind of its central character. By the end of the *Travels*, Gulliver is not even certain what it is to be human, and his behavior suggests as much.

Gulliver is the expert whose knowledge is limited, the sailor who knows little about the sea, the modern jingoist patriot who is also the national turncoat, the world traveler who speaks only to the horses in his barn, the surgeon who cannot operate, the translator who cannot locate idioms or contexts. What are we supposed to make of Gulliver, the linguistic expert, who derives the place-name of his third voyage, "*Lapute* was *quasi Lap outed*; *Lap* signifying properly the dancing of the Sun Beams in the Sea and *outed* a Wing, which however I shall not obtrude, but submit to the judicious Reader?"[4] Just *how* would the judicious reader know? More likely, the injudicious reader hears the Spanish *la puta*, or whore, which gets closer to Swift's satiric point about Gulliver inside his narration: it's all something like prostitution, a selling of one's narrative produce to all comers.

As narrator, Gulliver loses credit as his adventures develop. It is not that Gulliver exhibits the same greed, corruption, hypocrisy that constitute the satiric matter of his harangues against British life to his Houyhnhnm Master in the fourth voyage, but that he is self-infatuated, self-obsessed, and deranged. He begins by thinking moderately well of himself and ends by thinking himself a superior member of an inferior species. Swift constructs a narrative subject who ironically does all he can to invalidate the literary form that conveys him. Snickering readers have long joked about the satiric significance of Gulliver's medical mentor, a Master Bates, in this respect. It is fairly well established by now that the pun was at least possible in 1726, and if so, it means Gulliver was trained not only in surgery but in a sort of narrative onanism, the same impulse that marked the self-projecting capacity of the unstable narrator in Swift's *A Tale of A Tub*.

Gulliver has, in a modern idiom, an image problem. The narrative sets out to present him with one. He doesn't know whether he looks good small or big; he doesn't know whether the features of his face look better symmetrically disposed or awry; he doesn't know whether his pathetic body would serve him better shaped like a horse's; he doesn't know whether his sounds and smells are as offensive to everyone else as they are to him. In short, he is uncertain about the material reality around him. Even at the beginning of his voyages he is all too ready to adopt an unsettling perspective in relaying information. When he urinates in Lilliput he refers to the "Torrent which fell with such Noise and Violence from me" (9). Why does *he* choose such words? The Lilliputians have reason to record the noise and violence, but not Gulliver. Similarly, in Brobdingnag Gulliver describes the way whales from his world swim into Brobdingnaggian waters: "These Whales I have known so large that Man could hardly carry one upon his Shoulders" (89). What does Gulliver think when he makes such an observation? Swift's deadpan narrative ventriloquism encourages the question.

When Gulliver returns home after his voyages he assumes the most absurd things. Looking at his wife after his visit to the land of giants he concludes "she had been too thrifty, for I found she had starved herself and her Daughter to nothing" (124). It is one thing to think them small; it is another to misconstrue completely why they would look so. Gulliver gets worse and worse. At the finale of his narrative he is a bundle of nervous tics; he has difficulty filtering out human things; he thinks that horses speak to him (has anyone ever asked how English horses come to speak Houyhnhnmese, a language derived from an unknown place 10,000 miles away?). *Gulliver's Travels* is so thoroughly satiric that its resolution is its worst narrative crisis, and the hero's homecoming the most foreign and alienating experience of all. Gulliver returns home in exile, as detached from his land and time as the infamous Struldbruggs or immortals of voyage three of the *Travels*. Indeed, the pattern for the Struldbrugg episode is not unlike the mental pattern for the *Travels* at large. Gulliver is set up to represent the best hopes of progressive modern life and is brought through to the alien side where he can comprehend neither the values nor, in some cases, the language of his native land. The course of the Struldbruggs, though long in *their* lives and adventures, is shortened for Gulliver. At their end, the Struldbruggs live at home the way Gulliver will in his – "like Foreigners in their own Country" (183), despised and hated by one and all.

Gulliver is an Odysseus gone sour; a homecomer who, in a satiric version of narrative rest, is depressed and drained by his very resources as a human being. His last observation on his human life is a deeply contradictory remark about not wishing any yahoo with a tincture of pride – though all yahoos, including himself, possess it – to appear in his sight. This is also the last reference to the fictional subject in the *Travels* and the last reference to the form that inscribes the self, the novel. Gulliver wants nothing human to appear before him. The modern subject faces only the raw dilemma of being alive.

Swift's attack on modern consciousness was not new in *Gulliver's Travels*. For years he was associated with the famous Scriblerus Club (whose very name identifies and mocks modern writing). The primary task of the Scriblerians was to collect and satirize all forms of contemporary literary expression represented by absurdly imagined figures of eighteenth-century political and cultural life. Out of the club came John Arbuthnot's British proto-imperialist, John Bull, John Gay's highwayman spoiler, Mac-Heath, and Alexander Pope's (under Arbuthnot's direction) expert-in-every-thing, Martin Scriblerus. *Gulliver's Travels* was originally supposed to have been an early part of the Scriblerian enterprise in 1713. Pope proposed that Swift get busy on a chapter for the *Memoirs of Martinus Scriblerus* in which Martin would visit the land of pygmies, giants, and mathematicians before voyaging to a land where he discovers a "vein of Melancholy proceeding almost to a disgust of his Species."[5]

Swift dawdled with the assignment at the time it was given, but never abandoned it. He waited until 1726, changed characters, expanded the satire, but to a certain extent kept wearing his Scriblerian hat. At the Academy at Lagado during Gulliver's third voyage, we hear of a giant word machine (actually diagrammed in the text) by which "Contrivance, the most ignorant Person at a reasonable Charge, and with a little bodily Labour, may write Books in Philosophy, Poetry, Politicks, Law, Mathematicks and Theology, without the least Assistance from Genius or Study" (156). It is difficult to read such a passage, let alone imagine the random, whirling words tossed out by the machine, and not think Swift had a typical Scriblerian target like Daniel Defoe in mind.[6] Defoe represented the voice of modernity – the prolific journalism, the conduct books, histories, gazeteers, mock biographies, the novel. It was almost as if Swift needed to have the century produce the literary symptom of Daniel Defoe full-blown before he could scourge the malady in *Gulliver's Travels*. In this sense, Defoe's impulsive traveler, the narrating merchant-adventurer Robinson Crusoe, provided Swift with a better satiric model for Gulliver than Martin Scriblerus.[7]

It is no accident that so many of the specifics of Swift's narrative ingest and redispose the Crusoe story in a form more suitable to satire. A pointed example occurs late in the adventures when Gulliver considers for the space of a few paragraphs what for Crusoe had been a life's adventure.

> My Design was, if possible, to discover some small Island uninhabited, yet sufficient by my Labour to furnish me with Necessaries of Life, which I would have thought a greater Happiness than to be first Minister in the politest Court of *Europe*; so horrible was the Idea I conceived of returning to live in the Society and under the Government of *Yahoos*. For in such a Solitude as I desired, I could at least enjoy my own Thoughts, and reflect with Delight on the Virtues of those inimitable *Houyhnhnms*, without any Opportunity of degenerating into the Vices and Corruptions of my own Species.   (248)

For Crusoe, this is a fictional opportunity that generates an entire narrative. For Gulliver, a native islander shoots him in the knee with an arrow, and he swims off the island in despair. So much for Swift's commentary on the value of the Crusoe saga. Would that the novel form itself, as a literary phenomenon, had enjoyed such a quick demise. That it did not do so was yet another symptom for Swift of the corruption of values and literary tastes in his age.

Crusoe is an image of the reconstituted self that Swift so distrusted, the I-land whose fictional experience reinforces the idea of enterprise, liberty, and self-sovereignty in the modern world.[8] The novel – whether called the personal memoir, the true history, the life and adventure, the confession – generally builds character; it devises strategies to make character paramount and also to build confidence in character. Characters in the early novel work by repeating key impulses, and succeed by integrating those impulses with possibilities offered to them in the worlds in which they circulate. The desires, wants, compulsions of the ordinary man or woman become the stuff of fiction. Life is a series of calibrations and negotiations, compromises and accommodations. The relatively inconsequential self becomes the filter for human experience where, as Defoe puts it in his own musings on *Robinson Crusoe*, "all reflection is carried home, and our dear self is, in one respect, the end of living."[9]

Defoe lets us know that Crusoe's subjective "Story is told with Modesty, with Seriousness, and with a religious Application of Events to the Uses to which wise Men always apply them (viz.) to the Instruction of others by this Example, and to justify and honour the Wisdom of Providence in all the Variety of our Circumstances, let them happen how they will."[10] In his parody of the Crusoe-like subject, Swift makes a mockery of this egocentric contract for fiction, and any moral justification that would tag along with it. He parodies the language of modern fiction while debasing the enterprise:

> I hope the gentle Reader will excuse me for dwelling on these and the like Particulars, which however insignificant they may appear to grovelling vulgar

Minds, yet will certainly help a Philosopher to enlarge his Thoughts and Imagination, and apply them to the Benefit of public as well as private Life, which was my sole design in presenting this and other Accounts of my Travels to the World. (73)

Of course all these particulars – the circumstantial voicings of the modern narrative self – are about Gulliver's disposing of his excremental waste in Lilliput, perhaps one of the many images for Swift that serve satirically for the new forms of eighteenth-century fiction.

Swift's satire tends to suck the lifeblood right out of the novel, to ignore the nuances of character, to present human response as reflexive, to doubt the unique and individual workings of the human mind. It is almost axiomatic in satiric representation that the subjects under scrutiny participate in a kind of thoughtless, soulless arena where individuals do not really count. Swift's characters act as if no one in his or her right mind would judge and scrutinize human actions on the basis of particular contingencies or necessities. Satire is essentially about the ways in which individuals reveal their selfish and egotistical desires; character for the satirist is always comically distilled as nothing but self-seeking. In Swiftian satire, the subject is an embarrassing monster who is meant to provoke in us an almost visceral disgust with the ways in which individuals misrepresent their real motives. Characters are always invalidated by their actions, and satire means stripping them of their narrative bona fides that the emerging novel grants them so fully and readily.

II NARDACS AND LIARS

Gulliver is a Nardac. There can be no dispute about that. After his waylaying of the Blefuscuan fleet in the service of the Lilliputians, Gulliver is made a Nardac "upon the Spot, which is the highest Title of Honour among them" (34). So what, then, is a Nardac? Nardac seems an arbitrary name until other anagrammatic matters provide a retrospective license of sorts to rearrange the order of its letters. In Laputa, during a discussion about anagrams and excrement, Gulliver claims special knowledge because of his unnarrated travels in a place, "Tribnia (by the natives called Langden)" (163). "Langden" and "Tribnia" are, by the simple disposition of the anagrammatic draw, "England" and "Britain." Few readers have, or ought to have, trouble rearranging these geographically disposed letters. After all, the Laputa episode itself, whatever implications can be drawn from *its* letters, invites readers to scramble letters by diagramming a machine that does just that.

As is often the case in narrative, incidents that occur later in a sequence have a kind of throw-back potential in focusing questions that may not have even occurred at first. We can ask with good cause whether the order of the Nardac is anything more than a scrambled Canard?[11] A *canard* is a hoax or joke. It is a concoction, as Sterne might put it, full of cock and bull; or, as the Marx Brothers might swim in, duck soup.

The Order of Canard brings Swift's readers close, perhaps perilously close, to a series of tricky fictional questions in *Gulliver's Travels*. What honor ought the reader best bestow upon Gulliver's story? To what extent does that story look like a hoax consisting of jumbled territorial letters inside the head of a traveler who may now be a lunatic, sojourning in Tribnia, by the natives called Langden? Are all of the *Travels* a canard, part of whose fictional content is the notion that the traveler never leaves the mental spaces that literally project his ground? Is the possessive in *Gulliver's Travels* not only a function of grammatical belonging but of subjective parody? Do the travels belong to Gulliver in the sense that the distraction of his ego-driven mind is the only thing that could have really produced them? Is the actual fiction a much more complicated narrative satiric investigation about the kind of mind that would imagine fantastical places from the mixed up, local, and nonsensical jumble of experiences that constitute a version of modern or *nouveau* British madness? Though Gulliver seems hardly touched by the modern world – exactly the King of Brobdingnag's point when, in a backhanded compliment, he exempts Gulliver as a traveler from the corruptions of the odious little race of vermin to which he belongs – perhaps he is really driven mad by it *before* he ever voyages anywhere?

To put these questions differently, what happens to the standard reading contract of fiction – the naive one that asks us to give the narrator his or her due and believe what is told us – if we assume Gulliver never left England? If we dismiss the naive reading contract that allows the voyages their fictional credibility, what is the point of reading on in the narrative? But what if another contract offers a different way of reading the *Travels*? What if the attitudes Gulliver strikes – especially his behavior at the end – become symptomatic of the delusionary madness of a depressed and self-persecuted modern? Swift and his age knew madness under several names, one of them melancholy – maybe that is why Gulliver marries a woman named Mary Burton, who sports the surname of the greatest expert on madness in the seventeenth century, Richard Burton.[12] Swift named as melancholy what we would name depression in its less manifest state and paranoia in its raving state. Essentially paranoia is a form of overactive imagination, as Swift explained the malady (even if he did not identify it) earlier in *A Tale of A Tub*. The delusion of special grandeur brings all paranoid experience into its own special compass, and imposes its vision upon the world as a form of power, the power of self-projection.

Why would Swift want to include the possibility that the *Travels* are Gulliver's stay-at-home invention, the fancy of homebound lunacy? One argument, perfectly consistent with everything Swift ever wrote (and, more important, perfectly consistent with the manner or mode of Swift's approach to the satiric nature of narrative voice), is that madness approached the very condition assumed as necessary for the modern form of the prose memoir or novel: the obsessive self-centeredness of the narrator. The narrator in the early *Tale of A Tub* is an abstraction of the later Gulliver in this sense. We learn to read the whole of the *Tale* as a projection of the reality of a lunatic whose several returns to Bedlam are all homecomings. The result looks like a tale told by a crazed teller. Swift's earlier modern writer in the *Tale* was supposed to be at work on two treatises, one called "A Description of the Kingdom of *Absurdities*," and another, "A Voyage into *England*, by a Person of Quality in *Terra Australis*, translated from the Original." Perhaps Swift produced both years later in *Gulliver's Travels*, an account more like a voyage into England or, at least, into the subjective *terra incognita* of Gulliver's disturbed brain than it is the comic record of travels to which we extend fictional credit only because we are told they occur. The presumed person of quality voyaging into England is the satiric travesty of Gulliver as novelistic canard, a person returned from somewhere near the Australia of his mind bereft not only of quality at the end of his travels, but of his senses.

To pose the possibility that Gulliver never leaves England is to raise notions about points of access into any fiction. Readers generally proceed by following the terms of a fictional contract until it is violated or altered. The center of the new narrative tradition building around the time of Swift's *Travels* and continuing after it, was the contract of good faith established between writers and readers of novels based on a key premise: relatively unexceptional characters could produce a relatively engaging narrative if enough circumstantially probable things happened to them. Only under the narrative contract of veracity do these narratives gain credit. That is, if we believed them to be improbable, they would lose the credit they sustain by masquerading as true stories.

Defoe begins his narrative of Robinson Crusoe by insisting that he "believes the thing to be a just History of Fact; neither is there any Appearance of fiction in it" (3). By this he means that within its fictional contract, the events laid out are strictly probable. Even if the novel takes place within an imaginary topography – say, Crusoe's island – that topography bears a resemblance to a place that might well exist. Those reading the narrative can, by a none-too-wrenching leap of the imagination, credit the possibility of the story actually taking place somewhere and to someone. Swift has Gulliver's cousin Sympson make the same assessment in the *Travels*: "There is an Air of Truth apparent through the whole; and indeed the Author was so distinguished for his Veracity, that it became a Sort of Proverb among his Neighbors at *Redriff*, when any one affirmed a Thing, to say, it was as true as if Mr. Gulliver had spoke it" (viii). But the choices Swift makes in constructing Gulliver's narrative, the contradictions and inconsistencies he allows Gulliver, contribute to the reader's suspicion that the contractual truth of this fiction is really the delusionary nature of Gulliver's adventures.

Gulliver's diction is tangled throughout when the subject is truth-telling, even if by the time he writes the *Travels* he is liege to Houyhnhnm ideology where there is no word for "lie" in the language. How convenient! Nonetheless, Gulliver keeps bringing up the possibility of lying. Does anyone imagine him "so far degenerated as to defend my Veracity?" (vii). How far degenerated does one have to be not to defend one's veracity? Gulliver's repeated defense of his veracity is one of those clues that all may not be as it seems. That he protests his abiding veracity is evidence of the extent to which Gulliver believes the claim, however much the untruth may have entered his consciousness as vision. The lengths to which a narrative subject will go to convince himself that his beliefs are definitive is one of Swift's major satiric strategies in representing the modern object of fiction. When Gulliver fronts the issue of his veracity again, late in the adventure, he selects for support the words of that infamous snake-in-the-grass Sinon, the Greek deserter during the Trojan War. Sinon is in the midst of telling the grandest lie in literary history to the Trojans concerning a gift horse that bears some looking in the mouth. Of course Sinon is only lying about a horse whereas Gulliver thinks he is telling the truth about a Houyhnhnm. When the Trojans express doubts about his story Sinon protests, "Though Fortune may have made me wretched, she has not made me a liar," and Gulliver finds the sentiment apt just after his own ringing claim that in all things he "would *strictly adhere to Truth*": "– *Nec si miserum Fortuna Sinonem / Finxit, vanum etiam, mendacemque improba finget* [Though Fortune has made Sinon wretched, she has not also made him a liar] *Aeneid*, II, 79–80" (256). Actually, at the very instance that Sinon protests his veracity he may well believe, like Gulliver, that his wretchedness supersedes his lie, a belief based primarily on its articulation.

It is because Gulliver cannot and could not recognize the implications of the Sinon allusion for his own account of horse culture in Houyhnhnmland that is so very powerful. The strength of Gulliver's belief in his veracity is precisely what clues the reader to disbelieve it. Gulliver's is not the imposter's lie but rather the lunatic's lie. He remains convinced that what is in his head is true, and he is willing to cite any scrap of material that has also lodged itself in his memory to support it, even if that scrap of material is profound countertestimony for his readers. Gulliver is so deluded that Sinon serves him as a character reference, which is, in a way, what Sinon is.

Some would insist that the fiction of the *Travels* resists a reading that would posit Gulliver as having made up all his voyages because there are still unaccountable bits of fictional information left over from the naive reading contract that the reader must dispose. For example, the *Travels* had to have taken place because we are told how Gulliver digs into his pocket on the way home from Lilliput and Brobdingnag and actually produces live artifacts of those tiny and gigantic civilizations. But this is simply to give the prior contract – the naive one – too much credit. Paranoids are perfectly capable – within the reading contract that assumes madness – of imagining actions that seem perfectly real to them, and then imagining a cast of characters who, unlike the rest of world, partake of the very fantasies created for and by the lunatic. There is the famous joke of the paranoid who complains to his shrink that he is covered with butterflies. "Good god," the shrink shouts, "don't brush them off on me." This joke is based on a double fictional contract: the naive one that the butterflies exist and the revised one that the patient and the shrink *think* they exist. Such is the kind of double contract that gets written for *Gulliver's Travels* as part of its satiric agenda.

III SCURRY POINTS

When anything occurs in fictional narrative that challenges, threatens, or alters the terms of an original or naive reading contract, readers are well advised to seek counsel. Doubting Gulliver's veracity or unscrambling the letters of Nardac and, later, Tribnia and Langden, compel just such radical alterations of the reading contract. A word like canard, all jumbled up as a special honor bestowed upon the narrator, forces a readerly double take. Exactly who is swimming in the duck soup? Maybe Gulliver and maybe all travelers who have been adhering to the wrong clauses of the wrong reader's contract and who continue to do so as they read on.

The *Travels* are filled with hundreds of narrative words, phrases, and incidents that force the savvy reader to pay most attention at the very moment the reading contract appears in doubt or in jeopardy.[13] These are what can be called scurry points, where readers are sometimes explicitly asked and sometimes implicitly required to reconstrue the contracts under which they are proceeding. In its 1726 version, *Gulliver's Travels* begins narrative life as a voyage memoir. Whether actual or counterfeit, it is fair enough to say that the fiction seems to proceed as a faithful record of Gulliver's experience abroad until we encounter a race of people roughly six inches tall in a place named Lilliput. Gulliver, no more than his readers, is ready for the Lilliputians. He senses their abnormality, their deep strangeness. Even as a character inside a fiction he does not assume the suspension of the laws of probability; rather, he asks for the suspension on the basis of a new reader's contract that *has* to be rewritten because of things that have occurred to him. After all, he simply came upon the Lilliputians. Readers tentatively grant him fictional license to proceed with his record. This seems an acceptable addendum to the naive fictional contract, understood by readers as part of a general theory of literature.[14]

The amended contract does not demand that we should expect such a race as the Lilliputians (neither does Gulliver before he encounters them), only that we should credit Gulliver's surprise discovery. Nonetheless, there is another option based on a more radical scurrying of the reading contract at the beginning of *Gulliver's Travels*. We have to recall something about the method and sequence of the work's publication history here. In 1735, nine years after the original publication of the *Travels*, Swift added prefatory material – a letter from Gulliver to his cousin Sympson, and a letter from Sympson to the reader. When he did so, he was obviously concerned enough about readers missing the course of Gulliver's mental history that he reimagined it.

Presumably compiled from notebooks and journals written close to the time of the voyages, even the 1726 *Travels* are recollected after Gulliver is represented to have gone crazy or at least to prance and whinny like a horse in his stable. But we have to reach the end of the *Travels* before we can entertain any notion of the already disturbed Gulliver establishing the sequence of his own distraction. This is a nifty trick. The new prefatory material simply emphasizes the process Gulliver has already undergone and places it at the beginning of the narrative. Swift might have wished the reader to infer in 1726 the proposition he reinforces in 1735: Gulliver was entirely mad when he turned over his manuscript to his cousin Sympson. At the very least, the letter opens the prospect that Gulliver suffers from a sort of delusion whose major symptom is the travels themselves.

We now begin with a potentially different contract. Gulliver represents in writing the state of mind that, first and foremost, produces the *record* of the adventures, not the adventuring. The private vocabulary of the prefatory Sympson material scurries the narrative in stranger ways than Gulliver's own bewildering encounter with a race of little people. As readers we hear words in the first paragraph of the narrative that are completely alien: first

Houyhnhnm, and, a few lines later, *Yahoo*. No first-time readers could incorporate these into the clauses of any naive fictional contract without worrying over them. The difficulty resides not simply in the strangeness of the words, but in the way they are presented by the text as if readers *should* know what they mean. Gulliver speaks a kind of foreign language as if it is a lingua franca, circling around from the ending of the 1726 version to the beginning of the 1735 version. The *Travels* become satirically supplemented. By the narrative device of adding what can be seen as a coda to the preface, Swift begins with a paranoid hero rather than building to one. The implication is that we missed something the first time around. Indeed, we did.

Of course, Gulliver's letter is for his cousin, who, presumably, does know what the words mean. But even if Sympson knows full well to what Gulliver refers, there is still something in the tone and insistence of the references that renders Gulliver fictionally suspect. *Something* has made Gulliver insane or unsettled at home, and the travels are the fable we get from him as an explanation. If the Sympson letter scurries the narration long before the first odd marvel, the Lilliputians, pop into the text, just what sort of a person conceived and wrote these things in the first place? Who, after all, uses a private vocabulary with such urgency? Depending upon where readers pick up the narrative thread Gulliver is literally a different narrator within two reading contracts. Readers have the option of beginning where they once might have arrived. Gulliver is a traveler in one contract; a madman in another.

With this in mind it is possible to return to the anagrammatic aside in Laputa about "Tribnia by the natives called Langden." The letters of the anagram collapse the naive and the novelistic spaces of the narrative: the external territory to which Gulliver may travel, and the locally mapped place from which only his mind may wander. Two reading contracts become one. We begin to substitute the contract of insanity for the naive indulgence of the adventures. In the most subtle of satiric strategies, Swift takes the novelistic reading of the *Travels* a step further than it might wish to go. That is, he returns the plot to probable grounds. He takes away the fantastic and the marvelous by assuming that his main character has imagined all that he experiences, with the exception of the madness that has made him imagine it. This is a perfectly naturalistic reading with enough clues strewn about the narrative that it is both a likely and a contractual reading. But what does it do to the new subject of fiction? Exactly what Swift wished to do. It unsettles him; it loosens the mental screws that make such a subject reliable; it depicts instability where that other innovator of novelistic form, Daniel Defoe, depicts substantiation.

Defoe suggested in defending his Crusoe fable that an island scene "placed so far off, had its original so near home."[15] By this he means that the story novelists have to tell is always in some sense a version of the mental experience of the author. The topography of the plot is a plausible extension of the narrating or authoring self. As satirist, Swift goes Defoe one better – he not only writes a narrative in which faraway places reflect local experiences, but he writes a narrative about a man so mad that his projected adventures *become* the equivalent of the jumbled letters of his home. Gulliver himself points readers to those who think he made these journeys up as "a meer Fiction out of mine own Brain" (vi); and he imagines his countrymen will "believe that I *said the Thing which was not*: that I invented the Story out of my own Head" (206). He even admits that his flirtation with lunacy occurred to him during his voyages: "I feared my Brain was disturbed by my Sufferings and Misfortunes" (198). Moreover, some "will not allow me to be Author of Mine Own Travels" (vi). That is, he not only didn't write them but he didn't actually make them. He has no authority to foist them off, and he has authored them only insofar as he made them up.

Oddly enough, he says he was "very little Sunburnt in all my Travels" (71), without exactly explaining why. Later, when he speaks to horses in his stable, his readers may stumble upon the quixotic truth. All the languages that come back from his voyages are in a way local. He is the only translator. And at the end is he transcribing nothing more than horse sounds? *Yahoo* sounds like a horse, a sort of wheeze and sneeze. And *houyhnhnm* is obvious – it doesn't even need translation. Gulliver ends up talking to horses in his stable because he probably began that way. We do not hear much about Gulliver's life in England, but he says things in Lilliput that make us think of him as hopelessly paranoid, presumably as the result of experiences at home rather than abroad. There are hints early on that Gulliver has a reputation in England that is not easily explained. For instance, what does he mean when he seeks to justify his cleanliness to satisfy "some of my Maligners" (13). These maligners have no history other than as readers of the book – they are in England, not in Lilliput. But the English at this point are supposedly all yahoos with an inherent disposition to nastiness and dirt. What goes here? Is Gulliver making up the maligners? Or is he persecuted at home for being crazy rather than for being dirty?

Lilliput is his first delusionary place, a fantasy of power, a combination of niceness and prissiness and barely suppressed violence: eating, bashing, squashing. Gulliver's first projection miniaturizes the world for purposes of overpowering it. It is not for nothing that the first voyage of the narrative makes Gulliver into so dominating a figure. But he is even persecuted by the little people. To do so much and still to be blamed is the paranoid's greatest fear and, in a complex neurotic way, his greatest delight. Gulliver is both perpetrator and victim. His locutions are revealing. Of a leading Lilliputian minister he says, "Skyresh Bolgolam, who was pleased, without any Provocation, to be my mortal Enemy" (25). It sounds as if Gulliver has practiced this phrase often; it falls easily off his tongue. His sense of persecution folds neatly into his proclamation as a truth-teller. Of his Lilliput adventures he says that "Posterity shall hardly believe them, although attested by Millions" (66). Who are these millions? If millions attest, why wouldn't posterity believe? Posterity has believed much more from far fewer.

By the last voyage to Houyhnhnmland, the paranoid feast is expanded. Gulliver speaks as if England had been a nightmare of persecution for him in contrast to Houyhnhnmland: "here I did not feel the Treachery or Inconstancy of a Friend, nor the Injuries of a secret or open Enemy" (p. 241). There "was neither Physician to destroy my Body, nor Lawyer to ruin my Fortune; nor Informer to watch my Words and Actions, or forage Accusation against me for Hire" (242). All of modern civilization seems out to get Gulliver; more so at home than out of the country. But when did these things happen? Gulliver's travels seem to allegorize experiences in England for which we have no narrative record.

It is in the most strikingly modern land of the entire adventures, Laputa, the land of projectors, that Gulliver is most explicit about his circumstances. He, too, claims (like Defoe) to have "been a Sort of Projector in my younger Days" (152), and he unabashedly makes further proposals throughout this book, venturing his "poor opinion" on such paranoid matters as the possibility of swallowing information wafers or analyzing excrement for political plots. His treatment could be the most revealing clue about his state of mind in England that led him to make Laputa and the other places up: "I thought my self too much neglected, not without some Degree of Contempt" (147). This is a key to Gulliver's psyche. Gulliver has nothing – no dignity, no centrality, no stature – and his experience in the most modern place of his travels is, as he describes it, the most melancholy of all. The modern inhabitants of Laputa are, for good satiric measure, the closest to mad, suffering from a sense of exaggerated doom, moving too fast toward their own conclusion. That is, they are unsettled in ways similar to Gulliver, displaying "continual Disquietudes, never enjoying a minute's Peace of Mind" (137). They "neither sleep quietly in their Beds, nor have any Relish for the common Pleasures or Amusements of Life" (138).

What Gulliver says of Laputa can be extended metaphorically to the condition that inspires the projected travels of a madman: "I was weary of being confined to an Island where I received so little Countenance, and resolved to leave it with the first Opportunity" (147). This is a parable of Gulliver's life. He leaves his own native England by making up his travels, which then provide an imagined antidote for his insignificance as modern man within his own culture. The fervor with which he ends up attacking European civilization makes less sense had he actually traveled for so many years than if he never left – precisely the point made to Gulliver by the King of Brobdingnag. The extraordinary harangue Gulliver later produces about life in his own country for his Master Houyhnhnm, with barely the vocabulary to do it in his host's language, reveals the image of England he carries around in his head. Gulliver is so steeped in satiric details that articulating them makes them real. Metaphorically, cataloguing abuses is equivalent to an obsession with them. His *Travels* are, as is so often the case in Swiftian satire, the articulated version of his madness. The Master Houyhnhnm senses as much when he points out that the information provided by Gulliver is enough to turn even a sane horse mad: Gulliver's "Discource had increased his Abhorrence of the whole Species, so he found it gave him a Disturbance in his Mind, to which he was wholly a Stranger before" (215). The process, though not the timing, is something that Gulliver well knows. Of course he may have made up the Master Houyhnhnm to image himself as narrator. The greatest truth about Gulliver is his fullest lie, the abiding satiric contract of the *Travels*.

NOTES

1 James Joyce, *Ulysses* (New York: Random House, 1984), 52. Subsequent references are to this edition. To box the compass is to go virtually nowhere. Ships set their compasses before voyages by sailing back and forth between light beacons on coastal points.

2 In the anonymous *Gulliver Decypher'd: or Remarks on a late Book, intitled, Travels into Several Remote Nations of the World. By Capt. Lemuel Gulliver* (London, 1727), the *Travels* are said to be "design'd only for a Satyr upon those Writers that affect the marvelous and improbable, and upon the wild and monstrous relations of Travellers" (43). Of course, within such a frame, the *Travels* are demonstrably a reflection of the wider social, political, and ethical orders of England: the corrupt practices of Lilliputian court life begin the attack; the King of Brobdingnag widens it; the shades summoned from the republics of the ancient world in Glubbdubdrib reiterate it; and the Master Houyhnhnm rearticulates and sustains it.

3 J. Paul Hunter makes a cogent case for just such a notion in "*Gulliver's Travels* and the Novel," in Fredrick N. Smith, ed., *The Genre of Gulliver's Travels* (Newark, Del.: University of Delaware Press, 1990). Hunter writes, "the *Travels* work as a kind of parodic answer to the early novel and as a satire of novelistic consciousness" (56).

4 *Gulliver's Travels*, Norton Critical Edition, ed. Robert A. Greenberg (New

York: Norton, 1970), 135. All subsequent citations are to this readily available edition.

5 Alexander Pope, *The Memoirs of the Extraordinary Life, Works, and Discoveries of Martinus Scriblerus*, ed. Charles Kerby-Miller (London and New York: Oxford University Press, 1966), 165.

6 At the time Swift was given the Scriblerian assignment, he thought of Defoe as the archetypal downclass modern writer, his "mock authoritative Manner" being "of a Level with great Numbers among the lowest Part of Mankind" (*Examiner*, 15 [16 November 1710], reprinted in Herbert Davis, ed., *Prose Works of Jonathan Swift* [Oxford: Blackwell, 1966], III: 14).

7 Early on, Jonathan Smedley, in *Gulliveriana: or, a Fourth Volume of Miscellanies. Being a sequel of the Three Volumes, published by Pope and Swift* (London, 1728), recognized the connection: "This pious Author seems to have taken his Hint, if not from the celebrated History of *Tom Thumb*, from the Author who a few Years ago obliged the World with the Travels of *Robinson Crusoe* [*sic*]." Cited in Kathleen Williams, ed., *Swift: the Critical Heritage* (London: Barnes and Noble, 1970), 91.

8 Richard Braverman's "Crusoe's Legacy," in *Studies in the Novel*, 18 (1986): 1–26, has a great deal to say about the *I* in island.

9 *Serious Reflections during the Life and Surprizing Adventurers of Robinson Crusoe*, reprinted in G. H. Maynadier, ed., *The Works of Daniel Defoe* (New York: G. D. Sproul, 16 vols., 1903), III: 4.

10 *Robinson Crusoe*, Norton Critical Edition, ed. Michael Shinagel (New York: Norton, 1975), 3.

11 The question was posed to me exactly this way by a student in the mid-1970s, whose name has long since passed the territorial borders of my memory. I gladly credit that student with the question and its implications.

12 Richard Burton's great *Anatomy of Melancholy* is a book so diverse and grand that the critic Northrop Frye considered it a Menippean satire and names his own *Anatomy of Criticism* after it.

13 For example, consider the name of the Lilliputian capital, Mildendo. It sounds like mid-London, or, fitting for Lilliput, Demilond. Better yet, it suggests the inhabitants, Dildo men, which, when we ponder what later happens to Gulliver among the young maids of honor in Brobdingnag when he is of Lilliputian size, makes the fiction not only satirically prescient but prurient. Gulliver becomes a kind of dildo for one of the queen's young female attendants ("wherein the Reader will excuse me for not being over particular" [96]). Even though he refuses to dwell on the details, the earlier training Gulliver received from Master Bates enjoys a curious supplement. Gulliver becomes the instrument of his own earlier training.

14 The first translator of *Gulliver's Travels* into French, the Abbé Desfontaines, wrote in his 1727 preface to the volume of the fictional contract implicit in giving the improbable its space: "That is the poetic system. If we condemn it, we must now reduce all fictions to the boring intrigues of romances; we must look with utmost scorn at Ovid's *Metamorphoses*, and those which are scattered through the poems of Homer and Virgil, since all this is based solely on inventions which are wholly lacking in verisimilitude" (excerpted from Williams, ed., *Swift: the Critical Heritage*, 80–81). The theory is validated by

Aristotle (*Poetics* 1460a): "Homer has taught other poets to tell an untrue story as it should be told, by taking advantage of a logical fallacy. When one event is followed by a second as a consequence or concomitant, men are apt to infer, when the second event happens, that the first must have happened or be happening, though the inference is false" (*On Poetry and Style*, trans. G. M. A. Grube [New York: Bobbs-Merrill, 1958], 53). Augustine makes the equally pertinent distinction between fable and deception: "What I call the fabulous kind of falsehood (*mendax*), the kind which is committed by those who tell fables. The difference between deceivers and fabulists is this, that every deceiver wants to deceive but not every one who tells a fable has the desire to deceive" *(The Soliloquies of Saint Augustine*, trans. Thomas F. Gilligan [New York: Cosmopolitan Science and Art Service, 1943], 105). (2.9.16)

15 *Serious Reflections*, III: xiii.

READING LIST

Bullitt, John. *Jonathan Swift and the Anatomy of Satire*. Cambridge, Mass.: Harvard University Press, 1953.

Carnochan, W. Bliss. *Lemuel Gulliver's Mirror for Man*. Berkeley and Los Angeles: University of California Press, 1968.

Elliott, Robert C. *The Power of Satire: Magic, Ritual, Art*. Princeton: Princeton University Press, 1960.

Hodgart, Matthew. *Satire*. London: Weidenfeld and Nicolson, 1969.

Hunter, J. Paul. "*Gulliver's Travels* and the Novel," in *The Genres of Gulliver's Travels*, ed. Frederick N. Smith. Newark, Del.: University of Delaware Press, 1990.

Jack, Ian. *Augustan Satire*. Oxford: Clarendon, 1952.

Kernan, Alvin. *The Plot of Satire*. New Haven: Yale University Press, 1965.

Leyburn, Ellen Douglass. *Satiric Allegory: Mirror for Man*. New Haven: Yale University Press, 1956.

Paulson, Ronald. *The Fictions of Satire*. Baltimore: Johns Hopkins University Press, 1967.

Satire and the Novel in Eighteenth-Century England. New Haven: Yale University Press, 1967.

Price, Martin. *To the Palace of Wisdom: Studies in Order and Energy from Dryden to Blake*. Garden City, N.Y.: Doubleday, 1964.

Rawson, Claude. *Satire and Sentiment, 1660–1830*. Cambridge: Cambridge University Press, 1994.

Rosenheim, Edward. *Swift and the Satirist's Art*. Chicago: University of Chicago Press, 1963.

Scholes, Robert and Robert Kellogg. *The Nature of Narrative*. New York: Oxford University Press, 1966.

Seidel, Michael. *Satiric Inheritance: Rabelais to Sterne*. Princeton: Princeton University Press, 1979.

Sutherland, James R. *English Satire*. Cambridge: Cambridge University Press, 1956.

5

MARGARET ANNE DOODY

Samuel Richardson: fiction and knowledge

In the study of nature, men at first all applied themselves, as if in concert, to the satisfaction of the most pressing needs; but when they arrived at knowledge less absolutely necessary, they had to divide it up and each advanced in its course more or less at an equal pace. Thus several sciences have been, as it were, contemporaries; but in the historical ordering of the progress of mind, one can embrace them only in succession.

It is not the same in the encyclopedic ordering of our knowledge. This latter consists in collecting forms of knowledge into the smallest space possible, and in placing, as it were, the philosopher above this vast labyrinth in a highly elevated point of view from which he can perceive at once the principal arts and sciences; see with one glance the objects of his speculations, and the operations which he can perform on those objects; distinguish the general branches of human knowledge, the points where they separate or where they unite; and even catch sight of the secret routes which connect them.

(Jean Le Ronde d'Alembert, *Discours preliminaire* to *Encyclopédie*, 1751)[1]

Samuel Richardson belonged to the age of the *Philosophes*, of the wits and men (and sometimes women) of letters who created or contributed to the new projects of mind – the dictionaries, encyclopedias, grammars, histories, that gave order and definition to the pursuit of knowledge. Such landmark guidebooks, among which the great French *Encyclopédie* figures most prominently, are not only containers (as it were) for what is known; they also make possible the creative work of thought. Such works tend to be lengthy, in order to be thorough, like the *Encyclopédie* itself, or the multivolume histories such as Charles Burney's *History of Music* or Edward Gibbon's *History of the Decline and Fall of the Roman Empire*. Every work of Enlightenment knowledge is conscious of standing at a crossroads of times and influences. The most exciting point at this crossroads is the temporal one; to arrange one's thought or knowledge is to stand between the old and the new, the past and the future. The encyclopedist, the knowledge bringer or enlightener, must look in various directions, seeing different lines of influence coming towards the one point. The author who wishes to assemble a great deal of thought must not be hasty, and need not be brief. The Enlightenment certainly valued short works, such as *Candide*, but it gave serious place to multivolume attempts to come to terms with the world, and to make sense of the numerous phenomena that press upon us. The author can take his time. Burney's four-volume *History* appeared between 1776 and 1789. Gibbon's monumental *Decline and Fall* filled six volumes and appeared between 1776 and 1788.

When novelists like Henry Fielding and Samuel Richardson took to calling their works "histories" (the term "romance" having just fallen out of fashion), they gave themselves the same permission to extend in space and time as the world accorded to modern historians, such as Edward Hyde, Lord Clarendon, whose *History of the Great Rebellion* (three gigantic volumes in folio) had appeared in 1702–4. For Fielding and Richardson, the novel is to be acknowledged as an inquiry into life, and as a mode of knowing. Samuel Richardson is sometimes accused of writing novels that are too long. As Richardson's contemporary Henry Fielding shared with Richardson (despite other differences) the contemporary appreciation of grand design and amplitude of pattern, to set both *Tom Jones* and *Clarissa* (or *Grandison*) in our current fourteen-week university course is well-nigh impossible. If we want to understand the appearance of such generously sized works in the eighteenth century, we need to adjust our mind set to make room for the encyclopedic concepts of the period. The pattern of amplification on the road to completion is a common one. Pope adds a whole new book to the *Dunciad*. James Thomson starts off modestly with the poem *Winter* in 1726, a mere 405 lines; by the mid 1740s he had produced *The Seasons*, each *Season* enlarged, to a total of 5,423 lines. We are to take pleasure in moving in an organized way through a plenitude of well-represented material, enabling us to take in phenomena and their ramifications. The giant organization does not serve to make the reader meek; it is not authoritarian, but stimulative of surprise and debate, along with fresh accesses of knowledge.

Samuel Richardson (1689–1760) was born in an age that was undergoing violent change. Earlier in the century of his birth the English Civil War had meant literal violence. The accession of James II in 1685 had inspired Protestant revolt, as objectors to the Catholic James proposed Charles II's illegitimate son, the Duke of Monmouth, as the rightful (Protestant) heir. The attempt at revolution was put down in 1685, and the Duke of Monmouth was beheaded. Richardson refers to this episode in his one autobiographical writing of any length, his letter of 2 June 1753 to Johannes Stinstra, his Dutch translator. Richardson there says that his father was involved with the Duke of Monmouth, whom he knew personally, and that he "thought proper, on the Decollation of the unhappy Nobleman, to quit his London Business & to retire to Derbyshire; tho' to his great Detriment; & there I, & three other Children out of Nine, were born."[2] Richardson's most recent biographers, T. C. Duncan Eaves and Ben D. Kimpel, however, have discovered that the Richardsons' father had left London before the beheading of Monmouth, but kept an address in the City of London throughout his time in Derbyshire, at that time a rural county of England, well north of London.[3]

Richardson's father was a worker, belonging to the class of skilled artisans; he was a "joiner," that is a carpenter skilled in woodwork for domestic interiors. What the Richardsons lived on in the time of exile and why they chose Derbyshire has yet to be satisfactorily revealed. Samuel Richardson was born in the village of Mackworth, Derbyshire, where he was baptized on 19 August 1689. It is tempting to suppose that his actual birthday is identical with the date of birth he gave to his heroine Clarissa: 24 July. The year in which Richardson was born was a monumental year for England. In 1688 a new Protestant revolution had just succeeded where the revolt of 1685 had failed. The Protestant Prince William of Orange with his wife Mary, daughter of James II, invaded England and King James left it, his army having dropped away. This "Glorious Revolution" or "Bloodless Revolution," as the victors liked to call it, is often seen by modern historians as marking the true end of feudalism in England and the rise of the mercantile middle class into real and dominant political power. The arrangement by which William took the crown (he refused to take it as a right of *conquest*) involved a degree of artifice on the part of Parliament, which drew up the "Declaration of Right" declaring that William and Mary were the new king and queen. A certain amount of fudging went into the assertions that the line of inheritance was not broken and that this was no innovation. At the same time, the innovating committee made sure that the succession was spelled out, and that it was made clear that no one other than a Protestant could ever sit on England's throne. Parliament was now in effect superior to the monarch and could dictate the terms of kingly tenure. William and Mary were crowned on 11 April 1689. A revolution had completed itself a few months before Samuel Richardson's birth.

Richardson was born when England was still reeling from the impact of the last phase of its civil war. The world in which he came of age was to be very different, in many respects more prosperous and more stable, though the prosperity and stability did not advantage all. The Richardsons themselves lived in poor circumstances in areas of East London near the Tower, areas not noted for gentility. Richardson had some education at some point in a grammar school, probably in Derbyshire: he may have attended the celebrated Merchant Taylors' school in London, if only for a very brief time.[4]

Samuel's father obviously appreciated his talents and his desire to read. Richardson tells Stinstra: "He [Richardson senior] designed me for the Cloth. I was fond of this Choice. But while I was very young, some heavy Losses having disabled him from supporting me as genteelly as he wished in an Education proper for the Function, he left me to choose ... a Business, having been able to give me only common School-Learning."[5] In fact, in order to be ordained a clergyman in the Church of England, a man needed a university education, which meant attending Oxford or Cambridge. The Richardsons had some hopes of a patron for Samuel, the mysterious "Gentleman ... greatly my superior in Degree," the "Master of ye Epistolary Style" who wrote him letters describing his travels. This unnamed person in Richardson's life has been identified since the late eighteenth century with a shadowy figure who appears in some early versions of the sequel to *Pamela* : Mr. B's friend, the "fine Gentleman ... blest with an ample Fortune, and extraordinary Qualities, but not free from Faults as great as his Perfections."[6] This "fine Gentleman" is in love with beautiful but diffident Maria, who is persuaded by her uncle, "the old spiteful Knight," to reject him. Spiteful Uncle George treats the gentleman caller "with great Indignity" when he tries to see Maria: "following him with Outrage to the Top of a Pair of Stairs, he twirled him from Top to Bottom almost" (*Pamela*, III: 392). The young gentleman went off to the Continent and married another lady, but unhappy Maria later followed him, and he lived a bigamous life united with both women. As country rake and good landlord, the "Gentleman" in volume 2 of *Pamela* resembles Mr. B. As ardent rake, versifier, and certainly as lover scorned by crude relations of his lady, he resembles Lovelace. As the man caught between two women he bears a close connection even to the faultless Sir Charles Grandison, long suspended between his Continental and his English lady. It is tempting to think, as Richardson's daughters thought, that the career of the real-life gentleman was repeatedly mined by the novelist. Whatever more immediate "Expectation" young Richardson may have had of his superior friend was doomed to vanish. Yet in his correspondence during his apprenticeship, Richardson kept up the connection. If the daughters are right and the friend died in 1739, Richardson's career as a novelist may have blossomed right after this rake–friend's death. Perhaps now, with the death of his friend, Richardson felt free to explore the erotic and social content of the friend's life.

Whatever the complexities of the relationship with the gentleman "superior in Degree," Richardson had to rely on himself and his circle of coworkers rather than on upper-class patronage. The business he had chosen for himself was that of a printer, as it was "what I thought would gratify my Thirst after Reading." Richardson says this ironically, for he soon discovered that his master "grudged every Hour to me, that tended not to his Profit." The middle-aged Richardson still seems annoyed that his master did not give him the time off that his more unruly companions extorted. Samuel's virtue went unrewarded; Richardson was too proud to break any rules: "I stole from the Hours of Rest & Relaxation, my Reading Times for Improvement of my Mind ... even my Candle was of my own purchasing."[7] The reading matter published by young Samuel's master, John Wilde, consisted largely of almanacs and other stuff that would scarcely hold the attention of the mind. But as young Samuel Richardson worked his way up through his apprenticeship to the status of journeyman and then of master printer, he was getting closer to what he desired. In June 1715 he became a freeman of the Stationers' Company and a citizen of London. He worked as a proof-corrector and compositor, doing the free-lance work available to a journeyman during his twenties, a period still cloudy to his biographers. He assisted the widowed Mrs. John Leake in running her printing business. At her death he inherited a small legacy, but there was probably also some kind of family agreement that Richardson was to be allowed to buy out the business at an advantageous rate. He set up shop for himself, and married his first wife, the daughter of his former master, in 1721.

Robert Darnton in *The Great Cat Massacre* (1984) has reminded us of the difficulties of the life of apprentices and journeymen in the printing houses of Europe in the mid-eighteenth century. Masters withdrew themselves from the physical labor of the printing press, apprentices were treated shabbily, and journeymen hired and fired very quickly. The growth of the printing trade in the eighteenth century had led to an industrialized organization within what had once been a guild and family structure.[8] Richardson was old enough to adhere to something of the older ideal. A major compensation for the hardships of tackling the print trade was the growing importance in his life of the Stationers' Company and what it stood for. Richardson became a member of a powerful and varied "family" that took a strong interest in the life of its members. At the very best, the printers were themselves still inheritors of the Renaissance idealism and excitement that profoundly affected the print trade. As Elizabeth Eisenstein has shown, the printing press was an "agent of change" in early modern Europe, and the printers themselves had a consciousness of their role as agents of change. Those who worked the press (which still retained its novelty into the seventeenth century) knew themselves to be the transmitters of ideas. As Eisenstein points out, the very interests producing heated religious differences in the sixteenth and seventeenth centuries also nourished the development of an idea of toleration.

> Paradoxically enough, the same presses which fanned the flames of religious controversy also created a new vested interest in ecumenical concord and toleration; the same wholesale industry which fixed religious, dynastic, and linguistic frontiers more permanently also operated most profitably by tapping cosmopolitan markets. Paradoxically also, the same firms made significant contributions to Christian learning by receiving infidel Jews and Arabs, schismatic Greeks and a vast variety of dissident foreigners into their shops and homes ... such print shops represented miniature "international houses."[9]

The sense of a certain internationalism, and a brotherhood beyond frontiers, connected with a new religious sensibility even to the extent of creating in effect new sects, such as the "Family of Love" that grew up around the Antwerp printer Christopher Plantin. The early Familists were printers; their beliefs were the inception of Rosicrucianism. Richardson deliberately seems to recall this international heresy in the repeated phrase of *Sir Charles Grandison*: the Grandisons pronounce themselves "a family of love."[10] The phrase not only refers to the ideal of a loving family, growing out of companionate marriage rather than from arranged dynastic relations; it also refers to the internationalism that accepts other persons of other cultures as members of the same great "family." The printing fraternity was Richardson's most powerful immediate model of an international, diversified, and forward-looking "family."

Printing itself may be seen as the basis for Enlightenment. Before the Age of Industrialism set in, as Eisenstein observes, there was not the modern division between an intelligentsia, working in elegant retired seclusion, and the noisy thudding of the machinery. Thinking, writing, and printing were often performed on the same premises – not only by printers such as Samuel Richardson and Benjamin Franklin, but by writers who worked beside the press that was to send forth their words. "The 'secluded study' which now provides a setting for many sociologists of knowledge, should not be projected too far back into the past. Between the sixteenth and the eighteenth centuries, at all events, intellectuals, mechanics and capitalists were not out of touch."[11] The printing press as an *agent of change* was not thought of as monumental, but as flexible. The use of the press by people of the Renaissance through the early Enlightenment eras in many ways resembles modern use of the computer. Works are produced very rapidly. The word gets out – others respond, with questions, annotations, remarks.

A new version of the first work is quickly produced, as an answer to the original piece. Casual writers have access to the press: Boswell and his friends later in the century write up and print in the course of a day their criticisms of a current play. Certainly, a master printer like Richardson valued correctness and regularity in the printed product. But the press was a lively medium for exchange of knowledge and opinion.

Exchange of knowledge and opinion could receive severe checks from government interference. It is not often noted what a difficult period the 1720s were, the era when Richardson first set up his own shop. After the crash of the South Sea Company, the Whig government and the Hanoverian king were particularly vulnerable to criticism, and sensitive to signs of uprising. The government was most concerned that the crown would go peaceably to George II as successor to George I, who was visibly not going to last too long (in fact he died in 1727). Jacobite plots undoubtedly existed and the government was paranoiac about them. Francis Atterbury, friend of Pope and Swift, was arrested and tried for participation in an alleged Jacobite plot in 1722; he was banished, while another man, Kelly, was imprisoned in the Tower. Richardson printed a book defending Atterbury, and also printed an edition of Kelly's speech in his defense. Another printer secretly gave the Secretary of State, Lord Townshend, a list of disaffected printers, including the names of Richardson and his father-in-law, "Said to be High Flyers" (that is High Tories). Richardson was also a printer of the Duke of Wharton's *True Briton*, a periodical that was extremely critical of the government. John Duncombe later said that Richardson wrote the sixth paper of this periodical. The printer Thomas Payne put his name on the title page, and he was the printer arrested twice, and fined and imprisoned for "seditious libel." Richardson was one of those who went bail for Payne on both occasions of his arrest.[12] This was extremely brave, for the government was looking for printers to pounce on, and had they sent soldiers in to destroy Richardson's printing press he would have been without a livelihood and without resource.

Apparently he never forgot this lesson as to how those in power could treat dissent. The episode sharpened certain "Tory" perceptions in Richardson himself. The word "Tory" is now confusing, for many contemporary Tories (of the sort represented by the Thatcherite and Major administrations in Britain) are really Whigs, believing in the right to rule of those who possess property, and in the evil of any interference with moneymaking – the very opposite of true Tory belief. Even though he himself rose to a substantial business ownership and modest affluence, Richardson never forgot that the poor should have a voice, and that an unquestioned oligarchy that is all-rich (and all-male) is unlikely to produce the model society.

Richardson's sensitivity to censorship is acutely realized in his novels. In many respects, these are a printer's novels. The characters are all *writers*. Clarissa quotes Job, "O ... *that* mine adversary had written a book!" (*Clarissa*, VII: 46).[13] But the heroine herself is the one who makes the book – or rather she and her enemies and friends make the book together. Richardson's use of the epistolary mode of narration is most congenial to his interest in writing and expression. His heroines try to maintain their own identity and perspective in times of great trial by setting thoughts and opinions down on paper. It is the mark of a villain or an unreformed character in all of Richardson's novels that that person will try to interfere either with writing itself or with the transmission of another's writing in some way. In Richardson's last novel, *Sir Charles Grandison*, Clementina's cruel relatives contrive to take away her power of writing for a long period of time. Pamela and Clarissa fare better in that respect. But Pamela's master tries to write letters in place of hers, or to dictate what she must write (both forms of censorship). Pamela, like printers during the Civil War and on many subsequent occasions, is reduced to hiding her writing materials and shifting that which has been written into hiding. Clarissa also has to secrete pens and ink when her relatives try to cut her off from written expression. Lovelace, a more subtle oppressor, acts like a government spy in scrutinizing Anna Howe's correspondence with Clarissa, breaking secretly into Clarissa's belongings in order to have copies taken of her papers.

At the core of the Enlightenment vision of communication is an idea – a somewhat disturbing idea – that there is no absolute human authority, and no truth that is fully known to human beings. One view of learning – a view that is never dead – is that there is a precious body of lore which must be preserved and ingested by each generation. Any loss suffered by this body of lore, as also any addition or alteration, constitutes a hideous adulteration; we need to go back to canonical purity. That idea of learning was sinking under the weight of the printing press, although dissent from that authoritarian ideal of pure gold heritage certainly predated the Reformation and the press. Milton in the *Areopagitica* (1644) dynamically expresses the continuous search for Truth, which is never complete:

> the sad friends of Truth ... imitating the careful search that *Isis* made for the mangl'd body of *Osiris*, went up and down gathering up limb by limb still as they could find them. We have not yet found them all, Lords and Commons, nor ever shall doe [sic], till her Masters second comming [sic] ... To be still searching what we know not, by what we know, still closing up truth to truth as we find it ... this is the golden rule in *Theology* as well as in Arithmetick.[14]

To many persons in the 1640s, the 1740s or the 1990s it is frustrating and worrying to think of truth as something always to be *sought* rather than *possessed*. But printers must see the pursuit of truth as a process never-ending, still beginning. The work of printing and disseminating information in the first ages of print depended on an idea of knowledge always in process, in accretion and slow accumulation, knowledge reassembled in revisions, new commentaries, corrections, and amplified editions. As Eisenstein indicates, it was inevitable for the new print world to know each stage as partial and to think of knowledge as open-ended. "The closed sphere or single corpus, passed down from generation to generation, was replaced by an open-ended investigatory process pressing against ever advancing frontiers."[15]

Censorship of written material is an effort by a tenuous and temporary political power to stifle the advancement of knowledge. Authority wishes always to assume that it is in control not only of the expression of ideas, but of the ideas themselves. Richardson in his novels recognizes no right invested in any person to control the ideas of another. The authorities who are always rising to put others down are going to be in some sense overthrown in the course of each novel. But Richardson needed to choose for his central images and plots material accommodating the concept of an absence of absolutism. The ideal locus for working out these problems is the female human being. Women in Richardson's culture (and elsewhere) are not thought of as possessing absolute authority, or indeed absolute anything. Concepts of the contingent and relative may be better reflected in dealing with female than with male characters. The eighteenth century had invested so much in the idea of the autonomous and commanding male that it became hard to organize contingency around a masculine center. Shakespearean tragedy had to supply that lack, or comic characters like those in *Tristram Shandy* who could be considered too eccentric and ludicrous to offer general comment on male human beings.

Richardson, it shall be remembered, turned to novel writing very late in life. He had been a successful printer, and being appointed printer to the House of Commons in 1733 had given him his first financial security. He printed the Debates of Parliament for that House, and thus had a very clear idea about contemporary issues. Richardson had also tried to enter the Enlightenment dialogue of learning directly, with his own project. In 1730–31 he tried to raise money by subscription for the publication of *The Negotiations of Sir Thomas Rowe. In his Embassy to the Ottoman Porte, 1621 to 1628.* Richardson had come upon the letters of the seventeenth-century English ambassador to Constantinople, and thought it would be an addition to knowledge to investigate the relations between the Ottoman Empire and England, as well as the reactions of one Englishman to an entirely different culture. It is also probable Richardson had heard that Mary Wortley Montagu had written a book created from her letters from Turkey, to which Mary Astell had supplied a preface in 1724. Montagu's book still remained unpublished, but Richardson may have thought that a forthcoming book evoking new interest in Turkey would stimulate interest in the Rowe letters. There were too few subscribers, but eventually the Society for the Encouragement of Learning (for whom Richardson was printer) offered to underwrite the cost, and Richardson acted as editor. *The Negotiations of Sir Thomas Rowe*, published in 1740, represents Richardson's contribution to the world of learning. It is a piece of historical scholarship, the fulfillment of the duty to add more to the sum of human knowledge, like a doctoral dissertation. The work was certainly not popular, but it makes its own contribution to the novels that follow. Richardson is here, too, working with letters, and the *Rowe* papers, like the first parts of *Pamela* and *Clarissa*, describe the efforts of an individual to negotiate with an arbitrary power.

Richardson turned to novel writing almost at first by accident. He had been asked by two booksellers (the eighteenth-century equivalent of publishers) to prepare a small book of sample letters, "in a common Style," to be of use to "Country Readers" who know little about writing.[16] While in the course of composing this book of model letters, using fictionalized characters, Richardson wrote two letters based, he said, on an anecdote from real life: evidently these are numbers 138 and 139, "A Father to a Daughter in Service, on hearing of her Master's attempting her Virtue," and "The Daughter's Answer."[17] Richardson temporarily dropped the "letter-writer" he had been commissioned to produce, although that was later completed and published as *Letters Written to and for Particular Friends on the Important Occasions* (1741).[18] (This book is usually referred to now by the title Brian W. Downs gave it, *Familiar Letters*.) On 10 November 1739 Richardson began writing a novel about the girl in service whose master tried to seduce her. He finished the first draft of *Pamela* on 10 January, as he told his friend the dramatist Aaron Hill.

The novel, then, was evidently written in a white heat. As far as we know, it was Richardson's first attempt at sustained fiction. He had told stories to entertain his schoolfellows when he was a boy. He had prepared works of fiction for the press. He may have written a number of prefaces to novels.[19] He had published his own new children's edition of *Aesop's Fables* in 1739. But *Pamela* is not at all like such routine work, and the pressure behind its production seems very different. Richardson had suffered an almost crushing series of personal losses in the 1730s. While his working life flourished, his private life was riven by disease and death. All his children by his first wife Martha were dead when Martha herself died in 1731. The children by his second wife Elizabeth fared somewhat better; four girls lived to grow up, but the last of his sons died, and his apprentice and nephew Thomas, a possible successor to Samuel in his business, also died. Samuel lost his father in a lingering and painful death, as well as two brothers and a friend. He himself became ill at this time, probably as an effect of the continued stress and anxiety of grief and threatened grief. It has been suggested that his constant malady, "the Distemper that common curatives would not subdue," was Parkinson's disease.[20] He was shaky, his hands shook, he had to walk with a stick. He must have felt as if his own life was nearing its end; he could not know that the grandest part of his career was about to begin.

At the very end of that crushing decade (the 1730s), when many hopes were disappearing along with health, and possibly life itself, Richardson found a new lease on life by throwing himself imaginatively into the life, experience, and indeed the persona of a lively fifteen-year-old girl. Pamela is a wellspring of liveliness. Richardson endows her with physical presence, energy, and an assurance that in the eyes of some contemporaries crossed the border of impudence. Pamela is a poor servant girl whose parents have come upon very hard times. She has been in service to a good lady, Mrs. B., but when that good lady dies (as she does on the first page of the novel), Pamela is in danger of being left without a job. She is pleased when her master, the lady's son, assures her of employment: "For my Master said, I will take care of you all, my Lasses; and for you, *Pamela*, (and took me by the Hand; yes he took me by the Hand before them all) for my dear Mother's sake, I will be a Friend to you, and you shall take care of my Linen" (25).[21] The reader catches the comic and ominous intimacy expressed in the "Linen" (a general term for shirts, nightshirts and under-clothing). Mr. B. takes to heart all too well his mother's dying plea "Remember my poor Pamela!," although he does have the grace to wait for some while after his mother's death before making his first pounce. Pamela angrily resists and resents his advances, and hopes that things will return to the way they were. At length she realizes she must leave Mr. B.'s house, and he at last permits her to go. But instead of being driven home as she expects, she is abducted to Mr. B.'s estate in Lincolnshire, and kept a prisoner in the old manor house and its grounds, guarded by the raddled housekeeper, fat Mrs. Jewkes, who is perfectly willing to help her employer accomplish his rakish purpose.

Mr. B. raises a major theme with his promise "I will be a Friend to you." Richardson is fond of using words with ambiguous meaning; and ambiguity is indeed one of his devices throughout a narrative. He wants to be Pamela's sexual "Friend." This word has a sexual meaning that survives now in words like "boyfriend," "girlfriend" (likewise ambiguous). It is a euphemism in the eighteenth century and earlier, standing in for "sexual partner" as in Iago's jeering description "or to be naked with her friend in bed / ... not meaning any harm" (*Othello*, 5.1). But Pamela is justified in hearing another meaning, the ostensible meaning, now almost disappeared but in the 1740s the dominant meaning. Mr. B. as master of the house, landowner, and employer is entitled to speak of himself as Pamela's "Friend." According to this old usage, based on a feudal and hierarchical sense of relations and responsibilities, a person's natural "Friends" are the people in authority over that person or in a position to be benevolent to him or her. A boy's or girl's first "friends" (in this sense) are the parents, also grandparents, uncles, etc. The important "Friends" include great people like the parson of the parish or the landowner for whom the parents work or from whom they rent. Such "friendship" survives only in the use of our word "befriend," which never refers to friendship of equality. Clarissa commits the error of running away from her "Friends" in that sense. Her family are her "friends" because they have *rightful power* over her. Friendship is thus paradoxically invested with authority, a paradox Richardson is always interested in exploring in his investigation of contemporary culture.

There is of course a third meaning of "Friend," the meaning towards which the entire novel points. A true "Friend" is an equal, a sympathizer, someone to whom we speak frankly of our own concerns and feelings, and whom we hear sympathetically in return. A developing idea of marriage, important in modern times, is that man and wife should be friends, and such an ideal is emerging in the eighteenth century. But as Richardson's novel shows, it is difficult, perhaps impossible, to arrive at that point, for various hierarchies (including that inherited in the Marriage Service) stand in the way. Mr. B. has, in terms of contemporary society, every reason to regard himself as superior to Pamela. He is twenty-five years old, and thus of age, while she is still a minor. He is male, she is female. He is upper class, a member of the gentry, while she belongs to the working class. Mr. B. is not a nobleman, but he belongs to the ranks of true gentry. As a real gentleman, he is entitled to appear at court to celebrate the King's birthday, or to appear in a court dress in the drawing room of the nearest representative of the King. He dresses up in his gold lace suit while Pamela has to contrive to get some homespun clothes. Even if Pamela were male and of age, her social power would be very slight. She belongs to the bottom of the social pyramid; Mr. B. and others refer to her father as "Goodman Andrews," as he is not of the class entitled to be called "Mister." He is a master of nothing. Mr. B. orders, as a stroke of *politesse*, that the servants at the Lincolnshire estate refer to Pamela as "Madam," "Mistress Pamela," "Mrs. Pamela," as if she were entitled by rank to claim the dignity of a title. But she knows this is making a "May-game" of her (103). By birth she is mistress of nothing, and they are trying to make her a "Madam" and a "Mistress" in the sense of "whore."

Richardson makes us see the extent to which both hero and heroine of the novel are forced into roles and moulds by social convention, most especially by conventions of hierarchy. Everywhere she looks, Pamela is reminded of that hierarchy, often through the use of the very word "Friend." Mr. B., appearing to sympathize with the girl's parents, admits he has given "Concern to your honest Friends," but promises he will make amends. He threatens Pamela with the fear that her parents will be "fatally touched with Grief" (108) unless she writes to them in the terms dictated by him. His phrase "honest Friends" tells Pamela first that her family is low on the social scale – not honorable, merely "honest." Mr. B. then reminds her that she is at the very bottom of the social heap. She still owes a duty to them, as, even if lowly, her parents are her superior "Friends." Later he threatens her in signing off another letter, "in a little time you shall find how much you have err'd in treating, as you have done, a Man, who was once *Your affectionate and kind Friend*" (146). That is, he has withdrawn from her the protection that a superior ought to give to an inferior to whom he is bound by legitimate ties, such as employment, which is identified as a form of patronage. Eventually they get to the point where Mr. B. can utter his greatest speech (after their wedding): "let us talk of nothing henceforth but Equality" (294). The pair have, however, much ado to get to that point. Their arrival is achieved only through Pamela's revolutionary resistance – or, rather, the revolutionary voicing of her resistance. She writes the letters, she takes authorship upon herself and thus contrives an authority – she who by birth is entitled to no such thing. Pamela's resistance is spirited, various, and iridescent. She is by no means a model girl, and Mr. B. has some justification when he hurls at her all the unkind epithets for females he can think of: "Slut," "saucy Jade." She *is* saucy in her bounciness, and capable of aggressiveness that comes out in the language she uses. She finds a childish relief in the animated spite with which she can describe her jailor Mrs. Jewkes: "a broad, squat, pursy, fat Thing, quite ugly, if any thing God made can be ugly ... her Face is flat and broad; and as to Colour, looks like as if it had been pickled a Month in Salt-petre" (107). Pamela's language is, almost throughout, entertainingly disconcerting. Richardson's novel is a perversely brilliant turn of decorum, holding Pamela's language in the register the novel itself creates, so that we are convinced this is the tone and language of a girl raised in the country and truly coming from a lower-class background. Pamela sometimes speaks vulgarly ("like as if"). Her images come from the kitchen and the kitchen garden. The range of literary reference available to her includes some snatches of Shakespeare, but her basic reference work is the Bible, with a few of Aesop's fables. Mr. B. accuses the girl to her father of having her girlish head turned by reading romances, but it is Mr. B. who knows about romances and novels. Pamela herself seems quite ignorant of romances. She is not a reader, she is the reverse of a Don Quixote. Don Quixote has to contrive a self suitable to what modern critics have labeled "mediated desire" acquired through reflection of bookish ideas of the self. Pamela has to learn how to desire and create a constant self that is able to resist the pressure of the time, her social station, others' authority. Her lower-class resistance is revolutionary.

At the same time, she is engaged in the process of making a self. We can be persuaded that we see her growing. Richardson is a pioneer in modern fiction in finding ways of giving an impression that a character is developing and changing from within. When Pamela decides (sadly) that she really must leave B.'s household, she knows the villagers of her parents' parish will make fun of her. She makes herself, at considerable cost to her personal funds and with a good deal of labor, a country costume. She then tries it on, and looks at herself in the glass. Some critics have seen in this episode only an instance of Pamela's vanity and her desire to trap Mr. B. by her masquerading charms. But Pamela seems rather to be acting at herself, for herself. The person she seduces with her country garb is Pamela, so she can turn her back on the fine shoes and the French necklace. Pamela wants to love herself. Richardson presents this not as startling narcissism or reprehensible vanity, but as a natural response of the girl of fifteen. Morality does not exist in some prim, airtight box. We live our moralities in our experience: our sense of right harmonizes with our sense of ourselves.

For all her courage, Pamela has moments when courage fails her. She is afraid of the bull that is said to be loose in the grounds of the house in Lincolnshire. When she tries to escape at one point, she hesitates between house and garden, frightened back by the sight of the bull: "there stood that horrid Bull, staring me in the Face, with fiery Saucer Eyes, as I thought" (136). It would cost an author no trouble to conjure up a legion of bulls, or a congregation of fiercely slavering mastiffs. Instead, Richardson makes clear here that the obstacle to Pamela's escape resides within herself. Anticlimactically the fearful male bull, which even turns into two bulls in Pamela's terrified vision, turns out to be "only two poor Cows, a grazing in distant Places, that my Fears had made all this Rout about" (137). It is her own fancy that connects the bull with Mr. B., and the two bulls with B. and

Mrs. Jewkes. Richardson really invites us to interpret this puzzling situation, to see the depth of Pamela's psyche and the conflict within her of love and fear, sexual desire and sexual anxiety.

All of Richardson's personages are what the nineteenth century called characters; they persuade us they have inner depths, and irrationalities. On the conscious level, Pamela later realizes that her emotions are not altogether appropriate to the straightforward morality of her situation: "What is the Matter, with all his ill Usage of me, that I cannot hate him? To be sure, I am not like other People!" (157). She is in difficulties because she has to keep secret from herself her own growing sexual attraction to Mr. B. If she were to admit that, she would be lost, falling into the degraded position that Mr. B. wants her to assume, and injuring herself deeply. But Pamela's inner as well as outer conflict may awaken inquiry as to why society dictates such conflicts.

The core of *Pamela*, and the reason why it so shocked and appealed to the men and women of the eighteenth century, is its revolutionary message. That message is directly uttered by Pamela in her argument with Mrs. Jewkes:

> And pray, said I, walking on, how came I to be his Property? What Right has he in me, but such as a Thief may plead to stolen Goods? – Why was ever the like heard, says she! – This is downright Rebellion, I protest! (116)

"How came I to be his Property?" This is the great question, and its echoes raise the other questions. How can anybody be somebody else's property? Why do we have property analogies in so many human relationships, not to mention actual property owning of people in the widespread eighteenth-century institution of slavery? Is it not "stealing" to claim any property in another? These are tremendous questions. When we have entered into them, we have raised questions that even the abolition of slavery – still far away in Richardson's time – cannot satisfy. Why are women and children considered the property of somebody else? Any woman in the last 4,000 years might ask "How came I to be his property?" Women may still ask it, even in America, where certain groups apparently hold it to be self-evident that female bodies are a kind of public property, to be controlled and managed for the public good. Richardson's own novel in the end draws back, as it had to draw back in order to be acceptable enough to read, from such questions as these. It leaves them trembling on the air. After *Paradise Lost*, this is the first great Enlightenment consideration of sexual relations. Like all Enlightenment works, it is in itself a body of controversies. The controversies are never-ending. After all, the questions are asked by Pamela, not Richardson directly. And other people, not only Mr. B., Mrs. Jewkes, and Lady Davers, have answers different from the heroine's and from each other. The last part of the novel shows the folding out of discussion and debate that the Enlightenment loved. Even when Mr. B., who cannot long remain on the level of "Equality" but returns to the pleasant hierarchy of the husband, thinks he has solved the question of the ideal marriage and its conduct in the harangue he makes to Pamela, Pamela can break up his discourse into "Rules" and then offer her own commentary. The novel is open-ended, deliberately open-ended. It runs right past the normal ending, the Cinderella ending, the marriage of hero and heroine, and on into their early married life. We leave Pamela expecting a baby, still not born – so life moves onwards into the future that the Enlightenment loved to explore, in the hopeful belief that the future is to be different from the past.

Richardson's greatest novel, *Clarissa*, picks up the hints and opportunities that *Pamela* itself afforded. In first writing his own sequel to *Pamela*, stimulated by the production of sequels by other authors, Richardson worked without some of the conflicts that made the first part of *Pamela* so engrossing. He does, however, include the debates and discussions about domestic life and childrearing that are to appeal immensely to readers like Rousseau. Richardson taught Rousseau that the novel can be philosophic. The influence of parts 1 and 2 of *Pamela*, as well as all of *Clarissa*, can be seen in Rousseau's *Julie, ou la Nouvelle Héloise* (1761). In *Clarissa*, Richardson returns to the major conflicts of sex and class. *Pamela* had met with great acclaim, but also with derision, in parodies and rewritings, the best known of which is the *Shamela* (1741) attributed to Fielding. The author of *Shamela* is certainly offended by the miscegenation seen in a marriage of a servant and a gentleman; he indicates that any girl who holds out for marriage must be a designing hussy and a whore. The more reasonable version of this critique is the charge that *Pamela* should not have married a man who had made such determined attacks on her, and that she sees her fate too much in the terms of worldly success.

In *Clarissa*, no worldly success awaits the heroine. Neither is she a lowly servant girl, but a well-educated young woman of a family of great wealth. She offends her family because her grandfather made her heir to one estate, her "Dairy-house." The Harlowes, who have risen in the world through accumulation of land, through mercantile trade with the East and through coal mines, represent the crossing of the new wealth and the old. They are an ambitious family, still somewhat vulgar despite the marriage of James Harlowe senior to a woman of the aristocracy. In the first edition of *Clarissa* (1747–48), Richardson wanted to make clear that Clarissa is not quite a "Lady" as the aristocracy would accept the term. Yet although Lovelace is a true aristocrat, Lord M. (his uncle) is happy to negotiate for the marriage with the bourgeois Harlowes' daughter. Lovelace's family is anxious that its heir should marry and have children. If such a marriage is a condescension on their part, and will involve Clarissa's changing class and status, the change is not so very great. In an overreaching piece of stupid cunning, Clarissa's Uncle Antony first introduces Lovelace to Clarissa's plain older sister, Arabella, as if *she* were the lovely Miss Harlowe of whom the young man has heard so much. Lovelace cleverly gets out of this entanglement, but at the cost of the lasting enmity of Arabella; her brother James is likewise horrified at the prospect of little "Clary" taking some of the family money with her into her high marriage. James picks a fight with Lovelace, and has him forbidden the house. He then induces his father to try to force Clarissa into marriage with the ugly, elderly miser Roger Solmes, on the under-standing that the Harlowes will get Solmes's lands if he dies without issue of that marriage. Clarissa puts up a heroic resistance to that forced marriage, while Lovelace, motivated partly by revenge, at last contrives to get her to run away from home. Once she is in his power, Lovelace hopes to induce her to live with him without marriage; if he makes her his mistress, he will remain free, and triumph over the middle-class family who abased him.

In *Clarissa* the Whig and the Tory in Richardson himself, as it were, fight it out. While having no confidence in the older Tory race of landowners (like stupid Lord M.) and their ideas of settled hierarchy, Richardson mercilessly exhibits the flaws of the rising middle class in the Harlowes' greedy and limited behavior. The Harlowes exhibit every negative attribute of Whiggism – contempt and envy of those above them, contempt and suspicion of the poor, a desire to hoard wealth and to use all human relationships as means to a material end. Clarissa utters a spiritual insight that others around her cannot hold: "The world is but one great Family. Originally it was so. What then is this narrow selfishness that reigns in us, but relationship remembered against relationship forgot?" (1: 46). Clarissa, with her desire to act like the productive manorial lady of an older England, and her concern for responsibilities to those around her that are outside the family, seems like a "natural Tory" born into a world of Whigs. At the same time, she transcends Tory doctrines in her own belief in the value of freedom and in the liberty that must be accorded herself. Such ideas are derived in part from Whig doctrine, although political Whiggism was extremely reluctant to extend to women the rights of men.

Lovelace also has his political aspects. In his cynical rakishness, his view of sexuality as the remaining arena of conquest and control, he is playing out (like the hero of Mozart's *Don Giovanni* slightly later) the dwindling of the aristocracy as a true force. The last bastion of aristocratic right is the bedroom. Lovelace is, however, both a hunter and a Whig in his present relation to power: he visits Windsor, where he has hunted; he evidently has friends and contacts in the administration; and his very name "Robert" connects him firmly with Robert Walpole, the "Great Man" who ruled England as prime minister (and some said near-dictator) from 1720 to 1742. Robert ("Bob") Lovelace also connects himself with Robin or Robert Earl of Huntington, the legendary Robin Hood. He has a gang of three rakish friends around him, he likes playing gang leader and devising (at least on paper) audacious schemes for the punishment of pompous persons who stand in his way.

Clarissa in its range of reference is encyclopedic. The structure of the book is itself a mode of knowledge. Instead of the one dominant narrator of *Pamela*, we have four narrators, two major (Clarissa and Lovelace) and two minor but vital: the best friends, respectively, of heroine and villain, Anna Howe and Jack Belford. In their intercutting assertions, questions, commentary, and ripostes these four characters create a very rich pair of dialogues in which the exchanges between Clarissa and Anna are held in tension and counterpoint with those of Lovelace and Belford. The Enlightenment is attached to dialogue and epistolary forms in works of argument and persuasion. The dialogue is an important vehicle of philosophy from Shaftesbury through Berkeley and Diderot. In addition, the letter form allows for personal observation that is temporary and may be subject to change. Richardson, in the systematic and complex multidialogic system of his novel *Clarissa*, includes – or creates – a picture of England as a culture with a deep structure.

D'Alembert was to say that encyclopedic order entails getting the philosopher to some raised point elevated above "this vast labyrinth."[22] Novels, on the other hand, work through plunging the readers *into* a labyrinth, making them undergo the labyrinthine experience. In *Clarissa* we are plunged into the labyrinth of experience and feeling, and at first do not note the grand design. Yet we are being given a view of the various classes in their relation, and of the struggles of English history. We see a British history of civil wars, including the old wars between Scotland and England, as well as the English Civil War. The conflict between James Junior and Lovelace even carries the remnants of the Wars of the Roses with it – James is Yorkshire; Lovelace, Lancashire. The crossing lines of tradition, manners, history, and feeling are everywhere present. Cultural material is richly introduced – with references to Virgil, Hottentots, Aesop, and to Julius Caesar, with play on Renaissance church monuments and samplers, smuggling, and soap selling. London is a vividly present man-made world of churches and sedan chairs, coach timetables and inns, alleys and open spaces.[23] Yet Clarissa's London is also a vast illusion, where she is cheated into living in the midst of a brothel without noticing it.

Paradoxically, this most encyclopedic of novels is the novel that partakes least of Enlightenment optimism. The outlook from *Clarissa* is very dark, even though the novel itself (as one reads it) is not only engrossing but spirited, often very funny, very witty. The novel circles about a dark event: the rape of Clarissa. In *Pamela*, Mr. B.'s threats of rape really came to nothing, for he did not wish to carry through the act once Pamela did not join in playing the part he wanted in his scenario. Lovelace at first repudiates rape. He also holds the comforting traditional male view (to be reinforced by Rousseau in *Émile*) that there is really no such thing, as the woman always consents.[24] Lovelace maintains that his power of seduction will be superior to any need to rape. In excusing his deceiving of Clarissa, he gives himself credit for merely performing an experiment, in putting her to the *test*. A gentleman, in the world's opinion, owes it to himself to marry a perfectly chaste bride. The woman who could "fall," even to a Lovelace's persuasions, is unchaste and then not a fit bride for him. Richardson makes sure we see this double standard in all its hideous absurdity. But Lovelace's "test" is not one that he intends to allow Clarissa to win. If she remains free of his attempts at seduction, then he is *not* all-conquering and she does *not* love him – concepts that are unbearable. Clarissa does remain superior to his attempts at seduction, and begins to see through the tower of lies he has built around her. In a bold stroke, involving even the hiring of well-bred prostitutes to act as his own relations, Lovelace brings off the rape that will, he thinks, make Clarissa his forever.

Some readers, like Elizabeth Carter, Richardson's contemporary, have thought that Lovelace (if witty and attractive) is too villainous to be natural. Richardson's novel seems designed to make us see in Lovelace not a mere realistic "villain" but rather the embodiment of his society's dictates about sex. Lovelace's attitude to women reflects very faithfully the attitude of his own society. In *Clarissa* the rape act once performed exhibits the hideousness of beliefs that can be made to sound playful, rational, or natural. The rape denaturalizes a power structure. As Richardson was doubtless aware from the time of *Pamela*, in which there is an early reference to the "Rape of Lucretia" (42), a rape story told is a revolutionary story. The "Rape of Lucretia" (according to legend) brought about the fall of the Roman monarchy. On Lucretia's rape republicanism is built. Whig writers rather than Tory tend to allude to the "Rape of Lucretia," and it is useful to dramatists such as Nathaniel Lee in his *Lucius Junius Brutus* (1681), a play which was to appeal to the sentiments of 1688–89. To tell a "rape story" is a political act. A strong rape story is a story about the necessity for revolution. In *Clarissa*, the "revolution" pointed towards is not a further movement in the Whig or Tory direction so much as the movement for the liberation of woman. So many people feel that they own Clarissa: her father, her family, Lovelace. Lovelace merely utters a commonplace when he assumes that once he has penetrated Clarissa he must own her, and at the very least she will be only too glad to marry him. Clarissa after the rape utters the revolutionary statement: "The man who has been the villain you have been shall never make me his wife."

The end of the story involves Clarissa's death as well as the death of Lovelace. Since the novel first appeared there have been objections to the ending. Early readers, including Fielding, begged Richardson before he published the last volumes to let Clarissa live. Lady Echlin rewrote the catastrophe and the ending, sparing Clarissa the rape as well as the death. Some argued that Richardson was too fond of making the woman suffer; rationalists of the period of the French Revolution, like Holcroft, rewriting *Clarissa*'s plot in *Anna St. Ives* (1792), implicitly argue that there is no need for either party to die, but only for reform. But it is hard to see how Richardson could have ended his novel. He suggests other endings: Clarissa living a life of good works on her grandfather's estate; Clarissa marrying another gentleman who offers to wed her knowing the circumstances; even Clarissa emigrating to Pennsylvania (which is what her family wishes her to do). But all these possible endings would weaken the heroine's cause. It has to be shown also that Clarissa has none of the guilt attributed to Pamela, who is accused of looking out for worldly ends.

Richardson claimed to Aaron Hill that his novel was of "the Tragic Kind," and argued against the narrow application of "Poetic Justice" to works of imagination.[25] The Aristotelian idea of poetic justice as sketched out by the Académie Française had taken hold in an era that was nervous of the effects of both drama and published fiction on a mass audience; authorities wished nothing to appear that was not of an improving nature. In refining his narrative method of "writing to the moment," Richardson invites the reader into the temporal world of process, where all is changeable, nothing is assured; yet at the same time the reader who looks upon this web of correspondence sees "at a glance," like readers of the *Encyclopédie*, the relations of part to part, the connection of coal mines to Indian trades, of higher to lord, of Oliver Cromwell to marriage contracts, of brothel to country house. Nothing is successive, no history is superseded, and nothing is transcended on a secular plane. All connections on this mighty grid are points of anxiety and distress.

Clarissa is deeply moral, but startlingly pessimistic. Its deep pessimism arises from its encyclopedic analyses of modern English and Western culture, which is found to be deeply flawed at its very heart. The cultural enslavement of women poisons familial and social life. All our social structures, built on the model of the family, are based on a distressing analogy. Richardson in his way makes us see what d'Alembert wants the *Encyclopédie* to make us see: the hidden connections between one phenomenon and another. Cultural life and the life of knowledge alike feel like a labyrinth, but when you take a look at them organizationally, schematically, in a just (because large) system, then the hidden connections, the secret corridors between one thing and another, leap to the eye.

Elizabeth Eisenstein has noted that "The figure of Minerva, often in conjunction with Mercury ... and other special symbols, occurs repeatedly in frontispieces of works favored by freethinkers of a certain kind" (143).[26] It is noteworthy that Richardson does include, if not a pictorial figure of Minerva, a decided reference to her; Clarissa, listening at night to "the distant whooting of the Bird of Minerva," sets to music the "Ode to Wisdom" by Elizabeth Carter, a poem addressed to "PALLAS! Queen of ev'ry Art" (II: 50–54). The novel here keeps opening out its width of reference, including Minerva, female poetry, and a woman's music – even giving us an extra gift in the shape of Clarissa's music as a pullout sheet for our own harpsichords. Richardson was a devout Anglican, not an atheistic freethinker, but a certain degree of "freethinking" is involved in the installation of a feminine deity addressed by a woman who values learning and solitude. The "freethinking" appealed to here would lead to a justification not only of women's right to education but of their right to themselves.

The novel is also rich in pictorial emblems: Richardson uses in the third edition the figure of Europa as a printer's ornament for the endpapers of the post-rape volumes 5 and 6, not only signifying her rape by Jove but playing with the other meanings of Europa on her divine bull – the foundation of new lands, and the opening out of new territories. Other emblems include the horn of plenty, the holy dove, and angels or cupidons with a book between them. Clarissa herself turns designer, designing the ornament of her own coffin as the *ourberos*, the endless serpent of eternity and wisdom.[27] The use of such figures and emblems prods us towards asking what everything might *mean*, and moves us on from the simplicity of reading just a love story or just a story about a family. Phenomena are organized into significance and connection.

In *Sir Charles Grandison*, Richardson writes another encyclopedic novel that attempts partially to rescind or at least to modify the starkness of vision of *Clarissa*. One form this modification takes is the presentation of a male who is both powerful and good. Richardson in this ultra-Enlightenment novel offers a central character who is an Enlightener. Clarissa may have been named so because she is "most brilliant," "most famous" and "most shining," but although she should be "most clear" she cannot clarify in the sense of taking away the darkness that surrounds us; she shows us that there are shadows. Her light makes clear some very distressing truths. Sir Charles, as male Enlightener, has no distress to unveil. He too is "most brilliant" and "most shining" – very like the sun, in short. Sir Charles is perpetually referred to in terms of the sun. The heroine Harriet says "here comes the sun darting into all the crooked and obscure corners of my heart, and I shrink from his dazling eye; and, compared to Him ... appear to myself such a Nothing" (*The History of Sir Charles Grandison*, III: 132).

Sir Charles is a kind of political model of the wise ruler, an example of what "Bonnie Prince Charlie," the last Stuart hope, should have been but was not. Sir Charles invades England without bloodshed, in his return as the heir. Often challenged by outrageous persons who make some wrongful claim to land or to women whom he protects, he never loses his calm and his reason. Sir Hargrave Pollexfen abducts Harriet Byron from a masquerade; Sir Charles comes to the rescue of the strange woman who appeals to him for help, and magnificently throws Sir Hargrave under the carriage wheel. Later in the debate with Sir Hargrave, who wishes to fight a duel to retrieve his lost honor, Sir Charles resists the angry Sir Hargrave and the baronet's shady friends by his show of superior reason. Richardson makes Sir Charles consciously encyclopedic as he gathers together all the arguments against dueling in a harangue beginning with a historical survey:

> It was natural for me to look into history, for the rise and progress of custom so much and so justly my aversion , so contrary to all love divine and human, and particularly to that true heroism which Christianity enjoins, when it recommends meekness, moderation, and humility, as the glory of the human nature. But I am running into length.
>   Again Sir Charles took out his watch. They were clamorous for him to proceed. (II: 263)

We may find it hard to believe that the other men were not also looking at their watches, and difficult to entertain the notion that they would have "clamored" for three pages of antiduel discourse. But Sir Charles is an organized enlightener, who has his knowledge at his fingertips. He discovered, he says, "that this unchristian custom owed its rise to the barbarous northern nations"; he can clear the Romans of complicity in setting it up, even going into the Horatii and the Curatii, and glancing over later history, with a glimpse of modern Turkey as well as modern France. Sir Charles is the sort of man who gets informed by encyclopedias. But he himself has no longer any need to learn, for he now knows everything.

It is the men in the novel who still have much to learn – and much that they cannot omit to notice. Sir Charles could draw a veil over his father's faults (Sir Thomas sent him off to the Continent early with orders to stay there). The daughters who had to live with that father cannot avert their pious gaze from that father's defects, which directly affected their lives. Gestures towards hierarchy and piety are undermined within the novel itself, which ultimately persists, despite its own best intentions, in looking into deeper spaces than those Sir Charles can "penetrate" with his demanding sunshine. In the last part of *Sir Charles Grandison* the reader accompanies the newly married heroine Harriet to Grandison Hall. Sir Charles owns property, he is the landowner, the center of authority. The life he leads, that of the virtuous, independent, and wealthy owner of an estate, reflects the great (masculine) dream of eighteenth-century England. Sir Charles fulfills a deep cultural fantasy or desire – that the man of property, the estate owner, should be the man of moral excellence. Sir Charles at home is surrounded by the accoutrements of mercantilism and colonial possession. Here is the home to which encyclopedias come, the "Study" of a Grandison:

> The glass-cases are neat, and ... stored with well-chosen books in all sciences. Mr. Deane praised the globes, the orrery, and the instruments of all sorts, for geographical, astronomical, and other scientific observations. It is ornamented with pictures, some ... of the best masters of the Italian and Flemish schools, statues, bustoes, bronzes. And there also, placed in a distinguished manner, were the two rich cabinets of medals, gems, and other curiosities, presented to him by Lady Olivia. (III: 271)

Here is the collection, everything appropriately stored in a manner to please a d'Alembert. No base confusion here, although there is *profusion*, science and the arts in close proximity. Here is property – intellectual property.

Harriet Byron seems like a visitor in this grand home, of which she will be "Mistress" but of which she can never be owner. Truly she is no more an *owner* than her former rival, Clementina, the young Italian woman who was in love with Sir Charles and went mad upon being forbidden to think of him because of their religious difference. The ardent Roman Catholic Clementina receives full use of her intellects and a reunion with her family at what we are made to feel is the healthful air of Grandison Hall. The Hall is open to visitors from abroad. It is a true international center, a kind of international house, like the printing shop, where the "family of love" may meet friends and relations from Scotland, Wales, or Italy. It can act as this center of benevolent tolerance because its own values are certain, and because it is under very tight control. It is inalienable and orderly. The description of the grounds echoes that of Milton's Paradise, with the same hint of the theatrical. Milton's Eden is set amidst circling rows of trees:

> and as the ranks ascend
> Shade above shade, a woody Theatre
> Of stateliest view.
>
> (IV: 140–42)

So too is Sir Charles' Eden:

> The orchard ... is planted in a natural slope; the higher fruit-trees, as pears, in a semicircular row, first; apples at further distances next; cherries, plumbs, standard apricots, &c all which in the season of blossoming, one row gradually lower than another, must make a charming variety of blooming sweets to the eye, from the top of the rustic villa, which commands the whole.
>
> (III: 273)

Richardson has picked up hints from Milton, and expanded on the suggestions. The Grandisons have been encyclopedic gardeners, working their fruit trees not only into ranks but into categories, separating pears from apples. The encyclopedic order is an expression of obedience to the *command* that might emanate from the rustic villa which "*commands* the whole." The eye of command is everywhere in Sir Charles's garden. Foucault's observations in *Surveiller et Punir* on the eighteenth century's interest in "surveillance" are richly borne out in this and other parts of *Grandison*, with their emphasis on the penetrating and commanding eye. Everything is to master a point of view: "alcoves, little temples, seats, are erected at different points of view."

The labyrinth becomes the ordered and mastered garden, and the crossroads of difficulty are sublimed into the "little temple" to be "erected" and consecrated to the "triple friendship" of Clementina, Harriet, Sir Charles (III: 455). Meeting places of difficulty, desire, and ambiguity are to be resolved by structures. Sir Charles proclaims "Friendship ... will make at pleasure a safe bridge over the narrow seas: it will cut an easy passage thro' rocks and mountains" (III: 455). Friendship is an engineer, energetically made for structure and for assured connections.

In his last novel, Richardson has brought the encyclopedic connections and categorizing out into the open – they lie at the surface of his novel, and not in the deep structure. With this overt pattern of connections comes a new assurance that nothing is ambiguous or difficult. Such an assurance runs counter to the deepest insights of *Clarissa*. There, desire really does cross desire, and one knowledge runs counter to another. There is no master plan of the whole, and we truly descend into the labyrinth. Although

Grandison is very rich in many things that matter – not least in comedy, especially in the views and comments of Sir Charles's witty sister Charlotte – we may miss the sunless shades and its more painful intersections and blind alleys.

The accommodation with the world of mercantilist and progressivist values achieved in *Grandison* is not exactly (one cannot help noticing) favorable to women. Harriet will always be a guest in her husband's house, the approved conduit for the heir, the wife who cannot disturb her deceased mother-in-law's furnishings. In *Pamela*, the manor house in Lincolnshire, although it is Pamela's "prison," became for a while in some sense her territory. Pamela the prisoner performed Lockean activities on the land (fishing, planting cucumbers), so that we sense she has a certain claim to the place. Clarissa's well-defined claim to land, which she improved, turning "the Grove" into "the Dairy-house," is a source of her misfortune. Her grandfather's bequest of this small estate to her turns many in her family against her. Woman's lack of any claim to an abode or to any space is here felt as problematic. In *Grandison* the patriarchy provides, and no one should claim that there is any problem with property. Neither is there a problem with desire, for the regulated heart. In these sunny uplands above the well planned scheme of things, we may ungracefully sigh for the intricacies of the labyrinth, and the more troubling crossroads and meeting places of the farmyard and the brothel. There, at least, we knew that not all was known. In *Grandison*, at last Richardson, like the eighteenth-century's favorite image of Hercules at the Crossroads,[28] chose Virtue over Pleasure – that is, the virtue of civic order and smiling male responsibility.

NOTES

1 Dans l'étude de la nature, les hommes se sont d'abord appliqués tous, comme de concert, à satisfaire les besoins les plus pressants; mais quand ils en sont venus aux connaissances moins absolument nécessaires, ils ont du se les partager, et y avancer chacun de son coté à peu près d'un pas égal. Ainsi plusieurs sciences ont été, pour ainsi dire, contemporaines; mais dans l'ordre historique des progrès de l'esprit, on ne peut les embrasser que successivement.

Il n'en est pas de même de l'ordre encyclopédique de nos connaissances. Ce dernier consiste à les rassembler dans le plus petit espace possible, et à placer, pour ainsi dire, le philosophe au-dessus de ce vaste labyrinthe dans un point de vue fort élevé d'où il puisse apercevoir à la fois les sciences et les arts principaux; voir d'un coup d'oeil les objects de ses spéculations, et les operations qu'il peut fair sur ces objets; distinguer les branches générales des connaissances humaines, les points qui les séparent ou qui les unissent; et entrevoir même quelquefois les routes secrètes qui les rapprochent.

Jean Le Ronde d'Alembert, *Discours Preliminaire, Encyclopédie ou Dictionnaire raisonné des sciences, des arts et des metiers (articles choisis)*, ed. Alain Pons, 2 vols. (Paris: Flammarion, 1968), I: 112.

2 Samuel Richardson, letter to Johannes Stinstra, 2 June 1753, reprinted in John Carroll, ed., *Selected Letters* (Oxford: Clarendon, 1964), 228–29.

3 See T. C. Duncan Eaves and Ben D. Kimpel, *Samuel Richardson: a Biography* (Oxford: Oxford University Press, 1971), 5.

4 "A Samuel Richardson entered the second form of the Merchant Taylors' School in 1701, advanced to the third form, and left the school in 1702. This could well have been the novelist." (Eaves and Kimpel, *Samuel Richardson*, 9.) Boswell was told that Richardson was "brought up" in Christ's Hospital, but the novelist's daughter denied this (ibid., 10).

5 Richardson, letter to Johann Stinstra, 2 June 1753, Carroll, ed., *Selected Letters*, 229.

6 *Pamela*, III: 391. It is in his autobiographical letter to Stinstra that Richardson dilates on his "Correspondence with a Gentleman greatly my superior in Degree . . . who, had he lived, intended high things for me." Perhaps the Richardsons had expected this gentleman to support Samuel in an education for the Anglican ministry, and some such hope may be behind the delay in his undertaking an apprenticeship. Richardson emphasizes, however, that the correspondence went on while he was a printer's apprentice: "Multitudes of Letters passed between this Gentleman & me. He wrote well . . . Our Subjects were various." (Carroll, ed., *Selected Letters*, 229). Richardson's daughters, Anne Richardson and Martha Bridgen, in their correspondence of 1784 narrate their recollections of the story of Richardson's highborn acquaintance, the generous libertine and bigamist who died in 1739. The daughter of the bigamist is supposed to have given permission in 1741 for the narrative to be printed in the second volume of *Pamela*. The daughters' story is a reconstruction with a lot of speculation mixed in, and they too were relying on the third volume of *Pamela* as well as on hints from their father and fragments of correspondence. Quotations, here from the gentleman's story as told in *Pamela*, have been taken from the third volume of the third edition of *Pamela; or, Virtue Rewarded*. (London: S. Richardson, 4 vols., 1742). All further references to *Pamela* in the text are to the third edition. See A. D. McKillop, *Samuel Richardson: Printer and Novelist* (Chapel Hill: University of North Carolina Press, 1936), 108–18; and Eaves and Kimpel, *Samuel Richardson*, 12–13.

7 Richardson, letter to Stinstra, 2 June 1753, Carroll, ed., *Selected Letters*, 229.

8 Robert Darnton, *The Great Cat Massacre and Other Episodes in French Cultural History* (New York: Basic Books, 1984), 75–104.

9 Elizabeth L. Eisenstein, *The Printing Press as an Agent of Change: Communications and Cultural Transformations in Early-Modern Europe* (Cambridge: Cambridge University Press, vol. II, 1979), 139.

10 The phrase is sufficiently closely associated with Richardson's novel for Jane Austen to seize upon it in parody of *Grandison* in one of her early works: "The Johnsons were a family of Love, and though a little addicted to the Bottle and the Dice, had many good Qualities." See "Jack and Alice," in Margaret Anne Doody and Douglas Murray, eds., *Catharine and Other Writings* (Oxford: Oxford University Press, 1993), 12. Jocelyn Harris, in *Jane Austen's Art of Memory* (Cambridge: Cambridge University Press, 1989), defines and develops echoes of Richardson in Austen.

11 Eisenstein, *The Printing Press*, 155.

12 For Richardson's part in the Opposition cause during this difficult and dangerous time, see Eaves and Kimpel, *Samuel Richardson*, 19–36.

13 All quotations from *Clarissa* are taken from the eight-volume third edition as reprinted with an introduction by Florian Stuber (New York: AMS Press, 1990).

14 Milton, *Areopagitica*, reprinted in Douglas Bush et al., *The Prose Works of John Milton* (New Haven: Yale University Press, 8 vols., 1953–82), II: 549–51.

15 Eisenstein, *The Printing Press*, 687.

16 For Richardson's account of this assignment, see his letter to Aaron Hill of 1 February 1741 and his letter to Stinstra, 2 June 1753 (Carroll, ed., *Selected Letters*, 40-41, 332–33).

17 See Brian W. Downs, ed., *Familiar Letters on Important Occasions* (London: Routledge, 1928), nos. 138–39.

18 The full title of Richardson's "letter writer" is *Letters Written to and for Particular Friends. On the Most Important Occasions. Directing Not Only the Requisite Style and Forms to Be Observed in Writing Familiar Letters; But How to Think and Act Justly and Prudently in the Common Concerns of Human Life.*

19 Wolfgang Zach, "Mrs. Aubin and Richardson's Earliest Literary Manifesto (1739)," *English Studies*, 62 (1981): 271–85.

20 The first commentator to suggest that Richardson's malady was Parkinsonianism was Elizabeth Bergen Brophy, in an appendix to her book *Samuel Richardson the Triumph of Craft* (Knoxville: University of Tennessee Press, 1974). Richardson gives some glimpse of his state of health in his self-descriptive letter to Lady Bradshaigh, when she was to meet him for the first time, explaining that he does not go to public places, "not even to church, a benefit . . . I have as long been deprived of by my nervous malady, which will not let me appear in a crowd of people." He walks a good deal, but carries a cane "which he leans upon under the skirts of his coat usually, that it may imperceptibly serve him as a support, when attacked by sudden tremors or startings, and dizziness, which too frequently attack him, but, thank God, not so often as formerly" (Letter to Lady Bradshaigh, late 1749, Carroll, ed., *Selected Letters*, 134–35). Richardson associated the onset of the malady with a period of great stress and grief from repeated bereavements: "No less than Eleven concerning Deaths attacked me in two Years. My Nerves were so affected with these repeated Blows, that I have been for seven Years past forced, after repeated labouring thro the whole Medical Process by Direction of eminent Physicians, to go into a Regimen, not a Cure to be expected, but merely as a Palliative" (Letter to Lady Bradshaigh, 15 December 1748, Carroll, ed., *Selected Letters*, 110). He abstained from wine, meat, and fish, and tried many remedies including exercise and taking the waters at Bath and Tunbridge.

21 All quotations from *Pamela; or, Virtue Rewarded* are taken from the Riverside edition, entitled *Pamela*, the first edition edited by T. C. Duncan Eaves and Ben D. Kimpel (Boston: Houghton Mifflin, 1971).

22 Jean Le Ronde d'Alembert, *Discours Preliminaire* to *Encyclopédie*, 112.

23 See my essay "The Man-Made World of Clarissa Harlowe and Robert Lovelace," in *Samuel Richardson: Passion and Prudence*, ed. Valerie Grosvenor Myer (London: Vision, 1986), 52–77.

24 Le plus libre et le plus doux de tous les actes n'admet point de violence réelle, la nature et la raison s'y opposent: la nature, en ce qu'elle a pourvu le plus faible d'autant de force

qu'il en faut pour résister quant il lui plait; la raison, en ce qu'une violence réelle est non seulement le plus brutal de tous les actes, mais le plus contraire à sa fin.

[The most generous and sweetest of all actions admits of no real violence, nature and reason are opposed to it: nature, in that she has provided the feeblest woman with sufficient force to resist when she wants to; reason, in that real violence is not only the most brutal of all actions, but the most contrary to its object.]

Jean-Jacques Rousseau, *Émile. ou de l'education* [1762] (Paris: Garnier-Flammarion, 1966), 468.

Rousseau, who knew *Clarissa* well and is influenced by it, quite definitely refuses to admit its major premise. Indeed Richardson has to be quite bold to set out his story of rape in opposition to a general cultural belief that rape does not really happen, that any sexual congress, even if it *looks like* violence, involves the woman's real desire and inner consent. Lovelace expresses this view in the novel. We thus see why Richardson had to have Clarissa drugged and unconscious during the rape sequence. He has to exhibit that rape does take place. Had Clarissa been conscious, Lovelace *and* many readers would have agreed that she had really consented, and that any bodily and vocal resistance was just play.

25 See Carroll, ed., *Selected Letters*, 95, and "Postscript . . . In Which Several objections that have been made, as well to the Catastrophe as to different Parts of the preceding History, are briefly considered" (*Clarissa*, VIII: 277–99).

Richardson has to take on not only the sensibilities of readers, but proponents of the traditional neoclassical view that "Poetical Justice" is aesthetically necessary in a work of fiction. Richardson sinned against "Poetical Justice" in dramatic and other works can most readily be found in cultural circumstances involving authoritarian ideas and controls – like the France of Louis XIV, where the politically supervised Académie Française emphasized such propriety. Punishing the bad characters and rewarding the good not only reminds the audience or readers that they are being instructed, but also posits a morality already known and a system of social rewards worth having. Insistence of Poetic Justice almost always supports a politically authoritarian system. The killing off of Clarissa by Richardson has been objected to on feminist grounds from its own day, with objections voiced by Lady Bradshaigh and Lady Echlin, as well as by Terry Castle and other modern critics. But in discussing the ending of Richardson's novel we should take into account the political implications of averting Poetic Justice and thus implicitly condemning current society.

26 Eisenstein, *The Printing Press*, 143.

27 For a discussion of Clarissa's coffin designs, see Allan Wendt, "Clarissa's Coffin," *Philological Quarterly*, 39 (1960): 481–95, and Rita Goldberg, *Sex and Enlightenment in Richardson and Diderot* (Cambridge: Cambridge University Press, 1984); Goldberg reads the emblems on Clarissa's coffin as sexual symbols. There are numerous emblems and examples of *ekphrasis* scattered through *Clarissa*.

28 *Characteristics of Man. Manners. Opinions. Times* of Anthony Ashley Cooper, third Earl of Shaftesbury, contains an essay on the "Historical Draught or Tablature of the Judgment of Hercules" with an engraving of the Choice of Hercules. This is just one of the many appearances of the image, but it is certainly an important one. It also should be noted that Shaftesbury's book carries an image (by Gribelin) of both sun and *ourberos* combined in a device on the title page of the first volume. Richardson must have known this very well–

known book. The development of eighteenth-century ideas of the natural goodness of man, and our innate pleasure in social virtues, can be attributed in part to
Shaftesbury's essays; *Grandison* is the most Shaftesburyan of Richardson's
works.

READING LIST

Beebee, Thomas. *Clarissa on the Continent: Translation and Seduction.* University
Park, Penn., and London: Pennsylvania State University Press, 1990.

Braudy, Leo. "Penetration and Impenetrability in *Clarissa*," in *New Aspects of the
Eighteenth Century. Essays from the English Institute*, ed. Philip Harth. New
York: Columbia University Press, 1974.

Brophy, Elizabeth Bergen. *Women's Lives and the Eighteenth-Century English
Novel.* Tampa: University of South Florida Press, 1991.

Castle, Terry. *Clarissa's Cyphers: Meaning and Disruption in Richardson's "Clarissa."* Ithaca, N.Y.: Cornell University Press, 1982.

Doody, Margaret Anne. *A Natural Passion: a Study of the Novels of Samuel
Richardson.* Oxford: Clarendon, 1974.

"The Manmade World of Clarissa Harlowe and Robert Lovelace," in *Samuel
Richardson, Passion and Prudence*, ed. Valerie Myer. New Jersey: Barnes and
Noble, 1986.

"Richardson's Politics," *Eighteenth-Century Fiction*, 2 (1990): 113–26.

Doody, Margaret Anne and Peter Sabor (ed.) *Samuel Richardson Tercentenary
Essays.* Cambridge: Cambridge University Press, 1989.

Doody, Margaret Anne and Florian Stuber. "*Clarissa* Censored," *MLS*, 18, 1
(Winter 1988): 74–88.

Flynn, Carol. *Samuel Richardson: a Man of Letters.* Princeton: Princeton University
Press, 1982.

Gillis, Christina Marsden. *The Paradox of Privacy: Epistolary Form in "Clarissa."*
Gainesville: University Presses of Florida, 1984.

Goldberg, Rita. *Sex and Enlightenment in Richardson and Diderot.* Cambridge:
Cambridge University Press, 1984.

Gwilliam, Tassie. *Samuel Richardson's Fictions of Gender.* Stanford: Stanford
University Press, 1993.

Keymer, Thomas. *Richardson's "Clarissa" and the Eighteenth-Century Reader.*
Cambridge: Cambridge University Press, 1992.

Kinkead-Weekes, Mark. *Samuel Richardson: Dramatic Novelist.* London: Methuen,
1973.

McKillop, A. D. *Samuel Richardson: Printer and Novelist.* Chapel Hill: University of
North Carolina Press, 1936.

Sale, William M. *Samuel Richardson: Master Printer.* Ithaca, N.Y.: Cornell University Press, 1950.

Stuber, Florian. "On Original and Final Intentions, or Can There Be an Authoritative *Clarissa*?" *Text: Transactions of the Society for Textual Scholarship*, 2
(1985).

Warner, William Beatty. *Reading "Clarissa": the Struggles of Interpretation.* New
Haven: Yale University Press, 1979.

Watt, Ian. *The Rise of the Novel: Studies in Defoe, Richardson and Fielding*. 1957; Berkeley: University of California Press, 1964.

Wendt, Allen. "Clarissa's Coffin." *Philological Quarterly*, 39 (1960): 481–95.

Wilt, Judith. "'He Could Go No Farther': a Modest Proposal About Lovelace and Clarissa." *PMLA*, 92 (1977): 10–31.

Zomchick, John P. *Family and the Law in Eighteenth-Century Fiction: the Public Conscience in the Private Sphere*. Cambridge: Cambridge University Press, 1993.

6

CLAUDE RAWSON

Henry Fielding

Henry Fielding was born in 1707, into a family in straitened circumstances but of aristocratic connections. A family myth, based on forged papers, claimed descent from the Habsburgs. The combination of financial embarrassment and gentlemanly caste is emblematic of the whole atmosphere of his life, and is variously reflected in his writings. He turned to writing fiction for a living (and to practicing law for the same reason) after his career as a prominent and successful dramatist was ended by the Licensing Act of 1737, which his own antigovernment plays helped to precipitate. He is the only one among the early novelists whose origins were patrician, and the only one whose style and cultural loyalties were closely tied to the tradition we sometimes call Augustan. Early in his career he sometimes called himself Scriblerus Secundus, after the Scriblerian coterie of Swift and Pope. One of his earliest poems, however, was an unpublished mock *Dunciad* against these authors, discovered some years ago among the papers of his cousin Lady Mary Wortley Montagu, an adversary of Pope and his friends.

Nevertheless, his literary tastes and cultural outlook were extensions of theirs, even when personal ties or political allegiance pulled the other way. His praise of Swift's writings, and his sense of Swift as one of his own great literary masters, along with (and perhaps surpassing) Aristophanes, Lucian, Rabelais, and Cervantes, was strong. Swift is said to have admired Fielding's wit and to have confessed that one of the only two occasions in his life when he remembered having laughed was "at ... Tom Thumb's killing the ghost," in a play (as it happens) to which Fielding attached a mock commentary by Scriblerus Secundus, modeled mainly on Pope's *Dunciad* (1728), not very long after his mock-Dunciadic attack on Pope and Swift themselves. The remarkable thing, however, was not that Fielding appropriated specific routines from the Scriblerian masters, but that he later extended his deep assimilation of their stylistic manner into his novels; into a genre, that is, whose defining characteristics might have been thought outside the range of their literary sympathies and even antithetical to them.

His first two works of fiction, *Shamela* (1741) and *Joseph Andrews* (1742), were triggered by his dislike of Richardson's *Pamela* (1740–41), and treated its author as a low vulgarian, in a manner derived from the older satirists' treatment of the dunces and Grub Street hacks.

Fielding's antipathy was partly conditioned by a dislike of the veristic claims of Richardson's novel: its pretense of "to the Moment" narration by a participant in the thick of the action; its particularity of specification; and its way of thrusting readers into an intimacy with the narrative, which Fielding seems to have regarded as voyeuristic. It is the power that made Diderot cry out to warn Richardsonian heroines not to believe their deceivers, a power which seems temporarily to accompany all significant escalations, whether stylistic or technological, of the pursuit of "realism": the anxiety and grief that readers later conveyed to Richardson or to Dickens over the fate of Clarissa or Paul Dombey (whose death "threw a whole nation into mourning") is disconcertingly replicated in popular responses to radio and television soap operas. What Flaubert was to extol as novelistic "illusion" has obvious affinities with the hoax and other forms of vulgar verism.

Fielding saw Richardson's hothouse immediacies as undesirable exposures to unprocessed circumstance, intimate, indecorous and unmanaged. His distaste can be seen as a resistance to one of the most powerful animating forces in the evolution of the novel. That this has a cheaply sensational obverse enables us more easily to see the point of Fielding's recoil, even without imputing to him any special prescience. The example of Swift's prefigurations (often in the form of advance parody) of modes of modern writing not visible to the ordinary observer in his own time suggests that one should not rule out some intuitive awareness of future directions on Fielding's part. An ambivalent interest in literary hoaxes, and in the rewards, risks and even dangers of irony collapsing into a hoax through the naivety of readers, was common to both writers. If some Flaubertian model of fictional (or "dramatic") "illusion" had been proposed to Fielding, I think he would have understood it in lowered terms, as what later came to be called illusionism, a fairground quackery, one of the licensed deceptions of popular culture, on a level with soap opera; or, if you prefer, as a hoax without irony. Irony is a badge of caste, a coded language notionally meaning one thing to the few and another to the many. It indicates both command and aloofness, the imperiousness with which, in the irony of Fielding as of Swift, words are made to carry the speaker's meaning rather than submitting him to theirs; and a distance from the vulnerably literal or the merely particular, intimating a wise perspective *de haut en bas*.

The manner implied that Richardson, and with him a whole line of future novelistic development, was ill-bred. But if Richardson's intimate prolixities were regarded by uppish readers as solecisms, they were at the same time felt to be immensely affecting. Lady Mary Wortley Montagu wept copiously even as she despised, and Fielding experienced over *Clarissa* (1747–48) a more thoughtful and generous version of the same ambivalence. His last novel *Amelia* (1751) shows the influence of *Clarissa*. His earlier rejection of *Pamela* was more complete, though he must quickly have become conscious of the irony whereby his rejection of Richardson's novel was being expressed in novels of his own. It is a recurrent phenomenon in the history of literary forms, and especially perhaps of the novel, that an antiform quickly resolves itself into a member of the class it is subverting. Fielding brought to this task a manner shaped for other purposes by the Augustan satirists, urbanely interventionist rather than self-effacing, and designed to indicate authorial management rather than induce an illusion of unmediated reality. The formal structurings and closures of his periods and paragraphs, his highly personal blend of hauteur, irony, and fervour, his parodic set pieces and inventive grotesqueries, contributed to the establishment of a rival narrative mode. The style, though partly derived from nonfictional models, helped to turn Fielding into the principal inventor of the English comic novel and an early practitioner of the kind of fiction that is concerned, self-consciously and on a substantial scale, with its own writing.

Although Fielding is chiefly known as a novelist, he was in his day England's leading playwright, a political journalist of considerable power, a barrister and, in his last years, a highly influential magistrate, who had a hand in shaping what eventually developed into the Metropolitan Police. His writings on the legal and social aspects of poverty and crime are by-products of his magistracy. Like his other late works, including *Amelia* and the *Journal of a Voyage to Lisbon* (1755), they form an impressive body of work, still relatively little known, which, in its affronted recognition of social and personal disorder, differs greatly from the more genial and confident atmosphere of the earlier and better-known books. Fielding died in 1754, near Lisbon, where he had gone for his health.

Fielding is sometimes superficially characterized as a "manly" novelist, and in successive culture wars from their own time to the present Richardson has traditionally appeared as correspondingly feminine (honorifically or otherwise). Angela Smallwood argues in *Fielding and the Woman Question* that critics and editors have disguised the extent to which Fielding wrote on female issues, shows Fielding to have been more strongly and decently concerned with the "woman question" than many thought, and sees the two novelists not as antithetical monsters but as working within "the same eighteenth-century cultural consciousness for which women and ideas of femininity were of very great importance." The idea of the two novelists as antithetical was nevertheless fostered by both and important to their own projects of self-definition, and it would be wrong to ignore how much of what we would now call vulgar sexism there was on both sides. The unctuous fair-sexing of Richardson was as patronizing as the gallantries of Steele or Pope. Smallwood notes Fielding's promotion of a common view that women were made inferior by bad educational practice rather than natural defect, but he was equally capable of more rearguard attitudes. In a copy of the works of Horace inscribed to Jane Collier, Fielding complimented her "for an Understanding more than Female." The words were meant, and presumably taken, as a compliment.

Fielding's imagination, quite as much as Richardson's, was strongly woman-centered and highly sexed, though the patrician codes to which he was culturally conditioned were not conducive to sexually-charged expression, the incandescent obscenity of the Restoration poet Rochester being a special case. This was more a matter of worldly reserve than of prudery. Prudery and prurience were, from this perspective, solecisms of similar order, amounting to an equal and opposite, or a merely equal, loss of cool. Even Rochester's bawdy fervors come over with an aplomb of cultivated insouciance, and are more a case of verbal outrage than of close attention to erotic detail. Fielding expressly shrank from graphically sexual scenes, whether in pornographers or in the censorious Richardson, refusing to cater for readers whose devotion to the fair sex needed to be raised with the help of pictures. His accounts of the amours of Tom or of Booth make a point of closing such readers out, not always without fuss. "Here the Graces think proper to end their Description," he says at the end of *Tom Jones* (IX.5; 1749),[1] after the business between Tom and Mrs Waters had indeed, in Fielding's words, been "partly described," but with a stylized comic-opera *mise en scène* (visually familiar to the modern reader through Tony Richardson's film) that translates the material to a mode quite different from that of pictorial arousal; festive, witty, urbane in a Chaucerian rather than a Chesterfieldian way.

The morally cloudier affair with Lady Bellaston gets a more laconic form of reticence (XIII.9), and by the time of Booth's amour with Miss Mathews the reticence comes with an accentuated reminder of wrongdoing: "tho' we decline painting the Scene, it is not our Intention to conceal from the World the Frailty of Mr. *Booth*, or of his fair Partner" (*Amelia*, IV.1). Fielding notes extenuating circumstances and had earlier made the point, which underlies all Tom's amours also, that Booth "was a Man of consummate Good-nature, and had formerly had much Affection for this young Lady; indeed, more than the Generality of People are capable of entertaining for any Person whatsoever" (III.12). The comment suggests the extent, as well as the limits, of an insistence on the moral importance of chastity in his fictional universe, which should not be written off merely because it has been receiving some overemphasis. It may also reflect the *embourgeoisement* of a patrician cast of mind by the pressure of Richardsonian example and the continuing decline of libertinism as a culturally significant ethic since Rochester's time.

The declarations of reticence are partly, but only partly, factitious. Telling the reader that you're not telling is itself a way of telling, and the avuncular geniality or fuss suggests that a posture of worldly cool is being relaxed. A fuss about not making a fuss is still a fuss, but what is eliminated is Richardsonian censoriousness over the more venial forms of sexual mis-conduct (the idea that there are venial forms, let alone generous ones, is itself foreign to Richardson) and especially Richardsonian prurience in the graphic portrayal of sexual doings. The establishment of an appropriate tone for dealing with these topics, and the definition of a sexual code strongly grounded in moral considerations but not overridingly preoccupied with the imperatives of technical chastity, are of central importance in Fielding's writing.

An eroticized perception is evident in his discursive and fictional prose, early and late, and is not confined to, nor most characteristically visible in, the amorous episodes. Its changes are a revealing index of the evolution (and progressive darkening) of his outlook and style. A recurrent image is the fleeting appearance of a beautiful woman, followed by a shock of surprise or disappointment. A "beautiful young creature of about fifteen," in the *Champion* for 24 May 1740, shocks first because she appears "big with child" and then "more so when we found she had pulled off all her clothes and her big belly together," explaining "that it was the fashion for all young ladies to appear with child in the world she came from": she was applying for admission to Elysium, and the allusion seems to be to the fashion for hoop petticoats, which Fielding repeatedly satirized, or to some related fad which, as Fielding said in his play *Miss Lucy in Town* (1735), made fine ladies "spoil their Shapes, to appear big with Child because it's the Fashion." In a parallel Lucianic piece in the *Journey from this World to the Next* (1743), "a very beautiful Spirit indeed" makes eyes at Minos, boasts of having refused "a great Number of Lovers, and dying a Maid," and is turned back by Minos, who "told her she had not refused enow yet," a typically eruptive put-down of prudery and cant (1.7).

Two late examples are painful. *An Enquiry into the Causes of the Late Increase of Robbers* (1751), describing overcrowded houses that offer cheap lodging to the poor in conditions encouraging whoredom and drunkenness,

Fielding reports on "one of the prettiest Girls I had ever seen, who had been carried off by an *Irishman*, to consummate her Marriage on her Wedding-night, in a Room where several others were in Bed at the same time" (6).[2] Out of the same image of defeated expectation, Fielding has wrought an effect previously absent. The earlier cases show neat fabular reversals in which the women's beauty is countered by an arresting revelation of moral shallowness: each reflects a prevailing code (of worldly fashion, or prudery), but the situation comes over as largely insulated from the pressure of social circumstance, an effect compounded by the context of otherworldly fable. The later passage retains traces of the formulaically startling cameo portrait, but moves away from the fabular mode and eliminates the personal bizarrerie. The girl isn't odd or vicious, merely thrust into a grimly disillusioning predicament by the sheer force of social conditions. In *Amelia* there is a further development:

> A very pretty Girl then advanced towards them, whose Beauty Mr. *Booth* could not help admiring the Moment he saw her; declaring, at the same time, he thought she had great Innocence in her Countenance. *Robinson* said she was committed thither as an idle and disorderly Person, and a common Street-walker. As she past by Mr. *Booth*, she damn'd his Eyes, and discharged a Volley of Words, every one of which was too indecent to be repeated. (1.4)

This woman is a whore and evidently viewed as a malefactress, more sinning than sinned against. In such a case, you might expect both "beauty" and misconduct without any undue sense that the fitness of things was being violated. But the combination of a whorish beauty with an air "of great Innocence," belied in turn by a volley of obscenities, seems a more radical affront to expectation. The effect resides not merely in an accentuated sense of moral letdown but in a defiance of intelligibility – akin to the surreal impact of the revelation – in the preceding chapter that another inmate of Newgate, the obscenely deformed, disease-ravaged old bawd, Blear-Eyed Moll, was not only "one of the merriest Persons in the whole Prison," but had been "taken in the Fact with a very pretty young Fellow" (1.3).

Moll's merriment is said to be "productive of moral Lesson," doubtless to do with keeping up spirits in adversity, but the main impact is hardly homiletic. Her being with a very pretty young fellow may seem a release into bawdy geniality, however off color, but here again the chief feeling is of its not making sense. The potential for lifting the mood actually highlights the painfulness of the unnatural. Prison gaiety in *Amelia* is hardly a "Newgate pastoral" like Gay's *Beggar's Opera* (1728). The prison episode includes a scene of what would now be called gay-bashing, in which the merry Moll, and perhaps the girl with the innocent countenance, took part, and from which the victim had to be "rescued ... by Authority" (1.4). Fielding is neither endorsing the sport, nor especially concerned to condemn it: no evidence of compassion for the plight of homosexuals is on the agenda. The prevailing note is of all-round scabrousness, in a mystifying combination with merriment, old hags disporting themselves with pretty fellows and innocent-looking beauties shouting obscenities. The play of social forces is not explainable in the manner of the *Enquiry*, where shocking things may affront us and predicaments are horrible, but where they derive intelligibly from overcrowding and poverty and do not defy rational comprehension.

The paragraph about the girl occurs a few sentences before the rough handling of the man of "odious unmanlike Practices." These depictions form parts of a densely peopled prison reportage, in which the flow of disorderly circumstance and teeming activity, the phantasmagoric sequence of judicial malpractice and criminal misery, are powerfully displayed, and at the same time framed in a ghostly paradigm of orderliness. An atmosphere of fabular organization pervades these Newgate chapters, including episodes of misfortune compounded by cruel miscarriages of justice, whose ironic payoffs belong to a highly formal mode, common in the earlier writings from the *Champion* to *Tom Jones*, but whose coexistence with the tearaway realities of *Amelia* is startling.

This stiffened recourse to fabular form is stripped of the fable's pretence of being able to explain. The "very pretty Girl" episode is structured for a payoff, culminating in the volley of obscenities, but it declines to provide the last-minute glimpse of moral clarification around which the episodes from the *Champion* or the *Journey* were organized, as conspicuously as it withholds the sociological understanding offered in the *Enquiry*. Though its surrounding context provides something like the *Enquiry*'s range of circumstantial notation, there is a retreat from the latter's *circumstantiality*. The quantum of misery is particularized on a comparable scale, but instead of an atmosphere of specification, of recording events as such, there is a reappearance of an older explanatory mode in a new pseudoexplanatory or explanation-denying form. As the realities become increasingly offensive and absurd, the writing shows an accentuated reliance on set-piece structuring, symmetries of balance and antithesis, climaxes, anticlimaxes, and payoffs, but without the reassuring provision of meaning. The meaning turns out to be that there is no meaning. The surprise of the volley of oaths is what might once have been called "absurdist." Its relation to the girl's beauty or innocent countenance is neither causal nor countercausal, confirming or betraying some intelligible principle, but a gratuitous anomaly, in the raw. This is even truer of the array of phenomena involving Blear-Eyed

Moll, and the account of her, more extended than the paragraph-vignette, is also more emphatically subjected to stylized patterning, the architecture of her decaying, misshapen body strenuously evoking residual Palladian symmetries, while her character as the merriest person in the whole prison has its roots in the surprises of Fielding's imitations of the first century AD Greek satirist Lucian's dialogues. As circumstance or behavior are increasingly registered as incomprehensible and perverse, the stylistic aspiration is for structures of understanding or containment of which the ironic fable, the well-made scene, the patterns of couplet rhetoric in verse and prose were the official visible signs. The fiction of Defoe and Richardson provided an alternative in relation to which Fielding could only operate adversarially. But at the time of *Amelia* he had been impressed by the particularized immediacy of *Clarissa*, and he lurches between unsuccessful attempts to emulate this and a reactive mode which would, in its surreal blending of irrational circumstance and intensified and signposted artifice, mark a striking anticipation of some modern absurdist writing.

The successive vignettes about beautiful girls seem in their localized way to trace a curve. An early, "Augustan" Fielding projects a patrician sense that reporting details, or stories, for their own sakes, shows poor breeding. His determination to display authorial command over facts and events gradually but incompletely progresses towards a newer notation, factually and emotionally more unguarded, which we associate with the Richardsonian novel. An inconvenience of this scenario is that stinging remarks about the author of *Clarissa*, and sneers against trivial specification, continue in Fielding's last writings. Nevertheless, Fielding's last two considerable works, *Amelia* and the *Voyage to Lisbon*, mark a major break from the buoyancies of an Augustan manner that seemed his natural voice and reached its full flowering as late as *Tom Jones*, even as they assert an accentuated attachment to its forms. The leap, as well as the continuity, may be observed in the transition from the *Journey from this World to the Next* to *Amelia*, 1.4. Between the two, after *Tom Jones* and before *Amelia*, the example from the *Enquiry*, reporting events and commenting upon them without the parade of gentlemanly point scoring, marks the only moment when the notional curve appears in its simple form. Its special character may be due to the fact that the *Enquiry* is a sociological tract, not a fiction, or to the chronological circumstance that Fielding's admiration for *Clarissa* had established a change and a deepened perspective without yet generating reactive defenses.

The vignettes about women are also emblematic in a structural sense. Fielding's fictions, for all their supposed male orientation (it is an oddity of literary history that of his three major novels the first two are named after a male protagonist and the last after a heroine, an exact reversal of the pattern of Richardson's titles), often have a woman, or an idea of woman, as part of their central conception. *Joseph Andrews* in particular not only offers in the somewhat inconspicuous Fanny a counterpart to Fielding's view of Pamelaic innocence, but places its male hero in the Pamelaic and traditionally feminine role of defending his chastity against an upper-class seducer. Underlying that, as *Shamela* makes clear even earlier, is the idea of a woman who is not what she seems, the central indictment in Fielding's early responses to Richardson, as it is the central feature of the scenes I began with.

Shamela, a parody of *Pamela* probably written before Fielding knew the identity of the author, not only attacks deception or hypocrisy. It is also a critique of a mode of writing "to the Moment," in which events purport to be narrated in letters by the participants at the time they are actually occurring, whose claims to immediacy and unadorned reporting might, in such a context, be thought of as one of the deceptions to be exposed. Shamela's boast that "I write in the present Tense" (6), however, and her relentlessly enumerated consumptions of tea, sugar, and "hot buttered Apple-Pie" mimic styles Fielding would have deplored even when they were used, as in their curious way they are here, in the service of unadorned truth. The parody of Richardson's hot scenes, as when Squire Booby "steals his Hand into my Bosom, which I, as if in my Sleep, press close to me with mine, and then pretend to awake," makes a related point. Richardson's prurience became a satirical commonplace, fair game for suggesting that his morality was hypocritical cant, but one of the put-downs of Booby in *Shamela* is that, like Didapper in *Joseph Andrews*, he is not a very passionate profligate:

> he run up, caught me in his Arms, and flung me upon a Chair, and began to offer to touch my Under-Petticoat. Sir, says I, you had better not offer to be rude; well, says he, no more I won't then; and away he went out of the Room. I was so mad to be sure I could have cry'd. (vi)

"Began to offer to touch my Under-petticoat" is at four removes from actually doing anything, and the great rush of energy fizzles out in a tactical retreat that leaves Shamela disappointed and unsatisfied. She really prefers the more vigorous Parson Williams, so Booby is heading for cuckoldry, since her objective is to trap him into marriage. Her disappointment, however, comes over as not merely opportunistic. Her eye is on the main chance, but she clearly likes a bit on the side (which bit and whose side, since Booby is to become her husband, is a nice question), and the gusto with which she conveys this is one of her attractions. It is seldom remarked that Shamela is one of Fielding's most engaging creations, brassy, demotic, direct, and *unshamming*, with a more completely realized paradoxical geniality than that which suffuses another of Fielding's early unalloyed villains, Jonathan Wild.

This gusto would be unthinkable in Richardson, which makes Fielding's rewriting of *Pamela* splendid as well as unjust. Part of the point scoring suggests a patrician appreciation, outside the range of merchant sensibilities, of "low" demotic energies. Richardson responded by saying Fielding was "low" himself. Fielding expressed in *Tom Jones* and elsewhere a fondness for farces and puppet shows, and even ran a puppet theatre of his own. His stylized versions of popular forms are often startling, as when, after listing portraits of famous beauties as he describes his heroine Sophia, he tells the reader "if thou hast seen all these, be not afraid of the rude Answer which Lord *Rochester* once gave to a Man, who had seen many Things" (*Tom Jones*, IV.2), an allusion to the line, "If you have seen all this, then kiss mine A[rs]e." The appeal to Rochester, in whose *Poems* (1680) the line appears though the poem probably is not by him, shows the self-consciousness with which Fielding projected the association of lordly arrogance and demotic forms.

The blend is strong in *Shamela*, where exuberant use is made of farcical insult and repartee. Booby blows in and finds Shamela reading a book, which he takes to be "*Rochester's* Poems":

No, forsooth, says I, as pertly as I could; why how now Saucy Chops, Boldface, says he – Mighty pretty Words, says I, pert again. – Yes (says he) you are a d—d, impudent, stinking, cursed, confounded Jade, and I have a great Mind to kick your A—. You, kiss – says I. A-gad, says he, and so I will.

(6)

Both the idiom, and its accelerated tempo, a zany transformation of selected elements of Richardsonian dialogue, evoke the rhythms of farce rather than normal conversation. In the quick-time succession of "says he" and "says I," Fielding has transformed the purportedly neutral notation of dialogue, in which the author is notionally effaced, into something whose clockwork precisions are as exuberantly interventionist in effect as any of the explicit authorial displays and commentaries of the later fiction.

Shamela is a delightful and underrated prefiguration of Fielding's major fictions. Its interest in the surreal precisions of slapstick looks back to some of his plays and forward to such moments in *Tom Jones* as that in which Squire Western tells his sister that he despised her politics "as much as I do a F—t," a word he immediately "accompanied and graced with the very Action, which, of all others, was the most proper to it" (VII.3). The comedy of such things is the demotic underside of the never-never lands of fairytale and romance, in which coincidences and closures are forever assuring us of ideal congruences denied by the experience of daily life. Precision farting is a fairground routine of apparently enduring appeal, and scenarios of farce, as of cartoon films, in which random events and unprogrammed physiological processes occur at the most fitting moment in the most fitting place, are outrageous assertions of the power of artifice to impose its order on the reality principle.

In his next and more ambitious confrontation with *Pamela*, the *Adventures of Joseph Andrews*, he made much of his attachment to the *real*, "exactest copying of Nature." The preface is often taken as a landmark in the theory of the novel. But even Fielding's most literal-minded admirers do not usually see it as a manifesto of fictional realism, and this defensive and self-conscious document is particularly interesting for its contradictions and confusions. Fielding's protestation of "exactest copying" is ostensibly written in opposition to the assumption, routinely expressed in mainstream literary and aesthetic theory from Dryden to Reynolds, that art should not be merely lifelike: "there may be too great a likeness," as Dryden or Hume would say, the issue being not the individual lowness of a subject but a more radical discomfort with what is "copied faithfully and at full length."[3] The attitude rested on old doctrines that the business of art was to enhance or transcend particularity, an objective most prestigiously fulfilled by the heroic aggrandizements of epic and tragedy but attainable also by contrary stylizations in "low" genres. Dryden saw a use for "deformity," the "distorted face and antic gestures," in comic portrayals, and Hume insisted that "if we copy low life, the strokes must be strong and remarkable," so that the process of derealizing might as appropriately be achieved by reducing reality to the grotesque or ugly as by raising it to nobility.

Such doctrines are inimical to the fictional portrayal we associate with Defoe or Richardson and the kind of "realism" principally expounded in Ian Watt's account of the "rise of the novel." The claim of exactest copying might seem aligned with the new novelistic endeavor, especially since Fielding's preface rejects heroic romance and burlesque as twin distortions of honest fact. After denouncing romances as travesties of serious epic, Fielding offers the definition of his novel as "a comic Epic-Poem in Prose; differing from Comedy, as the serious Epic from Tragedy." His point is that comedy has a "more extended and comprehensive" range, drawn from everyday life and "Persons of inferiour Rank," and is amusing rather than elevated. Disavowing the use of burlesque, he declares:

> no two Species of Writing can differ more widely than the Comic and the Burlesque: for as the latter is ever the Exhibition of what is monstrous and unnatural, and where our Delight ... arises from the surprizing Absurdity, as in appropriating the Manners of the highest to the lowest, or *é converso*; so in the former, we should ever confine ourselves strictly to Nature.

By comparison with heroic romances, a claim of "exactest copying," even for a work as stylized as *Joseph Andrews*, would be sustainable on any commonsense view, as well as in terms of traditional conceptions of comic realism. But the claim would have no standing beside the work of Defoe or Richardson, a truth which Fielding would at all times be more disposed to publicize than to conceal. The claim is also compromised in other ways, and some of Fielding's distinctions need clarifying and indeed distinguishing from one another, including that between "appropriating the Manners of the highest to the lowest" and its opposite (*é converso*), and between burlesque of diction and a more substantive burlesque which he claims to reject.

The first distinction has its *locus classicus* in the assertion by the French poet Boileau that he had provided, in his poem *Le Lutrin* (1674), a *burlesque nouveau* in which low characters like clockmakers and fish-mongers speak in the high language of Dido and Aeneas, rather than one in which Virgil's protagonists were comically travestied in a low idiom. An English example of the older mode is the opening of Charles Cotton's *Scarronides* (1664), an adaptation of Scarron's *Viraile Travesti*: "I *Sing the Man* (read it who list, / A *Troian* true, as ever pist)." The new mode proposed by Boileau is that of the great Augustan mock-heroics, including Pope's *Rape of the Lock* and the *Dunciad*, whose first version begins with an imitation of the same Virgilian opening: "Books and the Man I sing, the first who brings / The Smithfield Muses to the Ear of Kings." Fielding, like Boileau, used the term "burlesque" for both, but a convention later developed of using "burlesque" for the older mode and "mock-heroic" for the new. Augustan theory valorized the latter, as lending grandeur to satire and making of it, in Dryden's words, "undoubtedly a species" of heroic poetry itself, whereas the other came to be downgraded as a lowering style.

Fielding's key distinction, however, is between both kinds of burlesque on the one hand and his own purportedly realist mode on the other, attaching special importance to this "because, I have often heard that Name given to Performances ... of the Comic kind, from the Author's having sometimes admitted it in his Diction only." Fielding was quite ready to blur this distinction in his preface to his sister Sarah's novel *David Simple* (1744), where full-scale mock-heroic poems like *Le Lutrin* and the *Dunciad* are called comic epics, an *ex post facto* witness to the ample presence of mock-heroic in *Joseph Andrews* itself, as though the teller had belatedly or inadvertently caught up with the tale (though the critics who persist in identifying "comic epic" with mock-heroic are misreading the preface to that work). But the distinction is already hedged in the preface to *Joseph Andrews* by a secondary distinction between a burlesque involving "Sentiments and Characters" and one involving "Diction" only, a type he considered admissible, and "of which many Instances will occur in this Work, as in the Descriptions of the Battles, and some other Places, not necessary to be pointed out to the Classical Reader; for whose Entertainment those Parodies or Burlesque Imitations are chiefly calculated." These are brazen slippages. There are so "many Instances" as to neutralize any suggestion that "exactest copying" is intended to mean any style in which notation of events takes precedence over displays of authorial performance. The claim that burlesque flights are only extra fun for learned readers is belied by their frequency, despite a downgrading of mere diction, "which as it is the Dress of Poetry, doth like the Dress of Men establish Characters, (the one of the whole Poem, and the other of the whole Man,) in vulgar Opinion, beyond any of their greater Excellencies."

This argument, invoking an old commonplace about not mistaking a man for his clothes, is in striking contravention of that decorum of suitable styles with which the image of language as the dress of thought was traditionally associated. The principle of matching style to subject is so deeply engraved in Renaissance and Augustan literary theory that Fielding's apparent repudiation can only signal a hidden agenda, and the tendency of his emphasis on an "exactest copying" clothed in the distorting garments of burlesque diction may perhaps be surmised from the example of Pope. In "An Essay on Criticism," Pope spoke about poets whose "glitt'ring" conceits showed them to be "unskill'd to trace / The *naked Nature* and the *living Grace*" and who "hide with Ornaments their Want of Art." The naked truth, like exactest copying, embodies values no writer would lightly disown. But the haste with which concepts of dress supervene is revealing. Pope instantly adds the famous line "*True Wit* is *Nature* to Advantage drest," and his talk of a *naked* nature is succeeded by several images of covering and clothing.

The unusual attachment in the eighteenth century to the image of the dress of thought, though overtly applied in support of the decorum of matching styles, reflected a more radical inhibition over styles that were indeed unduly naked, too submissive to bare fact or unguarded utterance, and tainted with the deeper indecorum of nakedness itself. Offending examples included Puritan sermon styles, the ideal of plain scientific discourse contained in Thomas Sprat's much cited and much satirized recommendation in 1667 of "a close, naked, natural way of speaking," and latterly the rise of the novel as described by Ian Watt. Both the pressures and the resistance to them reflect underlying values that were cultural in the widest sense, not merely "literary." Nor was the rearguard stance of Fielding or other writers of Augustan commitment clear-cut. Contrary impulses towards unadorned expression reflected the internalizing of adversarial pressures, as well as a habit of loyalty to whatever is spoken of as "naked truth."

Fielding's assertion of "exactest copying" had in any case to be hedged by signals that he was not writing a Pamelaic novel. The fuss over burlesque was secondary, partly the product of a need to distinguish his book, which contained mock-heroic features, from works of wholly parodic form, like some of his plays or the soon to be published *Jonathan Wild* (1743). The admission of burlesque of diction tells us that "exactest copying" did not really come straight and that he was using some traditional Augustan procedures to guard against it. *Joseph Andrews* contains parody of *Pamela*, as well as mock-heroic set pieces, and part of the preface's point may be to highlight the presence of a substantive nonparodic interest.

The element of anti-Pamelaic satire is sometimes underrated by readers who think they are defending the work by insisting on its nonparodic purity, a position especially anomalous at a time when parody is widely understood to be an integral element in fictional forms. *Pamela* may be formally forgotten for extended spells, but it is an active presence, especially at the beginning and end. Joseph is putatively Pamela's brother until a final *éclaircissement* in which he is revealed to have a more patrician provenance. Richardson's own heroine and her husband, as well as her parents, comically reincarnated as Gaffar and Gammar Andrews, make appearances in their own right. The fact that Joseph's surname Andrews, which is that of Pamela, is part of the novel's title and is assumed to be his real name for most of the duration, plays its part in ensuring a more or less continuous awareness of the Pamelaic presence. Many of the most important works in the Augustan tradition, including *Gulliver's Travels* and the *Dunciad*, as well as many of Fielding's own writings, are parodic in form though their central concerns transcend bookish purposes or the immediate object of mimicry. For writers in this tradition, parody was a means of self-definition, distinguishing an author from cits, dunces or canting vulgarians who wrote books about servant girls trapping their masters into marriage.

The anti-Pamelaic subtext in Fielding's novels functions not only as a disengagement from Richardsonian censoriousness and prurience, but is a focus for the articulation of an antiprudential morality whose sexual code values generosity and warmth more than a rigorous virtue. Some critics have read Joseph's chastity with a solemnity hardly justified by Fielding's witty invocation of the biblical prototype of Joseph and Potiphar's wife. Andrews's persistence in preserving his virtue against the seductions of Lady Booby and others is itself a running joke against *Pamela*, sometimes explicitly punctuated by reminders of their supposed relation. The gender reversal in which a strapping young man resists the advances of his female employer is material for comedy in a way that Pamela's situation was not, and Fielding's treatment of Joseph, affectionate and loyal in its way, is also *de haut en bas*. The Chesterfieldian idea that young gentlemen benefit from amours with worldly older women is one which Fielding would not have formulated with anything resembling that nobleman's cynical blandness. But any serious objections would have been to Chesterfield's lack of interest in the aspect of personal affection, not (as the treatment of Tom Jones makes clear) to the transgressive leeway it offered.

Joseph's role, throughout most of the novel, is that of an unemployed footman, not a gentleman. As in Tom's case, the social deficiency is corrected by last-minute information about his origins, which may suggest the importance Fielding attached to such things. (He turns out, not without piquancy, to be the son of Mr. Wilson, whose career is partly modeled on Fielding's own.) That he is *in effect* Pamela's brother for the bulk of the novel makes Fielding's presentation of him quite different from that of Tom Jones, putatively of equally low status but raised by his quasi-seigneurial erotic freedoms and his nonsubservient status in Allworthy's household. Joseph fails all gentlemanly tests, not least in his chaste rigidity, admirable in its way but really fit only for a heroine or a yokel. Heroines are all very well if they are women, but a male in a heroine's role of virtuous resistance is material for derision. Joseph is cast in Pamela's part, and the writing often insinuates reminders of his status as a proxy heroine:

> Mr. *Joseph Andrews* was now in the one and twentieth Year of his Age. He was of the highest Degree of middle Stature. His Limbs were put together with great Elegance and no less Strength. His Legs and Thighs were formed in the exactest Proportion. His Shoulders were broad and brawny, but yet his Arms hung so easily, that he had all the Symptoms of Strength without the least clumsiness. His Hair was of a nut-brown Colour, and was displayed in wanton Ringlets down his Back. His Forehead was high, his Eyes dark, and as full of Sweetness as of Fire. His Nose a little inclined to the Roman. His Teeth white and even. His Lips full, red, and soft. His Beard was only rough on his Chin and upper Lip; but his Cheeks, in which his Blood glowed, were overspread with a thick Down. His Countenance had a Tenderness joined

with a Sensibility inexpressible. Add to this the most perfect Neatness in his Dress, and an Air, which to those who have not seen many Noblemen, would give an Idea of Nobility.   (1.8)

For all the brawny shoulders, Joseph's "Hair ... in wanton Ringlets" and "Lips full, red, and soft" are a heroine's properties. Even an access of flat realism like "the highest Degree of middle Stature" correlates arrestingly with Sophia, "a middle-sized Woman; but rather inclining to tall" (*Tom Jones*, IV.2). Joseph's countenance, with its "Tenderness joined with a Sensibility inexpressible," closely resembles Fanny's in the corresponding portrait in II.12: "a Countenance in which ... a Sensibility appeared almost incredible." Tom has similar feminine qualities, indicating a kind of perfection in which male and female virtues complete each other, and seemingly more often invoked (as in Fielding's words to Jane Collier or Pope's to that "softer Man," Martha Blount) in compliments to women. The feminized variant became common in male portrayals (one would not be surprised to see it in Richardson's Sir Charles Grandison, or the heroes of some feverish fictions by lesser authors), but Joseph's case, if not Tom's, is genially undermined.

The portrait contains other comic subversions. The *sprezzatura* suggested by "his Arms hung so easily, that he had all the Symptoms of Strength without the least clumsiness," actually has something of the tailor's dummy about it, and the asserted absence of clumsiness is not readily assimilable to the blushing awkwardness of his sexual and social comportment. "An Air, which to those who have not seen many Noblemen, would give an Idea of Nobility," meaning that real noblemen are too degenerate to look like this, also hints that only inexperience of the higher ranks would make you think this amiable domestic might possibly be thought to belong to them. It is interesting that Fanny is correspondingly and less damagingly said to have "a natural Gentility, superior to the Acquisition of Art" (II.12). Perhaps she needs this since, unlike Joseph, she is not ultimately revealed to be of gentle birth, but is actually the sibling of Pamela that Joseph has throughout been thought to be.

An incest scare for a time suggests that Fanny and Joseph might be related, much as a similar scare near the end of *Tom Jones* suggests that Tom has unknowingly slept with his mother. Neither turns out to be true, and the complication of mistaken identities to which this belongs is a commonplace of comedy and romance plots from antiquity to the plays of T. S. Eliot, sometimes serving as a last-minute obstacle that heightens suspense by making the desired conclusion appear unattainable just when it had begun to seem within reach. In *Tom Jones*, the fanfare of fright may be thought of as a jokey punishment for having slept around, or alternatively as a frisson of anxiety, atoning not so much for Tom's sexual lapses as for the absence of any guilty fuss about them on the part of the narrator. Such explanations might not apply to Joseph, who does not lapse, unless we wish to entertain the speculation that he might be punished for not lapsing, in a species of implicit tease built into the plot. These are covert intimations at best, but both scenarios might be consistent with a style that refused to lose its composure, in the manner of the low Richardson, over people's private transactions.

Anti-Pamelaic parody is a continuous thread, interacting with the mock-heroic flourishes to which the preface paid attention. It is common for epic parody to be thus accompanied by, and in competition with, alternative parodic enterprises. An additional layer of parody is the Quixotic, in which "Imitation of the Manner of Cervantes" evokes mockery of heroic romances rather than epics, of which later romances were also regarded as debased derivatives. These figure in Fielding's preface, and the burlesque elements in his descriptions of heroines target them rather than epic poems. They offer a coded way of attacking heroic pretension through degenerate examples, loyalty to the great epics being an important sign of cultural affiliation, of a sort that marked one off from writers like Defoe and Richardson, who made no scruple of denigrating the ancient epics.

The Cervantic element is itself not so much parody as imitation of parody, since parody of romances was already built into *Don Quixote*. The character of Parson Adams, the clergyman who serves as the Quixote figure, is not a mockery of his Cervantic original so much as an upward reformulation, even an unparodying. Where Quixote's mind is crazed by bookish codes of honor, Adams's character is primarily one of Christian unworldliness and selflessness. Whether or not Fielding was aware of it, Adams is part of an eighteenth-century trend to turn Quixote from a crack-brained eccentric into a "sentimental" paragon whose oddities are the product of a deep unprudential goodness, a comic equivalent of the Erasmian holy fool. In this regard Adams looks forward to Sterne's Uncle Toby and a whole tradition of "amiable humorists."[4] He is Fielding's only attempt at the genre. His later counterpart Dr. Harrison, the good clergyman in *Amelia*, is not comically conceived, part of a narrowing in that novel of Fielding's conception of virtue into a serious business, and most of Fielding's virtuous exemplars lack the vitality that Adams derives from the comedy of his demonstrative kindness and his absentminded antics. Part of the satire is at the expense of a good breeding that looks down on Adams's behavior as socially contemptible, though there is a hint of patronage in Fielding's own treatment of him. If this patronage is an effect of the comedy it is also irradiated by it. Fielding is not otherwise successful in his portrayal of saintly types especially those, like the Heartfrees in *Jonathan Wild*, whose status is middling and whose manner lacks polite ease.

Mock-heroic, a favorite form, and in this period unlike any other a vehicle for writings of the highest imaginative engagement, became the best available tribute to the heroic, hedged by parodic defenses and ironic disengagement. It ostensibly attacked not the heroic but a modern reality lowered to subheroic proportions. All parody risks damaging what it touches, however, and one of the effects in *Joseph Andrews* of alternative and concurrent threads of anti-Richardsonian and Cervantic parody is to disperse the focus of derision away from any heroic evocations generated by burlesque diction. Similarly, Swift's mock-epic *Battle of the Books* is concurrently a piece of mock-scholarship and mock-journalese. Disquiet about heroic morality sometimes remains unneutralized, receiving explicit discursive expression in Pope's commentary to the *Iliad*, and surfacing in *Joseph Andrews* in "the Descriptions of the Battles." Adams rescues Fanny from assault in a scene that combines parody of chivalric romance with a slapstick species of mock-epic:

> lifting up his Crabstick, he immediately levelled a Blow at that Part of the Ravisher's Head, where, according to the Opinion of the Ancients, the Brains of some Persons are deposited, and which he had undoubtedly let forth, had not Nature ... taken a provident Care ... to make this part of the Head three times as thick as those of ordinary Men, who are designed to exercise Talents which are vulgarly called rational, and for whom, as Brains are necessary, she is obliged to leave some room for them in the Cavity of the Skull: whereas, those Ingredients being entirely useless to Persons of the heroic Calling, she hath an Opportunity of thickening the Bone, so as to make it less subject to any Impression or liable to be cracked or broken; and indeed, in some who are predestined to the Command of Armies and Empires, she is supposed sometimes to make that Part perfectly solid. (II.9)

Heroic doings and heroic stupidity are genially lowered to rural fisticuffs, but the potential rape of the heroine gives urgency to the scene, and the mimicry of heroic styles actually turns into an explicit critique of heroic qualities. Burlesque is clearly not confined to diction. The allusion to commanders of armies and empires hints at a disturbing real-life analogy with epic heroes that much Augustan writing was disposed to play down, and which is more fully developed in *Jonathan Wild*. This book is a political fable in which the eponymous hero, a real-life gangster and protection racketeer who was hanged in 1725, is made to represent the recently deposed prime minister Sir Robert Walpole. It extends the allegory of Gay's

Beggar's Opera, in which criminals and national leaders are thrust into a damaging equivalence, in a formula whose continuing vitality may be observed in several works by Brecht, including the *Threepenny Opera* (1928), the *Threepenny Novel* (1934), and the *Resistible Rise of Arturo Ui* (1941), in the latter of which the allegorized analogy is between Hitler and Al Capone. *Jonathan Wild* has an important place in this tradition, and more closely resembles Brecht's atmosphere of heavy thuggery than does Gay's opera, which was Brecht's immediate model.

It is Fielding's only sustained work of mock-heroic, in the sense that, like Pope's *Dunciad*, it is conducted as a continuous irony in which the language of heroic celebration is applied to evildoers, while the good characters are treated with mock contempt. Unlike the *Dunciad*, it is not an inverted epic fable, following the outlines of one or more ancient prototypes, but a fictionalized parody of a species of criminal biography not formally associated with heroic pretensions, another example of competing layers of parody. The mock-heroic thrust derives not from the story but from an insistent verbal irony in which the terms "heroic," "great" and "admirable" are formulaically applied to criminals and bullies, while the virtues of honesty, decency and compassion are spoken of as "low" and "foolish." The structural disengagement from epic story suggests a more abstract, thematically rather than imaginatively grounded, relation to epic. There is a compensating tendency to insist that the criminal deeds described as heroic have their ancient counterparts not in the heroes of the *Iliad* or the *Aeneid* but in real-life conquerors and tyrants, principally Alexander and Caesar, supplemented by some modern exemplars whose celebrants are ancient and modern historians rather than poets.

This emphasis is established from the first chapter, and entails a distinction between the order of life and the order of art which made it possible to argue that the real-life behavior of conquering thugs should not be confused with the great poems, whose celebration of not dissimilar behavior might be thought to be redeemed or transfigured by the poetry. As Addison said (in *Spectator*, 548 [28 November 1712]), Achilles was poetically rather than morally good. Pope and others made anguished distinctions between the times of which Homer wrote and the greatness of the poems. Fielding's determination to separate epic from history goes with an impulse not to separate them too much, sometimes introducing an epic evocation and then, as if by afterthought, switching pointedly to a historical one. Wild's henchman Fireblood is described as "the *Achates* of our *Aeneas*," a Virgilian quip immediately canceled by "or rather the *Hephaestion* of our *Alexander*" (III.4). The cancellation of epic allusion does not neutralize it, since once read it cannot be unread. The corrective is factitious, and the analogy with Alexander, whom the work persistently presents as a historical hoodlum, adds an emphasis of disrepute. What comes through is something of that likeness between epic heroes and conquering thugs, and of both to gangsters, which Auden and Isherwood were to make commonplace, but which some of Fielding's contemporaries and elders took pains to deny or disguise. He tells us that Wild "was a passionate Admirer of Heroes, particularly *Alexander* the Great," but only after making clear that, as a schoolboy,

> He was wonderfully pleased with that Passage in the Eleventh *Iliad*, where *Achilles* is said to have bound two Sons of Priam upon a Mountain, and afterwards released them for a Sum of Money. This was, he said, alone sufficient to refute those who affected a Contempt for the Wisdom of the Ancients, and an undeniable Testimony to the great Antiquity of *Priggism* [i.e. thievery] (1.3)

It is a skewed view of Homeric values, not presented as Fielding's own. But the episode is Homeric, and its collocation with Alexander, and Wild's admiration for both, do not predispose the reader to discount disreputable perspectives.

Jonathan Wild reflects a growing reluctance to see the modern decline from heroic grandeurs as self-evidently deplorable. Classical nostalgia remains, but something closer to Eliot's sense in *The Waste Land* that contrasts between a noble past and a lowered present also conceal continuities of depravity is beginning to take shape. At the same time, the idea of Wild as a grimly diabolical figure, which prevails with many readers, needs revision. While the rhetoric suggests titanic viciousness, the story presents a record of almost unremitting unsuccess, in crime and in love. Vast energies of bullying and fraud are expended on small pickings, of which Wild is usually robbed by a lover anyway, the despotic lecher tricked and deceived by every woman in his life. A set piece of heroic lamentation, which begins with the words, "How vain is human GREATNESS! What avail superiour Abilities, and a noble Defiance of those narrow Rules and Bounds which confine the Vulgar," revolves around the fact that he is so trapped in the compulsive need to have his hands in others' pockets that he cannot ensure the safety of his own (11.4).[5] At his final scene of greatness, drunkenly brazen on the scaffold and pelted by the crowd, his compulsiveness, more comic in a Bergsonian way than implacable in a Hobbesian, takes over one last time – as he steals the corkscrew that the parson carries, in Joycean fashion, in lieu of a crucifix:

> But tho' Envy was, through Fear, obliged to join the general Voice in Applause on this Occasion, there were not wanting some who maligned this Completion

of Glory, which was now about to be fulfilled to our Hero, and endeavoured to prevent it by knocking him on the Head as he stood under the Tree, while the Ordinary was performing his last Office. They therefore began to batter the Cart with Stones, Brickbats, Dirt, and all Manner of mischievous Weapons, some of which erroneously playing on the Robes of the Ecclesiastic, made him so expeditious in his Repetition, that with wonderful Alacrity he had ended almost in an Instant, and conveyed himself into a Place of Safety in a Hackney Coach ... We must not however omit one Circumstance, as it serves to shew the most admirable Conservation of Character in our Hero to his last Moment, which was, that whilst the Ordinary was busy in his Ejaculations, *Wild*, in the Midst of the Shower of Stones, &c. which played upon him, applied his Hands to the Parson's Pocket, and emptied it of its Bottle-Screw, which he carried out of the World in his Hand.   (IV.15)

The ostensible intention to make of Wild a monster of iniquity works as erratically as Pope's when he made Cibber the hero of the *Dunciad*, allowing a feeling for his busy geniality to attenuate the sense of engulfing menace. Wild's theft of the corkscrew is a victory of the little man, helpless and slightly absurd, asserting his shabby selfhood just when society has crushed him and death is about to snuff him out. In the least "novelistic" of Fielding's novels, and despite the sharp questioning of heroic values, it is this figure, not the titanic antihero or public enemy proudly identified with the worst epic thuggeries, who comes through, an arresting index of the early encroachment of novelistic perspectives in an unlikely place.

Of all Fielding's novels, *Jonathan Wild* is the only one not conspicuously in Richardson's shadow. Though published later, it may have been drafted earlier than *Joseph Andrews*, and parts of it perhaps were written before he had read *Pamela*. With *Tom Jones*, the Richardsonian presence is reasserted, though the relationship is less overt and the targeting less specific than in *Shamela* or *Joseph Andrews*. His writing had gained authority and his voice was more relaxed. By the time the novel was published, he had declared his admiration for *Clarissa*. *Tom Jones* nevertheless represents a reversal of the typical Richardsonian plot, in the sense that the seducers tend to be female, not male, that the male profligate is a virtuous soul, that the objects of his sexual attentions are hardly paragons of defenceless chastity, that the sexual transactions between them are persistently reported through a signposted withholding of the lubricious particularities it had become customary to impute to Richardson, and that the novel's strongly stated ethic of the good heart is antiprudential.

Prudence, the supreme virtue of Richardson's moral universe, dwindles in *Tom Jones* to a secondary thing, "a Guard to Virtue" (III.7) rather than the thing itself, that self-protective attention to one's own interest, which "is indeed the Duty which we owe to ourselves" (XVIII.10) but which ardent, affectionate and trusting natures tend by definition to lack. The wise presiding figure of Allworthy regrets the troubles that Tom's imprudence had caused, but it is not lost on us that this judicial character is hardly a model of prudence himself. His trustingness makes him vulnerable to villains like Blifil as well as imperceptient about Tom's character in ways which precisely indicate where the balance of the novel's moral sympathies leans: "thus is the Prudence of the best of Heads often defeated by the Tenderness of the best of Hearts" (XVI.6).

Even so, the dignified and magisterial role in which Allworthy is cast seems to have made Fielding uneasy. He is perhaps Fielding's closest approximation to that Richardsonian ideal of the good man that was to be elaborated in the character of Sir Charles Grandison, and it is almost as though the presentation had been affected by an anxiety of proleptic association. Not only is Allworthy's championship of circumspection hedged by signs of a generosity that lacks it, but there is an attempt to shore the portrait up with somewhat improbable assertions of an ardent nature that no part of the narrative actually reveals. Though older than Sir Charles, and not cast in the latter's role as a romantic lead, Allworthy had, we are somewhat gratuitously told, "possessed much Fire in his Youth." The reminder seems designed to ensure that his accesses of judiciousness are not mistaken for an unfeeling nature: "Allworthy was naturally a Man of Spirit, and his present Gravity arose from true Wisdom and Philosophy, not from any original Phlegm in his Disposition: For he had possessed much Fire in his Youth, and had married a beautiful Woman for Love" (VI.4).

These adjudications provide an instructive context for his admonitions about Tom's imprudence, and when at the end of the novel, we learn that Tom had "acquired a Discretion and Prudence very uncommon in one of his lively Parts" (XVIII.13), the news is not of a radical and long-awaited moral reformation but of a convenient tidying up. He has grown up, married his sweetheart, and will no longer get into scrapes. The change has sometimes been invested by critics with a moral and even a theological gravity inappropriate to the case, and it seems preferable to insist on the more low-key satisfactions, which derive from the assurance in romance and comic plots that the good characters may be expected to live happily ever after. There is nothing here of the paean to a block-capitaled "amiable PRUDENTIA" that clatters with noisy sanctimoniousness at the end of part 2 of *Pamela*.

It thus seems necessary to insist that the unchastities of Tom, while they are considered culpable in their way and would be inadmissible in the context of a fulfilled and married love for Sophia, have their own status as indices of generous and affectionate feelings, equally distinct from a cold chastity and the unloving appetites of coarse sensualists. This is a matter to which Fielding devoted several "doctrinal" pronouncements in his introductory chapters, including the chapter "Of Love" (VI.I). And the opening chapter of book 14, whose ostensible subject is the usefulness to an author of "having some Knowledge of the Subject on which he writes." This includes a glance at authors who like to write about the "upper Life" without a proper knowledge of it, a point regularly made about Richardson though he is not an explicit target in this context. Fielding goes on to say it is not a subject for his own comic work, as well as being "much the dullest" among the social strata, though the subtext conveys (as Irvin Ehrenpreis has perceptively written) that he is himself writing as an insider, well qualified to know.[6] The chapter concludes with a bravura piece of irony, in which his knowledge of high life is invoked to contradict those who have declaimed against its profligacy:

> There is not indeed a greater Error than that which universally prevails among the Vulgar, who borrowing their Opinion from some ignorant Satyrists, have affixed the Character of Lewdness to these Times. On the contrary, I am convinced there never was less of Love Intrigue carried on among Persons of Condition, than now. Our present Women have been taught by their Mothers to fix their Thoughts only on Ambition and Vanity, and to despise the Pleasures of Love as unworthy their Regard; and being afterwards, by the Care of such Mothers, married without having Husbands, they seem pretty well confirmed in the Justness of those Sentiments; whence they content themselves, for the dull Remainder of Life, with the Pursuit of more innocent, but I am afraid more childish Amusements, the bare Mention of which would ill suit with the Dignity of this History. In my humble Opinion, the true Characteristick of the present *Beau Monde*, is rather Folly than Vice, and the only Epithet which it deserves is that of *Frivolous*.   (XIV.I)

The range of this stinging irony extends far beyond Richardson. It expresses an ethos that could hardly be more unlike Richardson's, but is not especially preoccupied with him. Much of its discursive substance is concerned with playwrights, a group to which Fielding himself belonged and Richardson did not. Paradoxically, Richardson's novels tended to the "dramatic" in the sense that they are conducted in the language of the participants, ostensibly without authorial mediation, and notably without the sort of extended discursive interlude represented by Fielding's introductory chapters. It has more than once been suggested that Fielding's own playwriting suffered from the fact that the dramatic mode of the time restricted opportunities for authorial intervention, and that his adoption of prose fiction after some two-dozen plays provided an outlet for a mode of expression more congenial to his disposition and talents. Fielding as playwright and novelist is thus less "dramatic" than Richardson the novelist who wrote no plays, though, to apply a distinction that has acquired some currency, he may be thought more "theatrical."

Fielding's plays belong to highly stylized genres: polite comedy of manners with witty repartee; quick-time farce (whose traces survive in *Tom Jones* as well as *Shamela*); and the rehearsal-play, of which Fielding wrote several examples, typically containing a play-within-a-play, with an author-within-the-play or similar presiding figure who discusses or manages the production. Such authorial figures have been seen as simplified prototypes of the ostentatiously paraded narrators of the novels, who comment on the story and its writing. The theatrical elements that Fielding transferred into his novels were those which stressed the artifice of the stage, not its illusion of unmediated reality, the patterned and witty ordering of events rather than their unprocessed flow.

The novels use a wide repertoire of stage routines: coincidences, contrived meetings, comic misunderstandings, conversations overheard at cross-purposes. They show a keen sense of the well-shaped, tightly-ordered plot, remarkable in a work of such length and panoramic coverage as *Tom Jones*, and many local signs of theatrical organization: chapters and episodes framed as set pieces, analogous in shape and length to a scene in a play; comic reversals and resolutions; an ear for dialogue of a stylized and typifying kind, designed to bring out the cant of social groups or the character-revealing accents of vicious or foolish types.

The dramatic is not the only source of stylization. Many of Fielding's chapter headings signpost themselves as typifying set pieces, "Containing several Dialogues" (VII.3), or "Containing Scenes of Altercation, of no very uncommon Kind" (VII.8), the latter dramatizing a ballet of snobbish pique between two female servants, Mrs. Honour and Mrs. Western's maid: "'Hoity! toity!' cries *Honour*, 'Madam is in her Airs, I protest ...' The other Lady put on one of her most malicious Sneers, and said, 'Creature! you are below my Anger; and it is beneath me to give ill Words to such an audacious saucy Trollop ...'" The debate dramatizes a favorite irony about pride of caste among those one might have supposed too low for such pretensions: "Mrs. *Western*'s Maid claimed great Superiority over Mrs. *Honour*, on several Accounts. First, her Birth was higher: For her great Grand-mother by the Mother's Side was a Cousin, not far removed, to an *Irish* Peer. Secondly, her Wages were greater. And lastly, she had been at *London*." The capturing of pedantic zeal is masterly, and the ridicule once again thrives on the author's own sense of real caste as he looks down on pretenders and mimics.

Both the chapter and the individual dialogue condition us to think of the episode as self-contained. The expressions of social contempt are simultaneously made to function as a conversation within the narrative and as a satirical anthology of usage, an abbreviated version of Swift's *Complete Collection of Genteel and Ingenious Conversation* (1738). Swift's is a large-scale, seemingly "exhaustive" compilation, in a satiric mode that was to find its fullest expression in Flaubert's *Bouvard and Pecuchet* and his uncompleted *Dictionary of Received Ideas*. The suggestion is that the follies enumerated, like the human stupidity from which they emanate, are inexhaustible and their lists self-multiplying. Where Swift pretends to a deadpan listing of all vacuous society usages, Fielding's effect is of knowing selectiveness. His satirical "Modern Glossary" has the form of a dictionary without its pretense of completeness, as his dialogues in the novels approximate to the form of anthologized specimens, not of the catalogue. Terms like "Creature" and "some People" in *Tom Jones*, or the "Dissertation concerning high People and low People" (*Joseph Andrews*, II.13), seem to belong to mini-anthologies and look forward to the codifications of the "Modern Glossary" (CREATURE. A Quality Expression of low Contempt"). Chapter headings are acts of defining, judging or arranging; and in the text itself are phrases that in turn mimic the titles (like the "smart Dialogue between some People, and some Folks" in *Joseph Andrews*, II.5) and perform some of the same functions, externalizing as well as interventionist, from within.

The sense of standing outside the action rather than surrendering to its flow, as Richardson's novels and Swift's catalogues pretend to do in their several ways, is distinctively Fielding's. It is paradoxically internalized into the natural fabric of the writing. Fielding imported into his novelistic voice something of the judgmental command of the semiauthorial spokesmen of Augustan satire. But it was only in his novels (in a genre they would not write) that he captured the confident and witty authority which was a feature of their satire.

This authority traditionally sanctioned definitional exactitudes and satirical severities. A sentence describing the contrary ideas of mercy held by Thwackum and Square – "The two Gentlemen did indeed somewhat differ in Opinion concerning the Objects of this sublime Virtue; by which *Thwackum* would probably have destroyed one half of Mankind, and *Square* the other half" (III.10) – belongs to an established satirical rhetoric about adversarial groups sharing the same murderous proclivities, large-scale and often reciprocal, practiced by Swift before Fielding and by Gibbon after him. Swift's *Sentiments of a Church-of-England Man* contains an attack on opposed fanatics at the violent ends of Whig and Tory faction, in which the Tories would have us "rise as one Man, and destroy such Wretches from the Face of the Earth," while their opponents would "erect Gibbets in every Parish, and hang [the whole Body of the *Tories*] out of the Way."

Fielding might have been remembering this passage, but its mood is very unlike. "And this is *Moderation*," Swift concludes, "in the *modern* Sense of the Word; to which, speaking impartially, the Bigots of both Parties are *equally* entitul'd." A subtextual sting is that they are also "*equally* entitul'd" to the treatment each intends for the other, a feeling never far from the surface in Swift. Swift half participates in the aggression he rejects, and is not above extending it to the rest of us. Fielding's Thwackum and Square are nasty, but cannot be taken as unbalancing threats. They are comic grotesques playing a minority role on a large human canvas, sanctioned nuisances whose measure is confidently taken. Their fetid absurdity can be held at arm's length, a line clearly drawn around them, where Swift's fanatics by contrast have an energetic political potential, a fervid busyness all too ready to spill over into the wider fabric of human life: Swift's well-known concern with the contagion of fanaticism mirrors the contagious energies of his ironic aggression, and the definitional clarities and protective demarcations of Fielding's manner belong to a different satiric register.

This register is closer than Swift's to the mainstream of English Augustanism, and to the rhetoric of urbane authority and confidently managed complicity with a notional reader's wisdom and "politeness," which we associate with Pope or Gibbon rather than with Swift. Gibbon has occasion to portray large-scale cruelties in graphic detail, and is perhaps the only author among them who does not actively avoid such occasions. His pleasure in exposing sectarian or genocidal atrocities by Christians as greater than any persecutions against them reflects an Enlightenment disdain for Christianity that the others would have found distasteful. But his most horrific accounts release a species of confidence, a sense that whole sections of humanity exist outside the scope of damaging exposure: wise and cultivated pagans, the congenial reader, and the entire type of "polite" or "enlightened" gentleman for whom that reader conveniently stands. Fielding would not have shared the assumption of an identity between politeness and Enlightenment (with the latter term's secular and antireligious assumptions about human progress), but the moral, social, and stylistic configuration of his relations with *his* reader was very much like that of Gibbon, who was one of Fielding's most eloquent admirers.

On 15 October 1748, a month before the first two volumes of *Tom Jones* were printed and five months before the whole was published in February 1749, Fielding wrote to Richardson about the fifth volume of *Clarissa*, in which the rape of the heroine finally occurs, a strange letter in which uncharacteristically emotional outbursts of praise are mixed with protestations of not intending to flatter, recognizing their mutual rivalry, being innocent of "that Monster Envy," and feeling secure in his relations with "that coy Mrs. Fame" for whose favors they are both rivals. The latter point is made with the clammy insistence of an off-color joke: "as to this Mrs. I have ravished her long ago, and live in a settled cohabitation with her in defiance of that Public Voice which is supposed to be her Guardian." Equally uncharacteristic, in the context of their known feelings for each other, is the letter's ending "yrs most Affectionately," marking what Martin Battestin and Clive T. Probyn, the editors of Fielding's correspondence, speak of as a temporary "turn for the better" in their relations[7] Even more uncharacteristic are the Richardsonian accents, sometimes echoing *Clarissa* itself, in which the novel is praised:

> Shall I tell you? Can I tell you what I think of the latter part of your Volume? Let the Overflowings of a Heart which you have filled brimfull speak for me ... I am shocked; my Terrors are raised, and I have the utmost Apprehensions for the poor betrayed Creature. But when I see her enter with the Letter in her Hand, and ... clasping her Arms about the Knees of the Villain, call him her Dear Lovelace, desirous and yet unable to implore his Protection or rather his mercy; I then melt into Compassion, and find what is called an Effeminate Relief for my Terror ... When I read the next Letter I am Thunderstruck.

Fielding was not alone among mature men of letters to respond to *Clarissa* in emotional terms, and the received rhetoric, in both fiction and criticism, for expressing such sentiments would nowadays seem theatrical. Even so, the letter is well outside Fielding's normal range. It survives only in copies transcribed for Richardson, and one might be tempted to suspect it was a Richardsonian fabrication if Fielding's published review of the first two volumes in the *Jacobite's Journal* hadn't praised the novel in terms consistent with its substance if not its fevered style. The hyperbolic raptures, like the archness about Fielding's motives, seem to reflect his uneasy relations with Richardson rather than the nuances of his response to the book.

There is no doubt that *Clarissa* had a powerful impact on Fielding, complicated or heightened by elements of recoil and resistance and by an impulse to overcome these. His writings after *Tom Jones* no longer display the accents of buoyant assurance that had hitherto been a kind of signature. He did not, outside the letter, show much sign of wanting to write *like* Richardson, and his later works reassume the gestures of anti-Richardsonian-point-scoring that began with *Shamela* and continued to the end of his life. *Clarissa* seems to have stirred in Fielding a recognition of the value of an emotional particularity unhedged by ironic guards, and the letter represents a first stunned realization of the possibilities. It is not surprising that it seems strained, or that he did not sustain the unguardedness. But the fact that he attempted it at all, and in doing so went, by his own normal standards, over the top, suggests a significant shock of readjustment.

Clarissa was not the only sobering influence. Fielding's experience as a magistrate, and his declining health, placed him in intimate contact with the miseries of individual lives, and may have contributed to a sense that his old style of witty containment and his predilection for comic plots were no longer appropriate to his experience of reality. Apart from *Amelia*, the extended writings of his last years were sociolegal tracts, legal case histories, and a travel memoir, genres more conducive to sober reportage than to stylistic high spirits.

Amelia is the only one of the three strictly novelistic works whose several books are not prefixed by essays defining the author's role and his fictional enterprise. The opening chapter of book 1 entitled "Containing the Exordium, &c.," is a meditation on the conduct of life and the causes of misfortune, not a disquisition on a new species of writing or a display of the narrator's authority and wit. The titles retain something of the old gesturing, for example "Panegyrics on Beauty, with other grave matters" (VI.1), but the narrative switches at once to a plain circumstantiality in sharp contrast with it: "The Colonel and *Booth* walked together to the latter's Lodging." This writing sometimes takes in things Fielding had derided in *Shamela*, the frequent tea drinking, the cold chicken and "two Pound of cold Beef" and "hashed Mutton" that get eaten or not eaten (VIII.9; X.5), often with accretions of pathos.

The content of the titles is sometimes nil ("Being the first Chapter of the eighth Book," or "To which we will prefix no Preface" [X.1]), the shadow of old habits surviving as a nervous tic. The manner, even in its buoyant prime, was already a continual social ploy, which is to say a nervous tic on a cultural scale. It is integral to *Amelia*, an enabling condition for the release of unencumbered factuality, as well as a sign of embarrassment. The opening of the narrative suggests that gestures a reader might think empty were also studied ones:

> On the first of *April*, in the Year –, the Watchmen of a certain Parish (I know not particularly which) within the Liberty of *Westminster*, brought several Persons whom they had apprehended the preceding Night, before *Jonathan Thrasher*, Esq; one of the Justices of the Peace for that Liberty. (1.2)

The sharp factual economy and the focus on circumstantial essentials are especially remarkable in combination with the mannered withholding of both date and place. Novels often have undated or vaguely dated plots, set in unnamed or pseudonymously disguised cities, like Hardy's Casterbridge or Graham Greene's Nottwich. The idea may be to discourage applications to known persons or events; or to protect verisimilitude or "illusion" among readers whose local knowledge might find the description wanting, or whose lack of such knowledge might induce a discomfort of nonrecognition. Timeless or delocalized settings may also suggest a universalized generality such as Fielding called for in *Joseph Andrews*, III.1. None of these purposes seems active here. The atmosphere of these chapters is hardly concerned to disguise contemporaneity or specific applications, and the reference to the "Liberty of Westminster" seems designed to point the finger. If legal or other constraints required the omission of the parish, they neither precluded an invented alternative nor called for a pretence of being unable to remember. Nor, as many novelists have pointed out, is verisimilitude served by express reminders of the author's existence or the limits of his memory. "Generality" does not depend on withholding locations but on bringing out their typicality.

The passage looks back to the mannerisms of an earlier nonnovelistic rhetoric of Augustan men of letters. Like Pope's (in *The Rape of the Lock*) "This Phoebus promis'd (I forget the year) ...," Fielding's forgetting has a quite different force from that of Moll Flanders reporting that "we lodg'd at an Inn ... not far from the Cathedral, I forget what Sign it was at," a character's natural conversational slippage under the stress of more pressing preoccupations.[8] Ford Madox Ford saw the opening of *Amelia* as an example of a habit of English writers to be more concerned to project their gentility than to take pride in their craft. Fielding, he says, was trying to show that he was "too much of a great gentleman to bother about details."[9] Ford had a point, though Fielding had no pressing personal need to display class credentials, and it is arguable that social insecurity and ostentatious class consciousness are more awkwardly in evidence in the novels of Richardson, whom Ford regards as a superior model of authorial self-effacement. A received rhetoric of tones proper for a polite author to project certainly existed, and its accentuated presence in *Amelia* is striking in the context of the novel's perceived shift to a Richardsonian manner. When the narrator in *Joseph Andrews* says "*Plato* or *Aristotle*, or some body else hath said" (II.15), there is a display of mock-modesty ("I would quote more great Men if I could") reminiscent of Swift's Drapier. *Amelia*'s narrator makes no coy admission of deficiencies. In the same chapter of *Joseph Andrews*, Fielding reports the fact of a "delightful Conversation" between Joseph and Fanny, "but as I never could prevail on either to relate it, so I cannot communicate it to the Reader." The narrator's appeal to his own ignorance is replaced in *Tom Jones* and *Amelia* by a forthright indication that such matters are none of the reader's business and that nobody with a knowledge of the world would need or want to have them spelt out.

Amelia in such places shows a similar stylistic evolution to that witnessed in the passage about the very pretty girl shouting obscenities. The new particularity is allowed its head, but the guard dropped in the letter to Richardson is here reaffirmed, with a stiffened emphasis. The manner passes beyond, or outside, the sociological explanatoriness of the *Enquiry* and returns to a mode self-consciously preoccupied with displaying the narrator. The shocking unpredictability in the episode of the girl, or the sequence of Newgate vignettes as a whole, are stark counterparts of the uppish flippancy of not remembering the parish. The response to social horrors has gone beyond the scope of intelligible causality, but what is registered is not simple incomprehensibility but a sharply captured inversion of order, a negative pattern as stylized as Ionesco but simultaneously stamped with Augustan accents of authorial control. This arresting coexistence is a special and powerful feature of *Amelia*, and suggests that had Fielding lived longer, he might have opened up the range of English fiction even more than he did. Parts of this novel are informed by a sense of pained disconnection not found again until Dickens's grimmest portrayals of London life. It was not sustained and gives way in some later portions to a weary sentimentality, and a quarrelsomeness that resurfaces in his last book of all, *A Journal of a Voyage to Lisbon*. The stresses that activated these extraordinary creative defenses were equally likely to generate an embarrassed defensiveness and an unusual awkwardness in Fielding's handling of the reader, far removed from the assured genial bossiness of *Tom Jones*. Fits of mock-ingratiation hover uneasily between embarrassed jokeyness and angry sarcasm. A "Scene of a tender Kind" between Booth and Amelia, related by Booth to his mistress Miss Mathews, shows Fielding in a sub-Richardsonian mode, reminiscent of novelettish imitators, with hyperbolic exclamation, tears, a fainting heroine, a talismanic small object for the hero to keep, and an emotional tableau whose language has a recognizable relation to that of Fielding's letter about *Clarissa*:

> "I caught her in my Arms with Raptures not to be exprest in Words, called her my Heroine; sure none ever better deserved that Name; after which we remained for sometime speechless, and lock'd in each other's Embraces." – "I am convinced," said Miss *Mathews*, with a Sigh, "there are Moments in Life worth purchasing with Worlds." (III.2)[10]

It is not an idiom in which Fielding felt at home, and the unctuous comment by Miss Mathews at the end might almost have been planted to signal his sense of the falsity of his own writing. The chapter is punctuated by Miss Mathews's ingratiating expressions of complicity with Amelia's feelings and closes with a reminder by Booth of the role played by sentimental epicurism in the entire piece: " 'This I am convinced of, that no one is capable of tasting such a Scene, who hath not a Heart full of Tenderness, and perhaps not even then, unless he hath been in the same Situation.' " It is Miss Mathews who is best described as "tasting such a Scene," and one may wonder how conscious Fielding was that in appealing to his readers' connoisseurship in such things he was placing them on the same level with her.

Fielding spoke of *Amelia* as his favorite work. He was defending the novel against a barrage of critical hostility, so the judgment may have a tactical dimension. But it was spoken feelingly, and perhaps his developing attachment to a new manner blunted his sense of the quality of execution and of his self-division over his stylistic choices. He goes on to claim that in writing the book he had followed "the Rules of all those who ... have writ best on the Subject," that "neither Homer nor Virgil pursued them with greater Care," and that "the candid and learned Reader" would recognize that Virgil's *Aeneid* was the "noble model, which I made use of on this Occasion." He added that he would "trouble the World no more with any Children of mine by the same Muse."

Whether he would have abided by the latter resolution we shall never know, but the remark reflects the considerable emotional significance with which this novel, and its critical reception, had been invested. The invocation of the *Aeneid* as a model is a retrospective reversal of several elements in the epic analogy in the preface to *Joseph Andrews*. What that preface described as entertainment for "the Classical Reader" are no longer flourishes of diction but a structural principle. "The candid and learned Reader" of *Amelia* is to recognize Virgil's poem as the "noble model" of the whole book. The relation is one of parallel rather than parody, discreetly insinuated rather than bumptiously signposted. The play of epic reminder, from the twelve-book arrangement to the recognition of Booth's amour with Miss Mathews in prison as a scabrous reenactment of the episode of Dido and Aeneas in the cave, is understated, anticipating Joyce's *Ulysses* more than it recalls Fielding's own earlier practice. It is no longer a matter of low subjects in high language or vice versa: there is instead a leveling of both to an underisive reportage of ordinary life. One is reminded of Joyce's sense of Homer's *Odyssey* not as a heroic exemplar against which to measure the ordinary, but as itself a complete embodiment of nonheroic humanity, so that its modern rewriting is not a drop but an extension, with variations, in modern dress. "Noble models" no longer provide exemplary grandeur, only a cachet of universality.

A noble model is a noble model, however. The self-division over epic seems to have become for Fielding a personal, not merely a cultural, issue, and it was expressly bound up with the incomplete surrender to Richardsonian fiction that began with Fielding's response to *Clarissa* and continued with progressive escalations until the announcement, in the preface to the posthumously published *Voyage to Lisbon*, that "I should have honoured and loved Homer more had he written a true history of his own times in humble prose, than those noble poems that have so justly collected the praise of all ages." This is a long way from the scorn of the humble prose of novels that is blisteringly evident in *Shamela*, and the "noble poems" seem to have dropped some notches below the estimation of the Virgilian "noble model" expressed at the time of *Amelia*. Even in this last preface, the furthest Fielding went in repudiation of the epic, old loyalties are audible, and there is a restatement of the old resistance to reporting any "merely common incident ... for its own sake." The preface closes with a final swipe at the author of *Clarissa* as a canting vulgarian, a still recognizable avatar of the early hostile portrayals, whose project "of reforming a whole people" is effected "by making use of a vehicular story, to wheel in among them worse manners than their own." Since prefaces, though we read them first, are usually written last, these are probably the last words Fielding wrote for publication.

NOTES

1 All references to *Joseph Andrews*, *Tom Jones*, and *Amelia* are to *The Wesleyan Edition of the Works of Henry Fielding*, ed. William B. Coley, Martin Battestin, *et al.* (10 vols. to date; Oxford: Clarendon, 1967–).

2 *An Enquiry into the Causes of the Late Increase of Robbers and Related Writings*, ed. Malvin R. Zirker (Oxford: Clarendon, 1988).

3 For fuller discussion and references, see Claude Rawson, *Satire and Sentiment 1660–1830* (Cambridge: Cambridge University Press, 1994), 136ff.

4 See Stuart M. Tave, *The Amiable Humorist: a Study in the Comic Theory and Criticism of the Eighteenth and Early Nineteenth Centuries* (Chicago: University of Chicago Press, 1960), 155, 140–63.

5 *Jonathan Wild* (London: Oxford University Press, 1932).

6 Irvin Ehrenpreis, *Fielding: Tom Jones* (London: Edward Arnold, 1964), 15; reprinted in *Henry Fielding: a Critical Anthology*, ed. Claude Rawson (Harmondsworth: Penguin, 1973), 537.

7 *The Correspondence of Henry and Sarah Fielding*, ed. Martin C. Battestin and Clive T. Probyn (Oxford: Clarendon, 1993), 73.

8 Daniel Defoe, *Moll Flanders*, ed. G. A. Starr (London and Oxford: Oxford University Press, 1971), 144.

9 Ford Madox Ford, *The March of Literature* (New York: Dial, 1938), 585.

10 *Journal of a Voyage to Lisbon*, ed. Harold E. Pagliaro (New York: Nardon Press, 1963).

READING LIST

Alter, Robert. *Fielding and the Nature of the Novel*. Cambridge, Mass.: Harvard University Press, 1968.
Battestin, Martin. *The Moral Basis of Fielding's Art: a Study of Joseph Andrews*. Middletown, Conn.: Wesleyan University Press, 1959.
  Henry Fielding: a Life. London: Routledge, 1989.
Braudy, Leo. *Narrative Form in History and Fiction*. Princeton: Princeton University Press, 1970.
Campbell, Jill. *Natural Masques: Gender and Identity in Fielding's Plays and Novels*. Stanford, Calif.: Stanford University Press, 1995.
Cross, Wilbur L. *The History of Henry Fielding*. 3 vols. New Haven: Yale University Press, 1918.
Ehrenpreis, Irvin. *Fielding: Tom Jones*. London: Edward Arnold, 1964.
Hatfield, Glenn W. *Henry Fielding and the Language of Irony*. Chicago: University of Chicago Press, 1968.
Hunter, J. Paul. *Occasional Form: Henry Fielding and the Chains of Circumstance*. Baltimore: Johns Hopkins University Press, 1975.
McKeon, Michael. *The Origins of the English Novel, 1600–1740*. Baltimore: Johns Hopkinss University Press, 1987.
Paulson, Ronald. *Satire and the Novel in Eighteenth-Century England*. New Haven: Yale University Press, 1967.
  (ed.) *Fielding: a Collection of Critical Essays*. Englewood Cliffs, N.J.: Prentice-Hall, 1962.
Preston, John. *The Created Self: the Reader's Role in Eighteenth-Century Fiction*. London: Heinemann, 1970.
Price, Martin. *To the Palace of Wisdom: Studies in Order and Energy from Dryden to Blake*. Garden City, N.Y.: Doubleday, 1964.
Rawson, Claude (ed.) *Henry Fielding: a Critical Anthology*. Harmondsworth: Penguin, 1973.
  Henry Fielding and the Augustan Ideal Under Stress. London: Routledge, 1972.
  Order from Confusion Sprung: Studies in Eighteenth-Century Literature from Swift to Cowper. London: Allen and Unwin, 1985.
Rogers, Pat. *Henry Fielding: a Biography*. London: Elek, 1979.
Smallwood, Angela J. *Fielding and the Woman Question: the Novels of Henry Fielding and Feminist Debate, 1700–1750*. Hemel Hempstead: Harvester Wheatsheaf, 1989.
Watt, Ian. *The Rise of the Novel: Studies in Defoe, Richardson and Fielding*. 1957; Berkeley: University of California Press, 1964.
Welsh, Andrew. *Strong Representations: Narrative and Circumstantial Evidence in England*. Baltimore: Johns Hopkins University Press, 1992.

7

JONATHAN LAMB

Sterne and irregular oratory

Laurence Sterne has always been considered the least rule-bound of the British eighteenth-century novelists, and his *Tristram Shandy* is generally cited as the most eccentric production within the already varied collection of narrative types of eighteenth-century fiction. The common method of assimilating his work to the new province of novel writing is to assume that the digressions, apostrophes, typographical outrages and zany time scheme that make it so unaccountable are the result of a thoroughgoing parody of the conventions of realism established during the previous decade by Richardson and Fielding. Accordingly, when Sterne is not sporting with the immediacy encouraged by the epistolary novel by intimately addressing the reader, accumulating heaps of pointless minutiae, or confounding real time with narrative time, he is taking Fielding's modified neoclassicism to absurd conclusions by invoking the principle of selectivity to justify his missing chapters, or using that principle to authorize wild appeals to the reader about what to include and what to leave out, and by wickedly clever misapplications of the rule of *ut pictura poesis* (a poem should be like a speaking picture) in the shape of marbled and blackened pages, and waving lines intended to represent the flourish of a stick or the digressions of his story.[1]

That this sort of parody might not be construed as irresponsible trifling (as F. R. Leavis called it), critics such as Sigurd Burckhardt and John Traugott have assumed that Sterne is clearing away the debris of verisimilitude in order to celebrate the sudden and natural communion one soul shares with another when the mediation of art is sidestepped – such sympathy being Tristram Shandy's sole plot as a narrator who is determined to treat his readers as friends with whom he expects to "so manage it, as to convey but the same impressions to every other brain, which the occurrences themselves excite in my own."[2]

This recuperation of Sterne's more spectacular irregularities as means to spontaneous communication between narrator and reader reflects his own taste for reprocessing texts (such as his favorite source of arcana, Burton's *Anatomy of Melancholy*) as well as his opinions concerning the detestable effects of imposture and the value of an open heart; but at a price. For one thing, such stabilizing of Sterne's text depends on an improbable estimate of the dominance of the novel's realism, as if it were well enough established by the 1750s for its parody readily to be undertaken and appreciated: for another, this approach demands a rather naive view of Sterne's naturalism and of his valorization of sensibility, as if the appearance of spontaneity itself were not always mediated by art. Virginia Woolf, one of the first to read Sterne's fiction as a critique of realism, uses it to illustrate an argument about modernism and its relation to the last great realist novelists such as Bennett and Galsworthy.[3] These arguments in favor of Sterne as sentimental protomodernist largely ignore questions of the motives for composition and the reception of his fiction in the eighteenth century.

In this chapter I want to consider *Tristram Shandy* (and to a lesser extent *A Sentimental Journey*) as fictions embedded in a definite cultural milieu, responsive to determinate and particular moments of political and social pressure, and ambitious to exert real power over their readers. This involves taking seriously what Sterne himself said about his first novel, namely that it was a satire, and as such alive to the current practices of churchmen, lawyers, politicians, medical experts, and soldiers, as well as writers. If we take Sterne's work seriously as social and cultural critique, it is possible to discover how his radical modification of his satiric enterprise, and his improvement of its side effects into a success of a different kind, involves his engagement with the public sphere on terms that emphasize not the satirist's monitory guardianship of society's rules and norms, but the importance of an individual's eloquence in determining the power relations that govern both the private "world" of Shandy Hall and the world at large. Furthermore, I hope to show that Sterne's eloquence (which is both the subject of his novels and their governing style of presentation) requires from the reader a reconceptualizing of narrative so that it is neither sentimental nor satirically instructive. Instead of thinking of Sterne's novels as fables from which the moral is to be deduced – that is, stories with a meaning that eventually becomes clear by means of interpretation[4] – it is more accurate to think of Sterne's narratives as an unstable series of seized initiatives, designed not for interpretive symmetry but for local practical advantages in the engagement with the reader. What may look like an invitation to share moral agency with the author is in fact more likely to be a tactical immobilization of the reader's resistance to what is being proposed.

In this chapter I shall draw an extensive parallel between Sterne's narrative practice and the political eloquence recommended by thinkers such as Lord Bolingbroke and David Hume, an eloquence shortly to be exploited to devastating effect by William Pitt, leader of the war ministry when Sterne began writing *Tristram Shandy* (1760–67) and the patron to whom that novel is twice dedicated. I shall rely to a great extent on the work of Jonathan Clark and John Pocock, historians who have recently contributed to a fundamental reconsideration of politics in mid-century Britain, and who have also based their reassessments on what they see as a recurring set of narratives in the political and ideological discourse of the age. Their work offers to explain why and how Pitt exploits the principles of the disinterested patriot out of motives that are not principled and for purposes that are self-interested. This tactical eloquence of the politician and Sterne's redeployment of satiric techniques share a common ground in their provisional and expedient adaptations of normative language. I propose to approach Sterne's adaptations as practical narrative, like the politician's speeches rather than as the narrative form of a definite inter-pretable meaning.

In *Tristram Shandy* the narrator's father, an autodidact with pediatric ambitions along the lines of Cornelius Scriblerus (one of a set of characters invented by Pope, Swift, and their friends to satirize pedantry), is conceived as the occasion for a variety of satirical attacks on rigid principles of reasoning and belief whose validity is simply assumed, never tried. Walter Shandy is the type of thinker who shelters untested hypotheses and prescrip-tions behind a screen of jargon and abstraction. His implicit belief in the value of a priori rules governing childbirth, Christian names, noses, and auxiliary verbs is compared during the first part of the novel with French theoreticians, Dutch commentators, and inquisitorial torturers in the fero-city of its attachment to the conjectural foundations of "an argument a priori" (II.17). When Walter's arguments are overwhelmed by empirical facts and practice, he is inconsolable until he can fashion (as in the case of his child's accidental circumcision by a falling window sash) an a priori rule out of an a posteriori breach of the order he wants to prevail. At the end of the fourth volume, however, Tristram intervenes to beg that his stories not be mistaken for satirical analogues ridiculing the bigotry of systematic thinking:

> In the story of my father and his christen-names, – I had no thoughts of treading upon Francis the First – nor in the affair of the nose – upon Francis the Ninth – nor in the character of my uncle Toby – of characterizing the militiating spirits of my country ... nor by Trim, – that I meant the duke of – Ormond – or that my book is wrote against predestination, or free will, or taxes. (IV.22)

As for Walter's character, initially the vehicle of the satire against a priori systems, it develops a freestanding versatility and unexpectedness that Tristram expects his reader to find more and more sympathetic and interesting, and less and less generically ridiculous.

The displacement of what appears initially to be a satiric plan by the strengthening impulse to value oddity for its own sake results in descriptions whose particularity generates a self-subsistent comedy, presenting characters who are uninterpretable in any other sense than that of their own indisputable singularity, involves two tricky renegotiations of the original satiric position. Characters such as Walter are not simply represented as generic – the pedant, as Didius is the lawyer or "your reverence" is the prelate. He and the others in the Shandy family develop profiles whose interest lies not in their conformity to any norm, but rather in their freedom from all types and precedents. Talking of the unaccountable diversity of his father's whims, Tristram warns the reader, "Be wary, Sir, when you imitate him" (v.42). At the same time, the novelty of such characters cannot be so pure as to defeat all methods of recognizing and appreciating them. The growing inimitability of hobbyhorsical eccentricity, evinced in Toby's "unparallel'd modesty" (I.21) or the baffling unpredictability of Walter's reactions to events (v.24), requires this assimilation of private singularity to the terms of public and sentimental approval if it is not to disappear into pointless elaborations of irregularity and anomie. This double shift, from the public standards of satire to the privacies of unparalleled minds, and then back from these private particulars to their recognizably public value, is achieved by the persuasive force of eloquence.

Sterne first experimented with this double shift in his satire on the ecclesiastical politics of York, A Political Romance (1759). Delivered in two parts, the first telling the story of Trim and the watchcoat, which runs parallel with the row between John Fountayne and Francis Topham over the control of minor ecclesiastical offices in Yorkshire, the second offering the "Key", in which the satirical allegory is variously interpreted by a political club, the satire evolves into a dramatization of the reading it provokes in this particular audience. The point at issue ceases to be the real events represented by the allegory in that "a good warm watch coat" stands for the church offices that were being contested, and becomes instead the contradictory particularity of its interpretations:

> Thus every Man turn'd the Story to what was swimming uppermost in his own Brain; – so that, before all was over, there were full as many Satyres spun out of it, and as great a Variety of Personages, Opinions, Transactions, and Truths, found to lay hid under the dark Veil of its Allegory, as ever were discovered in the thrice-renowned History of the Acts of *Gargantua and Pantagruel*.[5]

The risible failure of reading as a decisive interpretive act leads to a narrative whose stake is no longer an accurate decoding of signs, but the plausible representation of a series of scenes which dramatize the comic futility of thinking that there is one correct reading. By making the point of ridicule the search for meaning rather than the meaning *tout court*, Sterne's assault on the a priori falls not on the fantastic claims of church lawyers (the ostensible object of the exercise) but on the reader who claims to understand it as such. The a priori is now the assumption behind the act of reading and interpreting rather than the governing assumptions behind what is read about; and this strategy leaves the field of narrative particulars free from all normalizing interventions: the story is what it is, not another thing, and all its purposes are served in triumphantly revealing to the reader that it has none. For his part, the narrator enjoys the emancipation of his skills – a satire on the interpretation of satire – that is derived from self-reference. The more he can incorporate interpretation as the primary material of his story, the less the reader is free to interpret it. The index of this swing of choices in the narrator's direction is his reflexive grasp on the capacity of narrative to include within its purview its own effects, and to make its own genesis, development and consumption the legitimate objects of representation.

Sterne shifts from the public object of satire to the private foibles that make impossible the unveiling and stripping away characteristic of satirical discourse, and that involves a parallel shift from the reader's competence based on his ability to interpret signs to the author's own narrative freedom based on representational self-reference. So, in *Tristram Shandy* Tristram defends the unimpeachable singularity of his characters against readers who might like to judge them according to an objective criterion. After his apostrophe to his Uncle Toby, who has almost killed himself trying to find in calculus the secret of projectiles, Tristram tackles the reader. He explains that "the best plain narrative in the world" would have been "cold and vapid upon the reader's palate" after "the last spirited apostrophe" (II.4). He fills up the space between the apostrophe and the next piece of narrative with an instructive maxim, namely that an author is like a painter in deeming it "more pardonable to trespass against truth, than beauty." A truth laid down like this in defiance of literal truth presents no problems for Tristram, who goes on to show that the truth of what he has said lies solely in its timing: "As the parallel is made more for the sake of letting the apostrophe cool, than any thing else, – 'tis not very material whether upon any other score the reader approves of it or not." The truth of this kind of "truth" at the expense of an objective truth is determined by the circumstances and the rhetorical effects of its telling, not what it tells. Sterne's narrative does not offer the reader a prescriptive standard, moving in advance of the story and designed as a reference point in the critical estimate of its execution, but the narrative serves rather as a mirror in that the narrator may plume himself at the reader's expense. Here the a priori that is to be demolished is not belief, truth, or even the aestheticization of truth, but the reader's assumption that any rule or standard of objective accuracy might have priority over narrative practice. The self-referential skill of the narrator allows him to convert rule and principle into further narrative material – to represent the theory of representation as part of the story – so that what comes behind is always in advance of what goes before. The strange time scheme of *Tristram Shandy* is inseparable from this unsettled relation of the moral to the fable. An event can be narrated only after a set of rhetorical choices has been made, and in narrative therefore the world being represented is subordinated in every sense to the demands of persuasively representing it.

The story of the conception and delivery of the infant Tristram is Sterne's largest experiment in narrative self-reference, and it works by constantly incorporating metaphors of representation as the substance of the narrative. The technique is based on the analogy between eloquence and childbirth. The best orators are like mothers or accoucheurs in the deft production of a small child:

> When a state orator has ... hid his BAMBINO in his mantle so cunningly that no mortal could smell it, – and produced it so critically, that no soul could say, it came in by head and shoulders – Oh, Sirs! it has done wonders. – It has open'd the sluices, and turn'd the brains, and shook the principles, and unhinged the politicks of half a nation. (III.14)

The bambino in Tristram's tale is of course himself; and like other by-products of systemic ways of thinking, he is both the object and channel of a stream of eloquence directed ultimately at the world at large, represented by the reader. When he draws another analogy between his mother's retentive-womb and Dr. Slop's bag, so tightly knotted by Obadiah that it cannot easily be delivered of its instruments of delivery, and wonders which shall emerge first, the bambino or the forceps, he postpones all accounts of himself "till I am got out into the world" (III.8). To get out into the world is to make the transition from the muteness of infancy to the passionate practice of oratory by acquiring the powers "which erst have opened the lips of the dumb in his distress, and made the tongue of the stammerer speak plain" (VI.25). These are the same "exquisite powers" already apostrophized as David Garrick's (IV.7), and in Tristram's case they are acquired when the instruments and the objects of delivery become indistinguishable as items of narrative interest. When forceps double up as the infant they are to deliver, and when the agency of representation (the orator producing a baby from his mantle) doubles up as the object of representation (the baby born in the third volume of the novel), narrative power is generated. Tristram does not sentimentalize this power. It has practical effects often indistinguishable from the confusion Walter has always seen on the far side of the a priori, such as the mangled body which Ernulphus's tremendous imprecation (an actual Roman Catholic curse or Latin sentence of excommunication by Ernulf, Bishop of Rochester from 1114 to 1124, that Walter finds amusing and that Sterne inserts in the text) seeks to create, or the unhinged politics and shaken principles which it is the aim of ancient oratory to provoke. Hume points out in his essay "Of Eloquence" that the greatest achievements in oratory are contemporary with the worst kinds of disorder and violence.[6]

Tristram is committed therefore to acting as the deliverer of his own delivery, thereby controlling and directing the destructive and unsettling effects of eloquence. Like the tautologous relation existing between the womb and the bag of instruments, or a midwife and an orator, Tristram's relation to his genesis is closely implicated in the instrumentality of the eloquence that will make it known to the world. Whatever comes before, in the sense of being historically prior, finds its value solely in what comes after, in the sense of that narration of it which is rhetorically posterior. Hence the equivocation on the right and wrong ends of Mrs. Shandy, suggestive of the fact that young Tristram has come foremost into the world by a hindmost route. He has made his way forwards backwards; he owes his rise to a bottom, and so on. Tristram plays with these paradoxes, which are both comic and profound in their implications.

Tristram and his author cling to this reversible metaphor through thick and thin: an hypothesis (especially an hypothesis about childbirth) is like a fetus, for "when once a man has conceived it . . . it assimilates every thing to itself as proper nourishment" (II.19); an abortion occurs when, after a sound conception, a man is forced to "go out of the world with the conceit of it rotting in his head" (I.22). Sterne told Stephen Croft that it was in Ireland that "my mother gave me to the world," and it is by a parallel act of motherhood that he attempts to give his own children to the world: "I am going to ly in of another child of the Shandaick procreation, in town – I hope you wish me a safe delivery." But sometimes he is unlucky: "I miscarried of my tenth Volume by the violence of a fever . . . I have however gone on to my reckoning with the ninth, of wch I am all this week in Labour pains."[7] A perfect circularity, or at least a consistent nonpriority, exists between all aspects of his work. Both end and instrument of what he fashions, Tristram exactly resembles the state orator's baby, so indistinguishably presented as the object and impulse of rhetoric that no soul can say he comes in by head or shoulders. All his audience knows for sure is that either as cause or effect of eloquence, Tristram's is an unhinged and unhinging case. Tristram makes no bones about this. He apostrophizes the force as power: "O ye POWERS! (for powers ye are, and great ones too) – which enable a mortal man to tell a story worth the hearing ..." (III.23) Tristram salutes the great actor Garrick's art as power, and he several times warns his reader not to take it lightly; after all, it is confusing and politically dangerous: "O my countrymen! – be nice – be cautious of your language; – and never, O! never let it be forgotten upon what small particles your eloquence and your fame depend" (II.6).

His most eloquent reflection on the dangers of eloquence follows Trim's remarkable speech on death. Trim ornaments a self-evident truth: "Are we not here now, and are we not gone! in a moment." But he does this not with a bambino but a hat, dropped so dextrously half way through the citation that its triteness is transformed into a stunning practice, a deathly gesture on the topic of death:

> The descent of the hat was as if a heavy lump of clay had been kneaded into the crown of it. – Nothing could have expressed the sentiment of mortality of which it was the type and fore-runner, like it, – his hand seemed to vanish from under it, – it fell dead, – the corporal's eye fix'd upon it, as upon a corpse.
>
> (v.7)

Then Tristram turns eloquently to the world Trim's eloquence has revealed, and apostrophizes it as follows:

> Ye who govern this mighty world and its mighty concerns with the engines of eloquence, – who heat it, and cool it, and melt it, and mollify it, – and then harden it again to your purpose – Ye who wind and turn the passions with this great windlass, – and having done it, lead the owners of them, whither ye think meet – Ye lastly, who drive – and why not, Ye also who are driven, like turkeys to market, with a stick and a red clout – meditate – meditate, I beseech you, upon Trim's hat.

What does such a meditation bring? Not, certainly, an impression of a comfortable intimacy with the force of eloquence, which is shown to flow through the most public parts of the actual world, as well as in the text we are presently reading, towards ends that are manifestly not altruistic, principled, or even safe. Whom then might Tristram have in mind as he talks of the governor of this mighty engine? Garrick is always associated with eloquence in Sterne's writing, but his power is limited to the theatre. It is hard not to think that Tristram is alluding to an orator thought by many of his contemporaries to be the modern equal of Demosthenes and Cicero, the friend of Garrick who, by Garrick's good offices, was to become the patron of the aspiring comic author[8] – namely William Pitt, to whom *Tristram Shandy* is twice dedicated, a state orator whose eloquence in the House of Commons was by this time legendary, and whose power was then at its height. I want to explore the connection between Tristram's paradoxical and comic reflections on eloquence and the leading Patriot politician of the day by unpacking from the two dedications the themes we have been following through the novel.[9] In the first, "the Author" addresses the secretary of state from a thatched house in "a bye corner of the kingdom," asking him not to protect the book but to read it when he himself goes into the country. The Patriot subtext is not difficult: a marginal figure with an ambition to "get out into the world" addresses a politically central figure who nevertheless idealizes the integrity associated with the retirement from which the aspiring author speaks. Pitt's politics were nurtured at Stowe, the great estate and country house of one of his political mentors, the Earl of Cobham, and he loved a country life. He wrote to his sister Ann as "her gentle loving shepherd," and to his brother John he confessed, "I long to be with you kicking up my heels – and looking like a shepherd in Theocritus."[10] The "Country" ideology locates the disinterested man, and even the disinterested book (which "must protect itself" and not be slavishly dependent), in a topographical and temperamental remoteness from the run of politicians, who are so busily scheming at court that they cannot enjoy the happiness that the author claims to share with the statesman. The dedication, composed as Sterne was beginning the third and fourth volumes of his novel, sets satire aside in order to praise the decent isolation from which an honest individual may speak to a sympathetic figure in the world.[11] The singularity of the man who loves privacy guarantees in him an equilibrium that nothing can upset or corrupt, because it is disinterested, unmortgaged to party or faction, and freely emanating in public spirit. Such an individual resembles a Shandean humorist, whose singularity coincides with integrity, and whose isolation is the guarantee of an innocence that can not be violated by the interpretation of the public, or a readership, not inured to the privacies of practical virtue.

The second dedication is very different, coming as it does after Pitt, the "Great Commoner" as he had been called, has accepted not only a peerage as the Earl of Chatham in 1766 but also a large pension from the Crown. When Obadiah has to tell Walter that he cannot ride the horse Patriot because "PATRIOT is sold" (v.2), and when Yorick tells the Comte de B— that "Our court is at present so full of Patriots who wish for *nothing* but the honours and wealth of their country [that] there is nothing for a jester to make a jest of,"[12] it is plain that Sterne is not blind to the pressures exerted upon individual integrity once it has got out into the world. The difference between Pitt and the Earl of Chatham he recognizes as in some way analogous to the difference between a priori and a posteriori: that is, between an untested principle and the practice of power.

> Having a priori, intended to dedicate *The Amours of my uncle Toby* to Mr. P— I see more reasons, a posteriori, for doing it to Lord — I should lament from my soul, if this exposed me to the jealousy of their Reverences: because, a posteriori, in Court-latin, signifies, the kissing hands for preferment – or any thing else – in order to get it. (IX.1)

Tristram notes without bitterness the passage from the ideal of retirement, which he claimed to share with Pitt in the 1750s, to the murkier reaches of power politics in which he now locates the state orator. The rural figure that the author cut in first greeting the Country party politician is now remodeled as "some gentle Shepherd," the sharpest antithesis to pensioners and Patriots he can think of, "whose Thoughts proud Science never taught to stray, / Far as the Statesman's walk or Patriot-way." However, it is evident that the gentle shepherd is not the author, and that the transition he marks from the simple patriotism of the first dedication to the compromised political positions of the second, is not the occasion for a reintroduction of the satiric project at Pitt's expense.[13]

The key terms "a priori" and "a posteriori" are brought into play to mock, if anything, the naive valorization of the singular private life that Sterne once thought could be brought into the world without any danger of confusion or corruption. The lesson he has learned is that the eloquence which reproduces the private oddity as a public performance depends upon a power that is dangerous both to the orator and the audience, in that it shakes principles, generates confusion, and arouses ambition. But he has not learned this simply by following and interpreting Pitt's career. The process of writing and publishing his fabulously successful book has kept pace with Pitt's acquisition of power, involving modifications to the cultivation of the singular and the particular until the risks involved in getting into the world are undeniable, embodied in Sterne's practice of a narrative manner that has overwhelmed all constraints and all readerly resistance and made him rich and famous.

In Britain of the 1750s the party distinctions of Whig and Tory had been discredited.[14] Walpole's administration, which ended in 1742, and the Jacobite rebellion of 1745 were cited as instances of the wicked extremes to which party principles could carry people. More realistically, it was understood that high politics was such a pragmatic and quotidian negotiation between the king and the House of Commons that the conventional language of revolution and liberty was too rough to distinguish the subtle differences between ambitious men who, although they would all call themselves Whigs, were divided by the means each pursued in getting power, not by the objectives to be pursued once it had been obtained.[15] The chief architect of this state of affairs was Henry St. John, Viscount Bolingbroke, the man addressed in Pope's lines in praise of the gentle shepherd that Sterne cites in his second dedication to Pitt. Bolingbroke had succeeded simultaneously in persuading the public that power such as Walpole's, exercised self-interestedly and without restraint, was corrupt and corrupting, and that a parliamentary opposition, founded on steady principles of public spirit, not only gave the politically marginal figure a public voice, but also entered on his behalf a plausible claim for political office. The first fruit of the opposition led by Henry Pelham was the administration of his brother, the Duke of Newcastle, who practiced the art of the possible unhindered even by notional loyalties to founding ideals. Bolingbroke's advocacy of principles transcending private interest, combined with his recommendation of parliamentary oratory capable of a practical "force and authority,"[16] was soon to be embodied in the career of Pitt, an orator remarkable for eloquence whose transcendent qualities carried him above all definable commitments to principle and fed an ambition that was limitless.

Sterne's early enthusiasm for Pitt did not include approval of Patriot political theory in general, or of Bolingbroke in particular. His political journalism in the 1740s defended Walpole's policies, even after his fall, and was couched in the language of Hanoverian Whiggism. In the *York Gazetteer*, he attacks the scandal and invective of Pelhamites, raked out of "the Kennels of Craftsmen and Journalists" and sedulously spread about once again by Caesar Ward in the pages of the *York Courant*.[17] The noise of "the CRAFTSMAN and COMMON SENSE" is the cacophony of "false Invective and false Panegyrick." "*True Patriots* are good for nothing but to sit safely in their closets and attaque the tender Characters of Men,"[18] while maneuvering for the plunder they deplore. Of Patriot rhetoric during the aftermath of Walpole's fall, when the mayor and aldermen of London were pressuring their MPs to hasten their dilatory prosecution of Walpole, Sterne writes, "Nothing can give a reasonable Man, a meaner or more despicable Idea of the Citizens of London, than to hear them, in the midst of the most abandon'd Venality and Corruption, perpetually declaiming against Venality and Corruption" (*York Gazetteer*, "Sterne's Politicks," 99). Although Sterne confessed that he wrote these paragraphs to please his powerful Uncle Jaques and to gain preferment, there is a thread running through all his work that twitches in response to the scandalizing of a vulnerable reputation. His own suffered at the hands of this same Uncle Jaques who, angered when his nephew refused to write any more paragraphs in defense of vulnerable politicians, had it put about York that Sterne had preferred to let his mother be lodged in the poorhouse rather than give her a subsistence.[19] Parson Yorick's blighted career (as summarized in the opening volume of *Tristram Shandy*) represents in its most acute form everything Sterne felt was most opprobrious and unjust about this sacrifice of innocents for the sake of an outraged public virtue. Such vengeful hypocrisy he seems to have considered the speciality of contemporary Patriotism, "For I make no Doubt, that a great Part of the Opposition and OutCry against standing Armies, &c. for some time past, has proceeded from a Jacobite Party, under Pretext of Patriots ... Glorious Patriots indeed! *O my Soul, enter thou not into their Secrets.*"[20]

As for Bolingbroke, he seems to have represented for Sterne the type of a spoiled political idealism. In one of his letters, Sterne plays at arranging antithetical pairs ("Our Sydenhams, and Sangrados, our Lucretias, – and Massalinas"), ending with "our Sommers, and our Bolingbrokes," (*Letters*, 88) setting the true Whig against the false Patriot. The reason for such pointed hostility lies in the difference Sterne marks in the *York Gazetteer* between the language of opposition and the practical calls of political office. The Pelhamites now in government, "who before were the only *True Patriots* of our Country," find themselves the objects of the same vituperation that was previously reserved for Walpole, "which shews how widely *Opposition* differs from Patriotism, and that Places will always make Men appear Criminal: As if Government cou'd exist without Places, and Men to fill them, or a Man was less a Patriot for taking a Place in a Ministry which he approves" (*York Gazetteer*, "Sterne's Politicks," 92).

J. G. A. Pocock and J. C. D. Clark have drawn attention to the anomalous nature of Bolingbroke's commitment to principle.[21] In his *Letters on Patriotism*, Bolingbroke constantly links the marginalized figure – the scorned and exiled sacrificial victim whom Sterne had no trouble identifying with[22] – to the systematic array of principles that Sterne associates with an unacceptable faith in the a priori. According to Bolingbroke, opposition is a process of reasoning "on principles that are out of fashion", "a moral system of the world", "a system of conduct" (3, 12, 59). Such a system avoids, or at least pretends to avoid, the least taint of a posteriori application. As the German political theorist, Jürgen Habermas has pointed out, and as Sterne divined, the rhetoric of Patriot opposition could enter the public sphere only on condition that it equated powerlessness with integrity, and place with corrupt influence.[23] This is the dream language of the political exile, designed to embarrass those whose place he cannot take.

With none but the most oblique claim on practice, patriotism and its inventor perpetrate, as far as Sterne is concerned, the worst betrayal of political practice by blackening the names of those who dare to act. And this scandal is spread with the authority of an impossible rule of conduct. From Sterne's point of view, Bolingbroke is describing himself when he characterizes continental philosophers like this: "Rather than creep up slowly, a posteriori, to a little general knowledge, they soar at once as far, and as high, as imagination can carry them. From whence they descend again, armed with systems and arguments a priori."[24]

With this degree of skepticism about patriotism, how can Sterne salute Pitt in the language of Country ideology? The short answer is that Pitt, like so many politicians of the mid-century, married the language of principle to adroit interventions into practical politics. Sterne's two dedications comprehend the a priori and the a posteriori of Patriot possibilities, from the language of exile to what Clark calls "the tactical implications of principled rhetoric." Once that marriage is made, there is (as Clark also points out) "no clear, mutually exclusive difference between the sincere and the insincere assertion of principles ... Assertions of policy and principle have their place in a theory of the explanation of conduct only in the more general sincerity of a common ambition" (Clark, *The Dynamics of Change*, 151, 19). There is the gentle shepherd who kicks up his heels, like a swain in Theocritus, and the gentle shepherd desperate not to lose his political influence, like George Grenville. If Pitt understood and exploited from the outset of his career the advantages of principled language in the day-to-day maneuvering for the prime objective – power – then Sterne came to understand the convenient alignment of invoked principle to practice in the process of writing his book, where the double shift from satire to particularity, and from particularity to public value, requires that the language of narrative principle be deployed for the ends of eloquence, not of authentication. In *Tristram Shandy* each triumph over the reader's desire to interpret a story or to judge a character marks a narrativization of the a priori. That is to say, Sterne's main narrative strategy is the self-referential conversion of occasions of judgments into opportunities for a brilliant delivery.

When he finds the language of Garrick electrifying because it acquires its power by going beyond the rules of grammar (III.12) he begins to apprehend the qualities in Pitt's delivery that Horace Walpole declared "would have added reputation to Garrick," and which always shone most brightly when he was "exposing his own conduct: [and] having waded through the most notorious apostacy in politics ... treated it with an impudent confidence, that made all reflections upon him poor and spiritless."[25] The collapse of an interpretable satiric allegory that eventually resolves itself into the rhetoric of Tristram's self-indulgent and erratic history of his life runs parallel to the instrumental eloquence Pitt finds in Bolingbroke's exilic dream language once he has emptied it of its meaning. The narratives each then goes on to produce have much in common in terms of that circular or tautologous symmetry characteristic of state oratory. Choice and power stand in a direct ratio to self-reference, such as the delivery of delivered infancy, the satire of satiric interpretation, eloquence upon eloquence, reflection upon reflection.

An example of Pitt's delivery of a bambino occurs in a speech on the Scottish magistracy that Horace Walpole instances as one of his finest. He paraphrases it in the third person:

> "When master principles are concerned, he dreaded accuracy of distinction: he feared that sort of reasoning; if you class everything, you will soon reduce everything into a particular; you will then lose great general maxims ... He would not recur for precedents to the diabolic divans of the second Charles and James – he did not date his principles of the liberty of this country from the revolution: they are eternal rights: and when God said, *let justice be justice*, he made it independent."[26]

Only on reflection can we see that Pitt has invented, or conceived, this originary establishment of justice and the donation of rights purely on his own account. In the passion of delivery it comes with all the self-evidence of the *fiat lux*, from which it is no doubt derived, in order to blind the audience to the absence of any objective principle either in the theme or the conduct of the oration. You cannot tell how "eternal rights" come in, whether by head or shoulders. All the audience is told is that rights are rights because justice has been announced as justice; and all they discover is that rights belong to the man whose voice so eloquently and magisterially produces and, in producing, legitimates them. The language of "great general maxims" and revolution principles is a stalking horse for this invention of right, and the figure of illegitimacy – "the diabolic divans of the second Charles and James" – serves like the bend sinister on the coat of arms on the Shandy coach simply as the detectable outside of an arbitrary act of conception and delivery.

Like the Shandean reduction to narrative and rhetorical manipulation of the principles needed to decipher signs and to make judgments, Pitt's speech includes principles as a further theme of oratorical practice, citing the a priori in order to emancipate the a posteriori from its control. Just as Sterne's undermining of narrative referentiality disturbs the verisimilitude of his novel, so Pitt's eloquence unsettles the relation of political agency to ethical imperatives by transforming his indicators of probity into the figures of his oratory. As J. G. A. Pocock says: "We must beware of supposing that the actors in high politics were motivated by the things they said, and we must beware of supposing that the categories of ideological rhetoric necessarily furnish either reliable description or reliable evaluation of the way the institution of high politics worked."[27] Pocock is responding to Clark's summary of the politics of the 1750s as *narrative*:

> Narrative is the mental language of political action appropriate to men who, in real situations, refrain from basing their actions on a generalised view of their predicament ... Narrative ... involves a submission to the partial blindness dictated by events evolving successively in an order which, if a sequence, is not necessarily a pattern, and to which "pattern" is ascribed in retrospect in a great variety of ways ... Narrative reflects an order given to events by an actor in them in order to take the next step: it displays the coherence, the sequence, the significant selection which the actor adopts as the substitute explanation (no full, ideal explanation being attainable) of his own next action.

It follows that "actions are intelligible only if they can be narrated" and that narrative is the spur for subsequent activity.[28] Narrative is what happens when the stream of history runs backward as eloquence, and the discourse of generalized views obedient to a priori principles is gutted for an essentially pragmatic a posteriori rhetoric that both precipitates and justifies actions that are convenient and opportune. Pitt's genealogy of eternal right is just such a narrative, in which the illusion of priority is served by a circular argument. *Tristram Shandy* is another. Narrative is the state orator's and the autobiographer's sleight of hand that delivers and legitimates the bambino in the one recursive flourish.

In writing histories of a decade in which narrative came into this new relation to practice, Horace Walpole and William Godwin were prone to reproduce the improvisational, circumstantial, and personal rhetoric that has so often been claimed as Sterne's peculiarity. Confronted with "this chaos of politics" and of administrations "unprincipled and disunited, made up of the deserters of all parties," Godwin has recourse to a dense particularity: "A thousand additional circumstances attract us, in the present case."[29] Walpole is likewise determined by one factor in writing his *Memoirs*: "They are the minutiae of which I have observed posterity is ever most fond"; his aim being, "to relate our story with exact fidelity to the impressions it made on me" (*Memoirs*, III.92; III.47). What but a redaction of this narrative position is Tristram's maxim of situational relativity: "The circumstances with which every thing in this world is begirt, give every thing in this world its size and shape" (III.2), and Sterne's confession, "I am governed by circumstances – so that what is fit to be done on Monday, may be very unwise on Saturday" (*Letters*, 194). It is an impossible simplification to assume that this circumstantiality is a serious, or even a parodic, contribution to the realism of the emergent novel. Similarly, to interpret Tristram's and Walpole's plan of striking the reader with their own impressions of circumstances as a straightforward exercise in provoking sympathy is to neglect the apperception of the power of narrative on which it is based.

Ian Watt assigns Sterne's "very careful attention to all the aspects of formal realism: to the particularization of time, place and person; to a natural and lifelike sequence of action; and to the creation of a literary style which gives the most exact verbal and rhythmical equivalent possible of the object described" to his reconciliation of Richardson's "realism of presentation" with Fielding's "realism of assessment."[30] This judgment does scant justice to Sterne's exploitation of the energies that arise from the subversion of accurate presentations and assessments. Similarly, Michael McKeon's summary of the mid-century novel as "a form sufficient for the joint inquiry into analogous epistemological and social problems" seems to be less urgent than novels such as *Tristram Shandy* deserve. More appropriate to them are his remarks on travel writing, in which the first person singular is engaged in a calculated act of persuasion, based on "hearsay reports mediated through narrative style," in which attention is eagerly focused on "the very instrument of mediation, within the shape of the style itself."[31] The versatile narrative shared by Pitt and Sterne/Tristram develops three connected aspects: a factitious identity in the narrator; a taste for tautologous phrases and self-referential turns; and a desire for self-presentation so unbounded that the story of it cannot end. The child (Tristram) who escapes the definitions of a priori pediatric systems in order that he might bring himself into the world in his own way, the orator whose delivery is successful precisely because he has "only passions to sacrifice, not principles," are uniquely unrestricted by previous models and precedents. They are singular, or, to use Godwin's term for Pitt, "unresembled" (*History of Pitt*, 237) in proportion as they are self-authorizing and self-produced, conceivers and deliverers of their own selves. William Warburton wrote of Sterne, "As now everyone *makes himself*, he chose the office of common jester to the many" (*Letters*, 96 n6). His close political associate, the Earl of Shelburne, accused Pitt of making himself: "What took much from his character was that he was always acting, always made up, and never natural." Good as his parts were, he was afraid to trust to them,[32] and was "a complete artificial character."[33] Significantly it is to Garrick, in the same letter in which he acknowledges his obligations to Pitt, that Sterne reports an event which gave him the hint for what later he called "Shandying it," and doing "a thousand things which cut no figure, *but in the doing*" (*Letters*, 157): " 'Twas an odd incident when I was introduced to the Count de Bissie, which I was at his desire – I found him reading Tristram" (*Letters*, 151). The queer sensation of being introduced to the man reading your book as the chief character in it – "ce Chevalier Shandy" (*Letters*, 157) – provides the basis for the scene in *A Sentimental Journey* where the same Comte de Bissy cannot tell the difference between the Yorick who has appeared in front of him and the Yorick in the pages of his Shakespeare to which the other Yorick points. It provides Sterne with the opportunity simultaneously to mock the French and Warburton for acting on the belief that the difference between the natural and the artificial man is worthy of discrimination and surprise.[34] It also allows him to show, both here and in the Parisian sections of that novel, that artificial characters are the only ones to be met with in circles of political and social influence. Gentle shepherds and pastoralizing Yoricks may pretend otherwise, fashioning themselves simple identities whose very simplicity is intended as a reproach to artifice, but this posing is always a perilous simplification. Tristram is still uncertainly negotiating these issues when he meets an officer of the king's posts in France, and has his expostulation cut short: "As sure as I am I – and you are you – And who are you? said he, – Don't puzzle me, said I" (VII.33).

The self-measurement of things and qualities has already been evident in satire upon satire, delivery upon delivery, reflections upon reflections, and so on. These tautologies are expressive of the narrative incorporation of all regulatory judgments, and of the triumph of selfish eloquence. Like the apparition of the "real" Tristram in front of the reader of the fictional one, tautologies proclaim the ever-widening circle of a self-justifying narrative to a reader experiencing growing difficulties in determining its boundary. Sterne's "Shandying it" in Paris is justified in no other terms "*but in the doing*." Just as political narrative revolves between the arbitrarily chosen events that it articulates and the actions that such articulation legitimates, so Shandean logic produces the duplicate of the "unresembled" thing as both its warrant and example. Considering the self-generating possibilities of the narrative he is engaged upon, the furthest Tristram ventures into language that reveals his awareness of this solipsism is to observe, "I shall lead a fine life of it out of this self-same life of mine; or, in other words, shall lead a couple of fine lives together" (IV.13).

If such tautologies are expressions of that circular or iterative form by which Sterne's narrative and Pitt's eloquence of the mid-century empower themselves, then something like interruption or aposiopesis (a figure of speech in which a thought or sentence suddenly breaks off) is the appropriate figure for political ambition which, as it has no authoritative source, can have no definite end. Godwin talks of Pitt's ambition as uncommon in its disinterestedness and inexhaustibility, "The mere possession of power was not calculated to gratify it." At the same time, Pitt's ambition is so importunate as to introduce that "feebleness and versatility" into his story which makes it impossible to wind up satisfactorily (Godwin, 73, 150). If Pitt's story turns and turns and gets nowhere owing to his growing fascination with the institution of Bolingbroke's dream language as a political reality, the parallel with Tristram Shandy's "life" is to be found in the effects of a vision as imperial, in its own way, as Pitt's.

Such dissatisfaction with the actual world on the part of novelist and politician stems from the self-proselytizing tendency evident among eloquent individuals. The power they establish over their audience, which is measured in terms of extensive worldly success commanded by their tongues, eventually washes back over them, committing them to a quixotic attachment to an improbable and unnarratable ideal. The moment of eloquence is triumphant but transitory, since it aims at nothing but an immediate and vivid effect rather than at an assertion of a solid reference to an external world. When Tristram announces that he aims to do nothing but write his life to the end of his life, he has arrived at the first stage of literary empire (IV.13); and when he says he will read no book but his own as long as he lives, he has come to the second (VIII.5). His narrative is fully tautologized as a self-delivery that will give both *Life* and life, in which he will function as the fascinated reader of his own writing and his audience will be forced to cooperate with that self-enclosure. Interruption such as dominates every page of *Tristram Shandy* guarantees, paradoxically, the continuity of eloquent self-delivery as a nonoriginary and nonteleological activity concerned with virtualities and effective artifice. Contrariwise, the over-investment in *Life* as *life* – a translation of the self-fashioned self into a naturalistic and biological existence improbably extending far into the future such as we expect novelistic narrative to deliver – is fated to encounter interruption as a guarantee of nothing but mortality. *Tristram Shandy* is thus profoundly antinovelistic, since it values the moment of joyous individual eloquence as the revelation of personality (*Life*) and rejects with horror the narrative of a "life" as it is lived as merely a tracking of the inevitabilities of death and dissolution. As long as Sterne's first person narrators remember that, their self-deliveries a posteriori will never be mistaken for true births, and their bambini will never be trapped in a narrative that dispatches them from a beginning to an end.

NOTES

1 This view has found its most influential expression in Ian Watt, *The Rise of the Novel* (Berkeley: University of California Press, 1957), 290–91. Its fullest theoretical airing is to be found in a formalist consideration of Sterne's use of the estrangement effect in Victor Shklovsky, "A Parodying Novel: Sterne's *Tristram Shandy*," reprinted in John Traugott, ed., *Laurence Sterne: a Collection of Critical Essays* (Englewood Cliffs, N.J.: Prentice-Hall, 1968), 61–79.

2 F. R. Leavis, *The Great Tradition* (New York: Doubleday, 1948), 10–11n; Sigurd Burckhardt, "Tristram Shandy's Law of Gravity," *ELH*, 28 (1961): 70–88; John Traugott, *Tristram Shandy's World: Sterne's Philosophical Rhetoric* (Berkeley and Los Angeles: University of California Press, 1954); *The Life and Opinions of Tristram Shandy, Gentleman*, ed. Melvyn New and Joan New (Gainesville: University Presses of Florida, 1978), IV.32. Subsequent references – to volume and chapter – are noted in brackets in the text.

3 Virginia Woolf, "Sterne," in *Granite and Rainbow* (London: Hogarth, 1958), 167–75; and "The 'Sentimental Journey,'" in *The Common Reader: Second Series* (London: Hogarth, 1932), 78–85.

4 As in contemporary accounts of verisimilitude, such as Samuel Johnson's *Rambler*, 4, Edward Young, a close collaborator with Richardson, defines the verisimilitude of his long poem *Night-Thoughts*, and, incidentally, of Richardson's longer novel *Clarissa*, as follows: "It differs from the common modes of poetry which is from long narratives to draw short morals. Here, on the contrary, the narrative is short, and the morality arising from it makes the bulk of the poem." *The Correspondence of Edward Young*, ed. Henry Pettit (Oxford: Clarendon, 1971), 349.

5 *A Political Romance* (York, 1759; reprinted Menston: Scolar, 1971), 45.

6 "It may be pretended, that the disorders of the ancient governments, and the enormous crimes, of which the citizens were often guilty, afforded much ampler matter for eloquence that can be met with among the moderns." Although Hume affects to dispute this argument, he does not contest its associated proposition, namely that eloquence flourishes in proportion as laws are few: "The multiplicity and intricacy of laws is a discouragement to eloquence in modern times." David Hume, "Of Eloquence," in *Essays Moral, Political and Literary*, ed. Eugene F. Miller (Indianapolis: Liberty Classics, 1987), 106, 103.

7 *Letters of Laurence Sterne*, ed. Lewis Perry Curtis (Oxford: Clarendon, 1935; reprinted 1965), 250, 290, 294. Subsequent references are in brackets in the text.

8 In a letter to Garrick acknowledging his help, he seems to include another debt of gratitude to him when he adds, "I am under great obligations to Mr. Pitt, who has behaved in every respect to me like a man of good breeding, and good nature." *Letters*, 152.

9 "Patriot" (along with "Country," as opposed to those who favored the "Court" interest) was the general name applied to those who thought of themselves as the opposition to the long (and corrupt) dominance of English politics by Robert Walpole from 1721 to 1742. As a term that signified political opposition on "patriotic" rather than self-interested grounds, the word lingered into the 1760s.

10 See Jeremy Black, *Pitt the Elder* (Cambridge: Cambridge University Press, 1992), 7, 17.

11 During his first trip to London after the publication of *Tristram Shandy*, Sterne is struck with the patriotic vigor of the new king, whom he applauds in the same terms as he salutes Pitt. He seems, he tells Stephen Croft, "resolved to bring all things back to their original principles, and to stop the torrent of corruption and laziness ... the K[ing] gives every thing himself, knows everything, and weighs every thing maturely, and then is inflexible — this puts old stagers off their game." *Letters*, 126.

12 *A Sentimental Journey through France and Italy*, ed. Gardner D. Stout (1768; Berkeley and Los Angeles: University of California Press, 1967), 227.

13 The person aimed at seems to be George Grenville, Pitt's cousin who earned the contempt of his more eminent relative when, in 1763, he stayed on in Bute's administration, and was active in support of raising fresh revenue. In the midst of a speech where he kept plaintively asking his colleagues where, where, he was going to lay new taxes, Pitt interrupted him by whining the refrain of a popular song, "Gentle Shepherd, tell me where!" After that the name stuck, and Grenville was known as the "Gentle Shepherd." See *Macaulay's Essays on William Pitt*, ed. R. F. Winch (London: Macmillan, 1898), 92–93.

14 To Stephen Croft, Sterne wrote, "We shall be soon Prussians and Anti-Prussians, B[ute]s and Anti-B[ute]s, and those distinctions will just do as well as Whig and Tory – and for aught I know serve the same ends." *Letters*, 126.

15 Although Pitt's clarion call "Not men, but measures" was offered as a corrective to expediency, Burke shows how it presents opportunism in a different form: "When people desert their connections, the desertion is a manifest *fact*, upon which a direct simple issue lies, triable by plain men. Whether a *measure* of government be right or wrong, is no *matter of fact*, but a mere affair of opinion." That is to say, it escapes all "*leading general principles of government.*" *Thoughts on the Present Discontents*, reprinted in *Edmund Burke on Government, Politics, Society*, ed. B. W. Hill (Glasgow: Fontana, 1975), 115–16.

16 Bolingbroke, *Letters on the Spirit of Patriotism* (London: A. Millar, 1752), 51–56. In Hume's opinion, Bolingbroke himself is a fine specimen of what is desiderated in the modern orator: "Lord BOLINGBROKE's productions, with all their defects in argument, method, and precision, contain a force and energy which our orators scarcely ever aim at." Hume, "Of Eloquence," 108.

17 *York Gazetteer*, 16 November 1742; reprinted in Kenneth Monkman, "Sterne's Politicks, 1741–42," *The Shandean*, 1 (1989): 100. Monkman gives his reasons for assigning the piece to Sterne.

18 *York Gazetteer*, 2 November 1742, reprinted in Kenneth Monkman, "Sterne's Politicks," 92.

19 See *Letters*, 32–41; and Arthur H. Cash, *Sterne: the Early and Middle Years* (London: Methuen, 1975), 2236–40.

20 *An Answer to a letter addressed to the Archbishop of York* (Edinburgh, 1745), reprinted in Kenneth Monkman, "Laurence Sterne and the '45," *The Shandean*, 2 (1990): 72. The ascription of this piece to Sterne is less certain than the articles in *York Gazetteer*, but the political opinions it expresses are close to Sterne's.

21 "In the *Craftsman* period he made the historical reality of principles a cardinal doctrine." J. G. A. Pocock, *The Machiavellian Moment* (Princeton: Princeton University Press, 1975), 482. "Bolingbroke ... was atypical in his willingness to

express his political stance in general terms." J. C. D. Clark, *The Dynamics of Change: the Crisis of the 1750s and English Party Systems* (Cambridge: Cambridge University Press, 1982), 8.

22 "I will not say, like SENECA, that the noblest spectacle which God can behold, is a virtuous man suffering, and struggling with afflictions: but this I will say, that the second Cato, driven out of the forum, and dragged to prison, enjoyed more inward pleasure, and maintained more outward dignity, than they who insulted him." *Letters on Patriotism*, 330–31. Seee also *Reflections upon Exile*: "Your name is hung up in the tables of proscription, and art joined to malice endeavours to make your best actions pass for crimes, and to stain your character." *Letters on the Study and the Use of History etc.* (London: Alexander Murray, 1870), 165.

23 Jürgen Habermas, *The Structural Transformation of the Public Sphere*, trans. Thomas Berger (Cambridge, Mass.: MIT Press, 1989), 64.

24 "A Letter to Mr. Pope," in *A Letter to William Windham etc.* (London: A. Millar, 1753), 471.

25 Horace Walpole, *Memoirs of King George II*, ed. John Brooke (New Haven: Yale University Press, 3 vols., 1985), II:111; I:64.

26 *Memoirs*, II:39.

27 J. G. A. Pocock, *Virtue, Commerce, and History* (Cambridge: Cambridge University Press, 1985), 244.

28 Clark, *The Dynamics of Change*, 17–18.

29 William Godwin, *The History of the Life of William Pitt, Earl of Chatham* (London: G. Kearsley, 1783), 146, 181, 283.

30 Watt, *The Rise of the Novel*, 291.

31 An argument congenial to this is Michael McKeon, *The Origins of the English Novel, 1600–1740* (Baltimore: Johns Hopkins University Press, 1987), 410, 104, 109. The argument most congenial to mine is John Sitter's concerning the effects of the speed of the mid-century's shifting premises. Satire gives way to "the melodrama of momentary intensities," "a program for thinking to the moment: a willingness to take any felt certainties which came one's way regarding 'particular points'" at a "particular instant," including a renewed interest in the sublime and other examples of language "in which the gap between word and deed had been closed." John Sitter, *Literary Loneliness in Mid-Eighteenth-Century England* (Ithaca, N.Y.: Cornell University Press, 1982), 26, 229, 68.

32 Walpole on Temple, *Memoirs*, II:184.

33 Cited in J. C. D. Clark, *The Dynamics of Change*, 283.

34 Now whether the idea of poor Yorick's skull was put out of the Count's mind, by the reality of my own, or by what magic he could drop a period of seven or eight hundred years, makes nothing this account – 'tis certain the French conceive better than they combine – I wonder at nothing in this world, and the less at this; inasmuch as one of the first of our own church, for whose candour and paternal sentiments I have the highest veneration, fell into the same mistake in the very same case. – "He could not bear, he said, to look into sermons wrote by the king of Denmark's jester."

A Sentimental Journey, 221–22, and notes 16–19

See also Jonathan Lamb, "The Job Controversy, Sterne, and the Question of Allegory," *Eighteenth-Century Studies*, 24, 1 (Fall 1990): 19.

READING LIST

Burckhardt, Sigurd. "Tristram Shandy's Law of Gravity." *ELH*, 28 (1961): 70–88.

Byrd, Max. *Tristram Shandy*. London: Methuen, 1985.

Cash, Arthur H. *Laurence Sterne: the Early and Middle Years*. London: Methuen, 1975.

Clark, J. C. D. *The Dynamics of Change: the Crisis of the 1750s and English Party Systems*. Cambridge: Cambridge University Press, 1982.

Fluchère, Henri. *Laurence Sterne: from Tristram to Yorick*. London: Oxford University Press, 1965.

Jefferson, D. W. "*Tristram Shandy* and the Tradition of Learned Wit." *Essays in Criticism*, 1 (1951): 225–48.

Kay, Carol. *Political Constructions: Defoe, Richardson, and Sterne in Relation to Hobbes, Hume, and Burke*. Ithaca, N.Y.: Cornell University Press, 1988.

Lamb, Jonathan. *Sterne's Fiction and the Double Principle*. Cambridge: Cambridge University Press, 1989.

Lanham, Richard. *Tristram Shandy: the Games of Pleasure*. Berkeley and Los Angeles: University of California Press, 1973.

Moglen, Helene. *The Philosophical Irony of Laurence Sterne*. Gainesville: University Presses of Florida, 1975.

New, Melvyn. *Laurence Sterne as Satirist*. Gainesville: University Presses of Florida, 1969.

Piper, William Bowman. *Laurence Sterne*. New York: Twayne, 1965.

Pocock, J. G. A. *Virtue, Commerce and History*. Cambridge: Cambridge University Press, 1985.

Stedmond, John M. *The Comic Art of Laurence Sterne*. Toronto: University of Toronto Press, 1967.

Swearingen, James E. *Reflexivity in Tristram Shandy: an Essay in Phenomenological Criticism*. New Haven: Yale University Press, 1977.

Thompson, David. *Wild Excursions: the Life and Fiction of Laurence Sterne*. New York: McGraw-Hill, 1972.

Traugott, John. *Tristram Shandy's World: Sterne's Philosophical Rhetoric*. Berkeley and Los Angeles: University of California Press, 1954.

  (ed.) *Laurence Sterne: a Collection of Critical Essays*. Englewood Cliffs, N.J.: Prentice-Hall, 1968.

8

MICHAEL ROSENBLUM

Smollett's *Humphry Clinker*

If Tobias Smollett is a more important figure now than he used to be, it is
not because his novels seem any better now than they did thirty years ago.
Neither the first, *Roderick Random (1748)*, nor the last, *The Expedition of
Humphry Clinker* (1771), have attained the superstar status of *Clarissa*
(1747–48), *Tom Jones* (1749), or *Tristram Shandy* (1760–67) – nor are
they likely to. But because the kinds of questions entertained by the
academy have changed so radically, the terms for assessing importance have
also changed. It no longer seems quite so pressing to make a case for one of
his "neglected" novels, or to assess his achievement in relation to that of his
rival Fielding's, or to ask whether the novels are best described as "picaresque," or romance, or satire, and in just what amalgam.[1] At least for now,
these questions, framed from the traditional perspective of "literature,"
have yielded to a different set of concerns. The sleepy "period" that used to
be "Augustan" has now become the "culture" of an "early modern
England" busily engaged in a multitude of simultaneous construction
projects; nationhood and empire: the literary market place and commodity
culture; turnpikes and the modern subject.

Whether or not Smollett has the stature of Defoe, Hogarth, or Dr.
Johnson, he shares their centrality in conducting the various enterprises of
this culture. Like Defoe, he churns out immense quantities of print as writer,
editor, and compiler of multivolume works like *The Present State of All
Nations* and *A Compendium of Authentic and Entertaining Voyages*, which
market literature and subliterature in new ways to a new audience. He is the
first to serialize a novel in a periodical (*Sir Launcelot Greaves* in *The
British Magazine*) and probably the first to do so with illustrations.[2] Like
Hogarth, he is a maker of images that have become ubiquitous: Smollett's
set pieces on the disorder and stink of Bath and London in *Humphry
Clinker* are as inevitable as "Gin Lane" or the tavern scene in "The Rake's
Progress" as representations of culture. All the novels have some version of
Ferrett, the character in *Sir Launcelot Greaves* (1760–62) whose "nostrils

were elevated in scorn, as if his sense of smelling had been perpetually offended by some unsavoury odour; and he looked as if he wanted to shrink within himself, from the impertinence of society."[3] If Hogarth has the best eye for the culture, Smollett (whom Sterne called Doctor Smelfungus) has its most acute nose.[4]

Finally, the somewhat grander comparison with the "Great Cham" himself (the title Smollett bestowed upon Dr. Johnson). Smollett is a younger and somewhat lesser Cham who presides over the institution of literature from his perch in Chelsea, then just outside London. Like Johnson, he is both Grub Street writer and cultural arbiter, making literature accessible to a broader audience in his popular histories (*A Complete History of England* [1757–58] and the *Continuation of the Complete History of England* [1765]), and *The Critical Review*, the journal which he founded and which remained influential long after his death. His aim in this enterprise was "to befriend Merit, dignify the Liberal Arts, and contribute towards the formation of a public Taste, which is the best Patron of Genius and Science."[5]

This is the pose of disinterestedness that Smollett strikes in the cameo appearance that he gives himself in *The Expedition of Humphry Clinker*: he is Mr. S— of Monmouth House in Old Chelsea, receiving his guests "in a plain, yet decent habitation, which opened backwards into a very pleasant garden, kept in excellent order," which showed "none of the outward signs of authorship, either in the house or the landlord, who is one of those few writers of the age that stand upon their own foundation, without patronage, and above dependence."[6] This is a Grub Street moved to the suburbs and transformed into an orderly society ruled by an imperturbable Master of the Feast. This pleasant fantasy of withdrawal and self-sufficiency is repeated later in the novel when Smollett takes his travelers to Cameron House, his ancestral home in the arcadian Highlands. There he appears in the novel again as Dr. Smollett born on the banks of the Leven and author of the pretty "Ode to Leven-Water" that Bramble inserts into his letter. Even Smollett's way of framing the novel with a negotiation between Jonathan Dustwich and Henry Davis takes him out of the picture: an innocent Welsh clergyman in possession of a packet of letters offers them for publication to a reluctant London bookseller, who claims that they are hardly more marketable than the batch of sermons the clergyman is also peddling; the only thing the publisher really wants sent from Wales is some cheese for his wife.

The real Smollett was writing most of *Humphry Clinker* at his villa at Leghorn, where for the short time that he had to live, he was indeed safely removed from the literary and political battlefield. The Mr. S— of the novel is so far above the fray that he can provide hospitality for his enemies, but Smollett through most of his career was very much in the fray as editor and contributor to *The Critical Review*, and as the defender in *The Briton* of the policies of Lord Bute, George III's Scottish prime minister, as he sought to make peace with France in the face of tremendous domestic opposition. Judged by its brief existence and its pathetically small circulation, *The Briton* was a failed enterprise, but if we consider the enormity of the forces it had to oppose in *The North Briton*, the popular journal published by the clamorous opposition to Bute that numbered among its contributors the politician and glamorous rake John Wilkes, we can appreciate the extent to which Smollet in 1762 was at the center of the ideological battles of his time.[7] And in our own time, when we like our figures to be embroiled, hegemonic movers and shakers, Horace Walpole's taunt that Smollett was a "hireling propagandist" no longer seems quite such an insult.

And so instead of asking how good a novelist Smollett was, I will ask instead on what terms a novel like *Humphry Clinker* can be said to give us "access" (however qualified) to the changes taking place within the culture of early modern England. What can Smollett's novels, and particularly *The Expedition of Humphry Clinker*, tell us about history? Thirty years ago (I use this as a convenient "when-I-was-in-graduate school" sort of marker) history was what was most obvious about and therefore least interesting in a text; it was as what the clever had to learn to go "beyond." Narratives like *Humphry Clinker*, for example, might seem to refer to some state of affairs, outside and prior to the text, but this was their most superficial aspect: they were more "making than matching" (E. H. Gombrich), or "ways of worldmaking" constructed out of prior "worldmakings" (Nelson Goodman), or terms referring to still other terms in a semiotic chain. Since then history, albeit a "problematized" history, has returned as what clever readers need to restore to a text, the something that can neither be fully present in a text nor effaced from it.

Narrative now is figured as a kind of representational "space" whose boundaries are authorized by the culture within which acts of representation take place. With the right kind of tinkering, what is "inside" the narrative field can be shown to refer to what is "outside" the field, to what lies beyond in the "space" of history. Because the borders of fictional works are no longer considered to be inviolable (they are, in Bakhtin's figure, "permeable" rather than absolute), events inside can be taken to refer to events outside, and events from history can provide the clues for what is really happening inside the novel. Thus the novel is "situated" in history, or is used to "recover" a lost history in ways that would have been considered naive or outrageous in the past.

But if the referential element of representation is once again interesting, it is interesting precisely because such referentiality is far from straightforward. In order to illustrate how the obliquities of representation get treated in recent criticism, I will begin by considering the way that Raymond Williams and Edward Said move strategically between the "space" of narrative and the "space" of culture and history. They show that although representation is always ideologically constrained, narratives can nevertheless be read in such a way as to make them yield the history that they also obscure. I then will consider Smollett's space of representation from this double perspective: the first considers the way in which Smollett limits what he chooses to narrate and describe so that what we might consider as history can be seen – but only briefly. From the second perspective, more spatial than temporal, history makes a less fleeting appearance within the narrative field. Said observes that we are so "accustomed to thinking of the novel's plot and structure as constituted mainly by temporality that we have overlooked the function of space, geography, and location."[8] I will be treating The Expedition of Humphry Clinker as this kind of movement through narrative space: we get fuller access to Smollett's sense of history by considering the essential movements through space that his narratives trace.

In The Country and the City, one of the most influential works of the last thirty years, Raymond Williams praises Cobbett for hearing "the voice of men who have seen their children starving, and now within sight of the stately homes and the improved parks . . . It was not a new experience; it had been there all the time, but only rarely recorded."[9] That is, there was something out "there all the time" prior to the act of representation, a state of affairs in the "aboriginal" world, as unequivocal as the sufferings of the rural poor, which was to be seen and heard and which therefore was potentially available for representation (indeed cried out for it). But Cobbett's acuity is not typical: more often Williams shows that representations are the record of something not fully seen or wilfully mis-seen, as when Goldsmith tries to describe the sufferings of the rural poor in "The Deserted Village" (1770). But even if Goldsmith's Auburn does not get the history of rural dispossession "right" in the way that Cobbett does, it nevertheless reveals the circumstances and motives of somebody displaced by the historical changes he is trying to understand. In this respect, all representations are referential because they inevitably refer to the historical circumstances of their own making. To understand the act of representation we must know who is framing the space of representation and with what motives; who is deciding what is worthy of representation, on what scale, and in what genre. Such decisions must be ideological in nature since the concept of representation itself is both "aesthetic or semiotic" (things that "stand for" other things) and political (persons who "act for" other persons).[10] As W. A. Speck observes, even if the figure of Fielding's Squire Western does not necessarily tell the historical truth about country squires (that they were illiterate fox-hunting Jacobites), it certainly gives us access to the historical reality of Whig ideology.[11]

Criticism in the mode encouraged by *The Country and the City* scrutinizes the frames defining the "space" of representation and is especially concerned with what lies beyond those frames that also might or should have been given representation. In the thirty years since Williams wrote *The Country and the City*, it has become clearer that what seemed beyond the frame might have been there all along. As Edward Said has argued in *Culture and Imperialism*, what occupies relatively little of the space or time of the narrative field may in fact have the most "signifying power," if we pay these seemingly incidental mentionings the right kind of attention. His well-known reading of *Mansfield Park* argues that what are "at most half a dozen references" to Antiqua in the text point to the crucial historical reality outside the text that everybody (all the other characters, their creator, and her readers) would know about. When Sir Thomas Bertram disappears from the novel he is off tending to the business on the slave-holding colony that makes possible the elegance of his English estate. To read the novel properly we must connect his niece Fanny's "domestic or small-scale movement in space" (89). Said's method of "contrapuntal reading" restores an otherwise hidden historical reality by linking two spaces, one domestic, fictional, and fully represented, the other colonial, historical, and barely represented. History is something that is concealed in the margins, peripheries, or palimpsestic depths of the text; or to switch from spatial to temporal modalities, it is something to be briefly glimpsed in the text before it gets covered over.

Which is precisely what John Richetti does when he looks at the moments in the narrative fields of Smollett and Fielding. The figure of the half-naked Humphry Clinker first introduced into the novel gives us access to "a rural proletariat for whom work was varied, seasonal, and uncertain and for whom the local welfare system in case of illness or disability was harshly inefficient."[12] But this "real" Clinker emerging out of these "exactly rendered sociohistorical circumstances" is quickly transformed into a generic comic servant whose fulfillment lies in service to his master. Playing Kent to Bramble's Lear, he pledges undying loyalty to his master. Thus Smollett's "overtly ideological construction" of Clinker covers over what E. P. Thompson would see as the salient fact about any real Humphry: as a plebeian, his interests were anything but those of his patrician master.

What Smollett does here, Richetti takes to be characteristic of Fielding and Smollett's representational strategies in general: their surveys claim to offer "a richly comprehensive social representation" (comprehending, that is, the actual experience of the underclass as well as their masters), but at most we get a brief glimpse of the "actuality in which there lurk other beings, the underclass from which the eighteenth-century servant class was in fact recruited" (Richetti, 86). For the particularities that might reveal an actual history, Fielding cavalierly substitutes "a synthesizing abridgment of an actuality that otherwise yields no knowledge worth having" (91). Smollett's "richly particularized, almost distractingly concrete manner" allows more history into the narrative, but not much more.

So it is not surprising that one of the most promisingly concrete episodes in Smollett's first novel retreats into literary convention just when it promises to be most revealing about the actual circumstances of plebian life. When Roderick Random and his sidekick Strap first arrive in London from Scotland, they find themselves practicing "the art of diving" in a cook's shop. There, Roderick is "almost suffocated with the steams of boil'd beef, and surrounded by a company consisting chiefly of hackney coachmen, chairmen, draymen, and a few footmen out of place or on board wages; who sat eating shin of beef, tripe, cow-heel or sausages, at separate boards cover'd with cloths which turned my stomach."[13] The description is interrupted when Strap tumbles down the stairs, knocking over the cook who in turn dashes a porringer of soup on a drummer in the kind of disaster familiar to readers of Fielding or Cervantes. For modern readers, this description of the underclass pursuing their subterranean gastronomic pleasures is far more interesting than the farce that cuts it short. But as the preface to *Roderick Random* makes clear, Smollett knows what he is doing even if it is not what we would have him do. Smollett is anxious that such "mean scenes" will forfeit the eighteenth-century readers' "favorable pre-possession" towards his hero. And so his preface assures them that such episodes will only be brief excursions into lowlife before the hero resumes his proper status as a gentleman.

Some of Smollett's most revealing comments about the limits of proper representation occur in the long episode in *Peregrine Pickle* (1751; 1758) describing the folly of the painter Pallet, an uncritical admirer of the Flemish school of painting. In Antwerp, Pallet is delighted by an artist who depicts a huge louse crawling on a beggar's shoulder as well as two flies "engaged upon the carcase of a dog half devoured." Pallet regrets the loss of his own commonplace book "in which he had preserved a thousand conceptions of the same sort, formed by the accidental objects of his senses and imagination."[14]

Whether or not Pallet himself is a caricature of Hogarth, as Ronald Paulson has suggested, Pallet's representational preferences suggest the inclusiveness and detail of Hogarth's art. Smollett, like Fielding and Sterne, pays tribute to Hogarth, but the Hogarth they invoke is mainly a connoisseur of the picturesquely grotesque, ludicrous scenes like Tabitha and Griskin quarreling or Humphry preaching to the prisoners. When, in the *Continuation*, Smollett praises Hogarth for his ability to give representation to "scenes from ordinary life," he is pointing to an aspect of Hogarth's art that is more problematic: Hogarth disturbingly extends representation "downward" to the mean and crowded scenes for which he is famous.[15] Instead of the "grading and differentiation of elements" of Joshua Reynolds's canvases, Hogarth celebrates, says Paulson, "the naive eye that looks at signboards, and perhaps the world, not from single-point perspective but with an episodic and egalitarian contemplation of each object for itself."[16] This aesthetic allows the representation of such accidental objects of sense as beggars, dogs, and flies. Or worse: Pallet boasts that "he had exhibited the image of a certain object so like to nature, that the bare sight of it set a whole hogsty in an uproar" (335). Once classical norms of representation are abandoned, you find yourself descending into excrement.

In other words, Smollett's representational choices fit the norms of the neoclassical generality that we associate with Johnson, Reynolds, and, among the novelists, Fielding. This squeamishness about what might figure within the space of representation qualifies the traditional view that the rise of the novel itself makes possible an expansion of representational space. As Ian Watt argued in 1958, and J. Paul Hunter more recently, the novel is a shift in time spacing that makes the new territory of the familiar and the present, the here and now, available for representation: as a genre it breaks with the established hierarchy of genres, overcomes the doctrine of the separation of styles, recounts ordinary doings of ordinary people rather than the extraordinary adventures of the exalted. However well such a program describes Defoe, Richardson, and Sterne, it does not describe Fielding and Smollett's intuitions about what circumstances merit representation. For these two novelists, whatever is familiar, whatever is an accidental object of sense perception, is "not worth narratizing" because "it falls below the so-called threshold of narratability (it is not sufficiently unusual or problematic)."[17] The "mean scenes" of a cookhouse or of rural misery have little claim to narrative space in a high-threshold culture proscribing "lowness" and "minuteness." The circumstantiality and particularity that we associate with the concreteness of real history are for them mere contingencies, the dross of what happened to have happened. They want to move beyond the contingent here and now to those essential and universally known states of affairs that alone yield a knowledge worth having.

The ideological basis of such an "aesthetics" has become increasingly apparent: in his *Travels in France and Italy* (1766), Smollett finds it unseemly that Michelangelo has "chosen his kings, heroes, cardinals, and prelates from among the *facchini* of Rome; that he really drew his Jesus on the cross from the agonies of some vulgar assassin expiring on the wheel; and that the originals of his Bambini, with their mothers, were literally found in a table."[18] The dispersed composition of Buonarroti's *Last Judgment*, in which "a number of people are talking at once," bothers him: a single figure and clearly separated groups are intelligible, "but the whole together is a mere mob, without subordination." In other words, the rules for representational space in art and politics are the same: maintain hierarchy and subordination and avoid the promiscuous intermingling that obscures difference.

Clearly Fielding's and Smollett's way of drawing the boundaries for proper representational space differs from our own because of their very different notion of what circumstances will yield an actuality that is worth knowing about. The experience that they notate briefly as the condition of comic servanthood or Cervantean farce is exactly what we want to see given sustained and problematic representation. Their narrative field accommodates the kind of history in which "we" are interested only in those moments to be glimpsed off in the margins of the field, before the particularities we take to be the signs of true history get converted into the comic generalities which (Williams and Richetti might say) protect Fielding and Smollett from true history. Richetti's way of finessing their narrative field makes it yield the history it both conceals and reveals: states of affairs that are barely represented can be restored (at least briefly) to the center of the narrative.

Where Richetti recovers an obscured history by looking to "moments" in which the actualities of rural poverty or urban chaos are represented, Said recovers a suppressed imperial history by tracking the movements of the fictional characters through narrative space: the spaces of *Clarissa* or *Tom Jones* can be seen both as a "domestic accompaniment to the imperial project for presence and control abroad, and a practical narrative about expanding and moving about in space that must be actively inhabited and enjoyed before its discipline or limits can be accepted" (Said, 70).

In Smollett's first novel this imperial movement is more overt than suppressed. The resolution of *Roderick Random* depends upon the hero's unexpected remeeting with his uncle, the feckless Captain Bowling, who has in the meantime become his rich uncle. Even more miraculous is Roderick's discovery of his ineffectual and long-lost father as a rich man in Paraguay. In writing of these recognition scenes some thirty years ago, I described them as throwbacks to the language of romance, pure wish-fulfillment fantasies unhindered by the reality principle. I must have noticed, but it did not seem worth pointing out at the time, that although the meetings themselves depend upon the extraordinary coincidences of romance, the text was quite explicit about the means by which three such innocent characters as Roderick, his father, and his uncle were able to get rich so quickly. Bowling tells Roderick that he "was just arrived from the coast of Guinea, after having made a pretty successful voyage," and is "ready to set sail on a very advantageous voyage, which he was not at liberty to discover" (398). Roderick soon learns the secret: the ship "is bound for the coast of Guinea, where we shall exchange part of our cargo for slaves and gold-dust; from thence we will transport our negroes to Buenos-Ayres" (i.e., Bowling has struck it rich via the slave trade and restores Roderick's fortunes by setting him up in it too). Roderick buys 400 negroes in Guinea and sells them when he arrives in Paraguay, regretting only that he did not buy and sell "five times the number" that they could have sold "at our own price" (410). Rodrick's father has recouped his fortune, "in trade," which would probably also be connected with the colonial traffic in slaves. Roderick does refer to "the disagreeable lading of Negroes, to whom indeed I had been a miserable slave," but the disagreeableness has more to do with the burden of tending the slaves during an epidemic fever than it does with moral judgment. Bowling's secret is not the charged secret that the doings in Antiqua will be fifty years later, but it too explains how estates back home (in this case Scotland) are made possible.

Yet even where the movement in Smollett's novels is neither implicitly or explicitly imperial, Said's way of aligning movements within a narrative field with the movements of history is suggestive. England (its culture, its history) is seen from afar, as if from a satellite in space. It becomes a great game board on which we can trace the movements of individuals or armies; if we back off further we see that the board extends to Ireland, Scotland, and Wales, and further yet, to the outposts of Empire. Seen close up, the movements of Robinson, Tom, or Clarissa seem spontaneous and idiosyncratic, but from a distance they abstractly choreograph the essential movements of the culture. For critics like Williams and Said everything (culture, history, narrative) is literally a matter of space, a matter of who appropriates the land, foreign or domestic, and by what means. Culture converts continuous land into discrete plots owned by the few and worked by the many. Seen from above, England is ruled into big and little plots, each of which is dominated by a relatively small number of "big houses" surrounded by parks that are linked to some middling houses and more peripherally, a vast number of small structures which, as Williams notes, hardly seem human habitations at all. To understand the culture, one must understand the terms that legitimate the ownership, and "improvement," of this land. As the century advances the parks get larger, the big estates consolidate, more of the commons get enclosed, and more of the land gets connected to London. London is the "center" in relation to the rest of England, just as England is the center in relation to the "Celtic peripheries" that amalgamate with England to become the nation of Great Britain. And as Said emphasizes, this nation in turn is the center reaching outward to the more remote peripheries (East and West Indies, America) that become the Empire. And always, across a narrow channel from "Lilliput" is "Blefescu", the adversary "Center" reaching out for many of the same peripheries.

In addition to demarcating space, culture prescribes the rules for movement: who moves and who does not, and along what paths? The figures inhabiting the "big houses" have the most mobility, making routine loops between country and city in accord with the demands of business or pleasure, the sessions of parliament or the hunting season. Less routine are the excursions to various spas and seaside resorts, or, as the turnpike system improves, the more remote regions of Wales and the Highlands. The biggest loop of all is that of the grand tour. Where patrician itineraries tend to be voluntary, pleasure-oriented, and circular (there is always the estate and the "big house" to return to), plebeian movements tend to be involuntary, necessary, and open-ended. The poor and the ambitious are drawn centripetally toward London, or centrifugally toward the peripheries of the Empire to make their fortune. To "know" a culture is to know its repertoire of essential movements. Sometimes these movements are exemplary, like the circuits of the commercial traveler in Defoe's *Tour through the Whole Island of Great Britain* (1724–26) or Mr. Spectator's 24-hour perambulation around London; or the centripetal/centrifugal tides of the Thames as they flow "for all Mankind" in Pope's poetic celebration of English expansionism in his 1713 poem "Windsor Forest"; or Addison's praise of the Royal Exchange in the *Spectator* as the center of the world. But sometimes these movements are sinister or tragic, as in Pope's *Dunciad* (1744) where the goddess Dullness draws all wit and learning down to her as she travels Westward, or as in Goldsmith's elegy in "The Deserted Village" for a simpler rural England in his depiction of Auburn as its inhabitants are pulled toward London or dispersed outward to the far reaches of the Empire. Perhaps the culture's definitive mapping of movement along the rising and falling axis is revealed in Hogarth's progress pieces, such as *The Idle Apprentice* or *The Harlot's Progress*, which take us in a series of pictures that follow the apprentice and the harlot through the crowded stations of London life and end unhappily in Bedlam and Tyburn.

Smollett is an exemplary and influential figure in the culture of early modern England because he both participates in and gives representation to so many of its essential movements. Along with his first hero Roderick Random, he is one of the many enterprising Scots drawn to London. But they suffer the misadventures of empire at the Battle of Carthagena – but they profit from it too; Roderick by dabbling in the slave trade and Smollett by marrying a West Indian heiress. In *Peregrine Pickle*, his second novel, Smollett gives an extended representation of the grand tour. But it is Smollett's final novel that offers the most comprehensive and intricate tracking of the essential movements of the culture. If we stand back from its spaces in the way that Said would have us stand back from *Clarissa* or *Tom Jones*, what kinds of movement are traced? First we see a family group, a Welsh landowner and his entourage, moving in a loop through England and Scotland (the departure from and return to Wales implied, but not directly represented). This is the containing frame of the novel, and it corresponds to a kind of movement that grows increasingly popular through the century – "the Tour."[19] The second movement is what Bramble refers to as "the Vortex"; the chaotic movement in and around Bath and London that the tour allows him to observe with impunity (though he fears getting sucked into it). Finally there is a countermovement, the "Return to the Estate," which provides a way of escaping the vortex by reversing its movement. Instead of the sinister convergence that Smollett associates with social, economic, and political change, this centripetal movement flows outwards toward many centers – the country estates run by gentlemen landowners.

I will begin with the tour; the sustained and deliberate patrician move-ment that gives the narrative its shape. Like Defoe and Fielding, Smollett constructs narrative by moving his protagonists along from one "scene of life" to another. (Richardson and Sterne's characters move, but only within the scaled-down tracks of domestic space.) *Humphry Clinker* is Smollett's "purest" travel fiction in that the motive for travel is a seemingly disinter-ested wish to observe the scene from which all elements of necessity have been purged. Unlike Random or Fathom (or Pickle towards the end of his career), Bramble and company are not seeking a job or patronage. They are, quite simply, tourists. Although subject to the normal hazards of travel, like overturned coaches, the gentleman traveler is otherwise invulnerable. He cannot, like Humphry, be hauled before a magistrate. Even far from home he has the unassailable credentials that the ownership of land confers. In *Launcelot Greaves* the upstart Justice Gobble interrogates Greaves whom he accuses of being a vagabond:

"What are you, friend? What is your station and degree?" "I am a gentleman," replied the knight. "Ay, that is English for a sorry fellow (said the justice). Every idle vagabond, who has neither home nor habitation, trade nor profession, designs himself a gentleman. But I must know how you live?" "Upon my means." "What are your means?" "My estate." "Whence doth it arise?" "From inheritance." (94)

To such a catechism, Bramble would be able to answer with confidence: formerly Matthew Loyd, heir to his mother's land in Glamorganshire, he is now Matthew Bramble of Brambleton Hall in Monmouthshire as his nephew is Jeremy Melford of Belfield, in the county of Glamorgan.

Moreover, his status gives the gentleman traveler the authority to give a comprehensive representation of the tour. Paul Fussell has suggested that travel "comes very near the heart of the dominant eighteenth-century idea of knowledge," because it allows "the sequential accumulation of sense particulars collected from a multifarious but verifiable objective reality."[20] John Barrell would add the qualification that the objectivity of such knowledge depends on who it is that is accumulating the particulars: "Only the gentleman will be able to *describe* those social connections that only he is privileged to *observe*" because he alone has the "impartiality" that a language not "contaminated by regional or occupational particularities" makes possible.[21] The fact that Bramble is a choleric Welshman given to alternate fits of sensibility and outrage does not really compromise his essential impartiality. His letters and those of his nephew Jeremy Melford – another quintessential gentleman-observer – provide the dominant and authoritative voices of the novel. Bramble fumes where Melford is amused, but they see pretty much the same scene, and it is the scene Smollett would have us see. Along the way they enlist the services of various tour guides: Dick Ivy, who leads them through the literary world; the courtier Mr. Barton, who praises everybody; and Captain C., "a man of shrewd parts whom the government occasionally employed in secret services," who damns everybody. These different voices may create different perspectives, but Bramble and Melford have no difficulty in making the proper adjustments to get what they take to be a balanced view. Although *Humphry Clinker* is sometimes treated as a venture in the gaps and indeterminacies of Richardsonian epistolarity, I think it is really more old-fashioned. The unrecorded replies of Dr. Lewis, Watkin Phillips, Mary Jones, and Mrs. Gwyllim pose no more of an interpretive challenge than does reconciling the differences among the accounts of Bramble, Melford, Lydia, Tabitha, and Win. The letters are as grounded in the authority of the gentleman as the tour itself is.

Touring also means encountering a group of characters who are definitely *not* touring. These are the stranded, the most notable of whom is Bramble's opposite, the dislocated vagabond Humphry Clinker himself. There are also more genteel types who have fallen upon hard times: the widow in Bath, Mr. Martin the highwayman, and Obadiah Lismahago. They belong to the larger number of minor characters in all Smollett's fiction whose prehistory is sketched in a few sentences: the feckless second sons who fail in business or professions; clergymen and the women who marry them; consumptives; naval men or soldiers who fail to get promoted or who die before they have provided for their families; those who are ruined by standing security for a friend; those whose marriage displeases their fathers. Although perfunctory, these highly conventionalized mini narratives imply Smollett's sense of social causation, of all the ways there are of rising and falling in society (mostly the latter). The gentleman-tourist sorts out the stranded and assigns them their proper place: the widow is relieved; Clinker and Lismahago become part of the estate; while Mr. Martin is dispatched to the wars of empire.

In contrast to the deliberate and orderly circular movement of the patrician tour, there is the chaotic and ubiquitous movement of the vortex, the characteristic motion of change. Its movement is centripetal, a motion sweeping from the peripheries of empire to the center (first it is Bath, then it is London; it does not really matter since both are microcosms of the same society).

> Every upstart of fortune ... presents himself at Bath ... Clerks and factors from the East Indies, loaded with the spoil of plundered provinces; planters, negro-drivers, and hucksters, from our American plantations, enriched they know not how; agents, commissaries, and contractors, who have fattened, in two successive wars, on the blood of the nation; usurers, brokers, and jobbers of every kind; men of low birth, and no breeding, have found themselves suddenly translated into a state of affluence. (36)

Those from the peripheries, the men of the "New Interest" associated with commerce and empire are swept towards the center in a tide that allows them to mingle with the representatives of the "Old Interest." *Really* mingle: they breathe the same air; drink and bathe in the same putrid waters. And when they dance together, the pairings are as heterogeneous as possible: a Scotch lord with a mulatto heiress from St. Christopher's; a colonel with "the daughter of an eminent tinman from the borough of Southwark." In London, Bramble sees a mingling even more intimate: "a dirty barrow-bunter in the street, cleaning her dusty fruit with her own spittle; and, who knows but some fine lady of St. James' parish might admit into her delicate mouth those very cherries, which had been rolled and moistened between the filthy, and perhaps, ulcerated chops of a St. Giles' huckster" (120). The blending of the spittle of St. Giles and St. James makes it clear that when you mix what should be kept separate (bodies, the various spaces of London and the classes which inhabit them, colonials and natives), the result is contamination.[22] When Melford asks the actor Quinn if the mixture of plebeians and patricians would not "improve the whole mass? – Yes (said he), as a plate of marmalade would improve a pan of sirreverence" (49). Melford comments that "the general mixture of all degrees assembled in our public rooms, without distinction of rank or fortune ... is what my uncle reprobates, as a monstrous jumble of heterogeneous principles; a vile mob of noise and impertinence, without decency or subordination" (47). And so when Bramble sniffs the air in the common rooms of Bath and swoons, he is responding viscerally not only to the bad air, but to the social and economic changes that have brought all those people into the same space. In one involuntary gesture, his body registers and rejects the new order.

To escape the vortex, it is necessary to retreat back to the stable and controllable space of the ancestral estate. Smollett's novels typically end with a solemn journey (or a journey in prospect) back to the estate from which the protagonist has been disinherited and exiled – recovery of the lost estate is accomplished by miraculously coincidental recognitions scenes, duels, and timely deaths. Since Bramble is already in full possession of his estate, the act of regaining and improving lost estates is played out at the Dennison estate and the neighboring Baynard estate. After the travelers suffer the discomforts of estates controlled by bad landlords (like Burdock, Pimpernel, or Oxmington) or a hen-pecked landlord like Baynard, the party winds up at Mr. Dennison's and stays there for the rest of the novel. Clinker's deliverance of Bramble from the flooded coach sets off a chain of extraordinary coincidences: the "lord of the manor" near the site of the accident "is no other than Charles Dennison, our fellow-rake at Oxford," who also turns out to be the father of "Wilson," Liddy's mysterious suitor. When Bramble uses his old name "Matthew Loyd" to identify himself to Dennison, Humphry is able to figure out his relation to the man whose life he has just saved. As Melford puts it, "The quondam Humphry Clinker is metamorphosed into Matthew Loyd" (306).

That Clinker and Bramble should both be "Matthew Loyd," that the fastidious body of Bramble should be connected (via the barmaid Dolly Twyford) to so unprepossessing a specimen (to all but Win Jenkins) as Clinker is Smollett's final variation on the father–son recognition scenes that run through his novels. This is a literary joke that Fielding and Smollett both liked to play, but here it is not necessary to resolve the plot, as it is in

Joseph Andrews and *Tom Jones*. Clinker is, in fact, in a constant state of metamorphosis throughout the novel. First, by his own insistence and Bramble's consent, the ragged peasant becomes a liveried servant. Later he becomes a Methodist preaching to his social betters, then a jailbird preaching to his fellow prisoners. Finally he exchanges his unambiguous status as servant for a status as not-quite-gentleman, not-quite-heir. Bramble does not know what to do with Clinker: should he make him a farrier? An apothecary like the reformed villain Ferdinand Fathom? A vestry clerk as Doctor Lewis suggests? If, as Richetti argues, the initial transformation of vagabond into literary servant is "ideological in the classic sense," so too is the even more extravagantly literary transformation of servant and master to son and father. Bramble literally becomes the father, the role that his position as landowner has implied all along.

In this part of the novel we have Smollett's most extended discourse of the estate, a little treatise on how to (re)create the right kind of social/political/ economic space. Here Bramble really comes into his own as a figure of authority, though his competence as landlord has been emphasized throughout in the references to his dealings with his steward, tenants, a poacher, and a candidate for his vote. The closing pages of the novel deal more with the resolution of estates than the characters' lives, which is to say that the lives of the characters are inseparable from the social order whose creation Smollett so insistently narrates. First there is an extended description of the present flourishing condition of the Dennison estate, followed by Dennison's long account of how it got that way. At this point, "understanding by the greatest accident in the world" that Mrs. Baynard is ill, Bramble "attended only by Loyd (quondam Clinker) on horseback" travels the thirty miles to Baynard's where he is greeted by the news of Mrs. Baynard's death. (Smollett is consistently shameless in using this kind of narrative magic to get the estate back in all the novels.) "Vested ... with full authority," by Baynard, the newly virile Bramble actively superintends the renewal of his friend's estate. The pattern for renewal is the same for both estates: spatially, the movement from London to the country; temporally, a before-and-after structure transforming a *"tower of desolation"* into a self-sufficient community. I doubt that most readers could keep the two narratives of the transformations of the two estates separate, nor is there any need to: what Dennison did "two and twenty" years ago is still what needs to be done.

Bramble presides over the restoration of Baynard's estate in the same way that the restoration of Dennison's estate and his initiation into country life was guided years ago by his neighbor Mr. Wilson (who, in his turn, was instructed by his father-in-law Farmer Bland). Wilson is an universal genius – his talents are really astonishing – He is an excellent carpenter, jointer, and turner, and a cunning artist in iron and brass. He not only superintended my oeconomy, but also presided over my pastimes. – He taught me to brew beer ... He understands all manner of games from chess down to chuck-farthing, sings a good song, plays upon the violin, and dances a hornpipe with surprising agility. (313)

This list of accomplishments recalls Humphry's list of his own qualifications when he is persuading Bramble to hire him. Humphry enters the novel a bumbler, but by the end becomes a figure of competence who makes good on most of his promises to Bramble. He is something of a universal genius on the order of Wilson/Bland – and, in the earlier novels, such figures of competence as Strap, Random's sidekick, and the ex-sailor Pipes in *Peregrine Pickle*. Smollett's model for order depends upon gentlemen landowners who, in collaboration with the local peasants and yeomen, take their responsibilities seriously. The new (old) order links gentlemen like Bramble and Dennison with figures like Wilson, the ex-seaman, the farmer Bland, and the peasant–foundling Clinker who (and this is Bramble's last suggestion for his son Loyd) will assist his steward Barns in "superintending the oeconomy of my farm."

Bramble binds the Dennison and Baynard estates financially by refinancing Baynard's debt with loans from Dennison, as well as loans from Bland, Liddy's marriage settlement, Tabitha ("four thousand at four per cent"), and himself. This is the right kind of credit: derived from the land, it returns to it. In an earlier episode in the novel, Bramble is delighted by Captain Brown, a soldier in the East India Company who returns to his native village in Scotland. He uses his accumulated capital to pension his parents, dower his sister, commission one brother and make another his partner in a manufacturing enterprise that will "give employment and bread to the industrious," and gives charity to the poor and feasts the town. This kind of circulation of capital from the peripheries is acceptable because, as in the case of the returned Roderick Random, the capital goes back to the dispersed centers of the estates rather than the city.

The order that Bramble establishes is clearly a throwback to old England and recalls Launcelot Greaves's efforts to revive the "Golden Age" in Yorkshire. It also recalls the model social order of the clans whom Bramble's party have observed on their Highland tour. In these societies everything depends upon the social cohesion provided by the patriarchal bond:

The connection between the clans and their chief is, without all doubt *patriarchal*. It is founded on hereditary regard and affection, cherished through a long succession of ages. The clan considers the chief as their father, they bear his name, they believe themselves descended from his family, and they obey him as their lord, with all the ardour of filial love and veneration; while he, on his part, exerts a paternal authority, commanding, chastising, rewarding, protecting, and maintaining them as his own children. (246–47)

How shall we evaluate the historicity of this patriarchal space that in one way or another is the final destination of all of Smollett's novels? For Byron Gassman, one of Smollett's closest students, this is a "Tory" and "Augustan" "mythic realm" that lies just "beyond the perimeters of history."[23] In order to counter the corruption of "Hanoverian and Whiggish rule," Smollett imagines instead another kingdom where "the beneficent landlord, presiding over his estate with fatherly concern, honored by his subordinates, exacting their due homage, but in turn devoting his bounty to the promotion of the whole society's welfare" (103). For E. P. Thompson, such a paternalist myth is less a wish to go beyond the perimeters of history than the way a "predatory society" dominated by patrician landlords tries to smooth over class conflict: a more apt model for the paternal landlord would be the slaveholder of colonial Brazil.[24]

But for historians like G. E. Mingay, and more recently J. C. D. Clark, this patriarchal/paternal kingdom is real history, both as living practice and as a way of imagining the common interests of patrician and plebeian. Clark argues that "traditional, hierarchical, deferential forms ... were neither antiquated, tenuous survival nor mere veneers or superstructures on a reality which was 'basically' economic, but substantive and prevalent modes of thought and behaviour in a society dominated still by the common people, by the aristocracy, and by the relations between the two."[25] In Clark's version of eighteenth-century society, patrician hegemony is so benign, so well-established, and so much to everybody's advantage as hardly to be in need of explanation. Within such a society, Humphry's assent to Bramble's rule is neither his mistake in understanding his own interest nor his creator's misrepresentation of the real relation of patrician landowners to their tenants.

I introduce this very different spin on the patriarchal bond not to suggest that Clarke's harmonious England is more plausible as a construct than Thompson's tense theatre of conflict, but to recall some familiar matters that can easily be ignored when contemporary critics speak of representations as referring (however obliquely) to history. Although we know that history is always "history," an ideologically motivated act of representation, attempts to "situate" texts sometimes sound as if there were only one kind of history to be "recovered." Representational fields open out, or can be made to yield "history," but *whose* history? When we read historians as forceful as Thompson or Clark, it is hard not to get swept up in their versions of history (to say nothing of the difficulties of choosing between them). And when we read literary critics as eloquent as Williams or Said, insistence that history is a matter of interpretation seems a fatuous response to their evocations of the human suffering caused by the slave trade, imperial wars, and rural poverty. That there were many real men as wretched as Humphry was when Bramble first encountered him is incontestable, but the causes of that misery or the wisdom of his willingness to throw in his lot with Bramble can be subject to analysis as different as Thompson's and Clark's.

And this is finally why *Clinker* is so interesting: it gives access not to history but to a number of possible histories. For Richetti, *Clinker* illustrates "the process whereby the historical (in the Marxist sense) is appropriated by fiction." A more old-fashioned "literary" view would see this "process" of "appropriation" by "fiction" as less inevitable and impersonal, more a matter of something that Smollett contrives to make happen and less something that happens almost in spite of him (neither the particularity in which history sneaks through nor the comic generality by which it is covered over seems quite within Smollett's control). If the history that it attempts to represent seems muddled, it is the muddle of those experiencing changes whose outcome is as yet uncertain (as it still is, to some extent, for us). And if the representation of history in *Humphry Clinker* is clearly ideological, the thrust of that ideology is far from clear.

The ideological position from which Smollett constructs his narratives is almost always described as "Tory" or "Tory/Country." Some qualifications are in order: historians debate the relevance of the term "Tory" to the politics of 1760, and Smollett himself scorns those who make too much of the Tory/Whig distinction. And certainly as Donald Greene and W. A. Speck have shown, Smollett's interpretation of the settlement of 1688/89 in the *History* does not follow the typical Tory pattern. Moreover, Smollett does not, like most Tories, ground his political and social views within a specifically religious framework. Nevertheless he is, as James Sack describes him, "a Tory of sorts."[26] Smollett attacks the corruption of Whig politics, upholds the "Old Landed Interest" against the "New Interest," which he describes in *The Briton* as "an iniquitous band of money-brokers, usurers, contractors, and stock-jobbers, who prey upon the necessity of their country, and fatten on her spoils."[27] He is relentless in attacking "the mob" (or "the vulgar") and those "reformers who have espoused the plebeian interests from an innate aversion to all order and restraint" (317). In the *Continuation*, Smollett urges that noblemen convicted of crimes be executed at the Tower rather than at Tyburn "to avoid any circumstances that may tend to diminish the lustre of the English nobility ... or to bring it into contempt with the common people ... already too licentious and prone to abolish those distinctions which serve as the basis of decorum, order, and subordination."[28]

Clearly such a stance "fits" Clark's account of the dominant eighteenth-century ideology as "patriarchalism," the politics of deference that is observed on the "estate" and violated in the "vortex." Smollett's Toryism fits Clark's description of a social and political order grounded in a loyalty that is "hereditary, personal [and] emotional." And yet Smollett's Toryism also "fits" into Thompson's very different account of cultural hegemony. For Thompson, the "largely Tory 'Country' tradition of the independent lesser gentry" was one of the few groups that offered resistance to the "patrician banditti" (33–34). In fact Thompson says his own "alternative view" of eighteenth-century society was actually anticipated by contemporary writers, most of them Tory: "It is, after all, the criticism of high politics offered in *Gulliver's Travels* and in *Jonathan Wild*; in part in Pope's satires and in part in *Humphry Clinker*; in Johnson's 'Vanity of Human Wishes' and 'London' and in Goldsmith's 'Traveler'" (30–31). Presumably the part that Smollett gets "right" is contained in Bramble's critique of the vortex; the part he gets "wrong" is the perpetuation of the myth of the paternal landowner. Thus Smollett's Toryism can be plausibly connected with both a Tory politics of containment and a Tory politics of resistance. On the one hand he gives us a representation of the gentleman on tour or reclaiming his estate; on the other he (or characters like Bramble, Ferret, Crabtree, and Medlar) keeps insisting that there is a fundamental and lingering injustice in the social order.

And finally, Smollett "fits" or almost fits yet another version of cultural hegemony, that of Linda Colley's *Britons*. Like Clark and unlike Thompson, she stresses the common interests of very different kinds of Britons. But their allegiance is not to Clark's traditional order, but to the new order of commerce and nation-building. The gloating Protestantism and militarism is unattractive, yet because everybody benefited or thought they benefited, Colley finds this an order that is widely subscribed to rather than imposed. Of course Smollett is not quite like Defoe, a novelist who, in John Bender's description, "enables" the new order; as I have been suggesting, Smollett's relation to change is mainly anxious, even adversarial. Nevertheless he does participate in some of the most important changes of the period: to the extent that he persistently mocks the French, or imagines the marriage of Scotland, Wales, and Ireland in *Humphry Clinker*, or urges the improvement of the Highlands, he can be seen as helping in building the nation or the empire.[29] Nor is Bramble quite as dogmatic a foe of commerce as Lismahago, who beats his nephew for setting up commercial looms in the great hall of the ancestral home. When Lismahago rails against the evils of unrestrained commerce, Bramble replies mildly that "by proper regulations, commerce may produce every national benefit, without the allay of such concomitant evils" (269). Perhaps this acknowledgment of a new economic order is implied by the projected final itineraries of the novel: Bramble insists on returning to Brambleton Hall in time for Christmas because "it must be something very extraordinary that will induce me to revisit either Bath or London" (335–36). He will take with him two of the three married couples, the Lismahagos and the Loyds, as well as Baynard (on whom Bramble keeps an eye lest he backslide). But the older and younger Dennisons led by Jeremy Melford are drawn back to Bath.

I have considered Smollett from a perspective which assumes that it makes sense to try to connect the movements within a fictional narrative space to a "history" that is outside it. This assumption seems to have displaced the earlier assumption that a great ontological divide separates what happens within the world of a novel from the world in which novels get written. The new willingness to reconsider the borders between history and the novel seems to me a helpful development. At the same time, I would also note that however "permeable" those borders can be made to seem, they nevertheless remain. When, in Cervantes' novel, Don Quixote rushes up onto the puppet stage and cuts the strings of the "Saracens," I would still say he is making a mistake about the status of representations rather than making a bold critical "intervention." Nor can we forget the provisionality and the variousness of the versions of history offered by historians (or forget that invoking Clark, Thompson, Colley, or Lawrence Stone is not quite the same thing as doing history) either. Given the contrasts between Clark's harmoniously stable England in which there is no real class conflict (nor even classes), Thompson's agon of patrician and pleb, or Colley's energetic Britons displacing all conflict outward, judgments about the way a given narrative field refers to history have to be tentative. When we say something is missing, or glimpsed in the margins, or a figure for something else that is not otherwise within the narrative, we are registering our sense not only of what was "there," but what we think deserves to be given representation, which is ultimately a judgment about what knowledge is worth having. *Humphry Clinker* shows us that what happens in a novel can be related to history, but it also reminds us of how tricky that relation is.

NOTES

1 Nor do the intervening but still early novels (*Peregrine Pickle* [1751; 1758], *Ferdinand Count Fathom* [1753], and *Launcelot Greaves* [1760–62]) seem any less difficult to get through. On the other hand, if they are unreadable, they are hardly more so than *Amelia* or *Sir Charles Grandison* (1753–54).

2 For a comprehensive account of this aspect of his career see James G. Basker, *Tobias Smollett, Critic and Journalist* (Newark: University of Delaware Press, 1988).

3 David Evans, ed., *The Life and Adventures of Sir Launcelot Greaves* (London: Oxford University Press, 1973), 22.

4 G. S. Rousseau calls Smollett "the Hogarth of eighteenth-century prose." See "From Swift to Smollett: the Satirical Tradition in Prose Narrative," in John Richetti, ed., *The Columbia History of the British Novel* (New York: Columbia University Press, 1994), 127.

5 Quoted in Basker, *Tobias Smollett*, 32.

6 *The Expedition of Humphry Clinker*, ed. Thomas R. Preston (Athens: University of Georgia Press, 1990), 123.

7 See Byron Gassman's introduction to his edition of *The Briton* in *Poems, Plays, and The Briton* (Athens: University of Georgia Press, 1993).

8 Edward Said, *Culture and Imperialism* (New York: Vintage, 1993), 84.

9 Raymond Williams, *The Country and the City* (New York: Oxford University Press, 1973), 117–18.

10 W. J. T. Mitchell, "Representation," in Frank Lentricchia and Thomas McLaughlin, *Critical Terms for Literary Study* (Chicago: University of Chicago Press, 1990), 11.

11 W. A. Speck, *Society and Literature in England, 1700–1760* (Atlantic Highlands: Humanities Press, 1983), 12.

12 John Richetti, "Representing an Underclass: Servants and Proletarians in Fielding and Smollett," in Felicity Nussbaum and Laura Brown, eds., *The New Eighteenth Century: Theory, Politics, English Literature* (New York: Methuen, 1987), 95. See also the claim of John Sekora that Smollett "laments the depopulation of Midland farms but is silent on the plight of the dispossessed farmers. He speaks of the desperate men besieging the roads but says nothing of the sources of their despair." *Luxury: The Concept in Western Thought, Eden to Smollett* (Baltimore: Johns Hopkins University Press, 1977), 147.

13 Paul-Gabriel Boucé, ed., *The Adventures of Roderick Random* (Oxford: Oxford University Press, 1979), 65.

14 James L. Clifford and Paul-Gabriel Boucé, eds., *The Adventures of Peregrine Pickle* (Oxford: Oxford University Press, 1983), 335.

15 Tobias Smollett, *Continuation of the Complete History of England* (London, 5 vols, 1765), IV: 131.

16 Ronald Paulson, *Popular and Polite Art in the Age of Hogarth and Fielding* (Notre Dame, Ind.: University of Notre Dame Press, 1979), 41.

17 Gerald Prince, "The Disnarrated," *Style*, 22 (1988): 22.

18 *Travels in France and Italy*, ed. James Morris, (Fontwell, Sussex: Centaur, 1969), 352.

19 See Carol Fabricant, "The Literature of Domestic Tourism and the Public

Consumption of Private Property" in Nussbaum and Brown, eds., *The New Eighteenth Century.*

20 Paul Fussell, *The Rhetorical World of Augustan Humanism* (London and New York: Oxford University Press, 1965), 263.

21 John Barrell, *English Literature in History, 1730–1780* (London: Hutchinson, 1983), 178–79.

22 For a treatment of how *Clinker* allays anxieties about contamination, see Charlotte Sussman, "Lismahago's Captivity: Transculturation in *Humphry Clinker*," *ELH*, 61 (1994): 597–618.

23 Byron Gassman, "*Humphry Clinker* and the Two Kingdoms of George III," *Criticism*, 16 (1974): 108.

24 E. P. Thompson, *Customs in Common: Studies in Traditional Popular Culture* (New York: New Press, 1991). See particularly chapter 2, "The Patricians and the Plebs."

25 J. C. D. Clark, *English Society, 1688–1832* (Cambridge: Cambridge University Press, 1985), 43.

26 James J. Sack, *From Jacobite to Conservative* (Cambridge: Cambridge University Press, 1993). For discussions of the relevance of "Tory" to Smollett, see Donald Greene, "Smollett the Historian: a Reappraisal," in G. S. Rousseau and P. G. Boucé, eds., *Tobias Smollett: Bicentennial Essays Presented to Lewis M. Knapp* (New York: Oxford University Press, 1971); and Speck, *Society and Literature.*

27 Gassman, ed., *Poems, Plays, and The Briton*, 324.

28 *Continuation of the Complete History of England*, III: 384.

29 For an account of Smollett's role in constructing "the myth of the Highlands" see Peter Womack, *Improvement and Romance: Constructing the Myth of the Highlands* (London: Macmillan, 1989).

READING LIST

Barrell, J. *English Literature in History, 1730–1780: an Equal, Wide Survey.* London: Hutchinson, 1983.

Basker, J. *Tobias Smollett, Critic and Journalist.* Newark: University of Delaware Press, 1988.

Clark, J. C. D. *English Society, 1688–1832: Ideology, Social Structure and Political Practice During the Ancien Regime.* Cambridge: Cambridge University Press, 1985.

Colley, Linda. *Britons: Forging the Nation, 1707–1837.* New Haven: Yale University Press, 1993.

Gassman, Byron. "*Humphry Clinker* and the Two Kingdoms of George III." *Criticism*, 16 (1974): 95–108.

Mingay, G. E. *English Landed Society in the Eighteenth Century.* London: Routledge and Kegan Paul, 1983.

Nussbaum, F. and Brown L. (eds.) *The New Eighteenth Century: Theory, Politics, English Literature.* New York: Methuen, 1987.

Rousseau, G. S. and Boucé, P. G. (eds.) *Tobias Smollett: Bicentennial Essays Presented to Lewis M. Knapp.* New York: Oxford University Press, 1971.

Said, E. *Culture and Imperialism.* New York: Vintage, 1993.

Sack, James J. *From Jacobite to Conservative.* Cambridge: Cambridge University Press, 1993.

Sekora, John. *Luxury: the Concept in Western Thought, Eden to Smollett.* Baltimore: Johns Hopkins University Press, 1977.

Speck, W. A. *Society and Literature in England, 1700–1760.* Atlantic Highlands: Humanities Press, 1983.

Sussman, Charlotte, "Lismahago's Captivity: Transculturation in *Humphry Clinker.*" *ELH*, 61 (1994): 597–618.

Williams, R. *The Country and the City.* New York: Oxford University Press, 1973.

Womack, P. *Improvement and Romance: Constructing the Myth of the Highlands.* London: Macmillan, 1989.

9

JULIA EPSTEIN

Marginality in Frances Burney's novels

The heroines of Frances Burney's four novels embody a set of contradictions so paradigmatic of the later eighteenth century that they might be said to define the ideological tensions inhering in the period's complex demarcations of woman's social place. Burney's heroines are proper, decorous, and innocent, yet preternaturally aware of social danger; diffident yet fiercely self-protective; publicly self-effacing yet bent on independence of thought and action; ambiguously presented as to class yet adhering to upper-class ambitions; apparently unknowing about social mores and expectations, yet acutely observant of others and conscious of their own desires. Many recent feminist critics have analyzed these contradictions in Burney's fiction and in her life.[1] The conflicts Burney's protagonists face energize the novel of courtship in the later eighteenth century. Burney insists that the period in which a young woman becomes quintessentially identified as marriageable – as single in several senses – forms a crucially liminal proving ground, a period during which fundamental social barriers are traversed.

The importance of Burney's novels for students of culture and society has largely resided in their astute critique of gender and class ideologies as they affected the daily lives of women in the later eighteenth century. In addition to their deployment of Burney's famous power of caustic satirical wit, her fiction explores a variety of themes and narrative techniques relatively new to fiction in general and certainly new to fiction by women. Burney's novels[2] skewer social hierarchies and class divisions in rare ways; only in the picaresque tradition of the wandering male hero had fiction investigated class mobility to the extent that Burney foregrounds this question. Burney was an accurate observer of the economic fissures in social categories as the new mercantile classes began to aspire to the status of the landed gentry. Her heroines, with the possible exception of Camilla, traverse classes as they constantly face the need to invent and reinvent themselves for public consumption. In addition, as Margaret Doody has shown in detail in her magisterial literary biography, Burney experimented importantly with narrative style, moving smoothly from a sophisticated use of epistolary form in *Evelina* to the inauguration of a *style indirect libre* in the third-person narrative voices of the last three novels.[3]

The eighteenth-century courtship novel focuses on the delaying actions that dot the road between a young woman's emergence from her father's protection and the subsumption of her identity into that of her husband. Thereafter heroines disappear into the domestic life of marriage. This courtship tradition is replete with dark moments. In the early part of the century, heroines in difficulties sometimes turned courtesan, in a line that runs, for example, from Aphra Behn's *Love Letters Between a Nobleman and His Sister* (1684–87), to Defoe's *Moll Flanders* (1722) and *Roxana* (1724). The more sentimental tradition produced the tragedies of Richardson's *Clarissa* (1747–48) and Rousseau's *Nouvelle Héloïse* (1761), with a gender reversal in the protagonist of Goethe's *Sorrows of Young Werther* (1774). Burney has sometimes been treated as a "transition" figure in the history of the novel, someone who moved the form's satirical techniques from their broad Smollettian outlines to the more pointed satire of Dickens, and who moved the domestic focus on private life from the dense interiority of Richardson to the wry irony of Jane Austen. But while not disagreeing entirely with these chronological positionings of Burney's novelistic art, I would argue that she also represents a writer whose work broke original ground for the novel by exploring the new territory of social marginality opened up by class shifts during the eighteenth century.

Burney's version of the dark strain in the courtship novel dissects the testing of romantic heroines by heroes. Burney's isolated heroines seek, and obtain, marriage in order to establish their own social respectability. Unlike the "'I was born' first-person novels" that define the genre's focus on individual subjectivity with respect to male protagonists,[4] Burney's fictions produce a female subjectivity that questions its own merit at the same time it asserts that merit. And while Evelina and Lady Juliet move beyond their novels' closure into an ambiguous but apparently satisfactory married life, Cecilia and Camilla do not achieve safety in marriage. As Kristina Straub has pointed out, "the relationship that ensures Evelina's self and security, renders Cecilia voiceless and powerless; ... she cries out that 'no one will save me now! I am married, and no one will listen to me!'"[5] And Camilla's prize is Burney's most rigid and least appealing hero, Edgar Mandlebert, of whom Mrs. Arlbery warns Camilla: "He is a watcher; and a watcher, restless and perturbed himself, infests all he pursues with uneasiness."[6]

There is a particular way in which Burney's highly virtuous young heroines ironically resemble their young male counterparts in narrative tradition: the picaresque hero of European fiction from the sixteenth century's Lazarillo de Tormes to the early eighteenth century's Gil Blas and the mid-century's Tom Jones. The male picaro survives by his wits through a series of often violent adventures and threats to his life, always remaining a marginal figure who resides half inside and half outside society. The concept of "liminality" that I am employing to discuss the courtship period in a young woman's life in the eighteenth century may also be employed with reference to the fictional mode of being of the picaro. The term comes from anthropology, where its most cited theorist is Victor W. Turner. Turner says of "threshold people," or liminal social beings, that they "are neither here nor there; they are betwixt and between the positions assigned and arrayed by law, custom, convention, and ceremonial."[7] Turner identifies three stages in social transition rites – separation, margin, and reaggregation – of which liminality is the second. As these stages are useful in thinking about the male picaresque career in literary convention, they work as well for Burney's young women, who are sent into the world in a state of orphanhood or other form of acute solitude, work their way through social obstacles without benefit of a secure social position, and finally become reintegrated into recognized social hierarchies when they marry into respectability. Whether they also achieve personal happiness through this reintegration into society remains ambiguous.

Burney's female protagonists enter the world from the protection of paternal or paternal–surrogate homes, and end the novels with anticipated marriages. With the exception of Camilla Tyrold, the heroine of *Camilla* whose childhood serves as the backdrop for her attachment to the censorious hero Edgar Mandlebert, the early childhoods of Burney's eponymous women are recounted briefly and only in retrospect as histories of shelter and adult management. Later, this management becomes radically called into question: does her guardian, the Reverend Villars, teach Evelina adequately about social life, or does his protectiveness backfire when she has to fend for herself in London? Has Cecilia Beverley's egocentric uncle in Burney's second novel, *Cecilia*, cost his niece her happiness through the name clause that is a condition of her inheritance? Where is Camilla's mother (the only visible mother in the novels other than the problematic surrogates Mme Duval of *Evelina* and Mrs. Delvile of *Cecilia*) when her daughter needs her advice, and why doesn't Sir Hugh Tyrold have better sense than to take Eugenia to a fair when she has not been innoculated against smallpox? And finally, why do Cecilia and Lady Juliet Granville, the incognito heroine of *The Wanderer*, end up advertised in the newspapers as lost lunatics? How has the protection afforded to women of good family been eroded so thoroughly that they are forced to wander the streets in search of themselves and of a social category they might inhabit?

It is especially in the dark moments of Burney's narratives – Evelina arm-in-arm with prostitutes at a public pleasure garden; Cecilia chasing distractedly after Mortimer Delvile then languishing above a pawnshop; Camilla hallucinating in the bedroom of an inn; Juliet lost in the forest – that her heroines reside on the cusp of a boundary and fail momentarily to locate themselves within an acceptable social construction of female behavior. Victor Turner's cultural analysis of socially marginal positions and their instability is again instructive; liminality is by definition a state of ambiguous identity. It represents a holding pattern, a moment of delayed crossing from one social category to another. It is this conditional terrain of betwixt and between, the gap in a woman's social identity, that Burney mines for her novels.

The defining characteristic of social liminality for young women in Burney's novels is the simultaneity of their sexual awakening and their need to hold their sexuality in abeyance until all the appropriate economic and social negotiations that will produce a husband for them may occur. This hovering sense of precarious social status is the key to courtship in the later eighteenth-century novel. Jane Austen deployed her laserlike irony to depict courtship and the marriage marketplace for women whose economic status made them less than perfect matches, but Burney's representations of this critical period in a woman's life are less analytic than those of her celebrated near-contemporary. A conduct book published in 1789, the Reverend John Bennett's widely read *Letters to a Young Lady*, contains this portrait of the courtship period:

> If I was called upon to write the history of a *woman's* trials and sorrows, I would date it from the moment, when nature has pronounced her *marriageable*, and she feels that innocent desire of associating with the other sex, which needs not blush. If I had a girl of my own, at this *critical* age, I should be full of the keenest apprehensions for her safety; and, like the great poet, when the tempter was bent on seducing our first parents from their innocence and happiness, I should invoke the assistance of some *guardian* angel, to conduct her through the slippery and dangerous paths.[8]

It is this sense of danger that motivates Burney's fictions, danger that emerges from the fine line between "that innocent desire ... which needs not a blush" and the always slippery path of a female sexuality that demands to be policed and controlled before it has even been granted existence.

Burney does not address the question of female sexuality straightforwardly. Rather, her heroines dread what they understand as public expo-

sure, an exposure akin to public nakedness. Some scenes from each of the
four novels will illustrate the covert ways in which Burney confronts her
heroines with sexual desire and its dangers. In each case, the heroine is
tested for fitness to marry. Indeed, one might argue that Burney's narratives
of female social liminality represent a test-marketing of her protagonists'
value as romantic heroines and, concomitantly, of their abilities to mask
and rechannel their sexual desires.

In 1778, when she was twenty-six years old, Burney published her first
novel, *Evelina; or a Young Lady's Entrance into the World*, anonymously
and to immediate acclaim. The young author's conflicted response to
sudden fame had ironically been forecast in her novel by the conflicts
Evelina experiences when her youth and beauty attract public attention.
Innocent of London's social mores and fashions, Evelina tries, with often
disastrous consequences, to blend into the crowd. Her attempts themselves
endanger her: she ends up trapped against her will in the libertine Willoughby's carriage, surrounded by a group of drunken men along one of the dark
paths at Vauxhall and, in the most striking scene of dangerous public
misapprehension, she takes the arms of two prostitutes when she finds
herself alone and frightened after a fireworks display at Marylebone
Gardens. Having earlier learned not to trust men to protect her when she is
publicly alone, Evelina appeals to these "two ladies" without recognizing
the import of their laughter at her request. Only when the socially
impeccable hero, Lord Orville, raises his eyebrows at her new acquaintances
does Evelina realize who they are.

The prostitutes at Marylebone play a peculiar and crucial role in *Evelina*.
Evelina describes her encounter with Lord Orville while arm-in-arm with
these women as "the most painful of my life." In typical form, she remains
mute and unable to express herself other than by looking at the ground,
"curtseying in silence," while "with what expressive eyes did [Orville]
regard me! Never were surprise and concern so strongly marked".[9] Margaret Doody has analyzed the complex ways in which Burney depicts
embarrassment in her fiction; and in an insightful reading of this scene,
Ruth Bernard Yeazell points out that the Marylebone adventure "emblema-
tically stages the risk that every young lady runs who ventures 'out' into
public spaces – the risk of being seen to be one who belongs in them, a
woman of the town, as the idiom has it, or one who walks the streets."[10]
Evelina has great trouble identifying herself as an independent agent. She
reads her identity, instead, in the gaze turned on her every move by Lord
Orville, who along with Villars represents the novel's tribunal of social
behavior. But the interesting contrast in the prostitute scene derives from the

very freedom of these women of the town who, unlike their young protégé, know precisely who they are and have no need of disguise. As I have argued elsewhere, they are among the novel's key portraits of autonomous women, and they are characterized by their ability to circulate freely, to choose their own company, and to define themselves for themselves.[11] Burney does not idealize this radical departure from social norms for women, but neither does she condemn it. Indeed, Orville's later admission that he had wanted to inquire into Evelina's connection with "those women" before he proposed marriage marks him as at odds with his creator in this instance (*Evelina*, 389).

The prostitutes, in fact, prove to be safer companions than either Willoughby or the drunks at Vauxhall; they conduct Evelina reliably to Lord Orville and her friends. They also represent quite wittily (especially in Evelina's grandmother's response to their finery) the precise constraints involved in young adulthood for unmarried women, and they serve to blast the social structures that make such companions Evelina's best means of social preservation. Prostitutes reside by legal decree in a liminal position on the margins of society, and they represent an uncomfortable merging of private and public self-presentation. Prostitutes are sexualized women, as Evelina cannot admit to being. Yet even in their open sexual display, prostitutes share Evelina's vulnerability. The law hounds them, and marriage offers them no protection from the law.[12] Their predicament embodies the worst fears for women in the eighteenth century, that the price of their independence will be an imprisonment in a kind of social purgatory, always outside looking in.

If the prostitutes in *Evelina* are unrelievedly and unashamedly themselves as sexualized women, naked and undisguised (in spite of their painted faces), the costumed revelers at the Harrels' masquerade in Burney's second novel, *Cecilia; or the Memoirs of an Heiress* (1782), embody hierarchies of social power in their costumes. Terry Castle has brilliantly analyzed the powerful masquerade in *Cecilia* as a locus simultaneously for social pleasure and moral disapproval.[13] Cecilia replays Evelina's outing with the public women in Marylebone by choosing to attend the masquerade in her own dress: that is, in a roomful of masks and elaborate disguises, she presents herself unadorned. As a consequence, her very ingenuousness, her public identification of herself as herself in a world of dissembling and mimicry, marks her paradoxically as different and draws unwanted attention to her. Cecilia's overexposure in this scene mimicks the larger theme of public selfhood in the novel represented by the unprecedented codicil to her uncle's will: she is to inherit his money only on the condition that when she marries, her husband is to give up his own family name and become Mr. Beverley.

Needless to say, Cecilia falls in love with the only scion of a proud but cash-poor family who see the loss of their name as a disgrace. In the end, she is obliged to relinquish her money and to become Mrs. Mortimer Delvile, a sacrifice analogous to the necessity for young women to avoid public conspicuousness.

Though Cecilia is disgusted and horrified at the Harrels' extravagance and in most cases tries to avoid accompanying them to lavish public assemblies, she actually looks forward to the masquerade with pleasant anticipation. She enjoys the scene's "novelty" and relishes the carnivalesque aspects of transgressive confusion that the masquerade hosts. Categories of sex, race, and class intermingle and become meaningless through sheer cacophony. The moral testing of social conventions thematized through costumes in this scene is echoed when the gadfly leveler Morrice literally "breaks up" the evening by pulling down the awning on the dessert table Harrel has had constructed for the occasion. Glass, papier-mâché, lamps and oil rain down on the shrieking crowd, and the affair comes to an abrupt close.

The chaotic ending of the masquerade scene in *Cecilia* spares the heroine further importuning from unwanted suitors in disguise, and it is important that it is here that she meets her future husband, Mortimer Delvile. Their courtship represents a prolonged jockeying for the upper hand of identity and the right to name each other. Framing this initial meeting scene is the chase scene at the end of the novel in which Cecilia pursues Mortimer through the streets of London trying to correct his misreading of her visit to Belfield's private rooms. Unlike Orville, who gives Evelina the benefit of the doubt even while inquiring for an explanation, Mortimer and Camilla's suitor, Edgar Mandlebert, assume the worst when they encounter a social arrangement whose appearance troubles them. So thwarted is Cecilia during her pursuit of her husband, that she ultimately loses her sanity and begins to babble incomprehensibly to passersby: " 'He will be gone! he will be gone! and I must follow him to Nice!' " she cries, adding " 'No, no – I am not mad, – I am going to Nice – to my husband' " (896, 897). By this time, the panting Cecilia has rushed into a shop and collapsed on the floor, where she remains speechless. She is carried upstairs "alone and raving" (898), and an advertisement is placed for her in the *Daily Advertiser* as "a crazy young lady" (901).

The masquerade scene that introduces the novel's lovers and the pursuit and advertisement sequence that separates then reunites the by-then married couple match each other in the intensity of the disorder they depict. In both scenes Cecilia is forced to assert her identity, first by realizing that the best public protection is a blending in, a social disguise, and in the second through the much darker necessity to cry out the name "Delvile" in her delirium, the name for which she has given up her identity as the heiress of the work's title. In both cases, her status on the threshold, at a masquerade but uncostumed, covertly married but thought to be single and mad, tests her identity and her agency in her own life as that liminal status at the same time permits the hero to test her mettle as a mate. As occurs with Evelina, in every instance in which Cecilia navigates through the social world alone, she marks out her own social marginalization.

The testing of a heroine's fitness for marriage occurs most explicitly in Burney's third novel, *Camilla; or, A Picture of Youth*, published in 1796. Camilla Tyrold and her childhood admirer Edgar Mandlebert come to an amorous understanding early in the novel, but Mandlebert's tutor March-mont sets his charge to questioning Camilla's worth. Marchmont's paranoid advice inaugurates one of the plot's complicated strains:

> Whatever she does, you must ask yourself this question: "Should I like such behaviour in my wife?" Whatever she says, you must make yourself the same demand. Nothing must escape you; you must view her as if you had never seen her before. (*Camilla*, 159)

Marchmont goes even further, and counsels Edgar to "become positively distrustful" (160). Camilla's female mentor, Mrs. Arlbery, evaluates Edgar's acceptance of Marchmont's advice in the previously cited passage in which she condemns him as "a watcher."

As Mortimer misreads Cecilia's motives and actions, so Edgar misunder-stands the circumstances in which he finds Camilla, and his capacity to put the worst face on appearances seems virtually boundless. A telling scene after Camilla has incurred a series of debts foregrounds this dynamic of watching, testing, proving, and judgment. With a companion named Mrs. Mittin, Camilla strolls along the quay at Southampton looking in shop windows. Anxious to see the wares without spending any money, Mrs. Mittin hits on the idea of inquiring about local sights, and uses this ruse to enter one shop after another. Nobody would have attended to the nonde-script Mrs. Mittin, "but Camilla, who, absent and absorbed, accompanied without heeding her, was of a figure and appearance not quite so well adapted for indulging with impunity such unbridled curiosity" (607). The shopkeepers, struck by the contrast between Camilla's beauty and fashion and her ordinary and older companion and by their progress from one shop to another, wonder about the women's motives: "Some supposed they were only seeking to attract notice; others thought they were deranged in mind; and others, again, imagined they were shoplifters, and hastened back to their counters, to examine what was missing of their goods" (608).

Ultimately, two townspeople place wagers on whether the women are thieves or simply mad, a wager reminiscent of the sequence at the close of *Evelina* in which the fashionable men in Bristol Hotwells place bets on a footrace they set up between two eighty-year-old women.[14]

The shopkeepers pursue the two women by repeating their progress from shop to shop. The loquacious Mrs. Mittin, answering copiously for Camilla's habitual silence, marks a contrast with "the pensive and absorbed look of Camilla" that strikes the onlookers "as too particular to be natural" (608). It is Mrs. Mittin, therefore, who perceives their danger. They escape this collective leering gaze and take refuge in a bathing room at the end of the quay. Enjoying the beach scenery, they continue to be pursued and to inspire wagers and scrutiny. There Camilla is spotted by Marchmont and Edgar, who finds her companion inadequately dignified to chaperone her. The locals inform these men of their wager while three gentlemen enter the women's hiding place and imprison them with gallantries until Edgar providentially, but quite belatedly, turns up to rescue her. But to be rescued by the hero in a Burney novel is also to be judged and found wanting. Edgar walks away with Camilla in silence as they are "mutually shocked by the recent adventure," and he waits for Mrs. Mittin to depart so that he can "point out the impropriety and insufficiency of such a guard" (616). In short, Edgar seems more frightened and in need of reassurance than the recently imprisoned Camilla.

The difficulty Camilla faces in this scene develops from the circumstances of her liminal social position. On the one hand, she needs youth and beauty to negotiate the marriage market and the social milieu to which she wishes to belong. On the other hand, these very attributes turn her into an object of the judgmental gaze and literally make a spectacle of her. And once again, Camilla resides in the no-win territory of the unmarried woman: if she pays too much attention, she is a coquette who transgresses propriety; if she remains heedless of her surroundings, she appears insane. Simply to walk down a street, albeit a bit absent-mindedly, positions Burney's third heroine as an anomalous character, a female with no clearly-defined social status about whose activities speculation is invited and enacted among a group of men ranging from working middle-class shopkeepers to gentlemen-aristocrats. The ultimate blow comes when the suspicions of strangers find an echo in the romantic hero's response to the heroine: Edgar too questions the propriety of Camilla's behavior. Young single women may not define themselves, but they also must guard against the usurpation of definitions imposed by others.

Burney's last heroine confronts the most profound problem of self-definition, self-presentation, and disguise. Lady Juliet Granville of *The*

Wanderer; or, Female Difficulties (1814) is known through much of the novel simply as "Ellis." First appearing in blackface, she becomes the protean shape-changer, embodying in herself the whole scenario of the masquerade from *Cecilia*. Various characters speechify on this subject. Mrs. Ireton accuses Ellis of mystification: "You have been bruised and beaten; and dirty and clean; and ragged and whole; and wounded and healed; and a European and a Creole."[15] And Riley adds: "What a rare hand you are, Demoiselle ... at hocus pocus work! ... you metamorphose yourself about so, one does not know which way to look for you. Ovid was a mere fool to you" (739). By the time Burney composed *The Wanderer*, she had radicalized the problem of single female identity so profoundly that her last heroine becomes virtually a free-floating signifier of Woman, a symbol system of female virtues and accomplishments in search of a way to exist in the world.

One of the most drawn-out of the operations of Juliet's quest to stabilize her identity occurs in the second volume of this long novel, when she faces a proposal that she perform in a public concert. By this time the mystifications surrounding her identity have been revealed, if not resolved, and she is heavily in debt with no apparent means of acquiring money. Despite this, it is telling that she holds firm initially to "unsuperable" objections: "never, most certainly never, can I perform in public!" (267). Juliet recognizes the oppressive paradox that it is acceptable for her to offer harp lessons to proper young ladies, but not to display her musical talents on the stage. Nevertheless, she becomes embroiled in a subscription concert plan, despite her ambiguous concern that "those to whom I may yet belong, may blame – may resent any measures that may give publicity to my situation" (284).

At the first rehearsal Juliet panics, plays poorly, and sings inaudibly before recovering her composure. Bent on "self-dependence," she remains frustrated by the "cruel necessity! cruel, imperious necessity!" (311) of exposing herself in public in order to pay off her debts. The final blow in this impossible situation comes from Albert Harleigh's objections: "How ... can I quietly submit," asks her eventual husband, "to see you enter into a career of public life, subversive – perhaps – to me, of even any eventual amelioration?" (316). Harleigh invokes the prejudices of his relations, who would be unable to approve an alliance with a public performer. He refers to the sullying of her reputation (in limbo as it is) and urges her not to "deviate[e], alone and unsupported as you appear, from the long-beaten track of female timidity" (322). Harleigh dogs her with his objections, but she resists his efforts to control her actions. On the day of the concert itself, he continues to follow and importune her. Greeted with thunderous applause when she arrives on stage, Juliet becomes transfixed by a cloaked and masked figure who turns out to be her protofeminist revolutionary alter ego, Elinor Joddrel. Glimpsing the shimmer of a steel blade, Juliet faints on the stage. The event abruptly ends when Elinor stabs herself, thus rescuing Juliet from humiliation just as Bertha Mason would later rescue Jane Eyre.

Given the extraordinary pressures on Ellis's identity and its politically-charged, gendered, and plot-driven mystifications, it seems at first glance odd that most of one of the voluminous work's five volumes should be taken up with the anguish that leads to this public moment. And when the moment comes, what occurs – fainting, stabbing, and screaming – is construable as far more scandalous than the mere fact of public presence on a stage, since Ellis has all along participated in private theatricals and concerts. But Lady Juliet Granville acquires her aristocratic status and proper social place, along with a judgmental husband, only after hundreds of pages of residing in the margins. Lady Juliet's protean physical body, with its facial and fashion disguises, takes on symbolic meaning as the figure of Ellis metaphorically straddles the borders between class and race.

Albert Harleigh, like his predecessor heroes in delayed romance, Lord Orville, Mortimer Delvile, and Edgar Mandlebert, observes and tests the object of his love. And the mystery in The Wanderer is a real one: Juliet had been forcibly married in France, and must rebuff Harleigh's advances. Yet her "female difficulties" are presented as universal for women in the world of Burney's last novel. While Ellis's social anomalousness makes particular problems for her, it clearly represents for Burney a paradigmatic instance of single female liminality. Woman is fringe and perhaps fringe benefit, but "self-dependence" remains both the unattainable goal and the unexercisable threat.

Lady Juliet Granville battles and finally overcomes a series of political and institutional obstacles to her romance with Harleigh. Throughout the novel Burney's narrator repeats the subtitle reference "Female Difficulties" to a set of scalable but imposing restrictions on young women: "Her honour always in danger of being assailed, her delicacy of being offended, her strength of being exhausted, and her virtue of being calumniated!" (836) The Wanderer ends with this description and its ambiguously encouraging rejoinder: "Yet even DIFFICULTIES such as these are not insurmountable, where mental courage, operating through patience, prudence, and principle, supply physical force, combat disappointment, and keep the untamed spirits superior to failure, and ever alive to hope" (836). Paradoxically, it is precisely the judgmental loyalty and dogged watchfulness of Burney's heroes that keep her heroines buoyed in their impossible circumstances by a peculiar combination of romantic fantasy and self-doubt. Romance in a Burney novel is ever-vigilant. One wrong social move can bring down the whole house of cards in which lodge the carefully orchestrated ideologies of gender expectations and propriety. Burney's complex plots marginalize her young women within the regulated liminal space of rites of passage that lead to an accepted status in the community. Her novels challenge the conventions of propriety in the test-marketing of their heroines for marriage with the romantic and socially impeccable hero. At the same time, the novels work finally to reintegrate their heroines into the conventional social structures of the upper-class institution of marriage.

The scenes I have examined in detail from Burney's novels each represent a moment in which the heroine stands symbolically naked before a judging public. The public discourse that takes place concerning the prostitutes in *Evelina* emphasizes their "finery" and the question of face paint. Cecilia, however, appears without a costume, in ordinary dress that functions as undress, in the masquerade scene of Burney's second novel. Camilla's presence in the local shops and on the quay at Southampton renders her vulnerable to the speculations of passersby. And the abortive stage debut of Lady Juliet Granville in *The Wanderer* occurs when Elinor rescues Juliet with her histrionics. It is as though Elinor's elaborately cross-dressed disguise, literally penetrated by her dagger, were intended to "cover" the plain white stage dress of Juliet's social discomfort.

Recent work on Burney's art and her place in literary history, much of it written by feminist scholars and critics, positions Burney's interest in the liminality of her heroines and the precariousness of their investments in romance in relation to social history. This new work began with the notion proposed by historians that the eighteenth century saw the birth of individualism and of the modern concept of the self. That idea has received its own challenges from social historians, and feminists have added questions about the constitution and origins of a specifically female subjectivity during the eighteenth century. In Frances Burney's novels, young women experience their entrance into the world as a gauntlet of male observation and judgment. In addition, they must apprentice themselves to trade in the kind of shape-shifting of which Ellis in *The Wanderer* is accused. In order to mold themselves into an identity that is acceptable to a social collectivity and at the same time that they can live with, Burney's women battle strictures on their appearance and dress, their movement, their social skills, and their economic abilities. Literally forced to make a living, they do the only thing respectable young women can do; they market themselves to the most genteel, to the most watchful, and to the highest bidders.

NOTES

1 See in particular, the work of Kristina Straub, Margaret Doody, Julia Epstein, Mary Poovey, and Ruth Bernard Yeazell.

2 Burney's plays should be included in this assessment, though it is unfortunate that her writings for the theatre have received only a little critical attention and virtually no performances. Her journals and diaries have received more, and also participate in the Burneyan satirical project.

3 Margaret Doody, *Frances Burney: the Life and Works* (New Brunswick, N.J.: Rutgers University Press, 1988), 124, 257. The most famous use of this complex interior style is perhaps in Gustave Flaubert's *Madame Bovary*, a novel of the mid-nineteenth century. It is instructive to consider the ways Burney's heroines anticipated the profound *anomie* that informs the search for self-knowledge in the figure of the tragic, and tragically deluded, Emma Bovary, with whom Flaubert himself ("Madame Bovary, c'est moi") so poignantly identified.

4 J. Paul Hunter, *Before Novels: the Cultural Contexts of Eighteenth-Century English Fiction* (New York and London: W. W. Norton, 1990), 327.

5 Kristina Straub, *Divided Fictions* (Lexington: University Press of Kentucky, 1987), 172–73.

6 *Camilla*, ed. Edward A. and Lillian D. Bloom (London: Oxford University Press, 1983), 482. All subsequent references are to this volume.

7 Victor Turner, *The Ritual Process* (Chicago: Aldine, 1969), 95.

8 John Bennett, *Letters to a Young Lady, on a Variety of Useful and Interesting Subjects, Calculated to Improve the Heart, to Form the Manners, and Enlighten the Understanding* (Warrington: the author, 2 vols., 1789), II:160; cited in Ruth Yeazell, *Fictions of Modesty* (Chicago: University of Chicago Press, 1991), 44.

9 *Evelina*, ed. Edward A. Bloom (London: Oxford University Press, 1970), 235. All subsequent references are to this edition.

10 Yeazall, *Fictions of Modesty*, 123.

11 Julia Epstein, *The Iron Pen* (Madison: University of Wisconsin Press, 1989), 112–13.

12 Mary Poovey offers a helpful discussion of prostitution and social ideology for a later period in *Uneven Developments: the Ideological Work of Gender in Mid-Victorian England* (Chicago: University of Chicago Press, 1988).

13 Terry Castle, *Masquerade and Civilization* (Stanford: Stanford University Press, 1986), 259–89.

14 For a discussion, see Earl R. Anderson, "Footnotes More Pedestrian than Sublime: a Historical Background for the Footraces in *Evelina* and *Humphry Clinker*," *Eighteenth-Century Studies*, 14 (1980): 56–68.

15 *The Wanderer*, ed. Margaret Drabble (London: Pandora Books, 1988), 37. All subsequent references are to this volume.

READING LIST

Armstrong, Nancy. *Desire and Domestic Fiction: a Political History of the Novel.* Oxford: Oxford University Press, 1987.

Bloom, Harold (ed.) *Fanny Burney's* Evelina: *Modern Critical Interpretations*. New York: Chelsea House, 1988.

Castle, Terry. *Masquerade and Civilization: the Carnivalesque in Eighteenth-Century English Culture and Fiction*. Stanford: Stanford University Press, 1986.

Cutting-Gray, Joanne. *Woman as 'Nobody' and the Novels of Fanny Burney*. Gainesville: University Presses of Florida, 1992.

Daughtery, Tracy. *Narrative Techniques in the Novels of Fanny Burney*. New York: Peter Lang, 1989.

Devlin, D. D. *The Novels and Journals of Fanny Burney*. New York: St. Martin's Press, 1987.

Doody, Margaret Anne. *Frances Burney: the Life in the Works*. New Brunswick, N.J.: Rutgers University Press, 1988.

Epstein, Julia. *The Iron Pen: Frances Burney and the Politics of Women's Writing*. Madison: University of Wisconsin Press, 1989.

Figes, Eva. *Sex and Subterfuge: Women Writers to 1850*. London: Macmillan, 1982.

Freiman, Susan. *Unbecoming Women: British Women Writers and the Novel of Development*. New York: Columbia University Press, 1993.

Grau, Joseph A. *Fanny Burney: an Annotated Bibliography*. New York: Garland, 1981.

Gutwirth, Madelyn. *The Twilight of the Goddesses: Women and Representation in the French Revolutionary Era*. New Brunswick, N.J.: Rutgers University Press, 1992.

Hemlow, Joyce. *The History of Fanny Burney*. Oxford: Clarendon, 1958.

Newton, Judith Lowder. *Women, Power, and Subversion: Social Strategies in British Fiction, 1777–1860*. Athens: University of Georgia Press, 1981; reprinted London: Methuen, 1985.

Poovey, Mary. *The Proper Lady and the Woman Writer: Ideology as Style in the Works of Mary Wollstonecraft, Mary Shelley, and Jane Austen*. Chicago: University of Chicago Press, 1984.

Rogers, Katharine. *Feminism in Eighteenth-Century England*. New York: St. Martin's Press, 1982.

Ross, Deborah. *The Excellence of Falsehood: Romance, Realism and Women's Contribution to the Novel*. Lexington: University of Kentucky, 1991.

Simons, Judy. *Fanny Burney*. Totowa, N.J.: Barnes and Noble, 1987.

Spacks, Patricia Meyer. *Imagining a Self: Autobiography and Novel in Eighteenth-Century England*. Cambridge, Mass.: Harvard University Press, 1976.

Spencer, Jane. *The Rise of the Woman Novelist: from Aphra Behn to Jane Austen*. Oxford: Blackwell, 1986.

Straub, Kristina. *Divided Fictions: Fanny Burney and Feminine Strategy*. Lexington: University of Kentucky, 1987.

Turner, Victor. *The Ritual Process: Structure and Anti-Structure*. Chicago: Aldine, 1969.

Yeazell, Ruth Bernard. *Fictions of Modesty: Women and Courtship in the English Novel*. Chicago: University of Chicago Press, 1991.

10

JANE SPENCER

Women writers and the eighteenth-century novel

Toward the end of *The Rise of the Novel*, Ian Watt makes a throwaway remark that has since become famous: that most of the novels of the eighteenth century were written by women.[1] A recent study of the eighteenth-century novel echoes Watt with the claim that "the numerical (if not qualitative) majority [of novels] were actually written by women."[2] Such remarks seem to be made less with a view to statistical accuracy than in order to belittle the women novelists' achievements as merely quantitative: they are the modern version of the eighteenth-century reviewers' complaints that women writers were engrossing the trade in novels and debasing the new genre with hastily written performances. The most recent statistical and bibliographical work does not substantiate assertions of female numerical dominance, but does suggest that the sharp increase in novel production in the final decades of the century was even steeper in the case of female writers than male, and that women novelists may have equaled or slightly outnumbered men in certain subgenres such as the epistolary novel.[3] This indicates such a high proportion of women writing fiction as compared to their share in the production of poetry or drama that it is not surprising that women were perceived as taking over, even though they were not. Such an unprecedented level of female participation in a literary genre deserves investigation.

In the last ten years interest has quickened in the women novelists of 1660 to 1800, and their contribution to the development of the new genre is now increasingly acknowledged. Scholar Press, Pickering, Pandora, Oxford University Press and Virago have made many of the texts more easily available, and historical studies of early women novelists have begun to appear.[4] Aphra Behn is now recognized as a major pioneer of the form. In *Love Letters Between a Nobleman and His Sister* (1684–87) she develops a form of amatory narrative in which to deliver a partisan account of contemporary political events; and in this and other novels, most notably *Oroonoko* (1688) and *The Fair Jilt* (1688) she experiments with the creation of narrative personae.[5] A number of recent studies have reinterpreted a novelist whom critics are now learning to call Frances Burney, and who has become unquestionably a canonical figure.[6] Other women novelists have been given detailed treatment. Eliza Haywood, one of the most prolific and popular novelists of the century, whose career spans more than three decades from 1719 to the 1750s, has been the subject of a full-length study.[7] Mid-century authors like Sarah Fielding, Frances Sheridan, and Charlotte Lennox are now regularly discussed, and Lennox's *Female Quixote* (1752) is emerging as a key work in the understanding of the relation between romance, female desire and the novel. The late-century women novelists continue to attract attention, and Ann Radcliffe, long famous as a Gothic novelist for *The Mysteries of Udolpho* (1774) and *The Italian* (1797) is now read alongside contemporaries like Charlotte Smith and Elizabeth Inchbald.

In this new climate, recent accounts of the novel's development are less likely than earlier ones to confuse general with male. Behn's, Manley's, and Haywood's work receives interesting discussion in Michael McKeon's work, and that of Haywood, Sarah Fielding, and Lennox in J. Paul Hunter's.[8] These books still do not pay much attention, though, to the author's gender as a determining factor in the development of narrative. In contrast, some recent feminist discussions of women's fiction aim to explain women's achievements in terms of their gender and to show the novel developing differently as a result of women's work. The complex relationship between the novel and romance is often the focus of these studies. Deborah Ross argues for the blending of romantic and realistic elements in the eighteenth-century novel, a blending particularly pioneered by women and affecting the development of the novel as a whole. She complains of the split in criticism between general accounts that pay insufficient attention to women and feminist accounts that deal only with female authors, calling for a more "complete, integrative history" of the novel;[9] and some recent work is moving in this direction, dealing with both male and female authors and attending to the influence of gender on both.[10]

The focus on romance in much feminist criticism contrasts with work that emphasizes the novel's roots in popular discourses, especially the journalism of the late seventeenth and early eighteenth centuries.[11] J. Paul Hunter has argued that to appreciate the newness of the new form we need to get away from thinking of it as the child of romance (Hunter, *Before Novels*, 28). However, the feminist emphasis on romance is not primarily a matter of the question of indebtedness to romance form. Though a few women novelists, like Jane Barker in *Exilius* (1715), look back specifically to the romances of the sixteenth and seventeenth centuries for their models, this is not the essence of their relationship to romance. "Romance" is rather the name for a certain attitude to women, embodied in a good deal of the feminocentric fiction of the eighteenth century, and particularly, though not exclusively, developed by women writers.

Charlotte Lennox's *The Female Quixote* brilliantly demonstrates that its heroine's passion for the French romances of La Calprenède and de Scudéry indicates a female desire for significant selfhood and public existence.[12] Clara Reeve's *The Progress of Romance* (1785), an early history of the novel often cited for its clear statement of the distinction between romance and novel, champions the romance as the location of a deference towards women and their concerns that is in danger of being lost in the modern world. The modern novelists praised are Samuel Richardson (seen as a champion of women and of virtue) and women novelists like Frances Sheridan, Sarah Fielding, and Elizabeth Griffith, who maintain the attention to a female viewpoint that Reeve likes in romance.[13] That women's concerns and desires are important, and that a woman's story can be the center of a narrative, are the claims that make eighteenth-century women's fictions "romantic," linking them to the genre today labeled "romantic fiction" and still devalued in comparison to other genre fiction such as the detective novel or science fiction.

If romance as attitude has particular importance for women novelists of the eighteenth century, it by no means provides us with a total explanation of their work. Janet Todd has emphasized the variety and disparateness of women novelists' techniques and concerns: they are not all telling the same story (Todd, *The Sign of Angellica*, 22–3). In the early part of the eighteenth century, especially, when the novel was not sufficiently established to have its own traditional set of expectations, popular novels varied widely in form and in tone. Eliza Haywood wrote many short tales of passion, usually narrated in the third person, and often introduced with a maxim about the power of love. Elizabeth Rowe's epistolary novels contained a number of stories set within the pious and moralizing letters of the main characters. Penelope Aubin's didactic tales were contained within long episodic romances of travel and adventure. Jane Barker and Mary Davys, two of the liveliest and most original novelists of the earlier part of the century, both produced collections of stories held together by a loosely autobiographical framing device. Mary Davys also wrote comic novels about the reform of faulty characters, such as *The Accomplish'd Rake, or Modern Fine Gentleman* (1727); and in *Familiar Letters Betwixt a Gentleman and a Lady* (1725) she challenged the notion that epistolary fiction should be an outburst of feminine passion by making hers comic and more concerned with discussion of contemporary politics than with love. It was not till the second half of the century that a framework of conventions for the novel was really established, and hence that a typical "woman's novel" could be defined.

Women were struggling for literary authority at the same time as the novel's generic identity was becoming established, and the two developments affected each other. Despite the dominance and widespread influence of the male novelists Samuel Richardson and Henry Fielding in the middle of the century, *contemporary* commentators on the novel persistently gendered the form as a feminine one. Although they appear everywhere in the novels of the time, both the didacticism and the sentimentalism that became its standard features were associated particularly with women. A variety of forms was still used, with the epistolary novel, the journal novel, and the third-person narrative all represented; but towards the end of the century the long (three- or four-volume) novel with a third-person narrator was becoming a dominant form, and one in which women writers were developing their own distinctive use of narrative voice.

The establishment of the respectable professional female novelist in the second half of the century depended on the repression of certain aspects of the novel's history. The early novelists Aphra Behn, Delarivier Manley, and Eliza Haywood were repeatedly rejected for their immorality in order to prove by contrast the virtue of more recent female writers. The struggle over the virtue of fiction and of the woman writer was already under way in the early eighteenth century, and the 1720s saw a rivalry between two popular novelists, Penelope Aubin and Eliza Haywood, as representatives of the "moral" and the "immoral" woman novelist. By the 1740s the novel as a genre tended to establish its morality by virtue of disparaging references to the scandalous works of the past.

The numerical increase in woman novelists towards the end of the eighteenth century accompanies a narrowing of the limits on their expression (Ballaster, *Seductive Forms*, 210). The bawdy references and the erotic prose common in earlier work are shunned by later women novelists. Moreover, while men retained the freedom of literary experimentation, the most striking example being Sterne's *Tristram Shandy*, women in the second half of the century were arguably constrained by the generic expectations that built up for the feminine sentimental novel.

The split between earlier and later women novelists should not be exaggerated, however. The impression of a sudden, mid-century turn towards restrictive morality and didactic fiction arises largely from a change in women novelists' self-presentation; they were not necessarily so different from their predecessors as they claimed to be. They continued to experiment with narrative, and the sentimental novel established as standard by the end of the century was a flexible form well able to accommodate, among many other things, stringent questioning of the moral limits placed on women's lives. Jerry Beasley has pointed out that early eighteenth-century novelists like Aubin, Haywood, Barker, and Davys, "by responding with ... urgency to anxieties over broad social issues as they were touched by political circumstance, ... did much to form and then sustain ideals of public virtue."[14] The women novelists of the second half of the century continued this tradition, and attempted to delineate a public position for the supposedly private virtues of femininity.

In her work on Behn, Manley, and Haywood, Ros Ballaster has emphasized the participation of these early women novelists in the supposedly masculine world of party politics. While presenting themselves as feminine writers interested in love, they used amatory fiction as a way of intervening directly in party politics. In *The New Atalantis* (1709) Delarivier Manley's allegories about the sexual misconduct and corruption of prominent politicians attacked the Whig ministry at a point of crisis just before it fell from power, and were seriously damaging to the government. Ballaster contrasts the public role claimed for the woman writer in this and similar texts with the later eighteenth-century view of the woman's novel as an "essentially private" form, in which the figure of the virtuous domestic woman plays an indirect political role precisely because she is used to establish the bourgeois ideology that sees family life as a realm separated from the political (Ballaster, *Seductive Forms*, 128, 206–7). Certainly fiction of the mid and late eighteenth century concentrates on an examination of domestic, family, and emotional life, and associates this with women. However this does not mean that it necessarily exemplifies or advocates the separation of domestic and political concerns. Rather, it partakes of the ambiguous mingling of public and private that is characteristic of an age which, in England as well as other European countries, saw the emergence of what Jürgen Habermas describes as the bourgeois or classical public sphere – a sphere of relatively informal institutions distinct from the authority of the state.[15]

The public sphere in this sense of the term is not public as opposed to private; it is rather the realm of civil as opposed to state power. The clubs, societies, coffeehouses, and expanding print culture that made up the new public sphere were private, not state institutions; Habermas's public sphere "developed within the private sphere."[16] Dena Goodman has argued that the public/private dichotomy was not fully settled at the time of the emergence of the public sphere. In the eighteenth century, "public and private spheres were in the process of articulation, such that no stable distinction can or could be made between them ... individuals needed to negotiate their actions, discursive and otherwise, across constantly shifting boundaries between ambiguously defined realms of experience" (Goodman, "Public Sphere and Private Life", 14). This instability has important consequences for women's relation to the public sphere. We cannot simply impose the model of gendered separate spheres – public for men – onto eighteenth-century life. This is not to deny either the centuries-old tradition of attempted confinement of women's concerns to the domestic and familial, or the intensification of women's domestic role in the eighteenth century. Rather, we need to recognize the new public dimension to domestic life, fostered especially by print culture. What is new about eighteenth-century experience, it has recently been argued, is not the confinement of women to the home but the new value placed on that home.[17] The new evaluation of privacy and domesticity encouraged by sentimental ideology contributed to the ambiguity of public/private distinctions; and the domestic sentimental novel of the late eighteenth century had an ambiguous role as the carrier of private concerns into public print.

Though the new public sphere was male-dominated, some parts of it were easier of access to women than others; publishing, and especially the publication of novels, was relatively open to them. In this chapter I will focus on three novels, from the mid and late eighteenth century, that illustrate women novelists' negotiations with a shifting discourse of public and private femininity. While domestic settings were often used and domestic virtues frequently praised, this was not a retreat from public issues, since discourse about domestic life was constitutive of the new public sphere. In their novels, women articulated their claim for a public role for the moral authority of the woman writer. They expressed their concerns about women's place in the power structures of society, examining the implications of domestic power and power in the state; and they suggested ways that an understanding of history would be modified by the inclusion of a perspective that saw female life as important. Sarah Fielding's *The Lives of Cleopatra and Octavia* (1757), written when the woman writer's moral authority was not fully established, shows how this authority is based on a rejection of the values ascribed to Behn, Manley, and Haywood. Frances Sheridan's *Memoirs of Miss Sidney Bidulph* (1761) concentrates on the familial concerns and the inner life of its passively virtuous heroine, in a way that serves to question rather than promulgate the new ideology of domesticity. Charlotte Smith's *Marchmont* (1796), written when greater consensus existed about the roles of novel and of female author, participates in the broadening and repoliticization of popular fiction.[18]

In *The Lives of Cleopatra and Octavia* a number of negotiations are taking place: between a classical scholar and the new, romance-influenced novel; between a woman writer and a male classical tradition, as well as with a more recent narrative tradition dominated by her own brother and by her friend, supporter (and generous subscriber to the volume) Samuel Richardson; and of a woman writer with the "immoral" women writers of scandal fiction, who, despite their own claims to be satirists revealing the truths of political life, have now to be rejected in order to affirm the woman novelist as the upholder of truth and virtue. It is in this implicit rejection of such female predecessors as Haywood and Manley that Sarah Fielding's authorial stance seems most reactionary; but the position she eventually claims is in some ways similar to theirs, in being both bold and public.

Through the stories of their lives, narrated by Cleopatra and Octavia themselves, Sarah Fielding offers dramatically polarized pictures of female vice and virtue, condemning Cleopatra's pursuit of political power through sexual power over successive lovers, and lauding Octavia's attempts to avoid the public arena and devote herself to husband, children, and domestic values. Octavia is devoted to truth and simplicity, and, like other Sarah Fielding heroines (Portia in *The Cry*, Cynthia in *David Simple*) is an intellectual who suffers from male prejudice against women of learning. She can be seen as a surrogate for her author, while the power-seeking, seductive manipulator of men portrayed in Cleopatra has much in common with her view of authors like Aphra Behn and Delarivier Manley, whose seductive works of passion camouflage their seizure of political power through writing.

Henry Fielding had implicitly contrasted the virtuous woman writer represented by his sister with the salacious earlier woman writer. In *Tom Jones*, while "Mrs. Behn" is named as the author of the "romances" read by Mr. Macklachan for sexual titillation, Sarah Fielding gets a discreet allusion as the young lady of good understanding and good heart who writes the novel praised by Sophia Western.[19] In this contrast, Sarah Fielding represents the new, modest woman writer, virtuous and anonymous. Sarah Fielding's own negotiations with the image of the woman writer, however, are different, and the position she takes up is a much bolder and more challenging one. She certainly embraces, in the character of Octavia, a female virtue explicitly linked by its possessor with submissiveness and domesticity. As author, though, she assumes the role of public truth-teller, aligning herself, in her introduction to the novel, with the canonical classical writers. Not only does she place herself as a learned writer adapting (and at one point correcting) Plutarch, she follows both Shakespeare and Dryden in offering a new interpretation of the character of the famous Egyptian queen. If her portrait lacks the charms of theirs, that is part of her point.

The Lives of Cleopatra and Octavia is based on a selection from Plutarch's *Life of Antonius* – the parts concerning the two women, who are given central place instead of being part of the story of Anthony (as Fielding calls him). Retelling stories from Roman history as feminocentric illustrations of the power of Love, Sarah Fielding is, in a way, rather close to the seventeenth-century French romances that had been mocked in Lennox's *Female Quixote* five years earlier. The technique is also similar to the one Delarivier Manley had applied to contemporary politics in *The New Atalantis*. No doubt because of these similarities, Fielding is particularly concerned in her introduction to differentiate her work from both romances and novels. Because her subject is "the Lives of Persons who have really made their Appearance on the Stage of the World," it can teach truths and inculcate morality better than the "false Coin" of fiction, which is "rather calculated to deceive, than profit us." Whereas most male writers of the time give female gender to the falseness of fiction, Sarah Fielding sees male writers as the authors of delightful but deceptive fiction, calling her brother's Joseph Andrews and Richardson's Sir Charles Grandison "romantic heroes" (*Lives of Cleopatra and Octavia*, iii). Her own heroines, however, are by her own admission the source of the "Mixture of Romance" that she has reluctantly introduced in deference to public taste: their lives are told, not impartially by a historian but "as supposed to have been delivered by themselves in the Shades below." For this fictional device she claims classical precedent. Like "*Homer, Virgil, Aristophanes, Lucan*, and others," she has been whisked away to Pluto's realm by a magician (iv–v). There, Cleopatra and Octavia tell their life stories. In this situation even Cleopatra, whose life on earth was one of continual deceit, can only tell the truth; she is forced to see and articulate unpleasant motives that, during life, were hidden, sometimes even from herself.

Despite the work's similarities to romance, Sarah Fielding is right to claim that she is doing something different. She does not use romantic attitudes to soften Cleopatra's character, but sticks fairly close to her source throughout, and offers a view of Cleopatra's motivation closer to Plutarch's than to Shakespeare's or Dryden's. Like Plutarch's Cleopatra, Sarah Fielding's is unambiguously manipulative, using Anthony for her own ambitious ends. She has none of the mystery of Shakespeare's Cleopatra, whose motives are ambiguous at crucial points, nor does she have any of the softness and genuine devotion to her lover portrayed by Dryden in *All for Love*. As she repeatedly informs us, her love for Anthony is a pretence; her passions and jealousies are carefully calculated performances; and she is ready to betray him whenever it becomes expedient. In her account of the battle of Actium, Cleopatra encourages Anthony to fight at sea, despite the known disadvantages, for the glory of her Egyptian navy and as advance provision for possible defeat. After her flight from the battle she gives her attendants detailed instructions to persuade Anthony that she has not betrayed him: "I ordered them to excite his Compassion, by strongly representing my Sorrow for what I had done, and by imputing the unfortunate Error of my flight to the Timidity and Fears of a Woman; at the same time charging them to take occasion of intimating the Beauty and Charms of my Person, even in Grief" (149). Cleopatra's femininity – her fears, her sorrow, her beauty, and her love – is a fiction that she takes care to present to Anthony. Their long separations are to her advantage as she uses them to send various representations of herself to him, all calculated to obscure the reality of her identity as a woman seeking power. At times Fielding is even more severe than Plutarch, who at least credits Cleopatra with genuine grief for the dying Antonius: "she dried up his blood that had betrayed his face, and called him her Lord, her husband, and Emperour, forgetting her owne misery and calamity, for the pitie and compassion she tooke of him."[20] Fielding's Cleopatra records the same actions with different motives: "if this Grief was to take on itself the Name of Pity, Pride, or Affectation, it would assume a false Character, for it was indeed such a Composition of all Three, as would render it difficult to determine which was predominant. A little Compassion for *Anthony*, and a good deal for myself, overwhelmed by Eyes with Tears of Sorrow" (167–68). Outstripping her male sources in condemnation of a power-hungry woman, Fielding is not simply adumbrating patriarchal values. Cleopatra, forced to be truthful, takes on the voice of the moralist, and shares with her creator the authority to reveal what masculine gullibility has concealed. Fielding mocks the susceptibility of men to Cleopatra's carefully deployed femininity, which has fooled not only Anthony but Shakespeare and Dryden, and even to some degree Plutarch. The illusions of romance, as Fielding hints in her introduction with its reference to men's romantic heroes, are problematic for men as well as for women.

While Fielding debunks romantic views of Cleopatra, her decision to center her work on women's lives means that, like romance, it offers an alternative to male-centered histories. In Plutarch's *Life of Antonius*, Cleopatra and Octavia are introduced at the points of their lives at which they become significant to Antonius; in Fielding's novel each woman tells her life story, and we learn of her family background and her relation to the power structures of her society. In both stories the brother–sister relationship is highly significant, being used as a figure for relations of power between men and women. Fielding invokes the idea of a lost brother–sister equality as the background to her examination of corrupt and oppressive gender relations in her protagonists' lives.

Fielding emphasizes that the struggle between Rome and Egypt is between two systems in which women play contrasting public roles. Women in

Rome are pawns in a man's game; being Caesar's sister brings Octavia no official power, only obligation – the obligation to marry to suit her brother's purposes and to attempt to mediate between the men who rule the world. Egyptian customs treat the brother–sister relation more equally. Cleopatra records that her father left the Egyptian crown to her and her brother, Ptolemy Dionysius, whom she was to marry. The intervention of Pothinus, Achillas, and Theodotus, "Three Men of ambitious Spirits (who wanted to divide between them all the Power and Revenues of the Kingdom)" separate her from her brother and set in train events that make her his rival (9). Pompey, helped by Ptolemy in his war with Caesar, decrees that Ptolemy should have the throne of Egypt to himself. To regain her throne, Cleopatra gets Julius Caesar on her side by seducing him – the beginning of the process by which power she was once entitled to by birthright has to be regained through sexual manipulation of men. Infatuated with Cleopatra, Caesar makes her sole ruler of Egypt, but political considerations soon overrule sexual ones and "in order to appease the Alexandrians" he makes her brother her partner again (12). After Ptolemy's death he makes her younger brother, eleven years old, the sharer of her throne. Cleopatra, now determined to rule alone, has this brother killed.

Thereafter Cleopatra aims for absolute power; but she finds that the Roman world as well as the Egyptian one is ruled by men of ambitious spirits. She turns repeatedly to seduction and manipulation of powerful men in order to consolidate her own power. After Caesar's death, political expediency makes her fix on Anthony as her "Prey" (17), and she describes in detail the wiles she uses to entrap him. Fielding emphasizes the losses involved in this kind of power, positing the existence of true female sexuality and womanly feeling that are lost in Cleopatra's faking of them. Cleopatra's seductive ploys are distinguished from free use of sexuality: she notes that while Anthony was more easily manipulated, and so more useful, than Julius Caesar, she had been more physically attracted towards Caesar. She becomes a rival to her sister as well as to her brothers, and manipulates Anthony so that he has her sister Arsinoe killed. The murder of this good, happy, and unexceptionable sister indicates the necessary death of good womanhood in the service of the fictional femininity by which Cleopatra holds power.

Fielding's version of Cleopatra's story can be read as a myth about declining female power, invented to find some way of coming to terms with women's position in Fielding's society. An initial state of equality between brother and sister is broken by ambitious men, and in seeking to regain legitimate power the sister becomes ambitious for single rule. She kills brothers and sister, and replaces good womanhood by a deceitful travesty of femininity. Octavia's story adds to this the myth of the good woman who is accommodated in patriarchal society. This myth may express some of the author's anxieties about rivaling her brother and fellow novelist Henry Fielding. In a wider sense it suggests the compulsion eighteenth-century women writers felt to examine the question of women's power in society, to distinguish between legitimate and illegitimate uses of power, and to find some proper ground for their own authority as writers.

The power Cleopatra gains is not only debased, but finally illusory. By the end of her narrative her power has so declined that she substitutes the means (power over men) for the end (her kingdom). When Anthony is defeated in battle, she reports, "I still flattered myself, that whilst *Anthony* was so much my Slave, I need not despair of Commanding the World; for I had joined those Two Ideas so strongly together, that it was very difficult to separate or disunite them" (149). Eventually, deprived of political power, she is left only with the power of the illusion she has cultivated. Driven to the decision to die rather than be led in triumph to Rome, she consoles herself with the thought that "at least I should have the glory of being thought, by the injudicious World, to have entertained a long and constant passion for [Anthony]" (176). As she dies, the woman who has boasted of using Anthony so as to rule the world herself is reduced to feeling "somewhat flattered in presuming I should attain Glory by dying with *Anthony*" (176).

Because we are used to a tradition in which the typical tragic woman is a (usually virtuous) victim, we may not easily respond to Sarah Fielding's active and wicked Cleopatra as a tragic figure. Yet her story can be read as a princely fall, a fall from male–female power sharing into the frantic and increasingly illusory exercise of a perverted form of power. The final degradation of Sarah Fielding's Cleopatra is that her best hope is to be misread by history in the way Dryden misread her, as a woman who lost the world for love.

Octavia's much shorter story offers a postscript to Cleopatra's; virtue's answer to vice. Octavia never questions her subordination to male power. The one indication of pride in her narrative, significantly, concerns the brother–sister relationship: she intervenes to correct Plutarch and insist that she is a full sister, not just a half-sister, to Augustus Caesar. Octavia never attempts to rival her brother, but accepts the Roman system whereby men rule and their sisters are objects of exchange. Her pathos comes from her commitment to virtue and sincerity in a world in which women only gain power through vice and deception. In her first, happy marriage, she was able to keep out of public life and cultivate domestic virtues. In her second marriage to Anthony, entered into out of a sense of public duty, she does what good she can by loving Anthony and caring for their children. Her consolation for a miserable life is the classical – and Augustan – one of retirement: she leaves the court, reads philosophy, takes pleasure in her extended family of children (her own and those of Anthony and Fulvia) and lives with a soul "clear as a limpid Stream" (218).

In Octavia's story Fielding seeks a muted consolation for the loss of female power charted in Cleopatra's. "Conscious virtue" (219) is Octavia's reward in a world that deprives women of legitimate routes to power. In Fielding's own assumption of authorship there is the hope of something more. Octavia's role is necessarily a public one, for all her preference for a private life; she is a pawn of the Roman state. Sarah Fielding too claims a public role, in the new sense of membership of the eighteenth-century world of letters. This means that she can go beyond being a worthy sister to her more famous brother. Her claim is to tell the clear truth about historical women whose stories have been distorted by masculine tradition.

Frances Sheridan's *Memoirs of Miss Sidney Bidulph*, published a few years after Fielding's *Cleopatra and Octavia*, explores similar issues of women's virtue, women's vice, and women's power, but in an eighteenth-century English setting. The narrative is set back in time, beginning in 1703, but the concerns are those of the later eighteenth century.[21] Women's power in the state is not an issue; the novel is firmly embedded in domestic and familial concerns. Sidney's life in her widowed mother's household, and later in her husband's, is the focus of attention. Her only entry into public life comes with her occasional visits to public amusements like the theatre, and these are not, as in Burney's *Evelina*, the subject of detailed attention. It is power in the domestic realm, and especially the moral – and immoral – influence of women in the family that concerns Sheridan.

The narrative forms, a series of journal-letters from Sidney to her friend Cecilia, makes Sidney's thoughts and feelings central. At the same time, the work is organized in a way that suggests that domestic life, in itself, is not entirely worthy of being recorded. Like a Richardson heroine, Sheridan's spends much of her time recounting domestic incidents and family conversations. She also apologizes for the triviality of such details; and Cecilia, who is responsible for turning Sidney's letters into the narrative we have, has cut out some parts of the journal which are in her view irrelevant to the main story. There is a four-month gap at the time of the birth of Sidney's first daughter, and a nine-month gap around the birth of her second. The happy domestic life that Sidney experiences at these times is "nothing material to her story" (*Memoirs of Miss Sidney Bidulph*, 106); it is only the disruption of domestic happiness that the narrative focuses on.

The novel is to some extent a response to Richardson's novels, especially

Clarissa. Like Richardson, Sheridan makes the point that virtue is not rewarded in this world. Sidney's extraordinary commitment to the feminine virtues of meekness, obedience, gentleness, and long-suffering bring her only misery; and while a heavenly reward is assumed to await her, the narrative does not dwell on this as *Clarissa* does. Like Richardson, Sheridan raises the question of the double standard of sexual morality, and explores what might happen if the same standards are applied to men as to women; but she does not offer the solution of *Sir Charles Grandison*, that a chaste man can become the new ideal.

The novel explores and questions female moral authority. Sidney's brother, Sir George, has of course inherited his father's estate, leaving his widowed mother with only her jointure to live on; at one point she and her daughter are reduced to poverty while he, estranged from them, lives in affluence. But while patrilineal inheritance laws give Sir George financial power, his mother holds firm to all the influence that moral authority allows her. In the early part of the novel she uses that influence to break down the gendered division between her children's experiences, encouraging her son to live with her and have a more sober, domestic life, while occasionally telling her daughter to go out and enjoy herself, teasing her, "I will make a rake of you" (12). When Sidney is courted by Orlando Faulkland, both mother and daughters show their interest in changing the definitions of masculinity. Sidney, praising Orlando's looks, wonders "why should not there be male as well as female graces?" (17) Lady Bidulph, more seriously, asks why there should not be male as well as female chastity. When she hears of Faulkland's seduction of Miss Burchill, she immediately decides he is not worthy to marry Sidney. The wedding is canceled; subsequently, Lady Bidulph befriends Miss Burchill and tries to promote a marriage between her and Faulkland.

Lady Bidulph is unusual in her sympathetic support of a seduced woman, but her evident intention of using female moral authority to right the wrongs men do to women achieves only harm. Refusing thoroughly to read a letter that explains Faulkland's actions, she does not find out the truth of his affair. It eventually transpires that Miss Burchill was seducer rather than seduced. This so changes things that Faulkland is considered an innocent victim of a rigid moral standard naively applied, while Miss Burchill is portrayed as a villainess. Lady Bidulph's mistake is the typical one of the eighteenth-century sentimentalist: as a good woman herself she is deceived by the apparent innocence of a bad one.

The novel, then, is profoundly mistrustful of the female power it describes. Lady Bidulph, despite the best of intentions, becomes a maternal tyrant who separates her daughter from the man she loves, and later encourages her to marry another man, Mr. Arnold, mainly in order to avoid the rumor that she has been rejected by Faulkland. Though Sidney, dutifully, manages to love Mr. Arnold, their marriage is made unhappy by his infidelity and his unjust suspicions that she is having an affair with Faulkland. Faulkland eventually marries Miss Burchill, in order to please Sidney; his wife is unfaithful to him, and, believing he has killed her, he persuades Sidney, now widowed, into a hasty marriage, which is soon proved null by Mrs. Faulkland's survival. Faulkland dies, probably by suicide, and Sidney is left miserable. The moral influence of good women appears to have done nothing but harm.

The novel is also peopled with less well-intentioned women who exercise familial and sexual power. Lady Grimston, under whose roof Sidney meets Mr. Arnold, encourages Lady Bidulph to exercise maternal strictness. She herself has made her daughter's life miserable because she married without her mother's consent. Miss Burchill uses a pretence of female innocence to gain Faulkland from her rival. Mrs. Gerrarde seduces Mr. Arnold and poisons his mind against his wife. The widow of Mr. Arnold's brother, another sexual miscreant who had lived apart from her husband, brings a lawsuit to get the inheritance that should go to the Arnolds for her own (probably illegitimate) daughter. Sir George Bidulph is married to a woman whose mean-mindedness influences his own behavior and his treatment of his mother and sister. Most female power is shown to be illegitimate and corrupt, and manipulative women are shown as generally successful in their schemes. Men like Sir George Bidulph and Mr. Arnold, despite their masculine social power, are morally at the mercy of the women who influence them.

A man's morality is defined in the novel by the kind of female influence to which he is susceptible. Orlando Faulkland's moral capacity is indicated by his readiness to be guided by a good woman like Sidney. In one remarkable episode he lures Mrs. Gerrarde away from Mr. Arnold in order to make Sidney's reunion with her husband possible. He deceives Mrs. Gerrarde with a pretence of love, and then keeps her prisoner till she agrees to marry his valet. This effectually disposes of her. The episode is unusual in that, for once, the power of a wicked woman is taken away from her. The incident allows Faulkland to exercise the power of a rake while maintaining the excuse of good intentions. He has no sexual relationship with Mrs. Gerrarde, but he certainly enjoys his power over her. He sounds like Lovelace as he boasts, in his letters to Sir George, of his treatment of a captive woman, describing in detail her defiance and tears, and his tricks and sternness (Spacks, *Desire and Truth*, 139). He describes the humbling of Mrs. Gerrarde as the action of a "hero of romance" (199). Faulkland is a hero of romance in another sense too. All that he does in this episode is in the service of his lady, the unattainable Mrs. Arnold, and his actions to help her will only make her more unattainable. Faulkland's masculine and ostensibly rakish power is subordinated to Sidney's feminine power, operative through the conventions of romance. His venture into romance helps bring about the eventual domestic harmony between the Arnolds, in which Sidney can exercise her good influence over her husband.

Romance conventions, Sheridan implies, are necessary for a domestic woman's good influence to have any effect. In a similar way she allows Sidney, just once, to be rewarded for goodness when she helps an apparently indigent relative who turns out to be rich and benevolent. This only serves to underline the normal state of affairs in which goodness goes unrewarded. The novel ends with Sidney's misery, and with the promise of more misery for the next generation, her daughters and the son of Faulkland and Miss Burchill – a promise fulfilled in the sequel to the novel, published in 1767.[22]

Sheridan's narrative thus expresses strong skepticism about the possibility of doing good by moral authority. Its implicit critique of the domestic ideology of the time is expressed as anxiety about female exercise of moral authority. However, the novel itself enacts the domestic-yet-public authority of the female novelist. Unlike Sarah Fielding, Frances Sheridan does not discuss this authority directly in an introduction, but represents it in the framing narrative of Sidney's memoirs. Cecilia, who has edited the memoirs, appears at the beginning and the end. At the beginning she gives an account of Sidney's family and character. At the end she returns to England to support Sidney in her grief; it is she who brings Sidney news of Faulkland's death. Cecilia, in her turn, is framed by another editor, an unnamed young man who meets her much later, when she is a venerable old lady. Like her son, through whom he meets her, he respects the maternal authority by which she pronounces the moral of Sidney's tale – that the virtuous are not rewarded in this life. She dies soon after their meeting; and he is the one who insists on making these private memoirs public.

Cecilia's absence from most of Sidney's life is more than a convenient device to allow for the writing of the memoirs. Cecilia lives abroad because when her brother goes on the grand tour, that eighteenth-century method of widening a young gentleman's political, social, and sexual experience, she goes too: her mother "thought a young lady, under proper conduct, might improve as much by seeing foreign courts, and the various customs of different nations, as a young gentleman" (6). In fact, the whole family travels together, thus domesticating the public realm as well as widening the private one. Cecilia does not break out of the family or her feminine role within it. She stays abroad because she marries a man living in Vienna.

Nevertheless, with her wider experience she is distanced from the restricted domestic life led by Sidney, and – like a woman novelist – she looks on it as an observer. Like a woman novelist, too, she takes on the moral authority to comment on women's role and experience. But it is not she who decides to make the story public. The novel thus expresses both Sheridan's interest in the widening of women's role and the role of domesticity, and her skepticism about the public moral authority that she herself takes up.

Both Fielding and Sheridan show the influence in their work of the sentimentalism that became dominant in the later eighteenth century. Fielding, emphasizing Octavia's compassion for the victims of public dissension, in contrast to Cleopatra's readiness to torture and kill in her quest for domination, expresses the new concern for humane rule. Sheridan's concern with the application of feminine standards of morality is part of the sentimental challenge to masculinity. The "culture of sensibility" drew on gender stereotypes but also changed them, feminizing the masculine ideal and influencing the development of the public sphere.[23] Charlotte Smith's novels, written in the age of the French Revolution, show the widening political role of the novel of sensibility at the end of the century.

The importance of the concept of sensibility in late eighteenth-century culture gave women, and novels, a license to comment on that culture and be taken more seriously than before. The highly politicized nature of the novel in the 1790s has long been recognized.[24] Even the rhetoric of conservatives about the importance of keeping politics out of the novel served a political purpose. Political purpose in the novel was now a case of influencing the opinion of a larger reading public on general social issues, rather than the more specific attacks on particular party figures carried out by Manley earlier in the century. Men as well as women, of course, wrote the new kind of political novel. Women, however, led in the movement to establish the active sensibility of the heroine as the model for a new kind of engagement with public issues, and this process was occurring throughout the late eighteenth century, with Burney's *Cecilia* (1782) one of the most important contributors. Women writers of the final decades of the century were not simply retreating to a domestic space: rather, they remade the novel into a feminized public space in which contemporary political issues could be discussed.

The sentimental heroine, however restrictive was the code of virtuous womanhood by which she was drawn, offered a focus for the late-century novel to comment on social issues. Margaret Doody argues that women writers in the late eighteenth century "invented a new kind of novel. Having as its center the character of the intelligent, compassionate heroine, the new novel turns outward, like its heroine, to discover society and history."[25] The more liberal and radical novelists at the end of the century use the mingled sensibility and reason of the sentimental protagonist as a way of developing new ways of reflecting on politics and history: ways which return to the contemporary political concerns typical of earlier scandal fiction, but with broader interests in the process and formation of history. In the work of a writer like Charlotte Smith, the notion of history is being transformed from the story of the powerful and their political and sexual careers, to the experiences of ordinary people.

We can see this in *Marchmont* (1796), one of Smith's later novels, which, like other works by radical sympathizers in the later 1790s, expresses disillusionment with the results of the French Revolution under Robespierre. In *Desmond* (1791), Smith had explicitly defended her right to write, and female readers to read, a novel about contemporary politics. In *Marchmont* she continues her treatment of this subject, setting it now against the background of broad reflection on English history, particularly the seventeenth-century revolution. Thus she joins the debate over the meaning of seventeenth-century history through which eighteenth-century political issues were frequently discussed.[26]

Discussion of the French Revolution comes late in the book. The hero, young Marchmont, forced to leave England to avoid being imprisoned for his father's debts, travels in post-Revolutionary France and offers some account of it in letters. He laments some of the changes made by the Revolution, especially the loss of churches where the unhappy could find refuge in prayer, and finds the luckiest people are those who are too poor, and too unreflecting, to be affected by the Revolution one way or the other (*Marchmont*, IV: 64; IV: 51). The emphasis, though, is less on the failure of revolution than on the resemblance between Robespierre's tyranny and the tyranny of English law and custom. Marchmont, liable to imprisonment for debts left by his father, is in no position to believe in the "boasted freedom of England" (IV: 70), and he writes bitterly against both the money-getting bourgeoisie and the lazy aristocrats, who, both lacking "genuine liberality and enlargement of mind," enjoy an undeserved respectability through the prejudices of English society (IV: 71).

Contrasting his own sensations to those of an unthinking peasant largely unaffected by the Revolution, Marchmont is glad, despite the pain it brings him, to have the "sensibility" to know and care about society. His use of the word is qualified "(I hate the word, it is so prostituted)" (IV: 52), and his reflections are evidently meant to indicate a new form of sensibility, not just susceptibility to feeling but a unison of feeling and reflection that allows for a sympathetic and intelligent response to contemporary events. While Marchmont has sensibility, the heroine, Althea Dacres, has the "energy of mind" that has been described as a characteristic ideal of 1790s novels, implying a uniting of masculine and feminine qualities in a thoughtful, feeling response to the world (Spacks, *Desire and Truth*, 175–202).

Charlotte Smith wrote from financial need and often expressed distaste for the kind of popular fiction her market demanded. In *Marchmont* she provided the requisite elements of sentimental plot, from the heroine's need to resist a distasteful marriage to the hero's rescue from penury by a long-lost relative. At one point her narrator comments sardonically that the heroine is "fated to undergo that sort of persecution which has filled so many novels, and either disoblige her only parent and protector, or devote herself for life to a man she detested" (1: 147). Within these established conventions, Smith uses the novel to reflect widely on the nature of English society and history. While the hero travels abroad and reports on his reaction to post-Revolutionary France, the heroine leads the more sedentary life that, she remarks at one point, is more suited to a woman's constitution, but this does not make her reflections on society any less valuable. Her movements within England take her to various houses of emblematic significance, standing for various possibilities for English society. English history is confronted through Althea's discovery of Marchmont's family history, which is used by Smith both to comment on the seventeenth-century revolution, and to indicate the importance of rereading history in its personal and family aspects.

After her mother's death, Althea is brought up by her mother's sister Mrs. Trevyllian. Her home seems to be the place of maternal nature; the building is less important than the "lightly interwoven roof" formed by trees in the garden, and after her aunt's death Althea fancies she hears her voice in "the hollow wind of evening sobbing among the trees" (1: 108). Althea has to leave this paradise because of patrilineal inheritance customs that ignore maternal influences: Mrs. Trevyllian's house goes to her brother's son rather than her sister's daughter. Capelstoke, the country seat of Althea's unsympathetic father and her stepmother, is a place of luxury and splendor, signifying the heartlessness of fashionable society. When she refuses to marry the lawyer Mohun, Althea is sent to Eastwoodleigh, an old mansion house in the Devon countryside that her stepmother has obtained by foreclosing the mortgage on it she held from the Marchmont family. Eastwoodleigh's fate suggests the decay of the old order of landed gentry, whose "hereditary honor" and "hereditary pride" have failed to preserve their inheritance (1: 169).

At Eastwoodleigh, Althea reads English history and hears about Marchmont family history. Royalists in the seventeenth century and Jacobites later, the Marchmonts have always supported hereditary monarchy and opposed any reform that would weaken the hereditary principle. The result has been a slow decline in power and wealth; eventually the family is ruined by clinging to its ideal of patrilineal inheritance. Marchmont's father inherited mortgaged estates that he could have retrieved by selling part of them, but he refuses to do so; and having a worthy son and heir only makes matters worse, for when "the opening merits of [the younger Marchmont] rendered the father still more anxious not to dismember his estates, he entered into projects to retrieve them, which unhappily failing, served only to precipitate the ruin of his family" (I: 170).

Althea contemplates the Marchmont family history with sympathy and respect but without approving their political views, valuing rather their loyalty, even in a mistaken cause (II: 53). For her, really significant history is the history of family and feeling. Learning of the story of one Marchmont daughter whose love for a Cromwellian led to tragedy, she finds it "more affecting than any relations of the progress of a siege, or a plan of defence" (I: 308). Official history shocks her by the barbarity it records. In an attack on Burkean glorification of the chivalric past, the narrator comments that there is very little to be proud of in Norman, Tudor, and Plantagenet times, when "the people were so continually the victims of the hateful passions of their princes" (II: 44). Knowledge of the Marchmonts' past allows her to make connections between "the details of public calamity ... [and] its effects on private life," and she laments "the sad consequences of civil war on domestic happiness" (II: 48).

Eastwoodleigh is said to be haunted by the ghost of an ancestral Marchmont killed in the wars – a rumor that allows Althea to display the "fortitude and strength of mind" of a typical 1790s heroine by disregarding it (I: 178). The real ghost is the present Marchmont, hiding from his creditors in a disused part of his old home. Having voluntarily made himself answerable for his dead father's debts, Marchmont is imprisoned in the past of his failed family. His motivation, though, was not hereditary pride but concern for the welfare of his mother and sisters, indicating that he represents an alternative, more hopeful mode of family attachment. In political terms, too, he is not just the son of his father. When Althea hears rumors from a neighbor that legal officers are hunting for "a Jacobine [sic], or Jacobite; I don't know, not I, what they call 'em" (II: 74), the mistake is an appropriate one because Marchmont is in a sense both. His ancestors were Jacobites but his own initial reaction to the "auspicious appearance" of the French Revolution aligns him with the Jacobins. Marchmont's receptivity to ideas of radical reform is important; at the same time, part of Smith's purpose is to suggest common ground between Jacobin and Jacobite as outsiders victimized within English society. In Smith's attempt to read history with compassion, political allegiances matter less than humane sympathy.

Marchmont most resembles his ancestors in suffering, and it is human suffering, according to Smith, that history should record and respect. When he and Althea meet at Eastwoodleigh, he tells her that the cavalier poet Richard Lovelace is among his ancestors. A footnote praises Lovelace's loyalty to his king and notes that he suffered for it. Marchmont quotes Lovelace's "To Althea, from Prison," remarking that his fate is likely to be like the poet's. Marchmont may share Lovelace's fate in that he is persecuted for loyalty and consoles himself with the love of an Althea, but the differences between the two are as significant as the similarities. Marchmont has none of the serenity of Lovelace's conviction that the mind can be free while the body is imprisoned: "stone walls do not a prison make" had only an ironical truth for him, since without being physically jailed he is mentally imprisoned by his anxieties about his family's welfare, and his compulsion to haunt the ancestral home that no longer belongs to him. Nor can Marchmont have the simple faith in a soldier's honor that Lovelace expresses in another poem. War has no honor in this novel: Althea sees it as a business of transporting men "in floating prisons pregnant with infection and death" to a foreign country where they have to kill men "with whom they cannot have the slightest cause of quarrel" (III: 64). Marchmont cannot love his mistress by loving honor more. There is no higher love in this novel than the domestic affection that is eventually established between the two, and Marchmont's honor is sufficiently proved to his benefactor by his considerate behavior towards Althea.

Marchmont anticipates Scott's *Waverley* (1814) in seeing the honor and heroism of a previous age as outmoded in a modern world in which the choosing of political allegiance is not a simple matter. At the same time it emphasizes the importance of knowing about and feeling for the past, challenging Edmund Burke's attack on political reformers for disloyalty to the memory of their ancestors.[27] Althea and Marchmont are both loyal to the past in a way that modern commercial society is not. The past that should be remembered with affection is family past, often represented in the novel by family portraits. Marchmont's family portraits have been sold along with the estate. One has been bought by the family of a young woman who shows the worst side of the successful bourgeoisie in her flippant remarks on it. In Capelstoke, another house that has come from an impoverished old family, the previous owner's family pictures are stored, uncared for, in the closet adjoining Althea's room. They are faded, and Althea cannot tell much about the people from the portraits. From this poignantly irretrievable past, she turns to a more personal past that is represented by another picture abandoned in the closet: a portrait of her mother painted before Althea's birth. The sight of it affects her deeply and this picture and a miniature of her aunt are her most treasured possessions, reminders of a maternal past.

Both Marchmont and Althea need to be freed from a past shaped by fathers. Marchmont needs to be freed from the debts his father left him and to build a life for his mother and sisters in the present-day world. Althea, too, is imprisoned by allegiance to her father. Though she refuses to marry Mohun, she expresses an exaggerated sense of filial obedience, professing herself willing to die for a father who has shown her no affection. She is eventually freed by her father's death. On his return from France, Marchmont persuades her to marry him against her stepmother's wishes, and Althea, now free of any unreasonable sense of filial obligation, agrees without guilt or regret. Marchmont himself eventually suffers the imprisonment from which he has been fleeing all along, but is freed by the intervention of Mr. Desborough, a type of rich, benevolent uncle. Mr. Desborough is a clothier's son and republican sympathizer, and was the husband of Marchmont's father's sister, who was cut off from her family for marrying him. Marchmont is freed, then, by discovering his female ancestry; but Mr. Desborough explains that he is only helping his nephew because, apart from their relationship, he deserves help. Family affection is highly valued in *Marchmont*, but ruling dynasties are rejected.

When, at the end of the novel, Althea and Marchmont have managed to regain possession both of Eastwoodleigh and Althea's aunt's house, they choose the heroine's childhood home for their residence. Marchmont is freed from the family obsession with patrilineal inheritance. While the denouncement is marked by that air of retreat from the gloomy scene of contemporary politics that pervades late-century work by radical sympathizers, it is not a retreat to a purely domestic ideal of femininity. The compassion and capacity for imaginative projection shared by hero and heroine are seen as the basis of a new social attitude for men and women: to value the past without being trapped *by it*. The heroine's reflections reach out to history and society; she develops a way of understanding beyond that of the historians who have recorded battles, and through her Smith helps transform the sentimental novel into a wide-ranging tool for commenting on human affairs with public authority and sympathy.

The work of Sarah Fielding, Frances Sheridan, and Charlotte Smith demonstrate that despite the constraints of an authorial position based on virtuous femininity, women writers of the sentimental novel were not narrowly domestic or didactic, but used the form as an instrument of wide-ranging social reflection. They are only three of the many women writing novels in their time, but in some respects their work can be taken as representative. Without collapsing the differences between novelists, I would like to suggest that the female novelists of the eighteenth century shared certain concerns: with the idea of romance as a way of approaching historical truth; with women's relationship, as family members and by extension as authors, to the patrilineal inheritance patterns of their society; and with the creation and examination of a female public role. Through their dealings with these questions they established the novel, by the end of the century, as a feminized part of the new public sphere, in which discussions of politics and of private life could meet.

NOTES

1 Ian Watt, *The Rise of the Novel* (1957; Harmondsworth, Penguin, 1977), 339.
2 Clive T. Probyn, *English Fiction of the Eighteenth Century, 1700–1789* (London and New York: Longman, 1987), 2.
3 Judith Phillips Stanton, "The Production of Fiction by Women in England, 1660–1800: a Statistical Overview" (paper given at the eighth International Congress on the Enlightenment, Bristol, 1991). See also Cheryl Turner, *Living by the Pen* (London and New York: Routledge, 1992), chapter 3.
4 See Jane Spencer, *The Rise of the Woman Novelist* (Oxford: Blackwell, 1986); Dale Spender, *Mothers of the Novel* (London: Pandora, 1986); Janet Todd, *The Sign of Angellica* (London: Virago, 1989).
5 See Ros Ballaster, *Seductive Forms* (Oxford: Clarendon, 1992), especially chapter 3; and Jacqueline Pearson, "Gender and Narrative in the Fiction of Aphra Behn," *RES*, NS 42: 165 (1991): 50–55; 166 (1991): 179–90.
6 See Kristina Straub, *Divided Fictions: Fanny Burney and Feminine Strategy* (Lexington: University Press of Kentucky, 1987); Margaret Anne Doody, *Frances Burney: the Life in the Works* (New Brunswick: Rutgers University Press, 1988); Julia Epstein, *The Iron Pen: Frances Burney and the Politics of Women's Writing* (Madison: University of Wisconsin Press, 1989).
7 Mary Anne Schofield, *Eliza Haywood* (Boston: Twayne, 1985).
8 Michael McKeon, *The Origins of the English Novel, 1700–1740* (Baltimore: Johns Hopkins University Press, 1987); J. Paul Hunter, *Before Novels: the Cultural Contexts of Eighteenth-Century English Fiction* (New York and London: W. W. Norton, 1990).
9 Deborah Ross, *The Excellence of Falsehood* (Lexington: University Press of Kentucky, 1991), 13. See also the discussion in Laurie Langbauer, *Women and Romance* (Ithaca, N.Y.: Cornell University Press, 1990).
10 See for example Patricia Meyer Spacks, *Desire and Truth* (Chicago: University of Chicago Press, 1990).
11 See Lennard J. Davis, *Factual Fictions: The Origins of the English Novel* (New York: Columbia University Press, 1983).
12 Charlotte Lennox, *The Female Quixote*, ed. Margaret Dalziel (Oxford: Oxford University Press, 1971).

13 Clara Reeve, *The Progress of Romance* (Colchester: W. Keymer, 2 vols., 1785; reprinted New York: Facsimile Text Society, 1930).

14 Jerry Beasley, "Politics and Moral Idealism: the Achievement of Some Early Women Novelists," in Schofield and Macheski, eds., *Fetter'd or Free?* (Athens: Ohio University Press, 1986), 234.

15 See Jürgen Habermas, *The Structural Transformation of the Public Sphere: an Inquiry into a Category of Bourgeois Society*, trans. Thomas Burger (Cambridge, Mass.: MIT Press, 1989).

16 Dena Goodman, "Public Sphere and Private Life: Toward a Synthesis of Current Historiographical Approaches to the Old Regime," *History and Theory*, 31 (1992): 14.

17 G. J. Barker-Benfield, *The Culture of Sensibility: Sex and Society in Eighteenth-Century Britain* (Chicago: University of Chicago Press, 1992), 37.

18 Sarah Fielding, *The Lives of Cleopatra and Octavia* (1757; New York and London: Garland, 1974); Frances Sheridan, *Memoirs of Miss Sidney Bidulph* (1761; London: Pandora, 1987); Charlotte Smith, *Marchmont* (London: Sampson Low, 1796). A recent edition of *The Lives of Cleopatra and Octavia*, edited by Christopher D. Johnson (London and Toronto: Associated University Presses, 1994) provides an annotated text and brief introduction.

19 Henry Fielding, *Tom Jones* (1749; Harmondsworth: Penguin, 1976), 265, 471. Although Sarah Fielding did not put her name on the title page of *Cleopatra and Octavia*, she did sign the dedication page, thereby in spite of her modesty formally assuming a public authorial role.

20 *Plutarch's Lives of the Noble Grecians and Romans, Englished by Sir Thomas North* (London: David Nutt, 1896), VI: 80.

21 Margaret Anne Doody, "Frances Sheridan: Morality and Annihilated Time", in Schofield and Macheski, eds., *Fetter'd or Free?*, 237.

22 *Conclusion of the Memoirs of Miss Sidney Bidulph* (London: J. Dodsley, 1767). This sequel is discussed by Doody in "Frances Sheridan."

23 See Barker-Benfield, *The Culture of Sensibility*, especially chapter 5.

24 See Gary Kelly, *The English Jacobin Novel* (Oxford: Clarendon, 1976).

25 Margaret Anne Doody, "George Eliot and the Eighteenth-Century Novel," *Nineteenth-Century Fiction*, 35, 3 (1980): 278.

26 Bridget Hill, *The Republican Virago: the Life and Times of Catherine Macaulay, Historian* (Oxford: Clarendon, 1992), 51.

27 Edmund Burke, *Reflections on the Revolution in France* (1790: Harmondsworth: Penguin, 1979), 192–49.

READING LIST

Ballaster, Ros. *Seductive Forms: Women's Amatory Fiction from 1684 to 1840.* Oxford: Clarendon, 1992.

Gallagher, Catherine. *Nobody's Story: the Vanishing Acts of Women Writers in the Marketplace, 1670–1820.* Berkeley and Los Angeles: University of California Press, 1994.

Langbauer, Laurie. *Women and Romance: the Consolations of Gender in the English Novel.* Ithaca, N.Y.: Cornell University Press, 1990.

Ross, Deborah. *The Excellence of Falsehood: Romance, Realism, and Women's Contribution to the Novel*. Lexington: University Press of Kentucky, 1991.

Schofield, Mary Anne and Cecilia Macheski (eds.) *Fetter'd or Free? British Women Novelists, 1670–1815*. Athens: Ohio University Press, 1986.

Spacks, Patricia Meyer. *Desire and Truth: Functions of Plot in Eighteenth-Century English Novels*. Chicago: University of Chicago Press, 1990.

Spencer, Jane. *The Rise of the Woman Novelist: from Aphra Behn to Jane Austen*. Oxford: Blackwell, 1986.

Spender, Dale (ed.) *Living by the Pen: Early British Women Novelists*. New York and London: Teachers College Press, 1992.

Todd, Janet (ed.) *A Dictionary of British and American Women Writers, 1660–1800*. New Jersey: Rowman and Allanheld, 1985.

Todd, Janet. *The Sign of Angellica: Women, Writing and Fiction, 1660–1800*. London: Virago, 1989.

Turner, Cheryl. *Living by the Pen: Women Writers in the Eighteenth Century*. London and New York: Routledge, 1992.

11

JOHN MULLAN

Sentimental novels

Perhaps the most surprising fact about the "sentimental novel" of the eighteenth century is that the category is not just the useful invention of literary historians. The declaration "A Sentimental Novel" actually appeared on the title pages of many works of fiction of this period, and was particularly common during the 1770s and 1780s. Yet the novels that advertised themselves in this way are no longer read, even if they might once have been largely responsible for the poor reputation that "sentiment" earned, and for a change in the meaning of the word "sentimental" recorded by the *Oxford English Dictionary*. At the end of the eighteenth century the use of "sentimental" turned from the approbatory to the pejorative; from "exhibiting refined and elevated feelings" to "addicted to indulgence in superficial emotion." Yet clearly this change cannot have been certain even by the 1790s, when some novels were still willing to declare themselves "sentimental."[1]

These novels, prominent in the now buried world of formula fiction of the late eighteenth century, must have been in Jane Austen's mind when she satirized the avid novel reader Sir Edward Denham in *Sanditon* (1817), the work that she began shortly before her death. "Sir Edward ... had read more sentimental Novels than agreed with him," she tells us, and makes him speak with ludicrous enthusiasm of their special qualities:

> The Novels which I approve are such as display Human Nature with Grandeur – such as shew her in the Sublimities of intense Feeling – such as exhibit the progress of strong Passion from the first Germ of incipient Susceptibility to the utmost Energies of Reason half-dethroned.[2]

We know that the action of *Sanditon* takes place after 1815; it would appear that, in order to be worth discrediting, sentimentalism must still have been exerting its influence on the consumption of fiction in Regency England.

Austen's satire is instructive not only because it implies that sentimentalism had more staying power than the *OED* would lead us to expect, but also because the expectations that are parodied in Sir Edward's frothy recipe owe a good deal to fiction that is still read and studied, fiction whose liking for "Sublimities of intense Feeling" goes with other qualities that literary critics have found easier to admire. Indeed, Austen tells us that "[Sir Edward's] fancy had been early caught by all the impassioned, and most exceptionable parts of Richardsons." The circulating library fiction of the last decade of the century, however forgettable in itself, had learned its appeal and its methods from the most successful, and the most respected, novels of the mid-century, including most notably Richardson and Sterne. If we trace back the development of sentimentalism, we find that the extremes of "feeling" that Sir Edward relished are copied from some of the most influential innovators of the period. We find not only that sentimentalism is inextricable from the development of "the novel" as a genre, but that sentimental representations were often considered to redeem an otherwise suspect new form.

It was not only novels that aspired to be "sentimental" in this period. It is telling that the earliest use of the word recorded by the *OED* is by Lady Branshaigh, writing to Richardson in 1749, and puzzling over an adjective that was not only modish but also, apparently, applicable to almost anything:

> What, in your opinion, is the meaning of the word sentimental, so much in vogue amongst the polite ... Everything clever and agreeable is comprehended in that word ... I am frequently astonished to hear such a one is a *sentimental* man; we were a *sentimental* party; I have been taking a *sentimental* walk.

It is also telling that she was writing to a novelist whose own highly emotive works of fiction were refined enough to be relished by "the polite." Richardson was a good authority to whom to turn, for he was fueling the very fashion for tenderness and pathos that gave the word "sentimental" its resonance. The *OED* still shows us the traces of this fashion, displaying not only some of the first uses of "sentimental," but also of "sentimentalist," "sentimentality," "sentimentalize," "sentimentally," and even (one of Richardson's noncewords) "sentimentize" – all apparently coined between the 1750s and 1780s. These entries, and Lady Bradshaigh's puzzlement, tell us of a polite culture's new needs and values; these needs and values were to find their strongest expression in novels.

As we might expect, other kinds of books were also able to call themselves "sentimental." Sometimes the word was used by the compilers of collections of "elegant extracts": anthologies of morally elevating and supposedly touching passages from approved authors.[3] In the last decades of the eighteenth century there were also sentimental "memoirs" and sentimental "tours," almost all of which were advertising the cultivated sensitivity of their authors. One can now hear, in this kind of advertisement, meanings of "sentimental" that are strange yet recognizable: a readiness to be touched (particularly by others' distress), to display tender feelings, to be susceptible to sympathy. In 1785 it was possible for the philanthropist Joseph Hanway to call his account of the working conditions of London chimney sweeps *A Sentimental History of Chimney Sweepers.*[4] It is "sentimental" because it campaigns for the reader's pity, and implicitly because it is evidence of the sensitivity of its author. Sentimental texts appealed to the benevolent instincts of a virtuous reader, who might be expected to suffer with those of whom he or she read. Such a reader, alone with his or her better nature, might share some tears with a novel's suffering characters.

It is important that, while there were other words for the characteristics that the virtuous characters and readers of these novels were supposed to share (notably "sensibility" and "delicacy"), "sentimental" was usually a description of a *representation*: a person possessed "sensibility"; a text was "sentimental." Although such vocabulary was certainly not used with any great precision, this distinction is significant. "Sensibility" had originally referred to bodily sensitivities, began to stand for emotional responsiveness in the early eighteenth century, and came to designate a laudable delicacy in the second half of the century. It was a natural human resource or faculty often displayed by characters in sentimental fiction. "Sentimental," by becoming a word for a type of text, promised an *occasion* for fine feeling. This fine feeling could be experienced by both the characters in a narrative and the reader of that narrative. A sentimental text depicted "sensibility," and appealed to it.

The flurry of novels declaring themselves to be "sentimental" seems to have been set off by the success of Laurence Sterne's *A Sentimental Journey through France and Italy by Mr. Yorick*, published in 1768, shortly before Sterne's death. Indeed, the earliest book listed in the *Eighteenth-Century Short Title Catalogue* that calls itself "A Sentimental Novel" was published in 1769.[5] Many works specifically acknowledged allegiance to Sterne's model.[6] Sterne's earlier success, *Tristram Shandy*, had also sparked off imitations and would-be sequels, but a large proportion of these had been parodic or provocative, drawing particular attention to the aspects of the original to which Sterne's contemporaries most often objected.[7] They highlighted (and often extended) this novel's innuendo and its facetiousness; they reminded readers of what one reviewer called Sterne's "obscene asterisks," the nudges and ellipses that were guilty of "setting the reader's imagination to work, and officiating as pimp to every lewd idea excited by your own creative and abominable ambiguity."[8] The imitative texts that followed in the wake of *A Sentimental Journey*, however, were most often homages, and confirmed the success of the text with critics who praised its exquisite pathos.

Sterne was acutely conscious of public taste and sensitivity (he wrote, as he himself said, "not to be fed, but to be famous").[9] Some have argued that we can see *A Sentimental Journey* as Sterne's attempt to redeem himself from earlier criticisms; as a reaction to the widespread praise of *Tristram Shandy* for its pathos, and the widespread condemnation of its suggestiveness.[10] Certainly the contemporary reviews will often surprise a twentieth-century reader who is ready to be amused by the conflation of sentiment and sexual titillation in the novel.

> What delicacy of feeling, what tenderness of sentiment, yet what simplicity of expression are here! Is it *possible* that a man of *gross ideas* could ever *write* in a strain so pure, so refined from the dross of sensuality![11]

And this from the same reviewer (Ralph Griffiths) who had previously attacked *Tristram Shandy* for its indecency. Most seem to have been delighted to have been able to discover fine feeling in Sterne's new novel. For those who did so, the narrative's pathos was conveniently heightened by the death of its author, only a month after its publication. His last testament was one of feeling, and he was installed as the leading prophet of sentimentalism.

At first it appears odd that such a clearly mischievous author as Sterne should have been installed, posthumously, as *the* exemplary sentimentalist. (In the entirely earnest *Sentimental Magazine*, which ran for four years from 1773, he is a kind of patron saint: "Laurence Sterne, commonly known by the name of Yorick ... who introduced the present mode of sentimental writing."[12]) In part, this tells us something about the special requirements of many eighteenth-century readers (and, not incidentally, about the special opportunism of Sterne). *A Sentimental Journey* provided a narrator who was ready to be touched by the humble sufferings of those whose stories travel writers would usually never hear. Any survey of the novel's reception – from criticism to imitation, to fashionable paintings of its pathetic scenes – would have to notice that it found consumers who were equally ready to be touched, and perhaps less prepared than Yorick himself to find anything ludicrous in this readiness.

Yet it would be wrong to think that we simply see through a sentimentalism by which readers of the past were happily beguiled. While Sterne gave pious critics the chance to be admiring, he also produced a narration that allowed, and still allows, a different kind of reader to be suspicious of the

JOHN MULLAN

easy delights of "feeling." His novel continually associates sentimental encounters with erotic excitement, as Yorick dwells exactly on the little contacts of eyes and fingers by which he communicates with the young women whom he meets. Indeed, it ends with a famously audacious joke about our willingness to associate sentiment with eroticism. "The Case of Delicacy," which concerns the narrator's efforts to preserve proprieties when forced by circumstances to share a bedroom with the evidently attractive Piedmontese lady and her "brisk and lively" maid, might serve as a parable to the text's supposed refinement of feeling. It ends with an ambiguous last sentence – a perfectly delicate indelicacy:

> So that when I stretch'd out my hand, I caught hold of the Fille de Chambre's.
> END OF VOL. II.[13]

The comedy of this episode, like that of others in the book, is in the narrator's protest against the association of supposedly fine feeling with sensual delight. Yorick delicately leaves the details of "the manner in which the lady and myself should be obliged to undress and got to bed" to the reader's devising, "protesting as I do it, that if it is not the most delicate in nature, 'tis the fault of his own imagination – against which this is not my first complaint."[14]

Certainly it is not, for this narrator's way is to include possibilities by protesting against them. Thus he can entertain the possibility both that fellow-feeling is mere self-satisfaction, and that sentiment is a pretext for erotic pleasure. Sentimentalism never got more sophisticated than this: absorbing into its drama the likeliest objections of skeptical readers. Very thoroughly does Yorick protest on behalf of his better inclinations; Sterne's contemporaries were not allowed simply to be blind to the possibility that a man of feeling might have ulterior inclinations.[15] Sterne's Yorick is determined to show us that he is more sensitive to his odd mixtures of feeling than any cynic, or any prude, ever could be; he knows that his feelings need not be base, and cannot quite be pure. A Sentimental Journey continues to be amusing because its narrator is alert to, and even himself taken aback by, the strange combinations of emotion that a sentimental traveler is likely to experience.

Perhaps the most knowing readers are therefore "sentimental" to the extent that Yorick is himself. He has his feelings, which he cannot guarantee to be the most dignified or proper ones, and then reacts to them or checks them – perhaps flinches from them, perhaps gives way to them. "I write not to apologize for the weaknesses of my heart in this tour – but to give an account of them."[16] The *present* tense of much of the narrative ("I write ... ") is the one in which the narrator exclaims at the feelings that he recalls, allowing the reader to be as suspicious as he or she would like about the wishfulness or self-gratification that might lie beneath the sentiment. A new attempt is made to fulfill the ambition of what Richardson had called "writing to the moment."[17] Indeed, some attempt to reproduce the very momentariness of feelings is often a feature of sentimental writing. Richardson's epistolary method was one model for this: his heroines write with shaking hands; their letters are graphs of their emotions whilst writing them. It is not surprising that the majority of those novels of the late eighteenth century declaring themselves "sentimental" are also written in letters – nor that, as the fortunes of sentimentalism waned, so did those of the epistolary form.

For all its playfulness, *A Sentimental Journey* is a good guide to the resources of sentiment in eighteenth-century fiction, and to the ideals of writers much less sharp-witted than Sterne. It makes particularly creative uses out of the idealized possibility that human communication and fellow-feeling can transcend language; this ideal is often invoked in novels with an investment in the sentimental susceptibilities of their characters. Sterne's sentimental traveler escapes his nationality to live in a world of sympathies where there are no language problems. Many of the fragments or episodes that constitute his story ("chapters" seems precisely the wrong word) leave us, like the book's end, in midair; the text is full of significant silences. Yorick's moments of sentimental delight, when he holds one woman's hand or feels another's pulse, are moments of speechless expressiveness, of emotion in suspension. Later sentimental novels also try, less wryly, to exploit fragmentary narration in order to isolate special moments of poignancy – moments whose significance an unsentimental narrative would never consider. (Henry Mackenzie's hugely popular *The Man of Feeling* [1771] clearly learned this much from Sterne.)

Sentiment lives at the edges of speech; it is felt most when words stop. It is not therefore strange that Sterne's earlier novel, *Tristram Shandy*, should have been renowned for its suggestiveness as well as for its sentiment. The intensest feeling, on the one hand, and the most improper implications, on the other, are equally known when a speaker cannot go on. Beyond a trailing sentence might be either the emotions to which words can only gesture, or the innuendo that is all too well understood. In *Tristram Shandy* the narrator discusses, in his mock-learned style, the importance of "that ornamental figure in oratory, which Rhetoricians stile the *Aposiopesis*" (II. 6). By breaking off in the middle of saying something (for this is what *aposiopesis* means), something unsayable is said. Significance of a sentimental kind is found by stopping at the edge of what might be said or done – as Yorick does, in all those moments of suspension – of travel interrupted.

This is why all the subtle sentimental understandings claimed by Sterne's narrators require the possibility of misunderstanding. Communication is the more delightful because of the mistranslation that hems it round. Sterne has Tristram liken writing to conversation, in which we respect another by leaving much unsaid (II. 11). A just sense of implication means seeing that things might have been misunderstood, but were not. To make the right inference means sensing what it would be to make the wrong inference. Any reader of *Tristram Shandy* is allowed, as is often remarked, to see complex paths of misunderstanding, usually a consequence of the "hobbyhorses" of particular characters. He or she is also allowed to know of an eloquence that is speechless, compensating for the verbal inadequacies and intellectual eccentricities of Walter Shandy, Uncle Toby, and Trim.

"Tears are no proof of cowardice, *Trim*. – I drop them oft-times myself, cried my uncle *Toby*" (IV. 4). The character who declares this may be foolish, but his is the folly of ingenuousness and virtue. It was not difficult for eighteenth-century anthology makers to plunder this novel for touchingly sentimental episodes, for in themselves the episodes contain no spirit of satire. Here is Corporal Trim sensing Uncle Toby's fellow-feeling as he attempts to tell of his brother's fate at the hands of the Spanish Inquisition.

> The Corporal blush'd down to his fingers ends – a tear of sentimental bashfulness – another of gratitude to my uncle *Toby* – and a tear of sorrow for his brother's misfortunes, started into his eye and ran sweetly down his cheek together; my uncle *Toby*'s kindled as one lamp does at another; and taking hold of the breast of *Trim*'s coat (which had been that of *Le Fevre*'s) as if to ease his lame leg, but in reality to gratify a finer feeling – he stood silent for a minute and a half. (*Tristram Shandy*, IX. 5)

"Pathetic" episodes like the death of Le Fevre (referred to here) were frequently treated as the highlights of Sterne's fiction. *The Sentimental Magazine* declared, "the story of Le Fevre is one of the most highly finished, and masterly examples of true pathos to be found in any language, and would have made its author immortal, though he had never written anything else."[18] On its publication, in volume 6 of *Tristram Shandy*, *The Monthly Review* declared that is "does greater honour to the abilities and disposition of the Author, than any other part of his work."[19] Indeed, episodes exhibiting "true pathos" were later separated out in many editions of *The Beauties of Sterne*, the first of which was published in 1782 (the subtitle of the first edition, "Selected for the Heart of Sensibility," gives a sense of what was supposed to be "beautiful" in his writing). These popular compilations exploited the fragmentedness of Sterne's fiction, selecting the touching passages that confirmed his posthumous reputation as a sentimentalist.

To a social historian, one of the striking characteristics of Sterne's fiction must be its endorsement of the tearful *man* of sentiment. An aspect of sentimentalism that was evidently thought to be novel at the time was its celebration of male susceptibility. This was not Sterne's invention, and was one symptom of a new genre's search for a new kind of "hero." One way of seeing the "man of feeling" is as the Novel's alternative, on the one hand, to the picaresque transgressor adapted by Fielding and Smollett, and on the other hand, to the traditional models of public virtue offered by older genres. The new "hero" had to be virtuous, but had to be a private, and in this sense unheroic, person. One of the earliest attempts to sustain such an invention is Sarah Fielding's *The Adventures of David Simple* (1744), a sentimental novel *avant la letter*. Like later sentimentalists, Fielding puts her highly sensitive protagonist not only through his own misfortunes, but through the sorrows of those whom he meets, and whose tales of suffering he eagerly elicits and pities.

The ready tearfulness of Sarah Fielding's "hero" now seems ludicrous, but it was the consequence of an ambition that was to continue to influence novels throughout Europe: the aim of making a male exemplar, with the proper qualities of a "gentleman." This was an especially important aspiration given the reputation of novels in general as "low" or "vulgar" books.[20] Some of the difficulties inherent in imagining the appropriate sensitivities of a "gentleman" can be sensed by looking at Samuel Richardson's last (and now rarely read) novel *Sir Charles Grandison* (1753–54). Richardson had, of course, based his two earlier novels on the sufferings of two kinds of heroine: Pamela and Clarissa, his women of feeling. His attempt, however, to follow their stories with "the Example of a Man acting uniformly well thro' a Variety of trying Scenes" was much less successful.[21] While Richardson's imprisoned heroines showed their virtue through their feelings, his hero is able to display his virtue in action; as a consequence, *Sir Charles Grandison* presents its protagonist without the minutely analyzed reflexes of emotion that brought his heroines to life. His very letters come contained and quoted within another character's letters: encountered as semipublic readings rather than private expressions of feeling.

Yet in the wake of Sarah Fielding, and then of Sterne, there was a masculine hero of sentiment on offer. His main activity was benevolence; his fate, to exercise a philanthropy that few observed and even fewer valued. Henry Brooke made a child the benevolent hero of *The Fool of Quality* (1764–70), driven by sympathy to recognize misfortune and relieve distress. In this extraordinarily tearful narrative, the capacity for fellow-feeling is equated with an innocence that the world has lost. Novels celebrating men of feeling are often torn between showing their protagonists as strange, marginal exceptions, or insisting that they are indeed modern examples, and can be imitated. In the preface to Sarah Scott's *The History of Sir George Ellison*, published anonymously in 1770, "the Author" offers us the novel's eponymous paragon as an alternative to the "great men" of whom we normally read. Instead we have "the life of a man more ordinarily good, whose station and opportunities of acting are on a level with a great part of mankind."[22] Sir George's actions are "within the extent of every gentleman's power."

Clearly, however, not every "gentleman" finds himself, like Sir George, inheriting a plantation in the West Indies, and therefore able to test the powers of benevolence on slaves. Equally clearly, Scott must have thought that, in glorifying feeling, she was part of a social movement as well as a literary fashion. There is no room for anything but earnest intent in something like the following; the account that Ellison gives his wife of the reactions of the slaves to his unexpected mercifulness:

> Had you, my dear, been present when they threw themselves at my feet, embraced my knees, and lifting up their streaming eyes to heaven, prayed with inexpressible fervency to their supposed Gods to shower down their choicest blessings on me, you would have wept with me; and have owned a delight which nothing in this world can afford, but the relieving our fellow-creatures from misery.[23]

As is the case in much sentimental fiction, the cadences of self-satisfaction are clear enough in the descriptions of the powers of feeling. "But of all Mr. Ellison's charities, none gave him such exquisite delight as the release of prisoners confined for debt";[24] "all his hours yielded him refined pleasures, because they were all spent in the exercise of benevolence."[25] The potential comedy of such passages is, needless to say, entirely inadvertent – and entirely destructive of the fine feeling that Scott was trying to capture.

Benevolent remedying of misfortune is invariably the activity of the sentimental protagonist, drawn "to afford succour to distress from the tender motives of humanity."[26] Perhaps only Sterne manages to catch at the rather mixed motives that impel a person to charitable action. Other novelists of the period predictably, and often implausibly, celebrate the alleviation of sufferings; Sir George Ellison is not the only man of feeling who is kind to slaves in eighteenth-century fiction. Henry Mackenzie's *Julia de Roubigné* (1777) also gave its polite readers the example of a virtuous man whose tenderness is reached by the West Indian slaves in his charge. And, like Ellison, Mackenzie's Savillon discovers that the exercise of compassion extracts unprecedented loyalty and hard work: "they work with the willingness of freedom, yet are mine with more than the obligation of slavery."[27] For a while, Mackenzie's fiction was highly regarded. It was his first novel, *The Man of Feeling*, that gave a title to the new hero of sentiment, and depicted him in his most extreme condition of sensitivity. By making his sentimental protagonist, Harley, a character scorned and ill-treated by "the world," he at least escaped the smugness of some other sentimental novels, and created a text that was widely admired for a couple of decades after its publication. As a contemporary reviewer put it, "By those who have feeling hearts, and a true relish for simplicity in writing, many pages in this miscellaneous volume will be read with satisfaction."[28]

Unlike most sentimental fiction, *The Man of Feeling* has remained in print since its first appearance, and it is still possible to see why. It is a polished and formally intelligent work, carefully exploiting episodic structure to produce its poignant moments. Yet, in an important sense, it is now unreadable. Students unversed in eighteenth-century fiction are liable to ask whether the extreme tearfulness of its hero is, perhaps, meant to mock or amuse. The question as to whether *A Sentimental Journey* is meant ironically enlivens that text; the same question asked of *The Man of Feeling* shows us that Mackenzie's novel has become a literary fossil. It is a fossil that tells us a good deal about the needs of eighteenth-century readers, but that also tells us that we can no longer read "for the sentiment," in the way that Mackenzie's first admirers must have done.

"You must read him for the sentiment" was Samuel Johnson's recommendation to James Boswell, when the latter admitted that he found the fiction of Richardson "tedious"; "consider the story as only giving occasion to the sentiment."[29] It may have been Sterne who allowed "sentimental" novels to become self-conscious, and to declare themselves, but it was Richardson, two decades earlier, who established "sentiment" as the very purpose of reading fiction. (Some might say, more drily, that he established "sentiment" as the best excuse for reading fiction.) Johnson's recommendation is itself an example of a complication in the meaning of the word "sentiment," a complication that was important to Richardson, and then to his many imitators. For "sentiment" can mean both *feeling* (we should read Richardson in order to be touched) and *precept* (we should read Richardson in order to be instructed). It was very much to Richardson's purpose to conflate these two meanings. Through the use of letters, his texts would trace the fluctuations of his leading characters' feelings; as he wrote in one of his prefaces to *Clarissa*,

All letters are written while the hearts of the writers must be supposed to be wholly engaged in their subjects (the events at the time generally dubious): so that they abound not only with critical situations, but with what may be called instantaneous descriptions, and reflections.[30]

Yet the same preface sternly assures "considerate readers" that this is not "to divert or amuse," and that the novel certainly will be thought "tedious" by "all such as dip into it, expecting a light novel, or transitory romance; and look upon story in it ... as its sole end, rather than as a vehicle to the instruction."

This sense of sentiments as precepts – as morals drawn from a narrative – is often clearer in the texts that Richardson wrote around his novels (prefaces, postscripts, footnotes, or letters) than it is in the novels themselves. One of the strangest examples of his need to show how morally edifying his stories of feeling and suffering could be is just such a supplementary commentary on his own achievement: his *Collection of the Moral and Instructive Sentiments, Maxims, Cautions, and Reflexions, Contained in the Histories of Pamela, Clarissa, and Sir Charles Grandison* (1755). This was made out of what were originally the indexes of his novels. Arranged in alphabetical order of topics, it lists sententious extracts from Richardson's fiction; in the case of his first two novels, this means mostly the moral reflections of Pamela and Clarissa themselves. It presents itself as if it were a distillation of the wisdom that the novels contain.[31]

This insistence on "moral and instructive sentiments" can seem simply untrue to the novels themselves and sound like little more than an official justification of the pleasures of fiction. After all, the whole force of *Clarissa* comes from its author's determination to place his heroine in situations where there seems no right choice – or no choice at all. Ever since the immediate success of *Pamela* in 1740, readers and critics have indeed argued about what to make of this moralistic intent, and disagreed about whether Richardson actually performed what he preached.[32] While his first readers were certainly grateful to be assured that reading fiction could be good for them, his novels were most of all renowned, even revered, for their hold over those readers' emotions. One of the characters with whom Pamela corresponds tells her, "you make our hearts and eyes so often overflow, as we read."[33] This seems both the book's prescription for its would-be effect on its readers, and a pattern that many of those readers were prepared to follow. *Clarissa*, in particular, excited vivid testimonies to its capacity to stir emotions, and touch nerves – testimonies with which Richardson's own correspondence is full.[34]

It is clear that Richardson, notably testy if he found his admirers interpreting his books out of the track of his intentions, was gratified by the intense feelings he had aroused. To encounter these feelings now is to glimpse strange evidence of what were once the "sentimental" powers of fiction. Here is Lady Bradshaigh, Richardson's favorite correspondent, who has just finished reading the last volumes of *Clarissa*:

> I verily believe I have shed a pint of tears, and my heart is still bursting, tho' they cease not to flow at this moment, nor will, I fear, for some time ... in agonies would I lay down the book, take it up again, walk about the room, let fall a flood of tears, wipe my eyes, read again, perhaps not three lines, throw away the book, crying out, excuse me, good Mr. Richardson, I cannot go on.
>
> (Barbauld, *Correspondence*, IV: 240)

Lady Bradshaigh's descriptions of her susceptibility to fiction replicate the sensibility of the heroine of whom she read so painfully and so avidly. "My hand trembles, for I can scarce hold my pen. I am as mad as the poor injured Clarissa," she wrote of the effect on her of Clarissa's rape (Barbauld, *Correspondence*, IV: 201). This tendency is not just one individual's fanaticism; it is also exactly that conflation of the experience of reading with the experiences being represented which is the appeal of sentimentalism. Richardson's use of letters allowed him to record the impact of Pamela's or Clarissa's accounts of suffering on other characters, and thus provide his public with some exemplary tearfulness. Weeping was recommended: as Belford, the reformed rake, says in *Clarissa*, "Tears ... are no signs of an unmanly, but, contrarily of a human nature; they ease the overcharged heart" (*Clarissa*, IV: 145).

Advocates and (eventually) critics of sentimental texts were equally conscious that these texts supposedly allowed the properly sensitive consumer to experience, in the very activity of reading, those "refined and elevated feelings" to which the *OED* refers. Richardson had made it possible to believe that delicate feelings were morally admirable, and could be tested and enlivened by reading. Here is an anonymous "essay on sentiment" from 1775:

> sentiment in all its latitude is a privilege of a favored few; of those exalted and refined spirits alone, who seem composed of purer materials than other mortals, whose exquisite sensations yield to ten thousand impressions, equally unknown and incomprehensible to the vulgar, of whatever condition.[35]

This very assurance, however, was open to an attack that is, arguably, still implicit in many of our uses of the word "sentimental": namely, the accusation that these "exquisite sensations" could be enjoyed without any real activity of fellow-feeling. This is the line taken by Hannah More's *Sensibility. A Poetical Epistle* (1782), which praises writers who stimulate "the finely fashioned nerve" (Richardson, Sterne, and Mackenzie are prominent), but denounces those whose sensitivities are confined to reading. These imagined consumers of the texts that More herself most admires, while they are "Alive to every woe by *fiction* dress'd," neglect "The social sympathy, the sense humane" that is true sensibility: "While FEELING boasts her ever-tearful eye, / Stern TRUTH, firm FAITH, and manly VIRTUE fly."[36]

By the time that More, herself a formidable Christian moralist, wrote this, sentimental fiction had become the regular business of the unnamed writers who supplied the circulating libraries, and Richardson's large claims for sentiment had become less compelling. It should be noted, however, that even this formulaic fiction was not shy of continuing such claims. Often it adopted a high moral tone, rebutting "all suspicion of its containing sentiments inconsistent with ... wisdom and virtue," as the dedication of *Emma; or, the unfortunate attachment. A sentimental novel* put it.[37] No doubt such pieties were frequently just a conventional necessity; throughout the eighteenth century, novels attached themselves to the cause of "virtue," often bemoaning the corrupting influence of other novels. Yet it is also symptomatic of a deeper need, which novels of the period – sentimental or not – were attempting to answer: the need to imagine how private individuals might understand each other, and learn to share each other's interests. If the novel developed as a genre that made significant the distinctive fate of a particular individual, then sentimentalism was the attempt to rescue that individual from isolation and selfishness.

This is one reason for the emphasis upon suffering and misfortune in sentimental fiction – on "virtue in distress."[38] No writer was able to outdo the slow death of Clarissa for tearful consequences, but those who followed in Richardson's wake returned again and again to the ennobling effects of distress, both for those who suffered, and those who watched. As one of the letter writers in *Emma; or, the unfortunate attachment* has it, "Grief ... improves the heart; it humanizes, it renders us more fit for society."[39] Novels of the 1770s and 1780s are full of similar recommendations, and boasts, of tenderness. Underlying sentimentalism is the belief that a capacity for deep, and even disabling, feeling renders individuals fit for society. To possess heightened sensibility is to feel more readily the pleasures and pains of sympathy, to be able to escape self-interest, and therefore to be virtuous. Sterne was alive enough to the gratifications of this formula to allow us to feel uneasy, about it, as Yorick tells us of the delight of mingling his tears with Maria in *A Sentimental Journey*. In *Clarissa*, Richardson made the capacity for feeling so exceptional that it was the doom as well as the privilege of his heroine, and therefore turned the formula into tragedy. The imitators of both novelists, however, tended to emphasize all that was simply consolatory in the equation of feeling and virtue.

That equation may have become platitudinous by the late eighteenth century, but the notion that "sentiment" was what rescued individuals from themselves was pursued with considerable intellectual rigor in the period. It is no coincidence that the moral philosophers who were the contemporaries of Richardson, Sterne, and Mackenzie produced complex analyses of "moral sentiments" (Adam Smith's major work of moral philosophy, published in 1759, is indeed called *The Theory of Moral Sentiments*). Hume and Smith, in particular, set out to describe the properties of "sympathy," the faculty by which "the passions and sentiments of others" become our own.[40] They too were trying to understand how the experiences of individuals were communicable, and how "sentiments" might be both vivid emotions and moral judgments.[41] Yet it is also important to note that these philosophers of moral sentiment showed little or no interest in novels, even though it is now clear that it was in novels that the powers of sentiment were being tested. Their "literary" interests remained conservative; they concerned themselves with the nature of "taste," and with the polite, collective consumption of literature. The pleasure of novels was widely supposed to be disturbingly private; readers were drawn onwards by the misadventures of a singular protagonist, experiencing sympathetic emotions that are treated as deeply suspect by critics of the new genre.[42]

Many sentimental novels themselves worried about where the capacities for sympathy and for strong feeling could lead. Long before Mary Wollstonecraft complained of the "romantic unnatural delicacy of feeling" that "the herd of Novelists" glorified,[43] those novelists themselves depicted the price that was often to be paid for sentimental susceptibility. Pamela and Clarissa are reduced to weakness or illness by their sensitivities, as is the virtuous Clementina in *Sir Charles Grandison* driven to "hysterical disorders" by all her fine feeling (568). Sterne's Yorick and Mackenzie's Harley are made weak by their better natures, and they, as well as we, must learn to value that weakness. Characters are often as self-conscious about the debilitating effects of "delicacy" as Frances, one of the correspondents in Elizabeth Griffith's *Genuine Letters between Henry and Frances* (1757): "I have, from my Infancy, been used to a fatal Delicacy … it has enervated every Faculty of my Soul, and superadded a thousand tender Weaknesses to the Weakest of the weaker Sex."[44] It was the pioneers of sentimentalism who themselves showed that the woman of sensibility and the man of feeling were made ill by all that they were able to feel.

Here again, sentimental novels seem close to other eighteenth-century inquiries into the private self. This was a period in which nervous disorders became a fashionable topic, and "the English Malady" was established as the malaise of those who were refined and sensitive – an illness that was also a privilege.[45] The association of feeling with affliction should warn us against presuming that sentimentalism derives from an optimistic creed of benevolence or humanitarianism. Even the least testing sentimental fiction doubts whether the capacity for sympathy, the social instinct that it celebrates, is common. The hero or heroine of sentiment is ignored or disdained by "the world." (Henry Mackenzie followed *The Man of Feeling* with *The Man of the World*, a novel named after a destructively unsentimental protagonist.) Sometimes he or she is simply too good to survive. Richardson's Clarissa and Mackenzie's Harley both die because of their virtuous sensitivities; outside England, sentimentalism's most famous victim is Goethe's Werther, whose suicide was a shocking acknowledgment that some feel too much to go on living. Sentimentalism in eighteenth-century novels seems much more like the consequence of an anxiety about the sociability of individuals, than the assertion of a faith in human benevolence. The novel, the genre that pays special attention to the texture of both individuality and social relations, is an appropriate place for this anxiety to find expression.

From the first, sentimental virtue had led to weakness or illness. Richardson's Pamela, a resolute heroine who endures suffering triumphantly, also sometimes collapses under the pressure of her feelings. The heroines who follow her, up to and including the Gothic novels of Ann Radcliffe, are made sick by their sensitivities. Time and again the protagonists of sentimental fiction fail to find a social space in which their sympathies can operate. They fall ill because their feelings are turned inwards. In a sense this is sentimentalism's acknowledgment of its own failure. For it tried to imagine the communicability of human sentiments, transcending all difference and leading individuals away from mere self-interest into the delights of sympathy. It found instances of that communicability in expressive speechlessness: tears, sighs, blushes, hesitations – that territory at the edges of speech which *A Sentimental Journey* so brilliantly explores. Often it behaved as if that speechlessness were simply a privilege, like this (pale) imitator of Sterne:

> Neither of us could articulate a word – yet though silent, we conversed – for the lady by degrees looking full in my face, our eyes spoke, and we perfectly understood each other – it was the language of *nature*, whose declarations were sincere.[46]

Yet the silence that was the fulfillment of sentiment was also its limit; it was the silence of feeling become private, visceral, debilitating. Sentimental novels behaved as if they were exemplary, but offered examples that were beyond imitation: Clarissa, the tragic victim; Harley, the weak, virtuous fatalist; Yorick, the wry epicure of emotion. All had to recognize that, in the logic of sentimentalism, the capacity for sympathy could only be realized in the most private experiences.

NOTES

1 See for instance *The conflict. A sentimental tale in a series of letters* (Newcastle, 1790); William Beckford, *Azemia: a descriptive and sentimental novel* (1797); *Tourville; or, the mysterious lover: a sentimental novel* (1800). Most fiction such as this was published anonymously; even Beckford's novel appeared under a transparently fictional pseudonym: "Jacquetta Agneta Mariana Jenks."

2 Jane Austen, *Sanditon*, reprinted in R. W. Chapman, ed., *The Works of Jane Austen* (1954; reprinted Oxford: Oxford University Press, 1987), 403.

3 See for instance *Sentimental beauties and moral delineations from the writings of the celebrated Dr. Blair, and other much admired authors* (London, 1782); *Perceptive, moral and sentimental pieces* (Manchester, 1797).

4 For a discussion of this, and Hanway's other activities, see Ann Jessie Van Sant, *Eighteenth-Century Sensibility and the Novel* (Cambridge: Cambridge University Press, 1993), chapter 2.

5 This is the anonymous *Margaretta, Countess of Rainsford. A sentimental novel* (London, 1769).

6 See, for example, *Unfortunate sensibility; or, the life of Mrs. L—. Written by herself. In a series of sentimental letters. Dedicated to Mr. Yorick* (London, 1784); *Sentiments on the death of the sentimental Yorick* (London, 1768); *A sentimental journey. Intended as a sequel to Mr. Sterne's* (London, 1793); *Sentimental excursions to Windsor and other places* (London, 1781). The last of these, by Leonard MacNally, admits, "I have imitated STERNE": 59.

7 The best account of this is to be found in Alan B. Howes, *Yorick and the Critics: Sterne's Reputation in England, 1760–1868* (New Haven, Conn.: Yale University Press, 1958). Samples from some of the contemporary burlesques are given in Howes' *Sterne. The Critical Heritage* (London: Routledge and Kegan Paul, 1974).

8 *The Monthly Review*, 23 February, 1765, 125–26.

9 See *Letters of Laurence Sterne*, ed. L. P. Curtis (Oxford: Clarendon, 1935), 90.

10 See in particular Gardner D. Stout's introduction to *A Sentimental Journey through France and Italy by Mr. Yorick* (Berkeley and Los Angeles: University of California Press, 1967), and Howes, *Yorick and the Critics*.

11 Howes, *The Critical Heritage*, 200–1.

12 *The Sentimental Magazine; or, General Assemblage of Science, Taste, and Entertainment*, January 1774, 4. The influence of *A Sentimental Journey* on periodical fiction is recorded in R. D. Mayo, *The English Novel in the Magazines* (Evanston, Ill.: Northwestern University Press, 1962), 341–45.

13 Stout, ed., *A Sentimental Journey*, 291. All further references to the text are to this edition, abbreviated as *SJ*.

14 Ibid., 290.

15 It is a possibility that Sterne's closest friend John Hall Stevenson makes much of in his own continuation and reinterpretation of the novel: *Yorick's Sentimental*

Journey Continued (London, 1769). Unlike other pastiches, this emphasizes the sexual ends of sentimental dalliance.

16 *SJ*, 90.

17 Richardson uses several, slightly different phrases for this standard of immediacy. This particular description can be found in his preface to *The History of Sir Charles Grandison*, ed. Jocelyn Harris (1972; reprinted Oxford: Oxford University Press, 1986), 4.

18 *The Sentimental Magazine*, January 1774, 6.

19 *The Monthly Review*, 26 January 1762, 32.

20 Such aspersions can be found everywhere in eighteenth-century discussions of fiction. Telling examples of these are given in Thomas Lockwood and Ronald Paulson, eds., *Fielding. The Critical Heritage* (London: Routledge and Kegan Paul, 1969).

21 Samuel Richardson, *Sir Charles Grandison*, ed. Harris, preface, 4.

22 Sarah Scott, *The History of Sir George Ellison* (London, 2 vols., 1770), I: v.

23 Ibid., I, 21.

24 Ibid., I, 208.

25 Ibid., I, 212–13.

26 *The Assignation. A Sentimental Novel. In a Series of Letters* (London, 2 vols., 1774), I: 17.

27 Henry Mackenzie, *Julia de Roubigné* (London, 1805), 136.

28 Cited in H. W. Thompson, *A Scottish Man of Feeling* (London: Oxford University Press, 1931), 127.

29 James Boswell, *Life of Johnson*, ed. R. W. Chapman (1904; reprinted Oxford: Oxford University Press, 1980), 480.

30 Samuel Richardson, *Clarissa; or, The History of a Young Lady*, third edition first published in 1751 (London, 1978), xiv.

31 This didactic ambition of sentimentalism attracts Oliver Goldsmith's mockery in *She Stoops to Conquer*. See especially the prologue to that play, and his "Essay on the Theatre: or, a Comparison between Laughing and Sentimental Comedy," in *Collected Works of Oliver Goldsmith*, ed. Arthur Friedman (Oxford: Oxford University Press, 1966), III: 209–13.

32 An excellent corrective to modern misunderstandings of Richardson's didacticism, and in my opinion the best critical discussion of *Clarissa*, is Tom Keymer, *Richardson's "Clarissa" and the Eighteenth Century Reader* (Cambridge: Cambridge University Press, 1992).

33 Samuel Richardson, *Pamela; or, Virtue Rewarded* (London: Cambridge University Press, 1978), II: 82.

34 Unfortunately, the only widely available edition of Richardson's correspondence, *Selected Letters of Samuel Richardson*, ed. John Carroll (Oxford: Clarendon, 1964), contains only letters *from* Richardson. To sample the accounts of reading his novels sent to him by some of his admirers, see *The Correspondence of Samuel Richardson*, ed. Anna Laetitia Barbauld (London, 6 vols., 1804). It should be noted that Barbauld's collection was intended to honor Richardson, and that her editorial principles were not scholarly.

35 *Dialogues from the German to M. Wieland. To which is prefixed, an essay on sentiment, by the editor* (London, 1775), iv.

36 Ibid., 282.
37 *Emma; or, the unfortunate attachment. A sentimental novel. In three volumes* (London, 1773), I: iv.
38 This is the title of one of the best books on sentimental novels in the eighteenth century, R. F. Brissenden's *Virtue in Distress. Studies in the Novel of Sentiment from Richardson to Sade* (London: Macmillan, 1974).
39 *Emma*, 249.
40 David Hume, *A Treatise of Human Nature*, ed. L. A. Selby-Bigge, 2nd edn, revised P. H. Nidditch (Oxford: Oxford University Press, 1978), 316.
41 I try to relate the undertakings of eighteenth-century moral philosophers to the sentimentalism of novelists in *Sentiment and Sociability. The Language of Feeling in the Eighteenth Century* (Oxford: Oxford University Press, 1988).
42 An excellent anthology of eighteenth-century criticism and comment is Ioan Williams, ed., *Novel and Romance, 1700–1800* (New York, 1970).
43 Mary Wollstonecraft, *A Vindication of the Rights of Woman* (1792; London, 1929), chapter 2, 37.
44 Elizabeth Griffith, *A Series of Genuine Letters between Henry and Frances* (London, 1757), 6.
45 See Roy Porter's introduction to his edition of George Cheyne, *The English Malady* (London: Tavistock/Routledge, 1991).
46 Leonard MacNally, *Sentimental excursions to Windsor and other places* (London, 1781), 38.

READING LIST

Bredvold, Louis I. *The Natural History of Sensibility.* Detroit: Wayne State University Press, 1962.
Brissenden, R. F. *Virtue in Distress. Studies in the Novel of Sentiment from Richardson to Sade.* London: Macmillan, 1974.
Conger, Syndy McMillen. *Sensibility in Transformation. Creative Resistence to Sentiment from the Augustans to the Romantics.* London and Toronto: Associated University Presses, 1990.
Crane, R. S. "Suggestions towards a Genealogy of the 'Man of Feeling.'" *ELH*, 1 (1934): 205–30.
Erametsa, Eric. "A Study of the Word 'Sentimental' and of Other Linguistic Characteristics of Eighteenth-Century Sentimentalism in England." *Annales Academiae Scientarum Fennicae*, series B, Tom. 74: 1 (Helsinki, 1951).
Frye, Northrop. "Towards Defining an Age of Sensibility," in *Eighteenth-Century English Literature: Essays in Modern Criticism*, ed. James L. Clifford. London and New York: Oxford University Press, 1959.
Goldberg, Rita. *Sex and the Enlightenment.* Cambridge: Cambridge University Press, 1984.
Hagstrum, Jean. *Sex and Sensibility. Ideal and Erotic Love from Milton to Mozart.* Chicago: University of Chicago Press, 1980.
Jones, Chris. *Radical Sensibility. Literature and Ideas in the 1790s.* London: Routledge, 1993.

Mullan, John. *Sentiment and Sociability. The Language of Feeling in the Eighteenth Century*. Oxford: Oxford University Press, 1988.

Rawson, Claude. "Some Remarks on Eighteenth-Century 'Delicacy,' With a Note on Hugh Kelly's *False Delicacy* (1768)," in *Order from Confusion Sprung*. London: Allen and Unwin, 1985.

Todd, Janet. *Sensibility, an Introduction*. London: Methuen, 1986.

Van Sant, Ann Jessie. *Eighteenth-Century Sensibility and the Novel*. Cambridge: Cambridge University Press, 1993.

12

JAMES P. CARSON

Enlightenment, popular culture, and Gothic fiction

In Ann Radcliffe's *The Italian* (1797), shortly after having escaped from her imprisonment in the monastery of San Stephano, the heroine, Ellena di Rosalba, accompanied by the hero, Vivaldi, and his garrulous servant, Paulo, travels toward Naples through the pastoral mountain scenery near Celano. In this scene between two imprisonments (the hero will shortly be confined in the prisons of the Inquisition in Rome), Ellena and Vivaldi, two characters whose aesthetic sense is a function of their genteel social status, admire the ruins of an ancient castle and the sublime and beautiful landscape. But their aesthetic sense is also determined differentially by gender. Vivaldi is typically more sensitive to the sublime, noting how the mountains appear "threatening, and horrid," "barren and rocky," "mighty" and dark.[1] Ellena observes how the beautiful – that which is sweet, soft, elegant, under cultivation, and under human control – contrasts with "the awful grandeur" of the mountains (158). The third observer, Paulo, apparently as a natural consequence of his low birth, sees nothing in these scenes to arouse aesthetic appreciation, admiring in the prospect only the things that remind him of his native city of Naples.

Two value systems intersect in the figure of Paulo: given the conjunction of cosmopolitanism and sentimentalism, Radcliffe mocks Paulo for his narrow nationalism and praises him for his local attachment. Vivaldi, the enlightened citizen of the world, bestows a patronizing smile "at this stroke of nationality" in his servant (159). Vivaldi's smile would seem to complicate the conventional critical judgment that the British Gothic novel indulges in popular chauvinism directed against despotic judicial and penal systems, papist superstitions, and, later, revolutionary mob violence in Italy, Spain, and France. Marilyn Butler, for example, sees Radcliffe as a political conservative and the Gothic novel as a form safely distanced, temporally and geographically, from progressive ideology, at least until the early nineteenth century and the appearance of books such as Mary Shelley's *Frankenstein* (1818) and Charles Robert Maturin's *Melmoth the Wanderer*

(1820).[2] On the contrary, in *The Italian*, rather than betraying her own British chauvinism or appealing to that of her "popular" audience, Radcliffe gently mocks the Neapolitan chauvinism exhibited by precisely the character most representative of the "people." But, along with a ludicrous patriotism, Paulo exhibits the sentimental virtue of local attachment. The period in which the gothic novel flourished witnessed a decline of a cosmopolitanism based on stoical ethics and a philosophical appeal to universal principles in favor of a local attachment associated with subjective responsiveness, sympathy, and the virtues of simplicity.[3] In terms of this second value system, Paulo's homesickness manifests, on a humbler level, the very same sensibility and capacity for humane feeling that the more refined characters reveal through the mode of aesthetic appreciation.

What Paulo recalls most fondly when he thinks of Naples is the "good" Mount Vesuvius, which provides a brilliant and impressive display on some dark nights. Vivaldi feels compelled to remind his servant of the great harm that a volcano can do. But within a few paragraphs, when darkness has obscured the beautiful and sublime scenery near Celano, Paulo reiterates the virtues of the good volcano: "here we have no mountain, that will light us on our way! Ah! if we were but within twenty miles of Naples, now – and it was an *illumination* night!" (160). The volcano, a figure for the sublime from the time of Longinus, proves to be a *good* mountain in two senses: first, it provides a spectacular show of light that fascinates the populace, and, secondly, this very show has the potential to guide benighted travelers. Radcliffe would like to make a similar claim for her Gothic novels: they simultaneously fascinate and provide moral guidance for the reader, though they fascinate more by means of darkness than light.

The Gothic novel, then, would resemble Paolo's "illumination night." In this chapter, I shall trace the associations of this Radcliffean phrase in order to define the Gothic novel, to explore its relation to popular culture and to the genre of the romance, and to attempt an account of why it arises when it does. Most critics tend to regard the Gothic novel as symptomatic of a discontinuity or sharp historical break, as a new development in fiction, an adumbration of the psychological focus of the nineteenth-century novel. I shall stress on the contrary the very apparent continuities between eighteenth-century "realistic" fiction and the Gothic form. There has been a tendency to structure books on the nineteenth-century novel with an initial chapter or two on the Gothic, as if it were merely a precursor form, bearing the same relation to the great novelistic tradition as what used to be termed "preromanticism" bears to Romantic poetry.[4] In emphasizing instead the continuities between eighteenth-century fiction and the Gothic, I am questioning the claim that there is a sharp break between the Enlightenment and Romanticism.

The phrase "illumination night" leads from the general atmospherics of an eighteenth-century aesthetic characterized by the appreciation of sublime landscapes, ruins, graveyard poetry, and "Gothic" architecture and literature, to the general aims of Enlightenment science (with an emphasis on combustion and electricity), to the specific institutions designed to promote universal visibility, to the peculiar phenomenon of "illuminations" – a phenomenon that embodies sometimes the cooperation of, and sometimes a conflict between, official festivity and popular culture. A reexamination of the relationship of Gothic fiction to both popular culture and Enlightenment thought will enable an assessment of the extent to which it is appropriate to term the eighteenth-century Gothic novel a "conservative" form.

The Gothic novel arises in 1764 with the publication of Horace Walpole's *The Castle of Otranto*. Henry Fielding's *Joseph Andrews* (1742) is a "comic Epic-Poem in Prose," and Fielding makes the Miltonic claim that this kind of writing has been "hitherto unattempted in our Language,"[5] and after Fielding claims in *Tom Jones* (1749) to be "the Founder of a new Province of Writing,"[6] Walpole with equal self-consciousness, in the preface to the second edition (1765) of his short novel, asserts his own originality. Walpole's "new species of romance"[7] reconciles the faithful representations of human nature from the new "realistic" novel with the extensive imaginative resources of the old romance. In the next major identifiably Gothic novel, *The Old English Baron* (first published as *The Champion of Virtue* in 1777), Clara Reeve situates her work in a tradition initiated by Walpole. In the 1790s the Gothic novel becomes the major fictional form in English, with the publication of Matthew Lewis's *The Monk* (1796), William Godwin's *Caleb Williams* (1794) and *St. Leon* (1799), five novels by Ann Radcliffe (1789–97), and the American novels of Charles Brockden Brown. After Mary Shelley and Charles Robert Maturin the Gothic novel declines, or undergoes transformation into such genres as ghost stories, vampire tales, sensation novels, historical romances, and detective fiction.

The Gothic novel is usually defined by its stereotyped characters, or formulaic plots involving the usurpation of a title or an estate, a hidden crime, or a pact with the devil. However, we might equally well define this fictional form in terms of the almost mandatory prefatory justifications for combining a representation of the manners of real life and the imaginative appeal of the marvelous. In their prefaces, Gothic novelists frequently claim to have undertaken a quasi-scientific investigation into natural human responses when characters are confronted with situations of apparently supernatural stress. Such prefatory justifications define Gothic fiction as a combination of novel and romance. The practice of early eighteenth-century novelists would not warrant a sharp distinction between these two terms. Moreover, few critics today would be tempted to use the identification of Gothic fiction with the romance form to dismiss it from serious consideration in the history of the novel.

Still, we need to account for Ann Radcliffe's insistence on the term *romance* in the titles and subtitles of her novels: *A Sicilian Romance* (1790), *The Romance of the Forest* (1791), *The Mysteries of Udolpho: A Romance*, and *The Italian; or, The Confessional of the Black Penitents: A Romance*. Radcliffe would seem to be drawing upon the distinction between novel and romance that Clara Reeve outlined in her 1785 work of literary theory and literary history, *The Progress of Romance*. Although Reeve attacks circulating libraries and the indiscriminate reading of novels and romances that they promote, she seeks to correct the sexist English misconception that romances are "proper furniture only for a lady's Library."[8] While Reeve echoes Fielding in her definition of romance as "an Epic in prose," she criticizes him for having "painted human nature as *it is*, rather than as *it ought to be*" (*Progress*, I: 13, 141). This distinction between realism and idealism, between mixed characters and exemplary ones, is fundamental to Reeve's opposition between novel and romance. Reeve quotes approvingly from Dr. John Gregory's *A Comparative View of the State and Faculties of Man, with Those of the Animal World* (1766): "Notwithstanding the absurdities of the old Romance, it seems calculated to produce more favorable effects on the morals of mankind than our modern Novels. If the former did not represent men as they really are, it represented them better" (II: 86).

Like other Enlightenment authors, Reeve worries about the enthusiasm and heightened imagination fostered by romance reading. However, she sees worse dangers than these, for when the enthusiasm that inspires glorious actions comes to be ridiculed, people will immerse themselves "in low, groveling, effeminate, or mercenary pursuits" (I: 103). Avarice, hedonism, and a decline of public spirit harm the state far more than the absurdities individuals may be led into by enthusiasm and an overactive imagination. Reeve's use of the word *effeminate* and her advocacy of public spirit indicate that she is drawing upon the classical republican critique of the corrupting effects of commerce on the once-autonomous citizen. Recourse to the romance form, for Reeve and Radcliffe, can potentially serve to mitigate the effeminating and corrupting effects of life in a commercial world.

However, women writers such as Reeve and Radcliffe are not attracted to the romance solely for its capacity to rehabilitate a masculinity threatened by commerce. The "Gothic" romance, in opposition both to the Greek and Roman classics and to life in eighteenth-century England, appears to offer women substantial power and respect. Reeve attributes to the "Gothic" age and to the later feudal institution of chivalry "that respectful complaisance to the fair sex, (so different from the manners of the Greeks and Romans)" (1: 34). In this respect women readers and writers would have been attracted to the Gothic romance for many of the same reasons that Arabella in Charlotte Lennox's *The Female Quixote* (1752) was attracted to seventeenth-century French romances. In these huge tomes Arabella found an idealized world of heroic women and men who lived lives and experienced adventures worth recording in history. In the eighteenth-century society of Bath and London, on the contrary, Arabella finds women who trifle away their lives in dressing and dancing, while they enviously compete in the marriage market, and men "with Figures so feminine, Voices so soft, such tripping Steps, and unmeaning Gestures" that they could never exhibit military virtue.[9] As Janice Radway has shown in her influential study of the readers of modern romances, twentieth-century women readers of "popular" fiction are less passive, escapist, and complicit with patriarchy than has usually been claimed.[10] The romance form in the eighteenth as in the twentieth century offers the potential for female creativity and the subversion of conventional gender roles.

In contrast to the *novelty* of "realistic" fictions and their proximity to newspapers, the early Gothic novel distanced itself from the world of its readers temporally, geographically, and by disruptions of normal causality. The "Gothic" story was initially characterized by a setting in medieval or feudal times, frequently in exotic locales such as Italy, Bavaria, or the Scottish Highlands. Italy was the ideal scene, not only for picturesque ruins and the requisite banditti, but also for tracing the decline of classical Roman virtue into luxury. For example, in *A Sicilian Romance*, the unfeeling Duke de Luovo, while pursuing the heroine, encounters robbers in whom he "could almost have imagined he beheld ... a band of the early Romans before knowledge had civilized, or luxury had softened them."[11] Even when set in the past, the Gothic novel typically differs from the historical novel in its tendency to ignore historical research, sometimes introducing anachronisms in the process. Fascinated with liminal states or with an undecidability between life and death, or between human beings and artistic representations, Gothic novelists tend to include in their stories statues and portraits that bleed, move, speak, or show other signs of animation. In many eighteenth-century texts the word *Gothic* was a pejorative term, synonymous with "barbarous," typically used as an epithet to modify "ignorance" or "superstition." However, even at the end of the seventeenth century – for example, in the writings of Andrew Fletcher of Saltoun – the "Gothic" age was sometimes idealized as an age of liberty, when virtuous and warlike barons imposed limits on monarchical power.[12] To the extent that this conception of the Gothic age is operative in the Gothic novel, the presentation of aristocrats who had not yet alienated their military capacities might stand as a civic humanist indictment of the corrupt times in which noble titles had come to be awarded for bureaucratic rather than military services or, worse yet, simply purchased.

The Gothic novel derives from Elizabethan and Jacobean drama a fascination with grotesque violence, and from erotic–sentimental novels plots that focus on a virtuous woman under sexual threat. The agent of this threat is often, like Lovelace in Richardson's *Clarissa* (1747–48), a hero/villain who would seem to be modeled partly on Milton's Satan. The character of the hero/villain permits novelists to study heartlessness or to join moral philosophers and proponents of solitary confinement in exploring the operations of the voice of conscience. The virtuous heroine, on the other hand, experiences her own insignificance in the face of sublime nature and Nature's God and learns of the transience of all human achievement. The Gothic novel thus explores the parallels between ethics and aesthetics upon which eighteenth-century moral philosophers insisted. The heroine's fears – sometimes imaginary, sometimes legitimate – produce claustrophobia and terror in castles, prisons, and caves, in which she often discovers moldering manuscripts, sees mysterious lights, and hears mysterious voices. Representations of the heroine's perspective and imagination reveal less a new psychological focus of the novel than they do a continuing exploration of the epistemological questions that dominate eighteenth-century British fiction.[13]

In addition to heroine and villain, Gothic novels usually contain a talkative and superstitious servant, whose literary progenitors would include Sancho Panza from Cervantes' *Don Quixote*, Hugh Strap from Smollett's *Roderick Random* (1748), and Benjamin Partridge from *Tom Jones*. That such servants tend also to be supremely faithful to their masters or mistresses permits Gothic novelists, like their counterparts in realistic fiction, to relive the anxieties of genteel readers who may fear that paternalistic relations of deference and subordination are yielding to those of contract and the cash nexus, and that the vertical ties of master and man are being replaced by class solidarity. The idealization of selected semifeudal or "Gothic" social relations may permit a nostalgic or "conservative" critique of the social relations in a society in which labour has become commodified.

Roman Catholic European settings provide opportunities for a Protestant attack on the apparatus of tyranny associated with papism and Continental absolutism. Still, the fact that the Reformation had reached England does not simply attenuate the criticism of despotism, as Judith Wilt would have it: "the point of the splendid overthrow of monkish tyranny that animates the early Gothic is surely that in the English mind it *has been overthrown*" (Wilt, *Ghosts*, 45). I would argue, on the contrary, that the Gothic critique is in no simple sense jingoistic, first of all because of the resemblance and, in some cases, indebtedness to the Continental Enlightenment and the revolutions it partly inspired. It has been long thought that the anticlericalism of Matthew Lewis's *The Monk*, for example, derives from "the French revolutionary theatre."[14] (One should not, however, discount the influence of a *popular*, as opposed to *enlightened*, anticlerical tradition, featuring proud and lascivious monks and priests.) Secondly, novelists often redirect their critique of "Gothic" tyranny toward feudal or barbaric survivals in Britain's own judicial or penal system. Hence Godwin and Mary Shelley echo the criticisms of the prison reformer John Howard, when they note the lengthy and inhumane pretrial imprisonment of Caleb Williams and Victor Frankenstein. Whereas the novels in which these title characters appear have contemporary settings, Godwin's *St. Leon*, a narrative about the sixteenth century, establishes a clear analogy between the Spanish Inquisition's suppression of heresy and the Pittite repression of political radicalism in the England of the 1790s.

In its critique of Continental despotism and in the redirection of that critique toward Britain, Gothic novelists are pursuing rather than departing from the sociopolitical aims of eighteenth-century "realistic" fiction. In *Pamela* (1740), for example, Samuel Richardson situates the rakish Mr. B.'s interrogation of the heroine in the context of the use of judicial torture in Continental criminal proceedings, prompting her objection in favor of British liberty: "Sir, said I, the Torture is not used in *England*; and I hope you won't bring it up. Admirably said! said the naughty Gentleman. – But I can tell you of as good a Punishment. If a Criminal won't plead with us here in *England*, we *press him* to Death, or till he does plead."[15] Although Mr. B. is merely making lascivious suggestions, the passage also reminds us of the menacing and archaic power of the law as it lingered into the mid-eighteenth century. Pressing to death or the *peine forte et dure*, one historian reminds us, "continued until at least 1741," shortly after the publication of *Pamela*; and it was not until 1772 that a statute was passed making "standing mute of malice" result in an automatic conviction.[16] To take one other example, within Fielding's beautiful and awe-inspiring "*Gothick*" house of Mr. Allworthy, the young Tom Jones undergoes a beating at the hands of his tutor, Mr. Thwackum, "so severe ... that it possibly fell little short of the Torture with which Confessions are in some Countries extorted from Criminals" (*Tom Jones*, 1.4, 42; 11.2, 122). What begins as patriotic praise of British justice modulates into a critique of an educational system in which sadists may assume despotic authority even in England. In eighteenth-century fiction, then, appeals to British liberty typically serve a corrective or reformist function, rather than simply a popular chauvinistic one.

In an obvious sense, Gothic fiction has no better claim than any other kind of eighteenth-century novel to be considered part of "popular" culture. Given the high, though decreasing, rates of illiteracy among the "people" and the high prices of novels, it would neither have been possible for many common laborers to have read them nor for any but a small elite to have purchased them. For example, an admittedly long novel like Radcliffe's *The Mysteries of Udolpho* was published in 1794, in four volumes, at a cost of £1 5s.[17] This amounts to more than a skilled English tradesman would have made in a week, and more than a common laborer would have earned in two. Even given the availability to a wider public through circulating libraries and in the form of reading aloud, Radcliffe could not be considered a "popular" artist in the sense, for example, that Peter Burke gives the term – one who, often anonymously and often in oral genres, "works mainly for a public of craftsmen and peasants."[18] In this sense, "popular" culture would include folk songs, folktales, broadsides, chapbooks, itinerant juggling, folk dances, alehouse games, animal baiting, and seasonal festivals. In addition to impersonality, "popular" culture tends to be distinguished by a local or regional and sometimes by a formulaic character, and its "discovery" by the elite in the eighteenth century tends to be associated with the rise of nationalism.

Now, while the Gothic novel is not itself part of "popular" culture, it is clearly contemporaneous with both the reform of popular culture and its rediscovery. The Gothic novel, moreover, appears in England at a time when literacy rates are rising and when more members of the lower social orders are beginning to possess more than minimal reading skills. Indeed, the increasing diffusion of print culture is one of the causes for the waning influence of traditional popular culture. The Gothic novel is part of the project of the recovery of popular culture to the extent that it appropriates the marvelous and supernatural from folktales. Perhaps it shares as well with popular culture an indictment of corruption and capitalism based on a nostalgic appeal to an idealized past. (If so, the Gothic novel might well be "conservative" in the same way that traditional popular culture is – critically opposing an older "moral economy" to the new political economy.) Still, it would be overstating the case to regard the Gothic novel as taking, in David Punter's words, "the form of an 'expropriated' litera-ture," with middle-class authors self-consciously reviving materials of folk belief that are, in his view, the "property" of the people.[19] Such an account ignores the long history of interaction between elite and popular culture, and the way such interaction necessarily alters the dominant culture. The rise of the Gothic novel – indeed, the rise of the novel itself – bears a significant relation to the withdrawal of the elite from popular culture, for when the elite participated in both, they viewed learned culture as serious and popular culture as play (Burke, *Popular Culture*, 28). The novel, in general, represents one mode of inserting play into learned culture, while Gothic fiction specifically draws upon popular cultural sources to provide the elite with substitutes for the ludic opportunities that have been lost.

In making the claim that the phrase "illumination night" serves as a description of Radcliffe's novelistic practice, I am doing something more than reasserting the conventional view that the Gothic novel represents the dark side of the Enlightenment or that it arises in reaction to an age of reason and light. This argument is complicated by Peter Brooks, who, drawing upon Freud and Rudolph Otto, finds in the ghosts and diabolical agents of Lewis's *The Monk* a dramatization of the return of the repressed, in which the Sacred, having been denied by eighteenth-century skepticism, returns, "atomized," in a horrific and primitive form, and internalized as psychological terror.[20]

The philosopher Noel Carroll has challenged the return-of-the-repressed model for the relationship between the Enlightenment and tales of horror. Rejecting a psychohistorical account, Carroll argues that tales of horror may have arisen when they did because a broadly accepted set of natural norms, such as that established by Enlightenment science, was the prerequi-site for recognizing the category violations that define the impure objects that arouse the emotional state of "art-horror."[21] That is to say, the taxonomic project of eighteenth-century natural history by its very success created the potential for a new sort of monstrosity. In the course of denying the analogy between horror and religious feeling, Carroll revises our under-standing of the literature of horror by focusing on its cognitive and ratiocinative components – emphasizing, specifically, both plots driven by curiosity and the numerous imitations of rationalistic explanations for the monstrous objects that defy categorization (Carroll, *Philosophy*, 163–66, 182). This account helps to explain the Gothic obsession with protagonists who seek "to penetrate the veil of mystery." Given Carroll's persuasive critique of theories of horror fiction built on Rudolf Otto's *The Idea of the Holy*, why should we revisit at this late date the account of the Gothic novel as representing a dark side of the Enlightenment?

Another account of Gothic fiction, by an author whose critique of the Enlightenment remains highly influential today, does justify an examination of Radcliffe's "illumination night." Michel Foucault attempts to explain why Radcliffe and the genre in which she wrote arise simultaneously with the reign of transparency that finds its institutional paradigm in Jeremy Bentham's Panopticon:

> A fear haunted the latter half of the eighteenth century: the fear of darkened spaces, of the pall of gloom which prevents the full visibility of things, men and truths. It sought to break up the patches of darkness that blocked the light, eliminate the shadowy areas of society, demolish the unlit chambers where arbitrary political acts, monarchical caprice, religious superstitions, tyrannical and priestly plots, epidemics and the illusions of ignorance were fomented ... The landscapes of Ann Radcliffe's novels are composed of mountains and forests, caves, ruined castles and terrifyingly dark and silent convents. Now these imaginary spaces are like the negative of the transparency and visibility which it is aimed to establish.[22]

For Foucault, the geography of the Gothic novel presents the dark negation of Enlightenment transparency. Following in the wake of Foucault's view of eighteenth-century history in *Discipline and Punish*, some literary critics and historians of the novel have attempted to show that the novel as it emerges is a force for regulating and controlling the individual's behavior, and in that capacity for such critics the novel is complicit with or even partly constitutive of the repressive forces of the modern state like the penitentiary and the police.[23] But the Gothic landscape as Foucault evokes it does not suggest that ideals of visibility are ultimately and absolutely ineffectual. Instead of revealing social, psychological, and spiritual territory that can never be fully illuminated, the Gothic novel for Foucault would seem to map out that dark terrain precisely so that it may be conquered. Brooks and many other critics present the Gothic novel as early evidence that Enlightenment science failed to dispel the dark mysteries of nature, the supernatural, and the human soul. The Gothic novel for Foucault, on the contrary, would seem to be a popular artistic tool that assisted the endeavors of science and humanitarian reform in the successful creation of a carceral network, which aimed to discipline bodies through the implementation of technologies for altering the human soul.

But the Enlightenment, whose inefficacy the Gothic novel marks, is a monolithic age of reason that never was. Foucault's account has the virtue of redirecting our attention away from a superseded history of ideas – in which light and darkness either create the chiaroscuro of Gothic settings or advance the rhetoric of scientific progress – to a history of the institutions designed to break up the early modern crowd and produce the subject of the liberal state. For Foucault the modern disciplinary regimes that Enlightenment thought and, probably, the Gothic novel helped to produce are monolithic, characterized by "total" institutions. In *Discipline and Punish*, Foucault equates modernity and rationalization,[24] and fails to take sufficient account of the contradictions within the dominant order and of the struggles and negotiations that inevitably enter into the creation of bourgeois hegemony. While he demonstrates how the disciplined bodies of individualized subjects serve the interests of emerging industrial capitalism, he oversimplifies the historical process by regarding this emerging mode of production as the economic base that determines social change, thus relegating to an epiphenomenal superstructure all of liberal political theory, Enlightenment science, humanitarian reform, and *belles-lettres*.

Foucault's monolithic account of modernity would obscure the extent to which the Gothic novel is at once complicit with and critical of the Enlightenment conceived of as a contradictory ideological formation and intellectual enterprise. The Enlightenment, even in France, did not simply promote the dominance of the bourgeoisie within centralized, bureaucratic states. Certainly, Enlightenment ideals include dethroning of tradition, elimination of prejudice, freedom of conscience, political liberty, and the optimistic view that the progress of knowledge and technology will lead to happiness for the many in this world rather than the next – a new optimism about the power of secular society to improve the human condition to be found in a line of Enlightenment thought stretching from the French Philosophes, such as the mathematician and philosopher Condorcet (1743–94), to the late eighteenth-century English radical philosophers and utopians, such as the political theorist and novelist William Godwin (1756–1836). These men envision a steady march toward the perfection of human social institutions. In their works the Enlightenment initiated a new secular study of human beings that led beyond mere sociological analysis to institutional efforts to reshape human nature for the better. What might be called "managerial rationality," the project of thinkers such as Jeremy Bentham in the late eighteenth century to transform human society along strictly utilitarian and rational lines, was only one facet of the Enlightenment, which was not as an intellectual movement simply a will to power that donned the masks of sensibility, humanitarianism, and science to accomplish its totalitarian ends.[25]

Nor did the Enlightenment foster possessive individualism in any simple sense. Appeals to sociability, community, and the emotions did not have to await the advent of Romanticism; indeed, Roy Porter argues that sociability was the "key felicific technology" of the English Enlightenment (Porter, "Enlightenment," 15). Nicholas Phillipson has shown how the Addisonian

ideal of coffeehouse conversation was developed by Scottish thinkers such
as Francis Hutcheson. In this view, Hutcheson is less a moral arithmetician
and utilitarian predecessor of Bentham than an Enlightenment teacher who
sought to inspire his students with "a 'spirit of enquiry' and a love of
'conversation' which would assist in the 'culture of the heart.' "[26] Gothic
novels, particularly those composed by Radcliffe and other eighteenth-
century women writers, certainly participate in this culture of the heart and
to some extent partake of the spirit of rational inquiry as well. What is often
called "male" Gothic fiction (such as M. G. Lewis's *The Monk*) features
horrific violence and destructive interaction between the natural and supernatural worlds; Gothic fiction by women such as Radcliffe stops well short
of such terrors. Female Gothic fiction tends to depict the abuse of power by
tyrannical patriarchs and their exploitation of women, and it is best understood as a subgenre within the novel of sensibility as it explores the
sufferings of persecuted young women. To put it another way, the female
Gothic focuses intensely on a violation of just those ideals of sociability and
rational intercourse that the Enlightenment prized and promoted. These
ideals of sociability and conversation were best realized in eighteenth-
century Edinburgh in the form of elite clubs and improvement societies,
which sought to assume "para-parliamentary" functions in facilitating the
transition to a new commercial world (Phillipson, "Scottish Enlightenment," 27, 35). In this respect it would seem that it was the dark side not of
rationalism and bourgeois individualism but rather of Enlightenment sociability of which Gothic novelists were aware – specifically, the danger that
societies of intellectual elites might attempt surreptitiously to control an
ostensibly open and increasingly democratic political process. Hence, the
focus in many Gothic novels on secret societies such as the Illuminati: a
utopian society, centered in Bavaria, that attacked the errors of religious
establishments and corrupt political institutions in order to advance the goal
of perfectibility.

In the transition to what we now think of as the modern period, Enlightenment intellectuals promoted a rejection of what they thought of as
popular superstition, and for economic as well as political reasons there was
an attempt by many governments to suppress or control traditional popular
culture, which was often seen by the emerging modern European states as
dangerously rowdy and potentially subversive. But the Enlightenment
historical project also authorized the collection and preservation, often
enough with nostalgic regret, of popular cultural artifacts. And historians of
the time came to understand crowd behavior as not merely irrational and
spontaneous but as governed by rituals that frequently created the discipline
essential for effective social action. In his description of the Porteous riots in

the Heart of Midlothian (1818), Walter Scott shows that he recognizes what recent students of the crowd have maintained: *pace* Foucault, discipline is the product not only of modern carceral institutions designed on the model of monastic asceticism and military ranks, but also of bells, drums, horns, disguises, bonfires, and tar barrels – the ritual accoutrements of the early modern crowd.

Such popular accoutrements, especially bonfires and tarbarrels, lie behind Paolo's "illumination night." The fires of Vesuvius in *The Italian*, at once beneficial to mankind and potentially destructive, offer a symbol of Enlightenment very similar to the sublime flash of lightning that destroys "an old and beautiful oak" near Belrive in a later Gothic novel.[27] For, in Mary Shelley's *Frankenstein* (1818), if the electricity associated with lightning does not actually provide the spark of life in Frankenstein's project of reanimating dead flesh, it at least inspires this scientific project designed for the benefit of the human race. In the context of Shelley's novel, the destruction of the venerable oak suggests the unnaturalness of Frankenstein's enterprise and the threat that Enlightenment science poses to natural beauty and fertility. So, on the one hand Mary Shelley is a critic of the Enlightenment. But the venerable oak surely also serves as a symbol of the British nation, and of its stability founded on naval strength and colonialist commerce (ships built of oak) and the hegemony of the aristocracy and landed gentry. Thus, on the other hand, Mary Shelley would have welcomed the power of Enlightenment to destroy the military force and the prejudices that sustained a corrupt political order. In *The Italian* the natural illuminations supplied by the volcano are associated with popular patriotic spectacle, while the enlightened Vivaldi objects that such sublime power may endanger human life. In *Frankenstein*, on the contrary, the sublime power of lightning is appropriated by the enlightened scientist, ostensibly for the benefit of the human race, while it threatens both the natural beauty that Shelley values and the patriotic prejudices that she does not. While there are certainly ideological differences between Radcliffe and Shelley, neither author can be adequately described as popular, patriotic, or anti-Enlightenment.

That the image of the volcano illuminates late eighteenth-century attitudes toward science and art has recently been shown in Susan Sontag's historical romance, *The Volcano Lover*, in which Sir William Hamilton notes that "like any object of grand passion, the volcano unites many contradictory attributes," among which he identifies the very ones Radcliffe found: "Entertainment and apocalypse."[28] Sontag, I think, has a better understanding of the relationship between the Enlightenment and popular superstition than many historians and critics. When her William Hamilton visits the fortune-teller Efrosina Pumo, he "was feeling rather, well, Voltairean: in an ethnological mood ... disdainful of all superstitions, magic, zealotry, irrationality, yet not averse to the prospect of being surprised, confounded" (49). In October 1770 the musician and music historian Charles Burney visited Hamilton at his Neapolitan country house, the Villa Angelica, on which occasion he compared the volcanic activity to fireworks,[29] another eighteenth-century form of illuminations. Model volcanoes featuring fireworks effects were constructed in the late eighteenth century most spectacularly at Wörlitz (near Dessau in Germany) and at the Ruggieri Gardens in the Paris suburbs. The Gothic novelist William Beckford, in addition to constructing a Gothic abbey at Fonthill, created in the 1790s a lake that he hoped would look as if it had been formed in the crater of an extinct volcano (Thacker, "Volcano," 77–81). Perhaps owing to the extreme volcanic activity of Mount Vesuvius in the last third of the eighteenth century (including major eruptions in 1767, 1779, and 1793),[30] elaborately designed models of volcanic eruptions formed a favorite subject of exhibitions of the late eighteenth and early nineteenth century. As Richard Altick notes, among the various spectacles of natural sublimity, "volcanic action was second only to sea storms in popularity."[31] (Readers of the Gothic will recall the sea storms in such novels as *A Sicilian Romance*, *The Mysteries of Udolpho*, and *Melmoth the Wanderer*.)

French festivals in the 1790s likewise employed explosive models of volcanoes, as metaphors for revolution.[32] The juxtaposition of natural and political cataclysms appears in the typically self-referential manner of Maturin in *Melmoth the Wanderer*. As a dying monk explains how the inmates of a monastery manage to survive the monotony of their mechanical existence by ingesting the poison of "innutritive illusion," one cannot help but recognize the conventional subjects of Gothic novels, Maturin's included, in these improbable fictions: the monks "dream that an earthquake will shake the walls to atoms, that a volcano will burst forth in the centre of the garden. They imagine a revolution of government, — an attack of banditti, – any thing, however improbable."[33]

The Gothic volcano leads us, first of all, into the midst of powerful and mysterious natural electrical and igneous phenomena that, in the eighteenth century, remained at the intersection of science, alchemy, and necromancy. Far from representing a return of supernaturalism following the repression of the numinous by Enlightenment rationalism, the Gothic novel shares an Enlightenment preoccupation with exploring phenomena at the margins of scientific knowledge: ventriloquism, somnambulism, mesmerism, physiognomy, phrenology, and reanimation of the dead. Among the most interesting recent studies of such subjects are Terry Castle's explorations of phantasmagoria and the "spectralization" of memory and thought. Castle apparently accepts a psychohistorical model not very different from Peter Brooks, in which "rationalists did not so much negate the traditional spirit world as displace it into the realm of psychology";[34] however, she not only brilliantly explores the confounding of Lockean mental images with supernatural apparitions but also argues that such a conception of mental operations and the emotional investment in the mental pictures of loved ones called forth technological developments such as the magic lantern, photography, cinematography, television, and holography.[35] Castle thus explores the interactions among Gothic fiction, scientific knowledge that sometimes overlapped with pseudoscience, and technological capabilities that formerly seemed almost magical.

Students of Gothic fiction have only recently begun to appreciate the connections between eighteenth-century science, the occult, and radical politics, even though these connections are fundamental to an understanding of the novels of Godwin, Brockden Brown, Mary Shelley, and others. Marie Roberts has argued that the "Rosicrucian" novel in English, a subgenre of the Gothic, explores precisely the overlap that the historian of science Charles Webster has seen between scientific magic and Newtonian mechanistic science.[36] We can now understand in a new way the device of the explained supernatural. In some instances, Radcliffe and other Gothic novelists leave the reader hesitating between a supernatural account and an explanation that draws upon Enlightenment research that today strikes us as pseudoscience. It is precisely such hesitation between the marvelous (the actually supernatural) and the uncanny (the bizarre event rationally explained away) that would situate a Gothic novel, for Tzvetan Todorov, in the genre of the fantastic.[37]

But "*illumination* night," the term Paulo uses to describe the volcanic fires of Vesuvius, also leads us to the contested ground on which the official displays of the dominant culture encountered the volatile festivities of the people. Radcliffe italicizes the word *illumination* because she wishes to emphasize that it has been wrenched from its normal context, in which it refers, to quote the *Oxford English Dictionary*, to "The lighting up of a building, town, etc. (now usually in a decorative way, with coloured lights arranged in artistic designs, etc.) in token of festivity or rejoicing." In fact, the *OED* cites Paolo's speech from *The Italian* to supply an attributive example for this sense of the word.

In 1797, the year *The Italian* was published, the English reader would most readily have associated "illuminations" with the officially sanctioned celebrations on the occasion of military victories in the war with France. Such illuminations were generally characterized by the lighting of bonfires and tar barrels in the streets, the placing of lighted candles in the windows of most houses, the firing of guns, the setting off of firecrackers, and frequently official civic fireworks displays. Large crowds would generally roam the streets at night, sometimes extorting money from genteel passersby and sometimes breaking the windows of houses that had not been illuminated by their owners or occupants. So for example in June 1794, following Lord Howe's naval victory over the French, "Three days of victory illuminations were ordered, and loyal mobs armed with sticks roamed the streets smashing any unlit windows which betrayed lack of patriotic enthusiasm." [38] Earlier in the century, when the news reached London of the Duke of Cumberland's defeat of the Jacobite rebels at Culloden (1746), Tobias Smollett and his friend Alexander Carlyle thought it prudent to remove their wigs, carry their swords in their hands, and conceal their Scottish accents by maintaining perfect silence, in order to avoid the insolence of the riotous London mob. Making their way through back streets, Smollett and Carlyle were nonetheless asked for sixpence by some boys around a bonfire.[39] Hence, even in the case of officially sanctioned illuminations, there was always the risk of the poor destroying or appropriating the property of the rich.

Handbills advertising late eighteenth-century illuminations reveal official awareness of the danger of riot. A notice for a general illumination, distributed in Bristol, England, on 5 September 1799, warned the people against the firing of guns and pistols in the streets, and "against committing any Outrage" on those "who, from religious Principles may not be disposed to testify their Joy by illuminations."[40] Illuminations, therefore, even officially sponsored ones, formed a site of contestation between expressions of popular sentiment and the increasing concern of the authorities to control the crowd. Thus, in *The Italian*, Paulo's affection for and Vivaldi's fear of volcanic illuminations play out a conflict between popular patriotic festivity and the concerns of the enlightened rich to protect the fragile property of landlords and householders, and to redirect and contain popular cultural manifestations within official channels.

But illuminations and bonfires were by no means confined to popular participation in officially sanctioned celebrations. They also served a ritual function in autonomous demonstrations of the early modern crowd and even in social and political protest. E. P. Thompson has argued that, from the time of John Wilkes, the English crowd used a threatening and seditious countertheater as a negotiating strategy against the patriciate's theatrical displays of paternalism. Thompson includes in the symbolic language of this countertheater "the illumination of windows (or the breaking of those without illumination)."[41] By the time of the French Revolution, the participants in British popular disturbances, even those supporting traditional grazing, gleaning, and provisioning rights, began to employ a new radical political rhetoric. In the political context of the 1790s, celebratory illuminations were occasionally held in Britain to mark not English victories but rather those of the armies of the French Revolution. For example, in Perth in 1792 an anonymous correspondent sent this report to the Home Office: "The Tree of Liberty was planted with great Solemnity in this town and a great bonfire with ringing of bells and a general Illumination upon hearing that General Dumourier had entered Brussels. The Lower Class of People talk of nothing but liberty and Equality."[42] The planting of the tree of liberty is itself a transformation of the traditional erection of maypoles, a transformation that indicates the politicization of popular culture (Burke, *Popular Culture*, 267). In 1797, then, an illumination night might not only be an occasion when the loyal ardor of "Church and King" mobs threatened to get out of control and put at risk the property and persons of gentry and householders. An illumination night might be the site of a fundamental clash of opposing social interests, which had come to be increasingly identified with opposing attitudes toward the French Revolution. Popular patriotic exuberance and popular revolutionary sentiment converge in the phenomenon of the general illumination, and hence, in the view of the authorities, this phenomenon had to be orchestrated and controlled.

The ideologically contradictory "illumination night" in *The Italian* does not lend itself readily to an account of Radcliffe as a conservative author, opposed to the French Revolution, writing an anti-Enlightenment fantasy, with a psychological focus. Rather, I have argued, the chauvinistic Paolo's local attachment to the Bay of Naples draws on similar Enlightenment sources to the cosmopolitan Vivaldi's aesthetics of the sublime. Even while Radcliffe gently mocks and patronizes her Gothic manservant, she uses his unquestioning love for his master to relive the anxieties aroused by the servant problem in the transition to capitalism. But the "illumination night" also hints at the power and potential threat of the crowd. As opposed to the dominant psychological tendency in criticism of the Gothic novel, which has shown how the subjective distortions of the heroine's vision derive from her simultaneous dread of and attraction to villainous paternal figures, historical criticism can reveal the way in which Gothic fiction participates in the social, political, and philosophical discourses of the late eighteenth century. As opposed to the psychohistorical model for conceiving the relationship between the Enlightenment and the tale of terror, the more local and particular insights of social history reveal the way in which Gothic novels give voice to social and political struggles.

The Italian ends with a paternalistic fete in celebration of Vivaldi and

Ellena's marriage. The setting is a villa, "a scene of fairy-land," where the gardens are said to be designed not in formal Italian fashion but in the wild, natural mode favored by English landscape gardeners: "On this jubilee, every avenue and grove, and pavilion was richly illuminated" (412). This fete is characterized not only by rich illuminations but by a mingling of social ranks, as if the elite could participate once more in the culture of the people. Paolo dominates the fete with his celebration of universal liberty after the experience of old regime inquisitorial imprisonment. An Enlight-enment science that borders on the occult also plays its part in the "felicific technology" of his sentimental communications: "the emotion which had nearly stifled him burst forth in words, and '*O! giorno felíce! O! giorno felíce!*' flew from his lips with the force of an electric shock. They commu-nicated his enthusiasm to the whole company, the words passed like lightning from one individual to another" (414).

Perhaps something of the difference between the female Gothic, or the Radcliffean tale of terror, and the tales of horror associated with male authors can now be illustrated through the treatment of illuminations. In contrast to the splendid illuminated groves and woods in *A Sicilian Romance* and *The Italian*, the most striking reference to illuminations in *Melmoth the Wanderer* is at once more learned and more horrific. Instead of a nostalgic appeal to the festive mingling of elite and populace, Maturin's Melmoth undermines the sentimental idealism of Immalee/Isidora, the child of nature who serves as the novel's major heroine, by offering as a comparison for the music of the spheres "the Christians, who had the honour to illuminate Nero's garden in Rome on a rejoicing night" (351). Maturin likely alludes here to Tacitus, who criticizes Nero, not for punishing Christians, which would have been in the public interest, but rather for indulging his private cruelty in the manner of their execution: "they were torn to pieces by dogs, or crucified, or made into torches to be ignited after dark as substitutions for daylight."[43] Maturin thus deploys his male educational privilege, his greater access, in the words of Clara Reeve, to "the manners of the Greeks and Romans," in order to reinscribe modern celebratory illuminations as a cynical and witty deflation of the sentiment-alism to which he nonetheless remains attracted. In the matter of illumina-tions, Radcliffe makes a manifestation of natural sublimity congenial to humanity, transforming a volcano by catachresis into a scene of popular festivity, whereas Maturin dehumanizes a modern celebration by alluding to a horrific ancient martyrdom.

One year after *The Italian* was published, Nelson's victory in the Battle of the Nile (1798) was celebrated by a general illumination in London. The occasion was also marked by a work with a better claim to be considered part of popular culture. Hawked on the streets of London was a one-penny broadsheet entitled *Illuminations, or The Orphan Boy and the Lady*, which, though it ends with the promise of paternalistic charity, looks upon patriotic celebrations from the sentimental but nonetheless critical perspective of the poor child of a sailor, one who was no doubt impressed into the King's service:

> Poor, foolish child! how pleas'd was I
>   When news of Nelson's vict'ry came,
> Along the crowded street to fly,
>   To see the lighted windows flame!
> To force me home my mother sought –
>   She could not bear to see my joy;
> For with my father's life 'twas bought –
>   And made me a poor orphan boy![44]

NOTES

1 Ann Radcliffe, *The Italian or the Confessional of the Black Penitents*, ed. Frederick Garber (London: Oxford University Press, 1971), 158. All further references are to this edition.

2 Marilyn Butler, *Jane Austen and the War of Ideas* (Oxford: Clarendon, 1975), 30, 50–51.

3 See Alan D. McKillop, "Local Attachment and Cosmopolitanism – the Eighteenth-Century Pattern," in *From Sensibility to Romanticism*, ed. Frederick W. Hilles and Harold Bloom (New York: Oxford University Press, 1965), 191–218.

4 See, for example, Elliott B. Gose, Jr., *Imagination Indulged: the Irrational in the Nineteenth-Century Novel* (Montreal: McGill-Queen's University Press, 1972); and Judith Wilt, *Ghosts of the Gothic* (Princeton: Princeton University Press, 1980).

5 Henry Fielding, *Joseph Andrews*, ed. Martin C. Battestin (Middletown: Wesleyan University Press, 1967), 4, 10.

6 Henry Fielding, *The History of Tom Jones*, ed. Martin C. Battestin and Fredson Bowers (Middletown: Wesleyan University Press, 2 vols., 1975), II: 1.77.

7 Horace Walpole, *The Castle of Otranto: a Gothic Story*, ed. W. S. Lewis (London: Oxford University Press, 1964), 12.

8 Clara Reeve, *The Progress of Romance and the History of Charoba, Queen of Aegypt* (Colchester, 2 vols., 1785; reprinted New York: Facsimile Text Society, 1930), I: xi. All further references are to this edition.

9 Charlotte Lennox, *The Female Quixote*, ed. Margaret Dalziel (London: Oxford University Press, 1971), 279.

10 Janice A. Radway, *Reading the Romance*, new edition (Chapel Hill: University of North Carolina Press, 1991).

11 Ann Radcliffe, *A Sicilian Romance*, ed. Alison Milbank (Oxford: Oxford University Press, 1993), 85.

12 See Nicholas Phillipson, "The Scottish Enlightenment," in Roy Porter and Mikulas Teich, eds., *The Enlightenment in National Context* (Cambridge: Cambridge University Press, 1981), 23.

13 See Michael McKeon, *The Origins of the English Novel, 1600–1740* (Baltimore: Johns Hopkins University Press, 1987).

14 Louis F. Peck, *A Life of Matthew G. Lewis* (Cambridge, Mass.: Harvard University Press, 1961), 22.

15 Samuel Richardson, *Pamela; or, Virtue Rewarded*, ed. T. C. Duncan Eaves and Ben D. Kimpel (Boston: Houghton Mifflin, 1971), 203.

16 J. H. Baker, "Criminal Courts and Procedures at Common Law 1550–1800," in *Crime in England, 1550–1800*, ed. J. S. Cockburn (Princeton: Princeton University Press, 1977), 34.

17 See Montague Summers, *The Gothic Quest* (London: Fortune Press, [1938]), 99.

18 Peter Burke, *Popular Culture in Early Modern Europe* (London: Temple Smith, 1978), 92.

19 David Punter, *The Literature of Terror* (London: Longman, 1980), 422.

20 Peter Brooks, "Virtue and Terror: *The Monk*," *ELH*, 40 (1973): 249.

21 Noel Carroll, *The Philosophy of Horror* (New York: Routledge, 1990), 56–57.

22 Michel Foucault, "The Eye of Power: a Conversation with Jean-Pierre Barou and Michel Perrot," in *Power/Knowledge*, ed. Colin Gordon (New York: Pantheon, 1980), 153–54.

23 See Michel Foucault, *Discipline and Punish*, trans. Alan Sheridan (New York: Pantheon, 1977); John Bender, *Imagining the Penitentiary* (Chicago: University of Chicago Press, 1987); D. A. Miller, *The Novel and the Police* (Berkeley and Los Angeles: University of California Press, 1988); and Nancy Armstrong, *Desire and Domestic Fiction* (London and New York: Oxford University Press, 1987). Armstrong explicitly states that "the novel provided a mighty weapon in the arsenal of Enlightenment rhetoric, which aimed at liberating individuals from their political chains" (98). For Armstrong, on the other side of such liberatory rhetoric lie new, and more effective, institutional strategies of control.

24 See Michael Ignatieff, "State, Civil Society and Total Institutions: a Critique of Recent Social Histories of Punishment," in Stanley Cohen and Andrew Scull, eds., *Social Control and the State* (Oxford: Martin Robertson, 1983), 83.

25 Roy Porter, "The Enlightenment in England," in Porter and Teich, eds., *The Enlightenment in National Context*, 7.

26 Nicholas Phillipson, "Scottish Enlightenment," 29; Phillipson is quoting from W. Leechman, "Some Account of the Life, Writings and Character of the Author," in *A System of Moral Philosophy* by Francis Hutcheson (London, 1755).

27 Mary Shelley, *Frankenstein; or, The Modern Prometheus*, ed. James Kinsley and M. K. Joseph (1969; reprinted Oxford: Oxford University Press, 1980), 41.

28 Susan Sontag, *The Volcano Lover: a Romance* (New York: Farrar, Strauss and Giroux, 1992), 129.

29 Christopher Thacker, "The Volcano: Culmination of the Landscape Garden," *Eighteenth-Century Life*, 8 (January 1983): 75.

30 Fred M. Bullard, *Volcanoes of the Earth* (Austin: University of Texas Press, 1976), 213–15.

31 Richard D. Altick, *The Shows of London* (Cambridge, Mass.: Belknap Press of Harvard University, 1978), 96.

32 Ronald Paulson, *Representations of Revolution (1789–1820)* (New Haven: Yale University Press, 1983), 75.

33 Charles Maturin, *Melmoth the Wanderer*, ed. Douglas Grant (1968; reprinted Oxford: Oxford University Press, 1989), 116. All further references are to this edition.

34 Terry Castle, "Phantasmagoria: Spectral Technology and the Metaphorics of Modern Reverie," *Critical Inquiry*, 15 (Autumn 1988): 52.

35 Terry Castle, "The Spectralization of the Other in *The Mysteries of Udolpho*," in Felicity Nussbaum and Laura Brown, eds., *The New Eighteenth Century* (New York: Methuen, 1987), 247, 151, 310 n.28.

36 Marie Roberts, *Gothic Immortals* (New York: Routledge, 1990), 5. "Rosicrucian" evokes a shadowy and secret society whose members share esoteric knowledge concerning such matters as the transmutation of base metals into precious ones, the prolongation of life, and power over the elements and elemental spirits. The name derives from the society's reputed fifteenth-century founder, one Christian Rosenkrenz.

37 Tzvetan Todorov, *The Fantastic*, trans. Richard Howard (Ithaca, N.Y.: Cornell University Press, 1975).

38 William St. Clair, *The Godwins and the Shelleys* (Baltimore: Johns Hopkins University Press, 1989), 125.

39 *The Autobiography of Dr. Alexander Carlyle of Inveresk*, ed. John Hillburton (London, 1910), 198–99; quoted in Lewis Mansfield Knapp, *Tobias Smollett: Doctor of Men and Manners* (Princeton: Princeton University Press, 1949), 58.

40 Quoted in Mark Harrison, *Crowds and History: Mass Phenomena in English Towns, 1790–1835* (Cambridge: Cambridge University Press, 1988), 238.

41 E. P. Thompson, "Patrician Society, Plebeian Culture," *Journal of Social History*, 7 (1974): 400.

42 "To Alexander Todd," 15 December 1792, in the Home Office (Scotland) Correspondence; quoted in Kenneth J. Logue, *Popular Disturbances in Scotland, 1780–1815* (Edinburgh: John Donald, 1979), 149.

43 Tacitus, *The Annals of Imperial Rome*, trans. Michael Grant (Harmondsworth: Penguin, 1956), 354.

44 *Illuminations, or The Orphan Boy and the Lady* (London: Printed for J. M. Flindall, ND).

READING LIST

Butler, Marilyn. *Jane Austen and the War of Ideas*. Oxford: Clarendon, 1975.

Ellis, Kate Ferguson. *The Contested Castle: Gothic Novels and the Subversion of Domestic Ideology*. Urban: University of Illinois Press, 1989.

Haggerty, George E. *Gothic Fiction/Gothic Form*. University Park: Pennsylvania State University Press, 1989.

Jackson, Rosemary. *Fantasy: The Literature of Subversion*. London: Methuen, 1981.

Kiely, Robert. *The Romantic Novel in England*. Cambridge, Mass.: Harvard University Press, 1972.

MacAndrew, Elizabeth. *The Gothic Tradition in Fiction*. New York: Columbia University Press, 1979.

Paulson, Ronald. *Representations of Revolution (1789–1820)*. New Haven: Yale University Press, 1983.

Sedgwick, Eve Kosofsky. *Between Men: English Literature and Male Homosocial Desire*. New York: Columbia University Press, 1985.

The Coherence of Gothic Conventions. New York: Methuen, 1986.

Tompkins, J. M. S. *The Popular Novel in England, 1770–1800*. London, 1932; reprinted Lincoln: University of Nebraska Press, 1961.

Wilt, Judith. *Ghosts of the Gothic: Austen, Eliot, and Lawrence*. Princeton: Princeton University Press, 1980.

INDEX

Addison, Joseph, *Spectator* (1712), 138, 184
Aesop's Fables (1739), children's edition
    published by Richardson, 99
Ainsworth, William Harrison, 52
Altick, Richard, 268
amatory novella, 3
Arbuthnot, John, 76
Aristophanes, and Fielding, 120
*Assignation, The. A Sentimental Novel. In a
    Series of Letters* (1774), 244, 252n
Astell, Mary, 99
Atterbury, Francis, 96
Aubin, Penelope, 214, 215, 216
Auden, W. H., 139
Austen, Jane, 1, 199, 201; and Defoe, 45;
    Mansfield Park (1814), and imperialism,
    179; parody of Richardson's *Sir Charles
    Grandison*, 115n; *Sanditon* (1817),
    satire of sentimentalism, 236–37
Austin, J. L., 62

Bacon, Francis, empiricism, 7
Bakhtin, Mikhail, 43, 54, 61, 177
Ballaster, Ros, 216
Barbauld, Anna Laetitia, ed., *Correspondence
    of Samuel Richardson* (1804), 252n
Barker, Jane, *Exilius* (1715), 213; 214, 216
Barrell, John, 186
Barthes, Roland, 49, 64
Battestin, Martin, 146
Beasley, Jerry, 216
Beckford, William, 268; *Azemia: a descriptive
    and sentimental novel* (1797), 251n
Behn, Aphra, 11, 27, 215; *The Fair Jilt*
    (1688), 212; *Love Letters Between a
    Nobleman and His Sister* (1684–87),
    199, 212; *Oroonoko* (1688), 212
Bender, John, 193
Bennett, Arnold, 154

Bennett, John, *Letters to a Young Lady*
    (1789), 201
Bentham, Jeremy, 264, 265
Berkeley, George, 107
Betsy Thoughtless (1751), Eliza Haywood, 25
Blount, Martha, 135
Boileau-Despréaux, Nicolas, *Le Lutrin*
    (1674), burlesque epic poem, 131–32
Bolingbroke, Henry St. John, Lord, 155,
    163–65, 170, 172n, 173n
Boswell, James, 245
Bradshaigh, Lady Dorothy, Richardson's
    correspondent, 116n, 237, 247
Brecht, Berthold, 138
Brooke, Henry, *The Fool of Quality*
    (1764–70), child sentimental hero, 243
Brooks, Peter, 263, 264, 269
Brown, Charles Brockden, American Gothic
    writer, 257, 269
Burckhardt, Sigurd, 153
Burke, Edmund, 172n
Burke, Peter, 262–63
Burney, Charles, 268; *History of Music*
    (1776–89), 90
Burney, Frances, 11; as minor writer, 34n;
    heroines in her novels and ideological
    tensions of the time, 198; liminality and
    the heroines, 200–1
    WORKS: *Camilla* (1796), 199, 200–1,
    205–6, liminal position of the heroine,
    206; *Cecilia* (1782), 199, 200–1, 203–5,
    masquerade in, 203, public issues and
    the heroine, 227; *Evelina* (1778), 200–1,
    202–3, 206, and social-cultural history,
    33–34, prostitutes in, 202–3; *The
    Wanderer* (1814), 200, 206–9
Burns, Robert, 56
Burton, Richard, 79; *Anatomy of Melancholy*
    (1621), 88n, 154